WAR in UKRAINE

Hal Brands is the Henry A. Kissinger Distinguished Professor of Global Affairs at the Johns Hopkins School of Advanced International Studies (SAIS), a senior fellow at the American Enterprise Institute, and a Bloomberg Opinion columnist. His previous books include *Danger Zone: The Coming Conflict with China* (2022), coauthored with Michael Beckley; *The Twilight Struggle: What the Cold War Teaches Us about Great-Power Rivalry Today* (2022); and *The New Makers of Modern Strategy: From the Ancient World to the Digital Age* (2023). He has been a special assistant to the secretary of defense, a member of the secretary of state's Foreign Affairs Policy Board, and a consultant to the US intelligence community.

WAR

IN

UKRAINE

CONFLICT, STRATEGY, AND THE RETURN
OF A FRACTURED WORLD

EDITED BY
Hal Brands

Johns Hopkins University Press
Baltimore

This book has been brought to publication with the generous assistance of
the America in the World Consortium and its supporters.

Johns Hopkins University Press
2715 North Charles Street
Baltimore, Maryland 21218
www.press.jhu.edu

Library of Congress Cataloging-in-Publication Data

Names: Brands, Hal, 1983– editor.
Title: War in Ukraine : conflict, strategy, and the return of a fractured world
    / edited by Hal Brands.
Description: Baltimore, Maryland : Johns Hopkins University Press, 2024. |
    Includes bibliographical references and index.
Identifiers: LCCN 2024008859 | ISBN 9781421449845 (paperback) |
    ISBN 9781421449852 (ebook) | ISBN 9781421449869 (ebook open access)
Subjects: LCSH: Russian Invasion of Ukraine, 2022– | Russia (Federation)—
    Politics and government—21st century. | Geopolitics—Former Soviet
    republics. | Geopolitics—Ukraine.
Classification: LCC DK5447 .W37 2024 | DDC 947.7086—dc23/
    eng/20240226
LC record available at https://lccn.loc.gov/2024008859

A catalog record for this book is available from the British Library.

*Special discounts are available for bulk purchases of this book. For more
information, please contact Special Sales at specialsales@jh.edu.*

Contents

Acknowledgments

I am grateful to the America in the World Consortium and its supporters for making this volume possible, and to the Johns Hopkins School of Advanced International Studies and its dean, Jim Steinberg, for hosting the conference at which these papers were first discussed. I am equally grateful to the staff of the Henry A. Kissinger Center for Global Affairs—namely Andrea Wise, Elizabeth Alexander Morales, and Nathaniel Wong—and to Wes Culp for their essential help with the project. Thanks also to Heidi Vincent, Barbara Kline Pope, and their colleagues at Johns Hopkins University Press for moving this book so speedily from concept to product. Most of all, I wish to acknowledge the efforts of the contributors, who put aside other important projects to contribute to this one.

WAR in UKRAINE

The Ukraine War and Global Order

Hal Brands

We don't yet know how the war in Ukraine will end. We do know, already, that this war has changed the world.

When Vladimir Putin sent his armies streaming into Ukraine in February 2022—the climax of a two-decade project to subvert and subordinate that country—he did more than trigger Europe's largest, deadliest conflict in generations. He also accelerated the emergence of a more fractured, rivalrous age.

Putin's assault intensified the great-power struggles that were already coming to characterize the 21st century. It reshaped alliances, deepened global cleavages, and sent economic turmoil washing around the world. The war created the first great-power nuclear crisis in decades; it saw sanctions, export controls, and other economic tools wielded as weapons of geopolitical combat. In these and other ways, the Ukraine War fostered an international environment more polarized and dangerous than at any time since the Cold War. Its outcome—whatever that outcome is—will profoundly influence the international balance of power, the struggle between democracies and autocracies, the alignment of countries on multiple continents, and the rules that govern global affairs.

Historians will be studying this war for generations to come.[1] In this volume—the product of a conference at the Johns Hopkins School of Advanced

Hal Brands is the Henry A. Kissinger Distinguished Professor of Global Affairs at the Johns Hopkins School of Advanced International Studies, a senior fellow at the American Enterprise Institute, and a Bloomberg Opinion columnist.

International Studies timed to coincide with the second anniversary of Russia's invasion—some of the world's leading analysts assess the conflict's origins, trajectory, and implications. They offer their appraisals of the most geopolitically consequential crisis of the 21st century so far.

Those appraisals are, necessarily, provisional: This volume is an effort to write history in real time. Coming to grips with a war in progress is like shooting at a moving target. Perspectives on events inevitably shift as time passes and the rest of the story plays out. A history of the US Civil War written in 1862 or even 1864 might have looked very different than one written after Robert E. Lee surrendered at Appomattox. A history of the Cold War produced in the 1970s might have yielded fundamentally different conclusions than one produced after the Soviet Union's collapse.[2] But if history in real time is hard, it is also essential. How else can policymakers and analysts make sense of—and react intelligently to—world-shifting events as they occur?

The chapters that follow represent a collective effort to explore the unfolding history and global significance of the Ukraine War.[3] The focus is less on providing a blow-by-blow account of the war—something that might well be outdated by the time you read these words—than on understanding its deeper causes and essential elements and explaining how this war is reshaping the world as a fraught new era begins. The takeaways from this effort are rich and varied. This introduction distills six core conclusions and themes.[4]

First, what we often call "the Ukraine War" didn't start in February 2022, even if that is when its most intense, calamitous, and globally resonant phase began. Just as Japan's invasion of Manchuria in 1931 was the prologue to its all-out invasion of China in 1937, the war between Ukraine and Russia began in 2014 with Vladimir Putin's taking of Crimea and his intervention—first through proxies and then with regular forces—in the Donbas. That war waxed and waned in the years thereafter, but it never really ended. As we will see, one reason Putin escalated to high-intensity conflict in early 2022 was because his strategy of lower-intensity warfare wasn't producing the desired political results. In fact, Putin's bid to control Ukraine, politically and geopolitically, dated back even further, to his failed effort to sway its presidential elections in 2004–2005. Moscow's methods changed over the next two decades, but its core objective never did.[5]

And as with most wars, this one had histories deeper still. The Ukraine War is simply the biggest of the many wars of the Soviet succession—the series of violent struggles involving the remnants of the Soviet empire since its collapse in 1991.[6] Decades before that, during the 1930s, Joseph Stalin made his own bid to crush Ukraine's identity and starve its population. Putin himself has weaponized the longer, tangled history of Russo-Ukrainian ties—arguing that Ukraine has never been a "real country" and has no right to exist as an independent state.[7] In this sense, the present war is simply the next phase of a longer-running struggle between Ukraine and a series of Russian empires—whether tsarist, communist, or Putinist—that have sought to dominate it.

The war is also part of a broader historical pattern in which Ukraine has been at the center of every major global clash, hot or cold, of the modern era. This isn't as surprising as it might sound. After all, Ukraine boasts some of the richest agricultural land on Earth. It possesses vital strategic frontage on the Black Sea. Most critically, it sits at the hinge of Eurasia, where the economically advanced European "rimland" meets the vast spaces and abundant resources of a "heartland" ruled by Russia. Any European empire seeking glory to the east must go through Ukraine. Any Eurasian power expanding into Europe must do the same. So the fate of Ukraine was a vital issue in every great Eurasian struggle of the 20th century: World War I, World War II, and the Cold War. It is no less central to the clash between Russia and the West today.[8]

Indeed, what sets the phase of the war since February 2022 apart is that it so hauntingly resembles something from these earlier, darker eras. Putin's invasion was not some limited land grab, some modest uptick in a long-running territorial dispute. It was an effort to topple Ukraine's government, kill or capture its leaders, and end its national existence. It was meant to shatter a whole set of norms and conventions underpinning the liberal international order—not least, the norm against the forcible conquest and annexation of territory—and thereby usher in an era in which neo-imperial powers engage in the most naked forms of predation.

The tactics Russian forces used in occupied areas—rape, murder, and torture; the kidnapping of Ukraine's children and the Russification of its schools—suggested a similarly totalizing ethos. So Russia's campaign, and Ukraine's desperate resistance, touched off a shockingly brutal conflict that has claimed hundreds of thousands of lives, consumed vast quantities of munitions and materiel, and produced geopolitical spillover around the world. If this war has proven so globally transfixing, perhaps that's because it reminds us of ugly realities—the viciousness of autocratic aggression, the destructiveness of large-scale war, the fragility of international order—we might prefer to forget.

Second, this war was the result of a double failure, years in the making: Putin's failure to ensure a weak, pliant Ukraine by means short of all-out conflict, and the West's failure to deter just such an all-out attack.[9]

Putin has long wanted to restore Russia as a great power, and ensure the stability of his autocratic regime, by making Ukraine a reliably docile, dysfunctional client state. Yet a quasi-genocidal conflict was not Putin's first choice for achieving that aim, even if, today, such barbarism seems to fit him like a glove. Between 2004 and 2022, Putin used an array of tactics—from poisoning and political meddling to covert wars and limited land grabs—against Ukraine. He eventually went for broke because those tactics were producing disastrous strategic results.

Putin's interference in Ukrainian politics in 2004–2005 backfired by triggering the Orange Revolution, just the sort of pro-democracy, pro-Western movement he surely hoped to avoid. Nine years later, Putin succeeded in coercing a more pro-Russian leader into jilting Europe and bringing Ukraine closer to Moscow—only to set off another popular movement, the Revolution of Dignity, that brought that government down. Putin responded by seizing Crimea and destabilizing eastern Ukraine. But in conquering a peninsula and roiling a region, he lost a country. The war encouraged Kyiv to seek tighter ties to America and Europe as a means of survival; it changed Ukrainian politics by stimulating the very nationalism that threatened Putin's neo-imperial agenda. In this sense, Putin tried to conquer Ukraine in 2022 because he was running out of other options—and because he was running out of time before a stubbornly defiant country made its future with the West.

Yet if Putin's invasion reflected a failure of coercion by Moscow, it reflected a failure of deterrence—or perhaps a failure to attempt deterrence—by the West. In 2008, NATO left Ukraine and Georgia in a perilous limbo by declaring that those countries would join the alliance *someday* but providing no concrete timetable and no military protection in the interim. Putin, all too predictably, exploited the ambiguity to dismember both countries in the six years that followed.[10] But even after Russia invaded and annexed Crimea in 2014—the most egregious act of conquest in Europe since 1945—it encountered only a half-hearted Western response.

The United States trained Ukrainian soldiers but took years to provide them with even a very modest amount of weaponry. Western sanctions, imposed reluctantly, never seriously hobbled Putin's economy. European countries, especially Germany, kept on cultivating their addiction to Russian oil and gas. If Putin thought he could perpetrate such a heinous crime in 2022, perhaps that's because he had gotten off easy for lesser offenses in the past.

Perhaps, also, it was because the West struggled to offer much resistance as the climactic crisis unfolded: A shambolic US departure from Afghanistan in 2021 had presumably not left Putin wowed by American strength and resolve. An unsettled political scene in Europe lent further opportunities to divide the Western coalition. President Joe Biden explicitly ruled out trying to stop a Russian invasion militarily. Even the threat of sharp, punishing sanctions was undermined by widespread disbelief in Europe that Putin would really try to conquer Ukraine and by public disagreement about how far America and its allies should go if he attacked.[11]

This was all perfectly understandable, in some respects. Ukraine was not a member of NATO. No US policymaker seemed to believe, before February 2022, that America had a vital interest in the territorial integrity of a distant, troubled democracy stranded between Russia and the West.[12] But the fact remains that in the years after Russia's taking of Crimea, and in the months before Russia's attack on Kyiv, the West never gave Putin much reason to believe he would suffer devastating consequences for assailing that country—which is perhaps why Moscow was so surprised when those consequences did, in fact, materialize.[13]

Among Putin's many failures was his inability to see how such a brazen, brutal escalation could catalyze international outrage—and international punishment— stronger than anything his regime had encountered before. The crucial, collective failure of America and its allies was their inability to make clear—or perhaps even to realize—how much Ukraine's survival mattered to them *before* a shocking invasion cast that survival into existential doubt.

The outcome of that invasion illustrates a third theme, which is that the course of the war was highly contingent and fairly predictable all at once. The opening phase of the war, certainly, was full of surprises, the most important of which was simply that Ukraine survived. If this book was written, in early 2024, at a comparatively low mark in Ukraine's fortunes, it is worth remembering that the country's fight for its existence was never supposed to go this *well*.

When the invasion began, most observers expected Ukraine to be defeated in short order. The Ukrainian military was outnumbered and overmatched; foreign governments were urging President Volodymyr Zelensky to flee. The collapse of Ukraine's government and the success of Putin's war plan were entirely possible.[14]

Yet Ukraine withstood the assault thanks to a serendipitous combination of factors, none of which were easily predicted in advance.

There was the extraordinary cohesion and sacrifice of the Ukrainian military and population, which demonstrated that Putin's enemy was a "real country" after all. There was the curiously slapdash way in which Russian forces planned and executed the most important military endeavor of Putin's long reign. There was the unexpectedly galvanizing leadership of Zelensky, who—after a generally unimpressive prewar performance—seemed to find his calling in crisis, as a manifestation of his country's courage and resolve. Not least, there was the extraordinary support that the United States and other countries poured into the fight.[15]

The West had been willing, for years, to tolerate creeping aggression against a country on the margins of Europe. It proved unwilling, in early 2022, to acquiesce in the outright destruction of the continent's second-largest state. European leaders thus surprised the Kremlin—and themselves—by signing on to harsh economic sanctions. Countries from Germany to South Korea would find creative, precedent-breaking ways of sending money and weapons to Ukraine. From the outset, arms and intelligence provided by the United States and other Western nations bolstered Ukrainian resistance in critical places at critical moments. Indeed, one reason prewar estimates underestimated Ukraine's prospects is that they underestimated the international backing that country would enjoy.[16] And when Ukraine, with Western assistance, turned the tide with successful offensives around Kharkiv and Kherson in late 2022, it seemed *Moscow* might be headed for a humiliating defeat.

But then the pendulum swung back, in ways that again confounded the expectations of many Western observers who had written Putin's ragged armies off.[17] Russian lines stiffened, thanks to the creation of prepared, layered defenses and an infusion of fresh troops. In 2023, Ukraine's much-anticipated counteroffensive—its biggest effort to retake territory and break Russia's occupation in the country's east and south—failed amid transatlantic finger-pointing over whether the West's slowness in providing aid, or Ukraine's inability to use it effectively, was at fault. Even the spectacular, if short-lived, mutiny of Yevgeny Prigozhin's mercenary army hardly changed Ukraine's fortunes. By early 2024, the difficult situation on the front lines was creating infighting in Kyiv; the future of American aid was growing more uncertain. Vladimir Putin, whose country was now economically mobilized for war, seemed more confident than at any time since the conflict's opening days. The period since February 2022 saw marked swings on the battlefield, which produced psychological swings more vicious still.

In other ways, however, the course of the war was not so surprising, for it simply revealed truths that a relatively peaceful post–Cold War era—an age in which major state-on-state warfare was fairly rare—made all too easy to neglect. The war showed that when strategies of rapid decision—such as the lightning strike Russia initially attempted—fail, they typically give way to grinding wars of attrition. It showed that sanctioning even economically anemic great powers such as Russia is far more difficult than punishing weaker rogue states.[18] It showed that breaking through well-prepared defensive positions is difficult and costly, as Ukraine discovered in 2023, and that Russia has deeper reserves of resilience than its enemies often expect. Above all, it demonstrated that victory in modern warfare is often a matter of mass and endurance—which means that such conflicts are ultimately contests of economic and societal mobilization—and that, for all its early successes, a Ukraine fighting against a larger, stronger Russia still faced a very tough road ahead.[19]

A fourth theme, reflected in the title of this volume, is that the Ukraine War produced a world more fractured than at any time in decades. Putin's invasion occurred as global tensions were already rising. The United States, accompanied by its regional alliance blocs in Europe and the Indo-Pacific, was waging parallel, intensifying competitions with Putin's Russia and Xi Jinping's China. For their part, those two autocratic giants had recently sealed a "no limits" strategic partnership meant to protect their illiberal polities and project their influence around the world.[20] The Ukraine War deepened and accelerated this process of global division. It pitted two coalescing, rival coalitions more sharply against one another, even as other countries resisted this polarization of world politics—or profited from playing both sides.

During the Cold War, an earlier case of shocking aggression—the Korean War—helped weld the nascent Free World together. At the close of the post–Cold War era, the Ukraine War had—for a time, at least—a similar effect. The sense that aggressive autocracies were advancing, that the very foundations of the international order were being menaced, had a galvanizing effect. European countries rushed aid to Ukraine and increased their own defense spending. NATO began the process of expanding to include Finland and Sweden; the European Union became a more tough-minded, strategic actor. Democracies in the Indo-Pacific—Australia, Japan, South Korea, and Taiwan, among others—also supported Ukraine and sanctioned Russia, for fear that aggression in one region might inspire emulation in others. "Ukraine today," said Japanese prime minister Fumio Kishida, "could be the East Asia of tomorrow."[21]

By late 2022, countries united by democratic values and support for the liberal order were enhancing their defenses from Eastern Europe to the western Pacific. They were strengthening their ties—military, diplomatic, and economic—to one another, while also circumscribing their economic connections to Moscow and, to a lesser extent, Beijing. A transregional coalition of advanced democracies was coalescing; President Biden pledged to lead this revived Free World to victory in another great struggle against tyranny and aggression.[22] At the same time, however, an opposing coalition was taking shape.

The invasion periodically strained relations between Xi and Putin—the former told the latter not to use nuclear weapons when Russia's plight on the battlefield seemed desperate in late 2022.[23] But for the most part, a war that drove the liberal order's primary defenders closer together had the same effect on its primary challengers. A Russia that increasingly found itself severed from, and locked in a deadly proxy conflict with, the West moved into closer alignment with the East. Technological, economic, and defense ties to China boomed after Putin's invasion. "Right now there are changes—the like of which we haven't seen for 100 years—and we are the ones driving these changes," Xi told Putin as he left their March 2023 summit.[24] Meanwhile, Moscow forged deeper military relationships with two other Eurasian revisionists, North Korea and Iran, whose artillery shells, drones, missiles, and other capabilities kept Moscow's marauding armies supplied.

The war produced a web of autocratic relationships crisscrossing the world's strategic core. It also produced a flurry of activity to develop trade and financial networks—such as the North–South Corridor linking Russia and Iran—that would be shielded from Western interdiction and Western sanctions. Most broadly, the war created a situation in which the Free World was facing off against the autocratic axis: a cohering group of autocracies located within Eurasia was competing against interlinked, US-led alliance blocs that ringed the supercontinent's margins.[25]

By most measures, the advanced democracies should have been well positioned for this struggle. In military spending, economic weight, and diplomatic influence, America and its key allies outstripped any combination of Eurasian competitors. Yet it was already evident, by the end of the war's second year, that cohering Eurasian alignments could create sharp strategic dilemmas. Deeper defense technological partnerships might turbocharge the development of disruptive military capabilities.[26] The ability of the Eurasian powers to threaten the existing order in multiple places simultaneously threatened to overstretch and disorient a democratic superpower, as when another severe security crisis erupted in the Middle East in late 2023. And, as of early 2024, with America's commitment to Ukraine wavering and the possibility of a second Trump presidency looming, it was harder to say which coalition might prevail in the end.

Complicating matters further was that the Ukraine War created a "three worlds" scenario, as a loose group of countries assiduously avoided choosing sides.[27] Brazil, Indonesia, India, Saudi Arabia, the United Arab Emirates, and Turkey, among other important players, rejected—or exploited—the polarization of global politics. They maneuvered opportunistically for advantage, cultivating relationships with both advanced democracies *and* Eurasian autocracies. They found ways to remind both sides that the choices these swing states make, on issues from sanctions enforcement to military partnerships, would do much to shift the balance of global advantage. Just as the Cold War produced nonalignment, the Ukraine War was producing a new nonalignment—creating another situation in which rival coalitions compete against each other, while also competing for the loyalties of more ambivalent actors around the world.

If the Ukraine War marked the return of a more divided world, it also marked—a fifth theme—the return of great-power nuclear crises. Before 2022, it had been decades since two great powers squared off in a crisis in the shadow of nuclear escalation. That changed when this war began.[28]

From the outset, Putin and his minions made threats, veiled and not-so-veiled, that Russia might use nuclear weapons if the West directly intervened in the conflict.[29] When the war turned against Russia in the summer and fall of 2022, Putin illegally annexed four Ukrainian oblasts and hinted he might go nuclear against any power that menaced the territorial integrity of his state.[30] Those threats elicited counterthreats from Washington that any use of nuclear weapons would lead to catastrophic consequences for Russia. They also spurred efforts by other powers—including India and China—to talk Putin off this ledge. The immediate crisis passed when Russia's military position stabilized. But even if nuclear weapons were not, at this stage, used in battle, they were profoundly influencing this war.

To be sure, Putin's nuclear threats didn't force Ukraine to surrender. They didn't stop Ukraine from carrying out attacks on Russian territory. They didn't deter Western countries from providing the arms, money, and intelligence that helped Ukrainian forces inflict a ghastly toll on the invaders. In these respects, Putin's nuclear coercion failed. But that coercion did give the Biden administration a powerful reason not to intervene more directly in the fighting, as US officials confronting a case of grievous aggression in Europe might otherwise have been inclined to do. His threats also dissuaded Washington from providing Ukraine with certain advanced capabilities, such as long-range missiles, during critical phases of the fighting.[31] In these respects, Putin's nuclear coercion was a success.

Yet the story becomes even more complicated because nuclear coercion worked both ways. The fact that NATO was backstopped by US military power—and US nuclear weapons—gave its members greater confidence that they could wage a bloody proxy war against Moscow without suffering greater Russian coercion or aggression in response. The course of events in Ukraine thus revealed the crucial, if sometimes subtle, effects of nuclear weapons on great-power crises—and offered a warning of more such crises to come.[32]

Putin's strategy of using nuclear weapons as a shield behind which to conduct conventional aggression raised the prospect that other revisionist powers might do likewise. If China were to attack Taiwan, for instance, it could try to use its own nuclear arsenal to deter US intervention in the conflict—especially as that arsenal comes to rival Washington's in the years ahead. And if Russia ultimately succeeds in dismembering Ukraine, it could increase pressures for nuclear proliferation in regions around Eurasia by convincing vulnerable states, from Poland to South Korea, that there is no surer way of protecting themselves from attack. If this were to happen, the Ukraine War's legacies would include a most dangerous combination: a world increasingly disordered and increasingly nuclearized at the same time.

This relates to a final theme, which is that the global legacy of this war is yet to be fully written. For if this conflict illustrates the contingency of major war, it also illustrates the contingency of global order.[33]

As we have seen, Ukraine was never guaranteed to survive the initial Russian onslaught. It is worth considering how different the world might have looked had Kyiv not surprised nearly everyone by resisting so well.

Had Russia subdued Ukraine following its prewar occupation of Belarus, it would have mostly reconstructed the European heart of the Soviet empire. A confident, assertive Putin would have held a position of intimidating strength from Central Asia to Eastern Europe; NATO would have faced vicious insecurity all along its eastern front. The new axis of autocracies would have had the strategic wind at its back, while the democracies—fresh off a chaotic US retrenchment from

Afghanistan—would have suffered another embarrassing retreat. The destruction of the Ukrainian state might well have ushered in a new era of anarchy and conquest. The road would have been open to the projects of imperial restoration being pursued by the likes of Putin and Xi.[34]

Ukraine didn't fold, of course, and for a time the global consequences seemed precisely the opposite. The West was revived and invigorated; Russia was bloodied and battered; China was diplomatically tainted by its close ties to Putin. The war in Ukraine appeared to be fortifying the international order. But self-congratulation of the sort that became common in Western capitals during this period proved misleading, and profoundly dangerous, because the question of what world the war would leave behind still hinged on who would win the war itself. And following the travails of Ukraine and its Western backers in 2023 and early 2024, the answer to both questions remained deeply uncertain.

As the war entered its third year, it was possible to imagine that Ukraine, if properly supplied and supported, could blunt Russian attacks, retake the offensive, and perhaps eventually win a tolerable peace. It was also possible to imagine that Russia, even if it never took Kyiv or conquered most of the country, might eventually succeed in grinding its enemy down. In 2022, US policymakers had declared, prematurely, that the conflict was *already* a "strategic failure" for Russia.[35] By early 2024, it was altogether too conceivable that Moscow might eke out a victory at tremendous cost.

Nothing that happens next is likely to fundamentally change the global fragmentation the war has caused. But how the conflict is resolved will have vast consequences for Ukraine *and* the world.

It will shape the balance of power in a vital region: a scenario in which Russia occupies large chunks of Ukraine and its Black Sea coastline presents a fundamentally different scenario for Eastern Europe and NATO than one in which it doesn't.[36] It will determine the degree to which Putin's Russia—already a vengeful, embittered revisionist—emerges from this conflict empowered or enfeebled.[37] It will shape global assessments of whether the advanced democracies that have supported Ukraine, or the Eurasian autocracies that have been complicit in its suffering, have the strength and persistence needed to thrive in this age of global competition.[38] It will determine whether the post-1945 norm against territorial conquest is strengthened or shattered and whether nuclear blackmail is seen to bring strategic benefits or self-imposed costs. A great deal is still at stake in Ukraine—most fundamentally, whether that conflict fortifies or fragments an international order that has served America and its friends so well.

NOTES

1. Not only historians, of course: many of the contributors to this volume hail from other backgrounds and disciplines.

2. See, for instance, John Lewis Gaddis, *We Now Know: Rethinking Cold War History* (New York: Oxford University Press, 1997).

3. For other valuable efforts to write early histories of the Ukraine War, see Serhii Plokhy, *The Russo-Ukrainian War: The Return of History* (New York: W. W. Norton, 2023); Simon Shuster, *The Showman: Inside the Invasion That Shook the World and Made a Leader of Volodymyr Zelensky* (New York: William Morrow, 2024); and Yaroslav Trofimov, *Our Enemies Will Vanish: The Russian Invasion and Ukraine's War of Independence* (New York: Penguin, 2024).

4. These conclusions draw on the chapters written by the contributors to this volume, as well as some of my prior writings, which are cited as appropriate.

5. See the contributions to this volume by Lawrence Freedman, Michael Kimmage, and Michael McFaul and Robert Person.

6. The term "wars of the Soviet succession" was originally coined by Charles King in "The Benefits of Ethnic War: Understanding Eurasia's Unrecognized States," *World Politics* 53, no. 4 (July 2001): 524, 525.

7. Yaroslav Trofimov, "How Putin's Obsession with History Led Him to Start a War," *Wall Street Journal*, February 11, 2024.

8. This paragraph draws on Hal Brands, "In Every Modern War, Ukraine Has Been the Big Prize," *Bloomberg Opinion*, January 1, 2023, https://www.bloomberg.com/opinion /articles/2023-01-01/russia-invasion-ukraine-has-been-the-prize-in-every-modern-war.

9. See, among other essays, the contributions by Michael Kimmage, Lawrence Freedman, Michael McFaul and Robert Person, and Kori Schake.

10. Ronald Asmus, *A Little War That Shook the World* (New York: St. Martin's Press, 2010).

11. Patrick Wintour, "Why Are Germany and France at Odds with the Anglosphere over How to Handle Russia?," *The Guardian*, January 26, 2022, https://www.theguardian .com/world/2022/jan/26/nato-allies-policy-russia-ukraine-analysis.

12. Robert Kagan, "A Free World, If You Can Keep It," *Foreign Affairs*, December 20, 2022.

13. See, for example, Victor Jack, "Sergey Lavrov Admits Russia Was Surprised by Scale of Western Sanctions," *Politico Europe*, March 23, 2022.

14. Shane Harris, Ellen Francis, and Robyn Dixon, "U.S. Stands Ready to Evacuate Zelensky, Russia's 'Target No. 1,'" *Washington Post*, February 25, 2022; Shuster, *The Showman*.

15. See the contribution by Michael Kofman to this volume; see also Hal Brands, "Ukraine and the Contingency of Global Order: What If the War Had Gone Differently— or Takes a Sudden Turn?," *Foreign Affairs*, February 14, 2023, https://www.foreignaffairs .com/ukraine/ukraine-and-contingency-global-order.

16. Dara Massicot made this point at the contributors' conference in February 2024. See also Alexander Bick's contribution to this volume on the prewar US planning that enabled this support.

17. See the contributions by Thomas Mahnken and Joshua Baker, Dara Massicot, and Michael Kofman on these issues.

18. See the essay by Daniel Drezner on the accomplishments and shortfalls of sanctions.

19. See the contributions by Michael Kofman, Dara Massicot, and Lawrence Freedman on this issue.

20. Presidential Administration of Russia, "Joint Statement of the Russian Federation and the People's Republic of China on the International Relations Entering a New Era and the Global Sustainable Development," joint statement, February 4, 2022, http://en.kremlin.ru/supplement/5770.

21. Agence France-Presse, "Japan PM: East Asia Could Be Next Ukraine," *Voice of America*, January 14, 2023, https://www.voanews.com/a/kishida-says-g7-should-show -strong-will-on-russia-s-ukraine-invasion/6918474.html. See also the essays by Kori Schake, Mark Leonard, and Alexander Bick.

22. Joseph R. Biden, "Remarks by President Biden on the United Efforts of the Free World to Support the People of Ukraine" (speech, Warsaw, March 26, 2023), https:// www.whitehouse.gov/briefing-room/speeches-remarks/2022/03/26/remarks-by -president-biden-on-the-united-efforts-of-the-free-world-to-support-the-people-of -ukraine/.

23. Stuart Lau, "China's Xi Warns Putin Not to Use Nuclear Arms in Ukraine," *Politico Europe*, November 4, 2022, https://www.politico.eu/article/china-xi-jinping -warns-vladimir-putin-not-to-use-nuclear-arms-in-ukraine-olaf-scholz-germany-peace -talks/.

24. "China's Xi Tells Putin of 'Changes Not Seen for 100 Years,'" *Al Jazeera*, March 22, 2023, https://www.aljazeera.com/news/2023/3/22/xi-tells-putin-of-changes -not-seen-for-100.

25. See the contributions by Andrea Kendall-Taylor, Ashley Tellis, and Bonny Lin and Brian Hart; see also Hal Brands, "The Battle for Eurasia," *Foreign Policy*, June 4, 2023, https://foreignpolicy.com/2023/06/04/russia-china-us-geopolitics-eurasia -strategy/.

26. Anthony Kuhn "Kim Jong Un Vows Full Support for Russia as Putin Pledges Space Tech for North Korea," *NPR*, September 13, 2023, https://www.npr.org/2023/09 /13/1199190066/russia-north-korea-putin-kim-jong-un-summit.

27. G. John Ikenberry, "Three Worlds: The West, East and South and the Competition to Shape Global Order," *International Affairs* 100, no. 1 (January 2024): 121–138. See also Ashley Tellis's contribution to this volume.

28. See Francis Gavin's contribution to this volume.

29. John Daniszewski, "Putin Waves Nuclear Sword in Confrontation with the West," *AP News*, February 25, 2022, https://apnews.com/article/russia-ukraine-vladimir -putin-europe-poland-nuclear-weapons-2503c0d7696a57db4f437c90d3894b18; Daniel Boffey, "Russia Reasserts Right to Use Nuclear Weapons in Ukraine," *The Guardian*, March 26, 2022, https://www.theguardian.com/world/2022/mar/26/russia-reasserts -right-to-use-nuclear-weapons-in-ukraine-putin.

30. Anton Troianovski and Valerie Hopkins, "With Bluster and Threats, Putin Casts the West as the Enemy," *New York Times*, September 30, 2022.

31. David Sanger, "Inside Biden's Reversal on Sending Long-Range Missiles to Ukraine," *New York Times*, October 17, 2023. These escalation fears also shaped the Biden administration's decision, in mid-2023, to send missiles with ranges of 160 kilometers (99 miles) rather than variants with ranges of 300 kilometers (186 miles), which Russian officials had warned would cross Moscow's redline. See Lolita Baldor, "Ukraine Uses US-Provided Long-Range ATACMS Missiles against Russian Forces for the First Time," *AP News*, October 17, 2023, https://apnews.com/article/atacms-ukraine-longrange-missiles-5fd95f32449d14da22b82d57d6ccab22.

32. Janice Gross Stein, "Escalation Management in Ukraine: 'Learning by Doing' in Response to the 'Threat That Leaves Something to Chance,'" *Texas National Security Review* 6, no. 3 (Summer 2023): 29–50, https://tnsr.org/2023/06/escalation-management-in-ukraine-learning-by-doing-in-response-to-the-threat-that-leaves-something-to-chance/; Hal Brands, "Welcome to the New Era of Nuclear Brinkmanship," *Bloomberg Opinion*, August 27, 2023, https://www.bloomberg.com/opinion/articles/2023-08-27/how-nuclear-threats-not-weapons-have-shaped-the-war-in-ukraine.

33. See, among others, the contributions by Stephen Kotkin and Anne Applebaum.

34. Jeffrey Mankoff, "The War in Ukraine and Eurasia's New Imperial Moment," *Washington Quarterly* 45, no. 2 (July 2022): 127–147.

35. Jim Garamone, "Russia Suffers 'Catastrophic Strategic Disaster' in Ukraine," US Department of Defense, November 9, 2023, https://www.defense.gov/News/News-Stories/Article/Article/3214909/russia-suffers-catastrophic-strategic-disaster-in-ukraine/.

36. Frederick Kagan et al., *The High Price of Losing Ukraine* (Washington, DC: Institute for the Study of War, 2023), https://www.understandingwar.org/backgrounder/high-price-losing-ukraine; Nataliya Bugovaya, *The High Price of Losing Ukraine: Part 2—The Military Threat and Beyond* (Washington, DC: Institute for the Study of War, 2023), https://www.understandingwar.org/backgrounder/high-price-losing-ukraine-part-2-%E2%80%94-military-threat-and-beyond.

37. On Russia's postconflict trajectory, see Andrea Kendall-Taylor's essay.

38. See the contribution to this book by Peter Feaver and William Inboden.

PART I / Origins and Overviews

Chapter One

Ukraine, Russia, China, and the World

Stephen Kotkin

An analyst who had been asked, in 1939, to assess the Soviet invasion of Finland in the Winter War, when shocking Soviet failures and stout Finnish successes were widely noted, might have looked quite the fool in 1940 when the Red Army smashed its way to victory with superior mass and firepower and Moscow imposed a draconian peace. Analyzing a war with the fighting underway requires utmost caution, not definitive statements. That applies no less to Russia's criminal aggression against Ukraine, which—as 2024 began—was entering its third year at full scale and tenth since the seizure of Crimea in 2014. That said, we can take stock of what has transpired and place events within a broad context.

Let us begin with a marvel: four great victories in 2022. First, Ukraine successfully defended its sovereignty and independence, preventing Russian forces from seizing its capital or overturning its elected government. Second, the members of the Western alliance achieved a higher degree of unity and resolve, and a strong sense of renewed purpose, responding vigorously to Moscow's aggression. Third, Russia's vaunted, large, and modernized military, and especially its president, Vladimir Putin, were humiliated—not defeated strategically but exposed for searing incompetence, corruption, and rot. Fourth, the Chinese leadership discredited

Stephen Kotkin is the Kleinheinz Senior Fellow at the Hoover Institution and a senior fellow at the Freeman Spogli Institute for International Studies at Stanford University. He is the author of a trilogy on Joseph Stalin and global history.

itself, particularly in the eyes of Europe but also East Asia, for its strong rhetorical and, soon enough, material support for Russia's wanton violation of international law, effectively blowing up its own grand strategy of inserting a wedge between the European Union and the United States on China policy. These four victories—Ukrainian sovereignty, Western unity, Russian humiliation, and Chinese self-discrediting—were astonishing. I certainly did not foresee them in 2014, or in early 2022. We should not lose sight of this marvel.

Worth noting here as well is a strategic irony. From the vantage point of Washington, Ukraine's valor and ingenuity, against Russia's criminal assault and Beijing's backing of it, managed to bring the entire nongeographic West—the community of states encompassing North America, Europe, and Asia's first island chain, down to Australia—into still firmer alignment on the basis of their shared values and shared institutions. The much-hoped-for American pivot to Asia, to counter China more systematically, turned out to involve enhanced Transatlanticism.

Any strategist would want to consolidate these four great victories. That is, they would want to take them off the table and make sure they were not at risk of reversal.

But the Ukrainians are the ones doing the fighting and the dying. These were fundamentally their victories, and they have a different view. Their view entails a just peace, which their president, Volodymyr Zelensky, defined as regaining all Ukrainian territory recognized under international law, extracting reparations for all the terrible destruction, and imposing war crimes tribunals on those responsible. One is hard-pressed to understand how such a peace would be feasible, short of marching on and conquering Moscow. At an emotional level, it is eminently understandable, given the accumulating documentation of Russian atrocities, from the deliberate killing of civilians to the annihilation and looting of Ukrainian cultural artifacts to wipe out evidence of the existence of a separate Ukrainian nation. Indeed, not only the individual acts but the entire war itself is an atrocity. A just but elusive peace has been allowed to eclipse an unsatisfying but attainable one, however. As a result, each of the four great victories of 2002 remains in play. One could even argue that they were placed at risk, effectively, for the aim of retaking the Sea of Azov littoral in 2023. In late 2022, Ukraine's leadership could potentially have threatened a massive offensive to demand an unconditional armistice while building up but also husbanding materiel and fighters. But Ukrainian societal expectations, whatever Putin's position, made such a farsighted strategy difficult.

Let us go deeper on this point, though. Economics wields very powerful tools, models with far-reaching explanatory power. There is a subtlety, however. The models depend on a qualifying phrase, "all other factors held constant." With that, the models obtain their analytical force. In geopolitics, all other factors can never be held constant. Something was going to happen somewhere, sometime, to alter the context for Ukraine. It could have been in a place few people were watching closely or a place nearly everyone was watching, and yet still transpired in surprising ways. During the entire first two years of the expanded war against Ukraine, I found myself declaiming that something, somewhere, was going to happen, and I've found myself admitting, again and again, that I was wrong: nothing momentous happened to shift the context around Ukraine. Until the bolt from the blue on October 7, 2023, when Hamas fighters from Gaza rampaged into Israeli territory. The revival of war in the region changed, not completely but partially, the context for Ukraine, and not for the better as far as Kyiv is concerned. Going forward, more events around the world, not to mention in Washington and European capitals, could affect the calculation of the stakes and the commitments for, as well as the course of events in, Ukraine.

For some analysts, such an observation might reinforce calls for still greater, still faster delivery of material support for Ukraine right now. For others, though, it might underscore the urgency of taking the four great victories of 2022 off the table before they can be undone. Ukraine's great victories, for itself and its partners, are perishable.

Every day the war continues is a bad day for Ukraine and, for the most part, a good one for Putin, which is why Ukraine needs an armistice. Putin and his forces are wrecking another country. He has his own country, and however rapaciously he covets Ukraine, ultimately he does not need it. Ukraine needs Ukraine. Even if Putin falls far short of his maximalist aims of installing a puppet regime in Kyiv, he wins a lesser but still major victory by denying a peaceful, prosperous Ukraine to Ukrainians. In other words, he wins even without winning.

All wars essentially begin as wars of maneuver. A belligerent attacks and, for a time, moves forward, taking territory, prisoners, and loot. Unless that aggressor attains a quick victory, the conflict devolves into a war of attrition. It can be a month. It can be three months, or six. At some point, absent a lighting victory, the parties find themselves in a war of attrition. Attempts to transform a war of attrition back into a war of maneuver—for example, with a miracle counteroffensive—

historically have proven exceedingly difficult.[1] And that's even before we take into account the advent of near total drone-furnished battlefield transparency.

To be sure, there are cases when, following a relatively quick battlefield victory, the defeated party refuses to accept its fate and mounts an insurgency, which usually provokes a counterinsurgency. The Arabs and Palestinians have been defeated in the war against Israel, beginning in 1948 and numerous times thereafter. Their leadership refuses to accept defeat, however, and has mounted a multigenerational insurgency. Each time renewed conflict erupts at scale, one could argue, it worsens the Palestinian position, with the costs imposed largely on their civilian population. By the same token, Israel has won the war but failed to win the peace. Yet this insurgency-counterinsurgency pattern, prevalent in the past as well as today, does not apply to the case of Ukraine and Russia, so far.

Wars of attrition are governed by just two variables, on each side: the capacity to fight and the will to fight. A country's capacity to fight is not what it has on the battlefield at any given time. It is what that country's population and draft board, as well as its defense-industrial complex and imports, can put onto the field to replace anyone and anything that gets annihilated. In other words, the capacity to fight is not the number of tanks or airplanes or drones a country has but the number of assembly lines and workers to produce them, or partners to sell them. It is not the number of soldiers on the front lines or even the number in reserve but the number available for call-ups, today and tomorrow. If the West supplies Ukraine with a tank, its life expectancy, even with luck, can be counted in weeks, perhaps days. Then it will need to go into the mechanical shops, if it can be salvaged, or harvested for spare parts.

On the Russian side, neither variable is sufficiently in play. Russia's defense production capabilities on home soil are not being bombed or sabotaged at scale. On the contrary, not only do they continue to turn out war materiel but they are doing so in a greater quantity now than before the wider invasion of February 2022. Geography also contributes to Russian resilience. China, North Korea, Mongolia, Kazakhstan, Kyrgyzstan, Turkey, the United Arab Emirates, Iran, and other countries that border Russia or that border countries that border Russia, whether out of self-interest, anti-Westernism, or both, have been serving as vigorous suppliers or transit points for Russia's war effort. It's impossible to blockade Eurasia.

To be sure, severe sanctions and export controls have been intended to exert pressure on Russia's capacity to fight. Others in this volume address the effectiveness of these measures, the feasibility of enforcing them strictly in the real world, and their perverse and unintended consequences. Suffice it to say that besides

Eurasian geography, relationships dating back to the Soviet era, the global demand for energy (particularly outside Europe), and the adaptability of Russian companies, among other factors, have significantly blunted the hoped-for impact of sanctions and export controls in the short and perhaps medium term.

Without direct bombing of Russia and a blockade across a major stretch of the earth, Ukraine can destroy vast quantities of Russian weaponry—which they have been doing—and still make little to no progress. Ukraine can kill or wound several hundred thousand soldiers fighting for Russia, which they have done, but if Russia can more or less replace them, one for one, which they have been doing, Ukraine can make little to no progress.

This leaves Russia's will to fight. The government has been able to pay recruits from the provinces, who otherwise have few if any career prospects, some nine or even ten times the median monthly wage, a highly attractive proposition. If they happen to be killed, their families receive payouts exceeding lifetime earnings in most cases. The regime has been extra cautious not to entangle in the war too many middle- and upper-class families of Moscow and St. Petersburg, where the war is not viewed as an economic opportunity and where political opposition could cascade. For some fighters, the Donbas and other locales resonate as historically Russian territories, in line with regime propaganda. (Several cities in southern and southeastern Ukraine date their founding to Catherine the Great, from Sevastopol to Dnipro and Kherson.) The regime also continues to draw from its prisons—murderers might not seem cut out to make good soldiers, unless the war is essentially murder. (In some instances, prisoners who have served their time at the front and earned pardons have gone back to Russia and committed more crimes, replenishing the prison population to draw upon.) True, the regime has bruited raising the eligibility age from 51 to 65, and to 70 for officers, which is above the male life expectancy, but for now Russian manpower needs appear to be sustainable.

Russia's will to fight is ultimately a question not solely of contract fighters and prisoners but of its leader, who shows few signs of feeling under pressure. On the contrary, Putin's trademark cockiness has been on full view. (More on that to follow.)

On the Ukrainian side, by contrast, both variables are at play. Ukrainian capacity to fight is under massive pressure, in part because so much of it still comes from outside the country. Ukraine is likely to remain dependent for weapons and war materiel on Europe and the United States. These backers have been sending stocks without, for the most part, significantly increasing production lines.

European stocks were already low and have come close to exhaustion, while any new production, at scale, of artillery munitions or other crucial elements of land-warfare fires has lagged, predictably. In a sign of the stock depletion trend, the United States borrowed munitions from South Korea, which constitutionally was not allowed to send them directly to a war zone. Washington was also compelled to supply Ukraine with American cluster munitions, which European countries have outlawed and which initially even the Americans had hesitated to contemplate.

War can be unpredictable, and individual battles can be highly contingent, but longer-term considerations structure outcomes more. No one could be surprised at the severe erosion of Ukraine's capacity to fight—it has been foreseeable since the end of 2022, if not longer. Simply put, Ukraine and its partners have not been able to replace what they have been expending and what the Russians have been destroying. Sure, some analysts have faulted the Europeans and Americans for failing to ramp up defense production lines to support Ukraine all this time while exhausting stocks. But the reasons that prevented timely investments in production of new munitions are the same ones that caused the situation whereby such belated increases became necessary. A lot of things that should happen do not happen.

Ukrainians' will to fight has remained strong despite the duration and intensity of the suffering on home soil (the war has barely touched Russia's territory). How long that endures remains to be seen. Unlike Russia, Ukraine is an open society and partially democratic system that cannot send its people into a meat grinder with little or no regard for casualty numbers. Moreover, Ukraine's will to fight lies not merely in its government and people but in its partners, in the United States and Europe, principally, and in East Asia and Australia. At the beginning of the war, I devised a simple equation to understand its trajectory.

Ukrainian valor/ingenuity + Russian atrocities = Western unity and resolve.

There was never a reason to doubt the persistence of Russian atrocities. And for a long time, Ukrainian valor and ingenuity held. But Ukraine's self-inflicted debacle at Bakhmut, a strategically meaningless city its civilian leadership opted to defend—for political and information-war reasons—unsuccessfully and at an exorbitantly high cost, began to chip away at that vital part of the equation. In some ways, the 2023 spring-summer-fall counteroffensive was meant to restore this variable to peak strength. But beyond the blatant fact that Ukraine (no more than Russia) could not execute a combined arms operation at scale, attempting to do so achieved more than Russia could have on the battlefield at the time: it struck a deep blow to Ukraine's fighting image and thereby softened Western unity and resolve.

A smaller country—a democracy, however flawed, whose casualties reverberate publicly—found itself in a ghastly attritional war against a far larger country—a dictatorship that does not value life or permit free public debate about it. What is more, the smaller country has been *fighting for territory* against one with immense strategic depth. If Ukraine's counteroffensive Hail Mary had been wildly successful in recapturing the territory it sought, it would have converted the current 600-mile-wide front into a 1200-mile one, for unless Russia's capacity to fight suddenly vanished and/or its will to fight was demolished, Putin's forces could continue to lob missiles and, at some point, come back in force. Putin does not require a pause to rebuild his war capacity: he has been doing so while fighting.

The key to any war is to win the peace. A country can win the war and lose the peace. The United States did just that in Afghanistan. Arguably, it also did that in Iraq, although differences of opinion persist over the outcome and it might be too early to assay a definitive judgment. Be that as it may, the principle holds: a battlefield victory can be squandered, as history has shown time and again. Paradoxically, a country can lose a war and win the peace. Arguably the United States did just that in Vietnam, for, notwithstanding the atrocities America committed there, Vietnam became a highly pro-American country over time.

So, Ukraine needs a plan not solely to win the war but to win the peace. Banal as this point is, one is hard-pressed to encounter it in most public discussions about supporting Ukraine. Let us venture a vision of winning the peace for Ukraine.

First, a caveat. I sit in an office at Stanford University, literally in a tower (not ivory but concrete: the Hoover Tower), on an idyllic academic campus in Silicon Valley, far away from the meat grinder front lines. I'm not under bombardment. I have not lost family members in this war. And yet, for me, the war does carry a certain intimacy. Just about every day, for the past two years, and for some years before that, I've been using primary source documents to write about war in these very territories—Kharkiv, the Donbas, Dnipro, Crimea, Odesa. That war took place some eight decades ago. It is a central focus of the final installment in my trilogy, *Stalin: Totalitarian Superpower, 1941–1990s*. By the way, Joseph Stalin presided over victory in that war but, in the fullness of time, he lost the peace. Russian troops, in the 1990s, completed a retreat from positions in Central and Eastern Europe—which were attained by the Red Army at incalculable cost—along the very same roads used by Napoleon, only in the opposite direction.

The *sine qua non* of Ukraine winning the peace is an armistice and an end to the fighting as soon as possible, an obtainable security guarantee, and European Union accession. In other words, a Ukraine, safe and secure, which has joined the West. This after all was the reason why so many Ukrainians risked life and limb to oppose domestic tyrants twice, in 2004 and 2013–2014, before standing up to an invasion by a foreign tyrant. Russia cannot be picked up with a forklift and moved away from Ukraine. Under its current and future governments, Russia needs to be deterred from repeating its aggression or, better still, incentivized not to.

What might constitute a security guarantee remains uncertain—but it cannot be fantasy: it must be obtainable. It should also be rooted in a treaty ratified by the legislatures and therefore the publics of the countries willing to provide it, not something delivered by a leader or group of leaders who are destined to change. It will not flow from sympathetic politicians or pundits who insist that it must happen and will happen because it is the right thing to do. So, it would take very considerable work to achieve. Ditto for EU accession. The EU redistributes considerable sums of money, from richer member countries to poorer ones, and every single recipient EU member, under current rules, would lose EU funds and become a donor state were Ukraine to be admitted. So, some very heavy lifting lies ahead. In Poland, one of Ukraine's most steadfast supporters, societal opposition to Ukrainian grain imports gives a taste of what might be to come. Ukraine, without a fundamental transformation of its current political culture, could outdo Poland or Hungary and Slovakia—other troubled democracies—inside the EU. Still, these challenges, which would follow from an armistice, are better than the unending grinding down from major fighting.

This is a war for Ukraine's sovereignty *and* its future. Consider the demographic devastation. Ukraine's population peaked in 1991–1993 at more than 50 million. Today, no more than 31 million people, and perhaps as few as 28 million, live in areas controlled by the Ukrainian government (almost 6 million live under occupation).[2] Ukraine's fertility rate was already the lowest in Europe before February 2022 (the country was counting 39 births for every 100 deaths). On top of catastrophic battlefield losses, Ukraine has seen the mass dispatch of women and children abroad as well as illegal male flight. According to the United Nations High Commissioner for Refugees (UNHCR), more than 8 million Ukrainians sought refuge abroad in the early days of the war. Significant numbers did return, but nearly 4 million Ukrainians registered as residents in the European Union, including around 1 million each in Germany and Poland; another 1 million made it to

Canada and the United States. The vast majority is gainfully employed, in economies with hunger for labor. Nearly 3 million Ukrainians, the largest single contingent, fled or were taken to Russia, according to UNHCR (how many have stayed inside Russia or moved on remains uncertain). Disabled Ukrainians now number more than 3 million. The war's mental health effects remain to be assessed.

True, by Eastern European standards, Ukraine retains a relatively large population, but not in vital younger age groups. More than half of Ukrainians aged 10 and under are in school abroad, studying in a foreign language, and for most this is their third year of such schooling—what will push them back into a broken country, if the war ends? As the war grinds on, how many more years of going to school in German, Polish, Czech, and other languages, will be necessary for assimilation? And large numbers of newborn Ukrainian children are not on the way: the country has a tiny generation of 20-year-olds because of very low 1990s birthrates during a collapse-induced economic depression, and even now, after massive casualties, Ukraine has at least double the men in their 40s as in their 20s. Why has the Zelensky government refrained from drafting 20-year-olds during the war's first two years? Not because it wants to lose the war, but because it wants to safeguard the country's precarious future.

Continuing the current strategy of indefinite attritional war against the odds, with so much already won and so much new damage daily, seems inexpedient, even if Western support at sufficient scale were to continue without interruption. What appears to be on offer from Putin, if he is taken at face value, is a "negotiation" that begins with Ukrainian recognition of Russian annexations as well as permanent infringement on Ukrainian sovereignty in its freedom to choose international alignments. Putin exhibits a "fixation on controlling Ukraine and its choices," wrote William J. Burns, the director of the Central Intelligence Agency (CIA) and former ambassador to Moscow, in *Foreign Affairs* in early 2024.[3] Ukraine needs an enduring armistice that abjures recognition of Russian annexations or compromises on its sovereign right to join international bodies such as the EU or NATO. History is long and circumstances can suddenly, unexpectedly, and radically change to afford resolutions to long-standing issues left unresolved, such as evicting occupiers. There is no imperative to trade land for peace. But given Putin's position, how would Ukraine possibly obtain a durable armistice on favorable terms?

No country is going to inflict a clean, comprehensive, once-and-for-all defeat on one of the world's two great nuclear powers. Nor is an abrupt—and enduring—

transition to a Russia governed by the rule of law with scrupulous respect for its neighbors' sovereignty on the horizon. Imposing enforceable concessions on Russia from a position of battlefield strength did not work in 2023, and Ukraine appears to lack the wherewithal to try again in 2024 (and possibly beyond). Holding on and waiting for a long-anticipated Russian collapse—whether among troops on the battlefield or on the home front—might not serve to secure from foreign partners the support necessary to carry out even a minimal plan of holding on and building up. True, Ukraine has made notable progress in its domestic manufacture of weapons, especially drones, and its new strategy of necessity—sabotage and striking behind Russian lines as well as on the sea—has raised hopes. So far, it falls some distance from shifting Russia's momentum.

It is long past time to open a more decisive political front.

Authoritarian regimes are both all-powerful and brittle at the same time. They fail at pretty much everything at some point. But they can survive as long as they excel at one thing: suppressing political alternatives. If a regime is highly effective at suppression, it can exhibit serial incompetence, even lose wars, and persist in power. Such a regime can lose more than one war. (Serbia's Slobodan Milošević didn't get kicked out until he lost multiple wars.) So, policy should entail cultivating, encouraging, and promoting political alternatives by overt and covert means. That is how one gets an authoritarian regime's attention. That is how one puts significant pressure on their will to fight. That is how one potentially obtains a more favorable armistice.

To be sure, one can understand the strong desire to avoid a NATO versus Russia war. There is no appetite for such a direct conflict among the governments or publics in Europe or in the United States. Depending on how it came about, it might enhance Western unity and resolve; more likely, it would fracture and undermine cohesion and commitment. What is more, such a direct conflict carries actual existential risks. Anyone can intuit what the US war plan is for major power conflict: Russia attacks, and if they're winning, we nuke them, then they nuke us. Or Russia attacks, and if we're winning, they nuke us, then we nuke them. There are important details, scenarios, and permutations, but boiled down, the war plan is sobering in its underlying simplicity. It is not a plan citizens want their leaders to be arguing back and forth about for real. No one in a position of authority should want to have such discussions in the Situation Room.

Nuclear blackmail is frustrating, and some analysts assert that the threat has been exaggerated, that Putin has been bluffing, that Ukraine's partners have hamstrung themselves. Perhaps. But when an adversary possesses such capabilities, no matter how suicidal or irrational one might think using them would be, their use cannot be ruled out. Whatever probability one might want to assign to nuclear risk in a war between nuclear powers, it is not zero. Even the dual-key system, whereby a president's orders to launch must be matched by similar orders of the defense minister, bears minimal reassurance. Ask yourself why, despite the abject failures of Russia's initial war plan and execution, and much else since, Sergei Shoigu still occupies the position of Russia's defense minister. One reason is that his blatant impotence signifies Russia might effectively be a single-key launch system.

Despite these considerations, the US administration and the Europeans have chosen to incur the risk of Russian escalation and a direct military confrontation with Russia by supporting Ukraine on the field of battle. That has been done, gradually, as the United States, Europeans, and other partners have supplied larger and larger quantities of heavier and heavier weapons with greater and greater reach in the teeth of Russia's threats to respond.

Incurring escalation risks on the battlefield, where Russia is stronger, has been accompanied by a refusal to incur escalation risks in the political arena. Russia's political system is potentially vulnerable, and yet discussions of regime change, let alone bold measures to that effect, have been ruled out as excessively escalatory. All the while, public criticisms of Western policy by backers of Ukraine have mostly chastised hesitancy in supplying weapons systems. Let us note that Ukraine did not come close to running out of Western-provided heavy weapons before calling off the 2023 counteroffensive, so purported issues with their supply did not determine the disappointing outcome. Russia's robust antiaircraft capabilities, moreover, continue to render questionable the pundit-anticipated impact of F-16s (independent of what quantity of supply would be realistic). No doubt some capabilities could have been furnished earlier and in greater quantity. But it is remarkable that critics have by and large not taken up the glaring hesitancy to pressure Putin's regime politically.

Western partners are escalating on the battlefield; they should escalate in the political space. Both the American CIA director and the director of British intelligence (MI6) have publicly boasted about their successes in recruiting Russian defectors, while providing mechanisms for more to do so, including on Telegram. This trolling has drawn infuriated responses from Russian security officials behind the scenes, an encouraging sign. But should that, or could that, effort be taken several steps further? Russian officials and propagandists already obsessively accuse the United States and NATO of fomenting regime change in Moscow—why not commit the offense for which one has already been charged and convicted?

Consider the possibility of constituting some form of a Russian government in exile or a committee of concerned patriots, located in and perhaps rotating through European capitals. I do not mean inviting the pro-Western democratic opposition—which has many courageous activists, but which is also highly fractious and, with exceptions, ineffective in rallying support inside the country—to form a government abroad. Arguably, if they were capable of doing this, they would have done so. (We'll have to see what they do next.) Instead, I mean Russian military and security officials, men in uniform, their medals prominently displayed on their chests: defectors from Putin who are unapologetic Russian nationalists, authoritarian, anti-Western, and evincing little or no affection for Ukraine, but who have concluded, correctly, that the war is badly damaging Russia.[4]

Putin will choose his personal regime over the war every time. How do we know? Look at what happened to General Sergei Surovikin. He remains alive and could be recalled should the war front appreciably deteriorate. But Putin sacked him even though he was by far Russia's best-performing battlefield commander in Ukraine, responsible for the well-executed retreat and tightening lines at Kherson, when Russia got out all its troops and heavy weapons, and for Russia's stunningly successful, well-built defenses in Ukraine's southern regions. But he was viewed as disloyal because of vague associations with the June 2023 mutiny of Yevgeny Prigozhin, the head of the death squads known by the unfortunately romanticizing name Wagner Group.

Prigozhin staged an unwitting referendum on the regime. Once he launched his forces on Moscow, major military brass and security officials, propagandists, elected and appointed officials, almost the entire establishment, mostly kept mum—they did not publicly and vociferously defend Putin and his regime. This exposed the regime's hollowness despite its repressive strength and macroeconomic expertise. At the same time, no commanding officers publicly joined Prigozhin's mutiny, which is perhaps why he called it off. All coups fail, until they succeed; and that happens only when some people take the leap, prompting others to join, in a bandwagon effect, and breaking through the severe collective action challenge. For anyone incurring that extreme personal risk, there was nothing on offer economically from Europe, no proposal for a dialogue about Russia's place in the international order, nothing concrete to salvage the country's future. Note that American intelligence officials publicly hinted they knew beforehand that Prigozhin planned to seize Russia's southern military headquarters in Rostov, where the war in Ukraine is being overseen, but then stated, *in medias res*, that the episode was an internal Russian affair and the United States would not become involved.

Putin sacrificed Prigozhin for his disloyalty—having him assassinated, with implausible deniability, once the mutiny had been thoroughly contained—even though his fighters have been indispensable to the war effort in Ukraine, as well as to maintaining Russia's valued positions across much of Central Africa. Again, Putin chose his regime over the war. Ukraine and its supporters need to put this variable in play.

To be sure, Putin's war has consolidated groups with vested interests in its continuation. They continue to expand their power bases and enrich themselves, while others fall out of windows. But even some of the regime beneficiaries know that Putin is ruining their beloved Russia—hemorrhaging invaluable human capital, failing to ensure even minimal inward technology transfer, isolating the country from traditional partners in Europe, failing to invest in anything but killing machines, mortgaging the future. Prigozhin said two things during the mutiny: (1) if Russia was going to wage war, it should do so with far greater competence; and (2) the war was launched for invalid, corrupt reasons and was a terrible idea. Analysts have focused almost exclusively on the former rather than the latter. They have wrongly asserted that he was a supporter of the war; he was a proponent of his own fame and fortune and of a different, better war, which, he knew, Putin's Russia was unable to fight. He was power-hungry and a war skeptic.

Since Prigozhin's demise, the physicist and former parliamentarian Boris Nadezhdin publicly called Russia's attack on Ukraine a "fatal mistake," and he drew tens of thousands of people, in highly visible public queues, to sign petitions to qualify him to run against Putin in the March 2024 presidential elections. Predictably, the apparatus abruptly disqualified him after he submitted sufficient names. "Dictatorships don't last forever," Nadezhdin declared, giving voice to millions: "And neither do dictators." Eager to use a liberal candidate to portray liberals' supposed impotence, while legitimating the election with ostensible choice, the regime had staged a second unwitting referendum on itself. Any perceived alternative to Putin breaks the regime's information monopoly and reveals its vulnerabilities. Perhaps that explains the suspicious death, at age 47, of Russia's most successful opposition politician, the anticorruption crusader and liberal nationalist Alexei Navalny, who even in an Arctic prison retained enormous influence via social media channels in the run-up to the presidential election.

Navalny's bravery, inventiveness, and moral clarity will define this epoch of Russian history, as much and perhaps more than the role Putin assigns to his own misrule. With his bungled invasion of Ukraine, Putin wrecked his own mystique, losing forever his reputation as a supposed master strategist. He retains control over formidable levers of power, with severe repression and pressures for conformity, but Navalny, to a much lesser extent Nadezhdin, and Prigozhin with his march irrevocably demonstrated in different ways the live possibility of an alternative.

Top-level defectors should not call for Russia's defeat—the vast majority of Russians do not want to see their country defeated—but an end to the fighting. They would not have to praise or make concessions to the West beyond agreeing to an armistice without annexations or sovereign infringement on Ukraine, for Russia's sake. Men in uniform, the ones who are willing to defect, or have already defected but stayed in place, would appeal to their counterparts still in Russia who are fed up with the depth of the Putin regime's self-harm to Russian interests, a kind of Prigozhin episode redux. But this time, they would be greeted with policy levers to help arrest Russia's downward spiral. That would enhance their appeal to the mass of patriotic, nationalist Russians who could be drawn to an alternative to the current personal regime or at least the current course of the regime.

Uniformed defectors need to be given a platform and protection abroad, help to make speech after speech overflowing with insider information about how the war is damaging Russia, and assistance with communications technology to diffuse those messages throughout Russia's public sphere without consequences for those receiving them. This approach would need to be accompanied by a promised package of sanctions relief and investment for Russia in the event of a lasting armistice without conditions. Many European business and government leaders would be relieved to be able to resume partnerships with a Russian government that ends the aggression against Ukraine to rescue Russia. Such a turn of events could possibly dampen the appeal of far-right pro-Russian movements in Europe as well.

Let me be clear: the Western policy goal in support of Ukraine does not need regime change to succeed. It needs to raise the credible threat of regime change, to put pressure on the regime, to expand the public perception and concrete manifestations of political alternatives, to build on what Prigozhin demonstrated, Navalny achieved, and Nadezhdin reconfirmed. To enable Ukraine to obtain an armistice on favorable terms, Putin needs to feel that his regime is at serious risk.

Such a proposal will be treated skeptically, and that is understandable. It suffers from uncertain prospects for success. But what is the better plan? To continue with the existing strategy—which lacks a clear articulation of an attainable victory, let alone for winning the peace—and, as a result, see a softening of the political will to continue backing Ukraine? No supporting country is going to supply Ukraine with the five hundred thousand men and women aged 18–29 it needs, and Ukraine's own ability to do so is circumscribed, physically and politically, in these slaughterhouse conditions. No supporting coalition of countries is able to produce munitions or antiaircraft missiles or other direly needed supplies in the short or perhaps even medium term in sufficient quantities to outgun Russia. And even if, by a miracle, supplies do increase to required levels, a prolonged war of attrition remains a staggering prospect. No miracle weapon system, even in quantity, holds the power to turn the tide decisively. Not even the US superpower calling upon its many alliances can blockade Eurasia.

Applying political pressure systematically, and institutionally, does not preclude continuing to support Ukraine on the battlefield as well, obviously. This is not a substitute set of measures but additions to the tool kit, a ratcheting up of the acknowledged pursuit of defections. As long as Ukrainians are willing to defend their sovereignty, Western countries should live up to their promises to continue vital support—but to be sustainable, all efforts must be undergirded by a strategy that is easily communicated and possible to achieve in order to maintain political backing in democratic polities.[5] That goal, to reiterate, should be an armistice without annexations or sovereignty infringement. For those who argue that any agreement signed by Putin is not worth the paper on which it is printed, that might well be true, but not if he signs it in Beijing, or at least with Xi Jinping at the ceremony.

For the American public, Russia's war against Ukraine needs to be placed in global context. The current US-led international order for decades has had three areas of *territorial* vulnerability: Crimea/Ukraine, Israel, and the South China Sea/Taiwan. (South Korea is protected by a US defense treaty and nuclear umbrella and so are Poland and the Baltic states.) These areas are directly related to the three illiberal Eurasian land empires that view themselves as ancient civilizations predating the US-led liberal order by a millennium or more, and are unwilling to submit to that order as currently configured: Russia, Iran, China. Two of the three vulnerable areas are experiencing renewed conflict at scale, and each runs the risk of still wider war. Conflict in the third, so far at a lower level, could escalate to a world war between the United States and China, which could also have implications for Ukraine as well as Russian assertiveness in other places not protected by an American-led defense treaty and nuclear umbrella. In some ways, everything in the world, no matter how tragic from a humanitarian perspective, no matter how important from a strategic perspective, falls short of the question of managing risks with China. Avoiding either a global war or capitulation in East Asia must be the top US strategic priority.

In this light, too, an indefinite attritional war in Ukraine appears to defy strategic logic no less than capitulation there. True, some analysts argue that credibility is indivisible, so a US failure in Ukraine would reverberate globally, emboldening adversaries. But this latest version of a domino theory does not stand up to the historical record, certainly with regard to the aftermath of Vietnam. The regime in Beijing has zero doubt that the United States will join a war over Taiwan and demonstrates that conviction by assiduously preparing accordingly. US commitment to Ukraine is about that country, not about US credibility. The United States has no treaty obligations vis-à-vis Ukraine.

US support for Ukraine has been impressive. The approach—a version of lend-lease for Ukraine twinned with sanctions against Russia—fits a familiar pattern. The United States is an expeditionary force, with a military that is phenomenal on the water and even better under the water, in the air, and in space. Land is a different matter. When the United States has had to face a large-scale land war in modern times, it has rented a land army. In the Second World War, America effectively rented the Red Army to defeat the Wehrmacht on land. D-Day was an expeditionary action, followed by a comparatively limited land war, not all of which went swimmingly. In East Asia, the United States effectively rented the Chinese land army, and the Japanese had their teeth broken in China. After a US campaign on the sea and much island hopping, an invasion of Japan's home islands was obviated by the dropping of two atomic bombs, on Hiroshima and Nagasaki, and the Soviet land army's bludgeoning of Japanese land forces in Manchuria and on the Korean Peninsula. Subsequent US fighting in Korea and Vietnam, land wars, did not go all that well, with high casualties by American standards. The Gulf War was fought in expeditionary style, using shock-and-awe tactics. Afghanistan, too, resembled an expeditionary war before devolving, like Iraq, into a counterinsurgency.

To be sure, the US Army is a highly competent, dedicated service, with formidable capabilities, but casualties in land warfare exceed those of expeditionary or maritime warfare by many orders of magnitude—a difficult proposition for a democracy, not to mention a military that prioritizes force protection. The US land army is now at its smallest since 1940. Today the United States is, consciously or not, renting the Ukrainian land army to degrade Russia's land army to sizable effect. (The same posture could be said to apply to the position of Germany or even Poland and Finland, which, unlike Germany, have real armies.) This looks like American strategic DNA. But instructing Ukraine to suffer land-war-scale casualties against Russia, a land power par excellence with a regime that does not value human life, never struck me as a persuasive strategy in this war. Consider, finally, that although the East Asian theater is more water than land, land warfare there cannot be ruled out. And yet, there is no obvious option, as it were, to rent. (We could add that the United States has lost its shipbuilding capacity.) Whatever the outcome of Ukraine's noble fight, the lesson for America is already sobering.

Needless to add, any "strategy" worthy of the name entails matching means to ends. The United States does not seem clear about what it wants to achieve, let alone how. That analyst of the Winter War in 1939, by the way, was Adolf Hitler's general staff. They miscalculated.

NOTES

1. This was laid out in typically brutalist style in John J. Mearsheimer, "Bound to Lose: Ukraine's 2023 Counteroffensive," *John's Substack* (blog), September 2, 2023, https://mearsheimer.substack.com/p/bound-to-lose.

2. Ella Libanova, "Ukraine's Demography in the Second Year of the Full-Fledged War," *Focus Ukraine* (blog), Wilson Center Kennan Institute, June 27, 2023, https://www.wilsoncenter.org/blog-post/ukraines-demography-second-year-full-fledged-war; Jadwiga Rogoza, "Ukraine in the Face of a Demographic Catastrophe," Center for Eastern Studies, July 11, 2023, https://www.osw.waw.pl/en/publikacje/osw-commentary/2023-07-11/ukraine-face-a-demographic-catastrophe; Olena Harmash, "Ukrainian Refugees: How Will the Economy Recover with a Diminished Population?," *Reuters*, July 7, 2023, https://www.reuters.com/world/europe/however-war-ends-ukraines-diminished-population-will-hit-economy-years-2023-07-07/.

3. William J. Burns, "Spycraft and Statecraft," *Foreign Affairs*, January 30, 2024.

4. Such views are well articulated by a Federal Security Service general. Mariia Litvinova, " 'Putin Has Done More Damage to the Country than Any Other Sovereign Has Done in Its Entire History.' Retired FSB General Yevgeny Savostyanov on the Confrontation with the West and the Future of Russia" [" 'Putin nanec strane takov vred, kotoroyi ne nanosil ni odin gosudar' za vsiu ee istoriiu": general FSB v otstavke Evgenii Savostianov o protivosostoianii s Zapadom i budushchem Rossii"], *Republic*, February 11, 2024, https://republic.ru/posts/111434.

5. Ivan Krastev and Mark Leonard, "Wars and Elections: How European Leaders Can Maintain Public Support for Ukraine," European Council on Foreign Relations, February 21, 2024, https://ecfr.eu/publication/wars-and-elections-how-european-leaders-can-maintain-public-support-for-ukraine/.

Chapter Two

Why Putin Invaded Ukraine

Michael McFaul and Robert Person

On February 24, 2022, Russian president Vladimir Putin launched a full-scale invasion of Ukraine, expanding dramatically the war against Ukraine he began in 2014 and starting the largest war in Europe since World War II. Hundreds of thousands of Ukrainian and Russian soldiers have already been killed or wounded. More than ten thousand Ukrainian (and a handful of Russian) civilians have died and many more have been wounded. Tens of thousands of tanks, artillery, aircraft, and ships have been destroyed. The war has done deep damage to, first and foremost, the Ukrainian economy but also the Russian economy. Some worry that Ukraine is the first front of a larger war in Europe that will eventually expand to Moldova, Estonia, Latvia, Lithuania, and even Poland, thereby dragging the United States and NATO into war with Russia. Understanding why this war

Michael McFaul is director at the Freeman Spogli Institute for International Studies, the Ken Olivier and Angela Nomellini Professor of International Studies at Stanford University, and the Peter and Helen Bing Senior Fellow at the Hoover Institution. He served for five years in the Obama administration, first as special assistant to the president and senior director for Russian and Eurasian affairs at the National Security Council at the White House (2009–2012), and then as US ambassador to the Russian Federation (2012–2014). Robert Person is an associate professor of international relations at the United States Military Academy and director of West Point's curriculum in international relations. He is a resident fellow at West Point's Modern War Institute and a member of the Council on Foreign Relations.

The views expressed in this chapter are those of the authors and do not represent the official policy or position of the US Army, Department of Defense, or US government.

started, therefore, is important not only to scholars of international relations but to policymakers, present and future.

In this chapter, we argue that three factors—power, regimes, and individuals—interacted to cause this war. Specifically, we argue that the perception of an asymmetric balance of power provided a necessary, permissive condition for starting this war. A more powerful Ukraine and a less powerful Russia would have made war less likely. Second, regime types played a role too. Over the last twenty years, Russia has become more autocratic while Ukraine has become more democratic. Those divergent regime trajectories fueled growing tensions between the two countries. However, shifting balances of power and changing regime types were necessary but insufficient causes for starting this war. A third factor—Putin and his ideas—was essential. Enabled by a growing personalistic dictatorship, Putin and his distinct world outlook played a direct causal role in launching this invasion.

In focusing on power, regimes, and individuals as the causes of this war, we reject two alternative explanations—NATO expansion and innate Russian imperialism. NATO expansion has been a source of tension between Moscow and the West for a long time, dating back to the alliance's creation in 1949. But this tension has not been a constant driver of conflict over the decades; rather, it has been a variable. And it was most certainly not the main reason for Putin's decision to invade Ukraine in 2022: there was no movement underway to offer Ukraine membership in NATO at the time. There had not been since 2008.

Russian imperialism is a more powerful alternative explanation—a hypothesis supported by hundreds of years of history. Russia has expanded when it has the means to do so, irrespective of regime type or leadership, so the argument goes. True, Putin has invoked imperial legacies to help mobilize support for his invasion of Ukraine in 2022. That many Russians support his war underscores the fact that imperialist ideas are deeply rooted in Russian society. But there is evidence to undermine this argument of imperial continuity. Russia in the post-Soviet era has not always sought to attack or annex its neighbors. There has been variation, and that variation has been driven by power, regimes, and individuals. A less powerful Russia, a more democratic Russia, or a Russia ruled by a leader other than Putin would have been less imperial and less bellicose toward its neighbors, including Ukraine.

The Balance of Power

Any explanation of war must begin with an analysis of the balance of power, both real and perceived. The distribution of the material means of war always plays some role in starting wars. In fact, some realist theorists believe that the balance of power between states is all one needs to know to explain the behavior of states in the international system. In their view, regime type and individuals play no role. For example, when explaining the clash between Great Britain and Germany in the 19th century, Eyre Crowe, the British Foreign Office's leading expert on Germany, concluded "that Germany's intentions were irrelevant; its capabilities were what mattered."[1] The changing map of Europe over the last thousand years shows that strong states grow at the expense of their weaker neighbors. Set against this historical pattern, Russia's invasion of Ukraine in 2022 is nothing unusual—it's just what great powers do.

Power Asymmetries. The shifting balance of military capabilities between Ukraine and Russia over the last thirty years most certainly played a role in triggering this war. In the wake of the collapse of the Soviet Union (USSR), Russia's military and economic capabilities were weak. Some at the time even fretted over the collapse of the Russian Federation itself. Amidst the post-Soviet economic meltdown, Russia simply did not have the means to invade Ukraine. Even a decade after the USSR's dissolution, many analysts concluded that Russia was "finished" as a significant player in international politics. As Thomas Graham wrote in 1999, "We are witnessing a geo-political and geo-economic shift of historic dimensions, one in which Russia will become less and less an actor in world affairs, while running the risk of becoming an object of competition among more advanced and dynamic powers."[2]

Since the mid-1990s, however, Russia has strengthened politically and economically, even if events like the 1998 or 2008 economic meltdowns slowed its growth temporarily. Russia's economy in 2022 was much larger and stronger than thirty years earlier. Moreover, because of the extensive military modernization reform known as "New Look" in 2008, the Russian army became smaller but better armed and trained than its Soviet predecessor. Putin and Russia's minister of defense Sergei Shoigu also devoted significant resources to revamping military equipment, enhancing military training, and strengthening Russia's power projection capabilities more broadly. Before the invasion, Russia had over one million soldiers on active duty and regularly spent more on defense as a percentage of GDP than the United States. Since 2022, Russian military expenditures could now be over 6%–8% of its GDP.[3]

As Russia became more powerful in the three decades after the collapse of the Soviet Union, Ukraine did not keep up. By most measures, Ukraine's power was growing too but not as fast as Russia's. This was especially true concerning military capabilities: Ukrainian defense spending remained flat until 2014. On other basic metrics of power such as fighting-age male population, size of the economy, and raw materials, Russia also maintained an advantage that grew over time.

If a state cannot balance against the power of an opponent alone, allying with more powerful states is another option. That choice, however, was not available to Ukrainian leaders since Ukraine has never been issued an invitation to join NATO. Until 2022, NATO countries had done little to help Ukrainians defend themselves and a lot to weaken Ukrainian deterrence. In 1994, the United States and the United Kingdom collaborated with Russia to convince Ukraine to give up its nuclear weapons in exchange for security assurances, as well as financial assistance to dismantle its nuclear weapons. In compelling Ukraine to sign the Budapest Memorandum, the West was disarming, not arming, Ukraine.

Just a few years later in 2008, Russia invaded Georgia. Six years after that, Russia attacked Ukraine, annexed Crimea, and stoked a separatist war in the Donbas. Even after this Russian aggression, however, the United States and other NATO allies consistently refused to provide lethal military assistance to Ukraine. Only in March 2018 did the Trump administration finally decide to send anti-tank Javelin missiles to Ukraine, but on the condition that they would be stored in western Ukraine, far from the front lines in the east. NATO also took no definitive steps to accelerate Ukraine's membership in the alliance in the decade leading up to the 2022 war. Any objective assessment of the balance of power between Russia and Ukraine in early 2022 would have concluded that Russia had a decisive advantage.

Perceptions and Misperceptions of the Balance of Power. The objective balance of powers matters but so do perceptions (and misperceptions) of capabilities. Before the full-scale invasion of Ukraine in 2022, Putin already had used military power successfully several times, thus fueling the perception that Russia's armed forces had growing capabilities. In the Kremlin's view, Russia had used military power effectively in Chechnya in 1999–2000, Georgia in 2008, Ukraine in 2014, and Syria in 2015. Successful information operations against Ukraine, Europe, and the United States from 2014 onwards also fueled Putin's propensity for risky but successful behavior, leading him to believe in his intelligence services' ability to pave the way for successful military action.

This run of apparent successes boosted Putin's confidence in the ability of Russia's military to win easily again in Ukraine in 2022. His confidence in a quick decapitation strike against Kyiv and easy victory in Ukraine is apparent in the array of military units and weaponry that formed the first wave of Russia's 2022 invasion: these were largely "administrative columns" of infantry and mechanized forces equipped to advance quickly in the face of minimal resistance. They were accompanied by numerous Rosgvardia (Russian National Guard) troops to stabilize and establish political control over quickly conquered Ukrainian territories.

Putin was not the only leader with these expectations of a quick, decisive Russian victory. President Joe Biden and his administration shared the same assessment, as did many other leaders in Europe. Once the war began, US intelligence—at least according to information leaked to the press—believed that Russian soldiers would conquer Ukraine easily. This assessment was made by counting both the number of Russian soldiers and tanks but also Ukrainian soldiers, tanks, and the like. Variables like "resolve," "will to fight," or "preparedness" are more difficult to measure and did not factor prominently in these analyses, perhaps due to a misreading of the collapse of Afghanistan just a few months prior. Ukraine's Territorial Defense Forces—reservists and volunteers who took up arms to defend their local cities and villages—also did not feature prominently in the initial balance-of-power assessments.

Since many predicted that Russian soldiers would be patrolling downtown Kyiv just weeks after the war began, American and European leaders encouraged the Biden administration to withdraw its diplomatic mission from Kyiv accordingly and destroy sensitive equipment at the American embassy in the Ukrainian capital—they didn't think they would be back anytime soon. We now know that these assessments made in Moscow and Washington were incorrect, but this became evident only after we witnessed Russia's military on the battlefield.

Leaders often initiate wars when they assess (accurately or not) the balance of power to be in their favor. Even relatively equal distributions of power can tempt leaders into believing that they can benefit from war. Furthermore, leaders may be more likely to start wars when they believe that changes in the long-term balance of power favor decisive action now, rather than waiting to fight in the future when the adversary might be stronger. This "better now than later" logic sits at the heart of preventive war strategies. But the farther a leader looks beyond the horizon, the greater the role of perception (and misperception) in assessing the likelihood of future conflict and the balance of power. Extrapolating from trends in Russian, Ukrainian, and Western power (as he saw them), by 2022 Putin came to the conclusion that the balance of power favored bold Russian action.

Capabilities, Resolve, and the Failure of Deterrence. Ukraine and the West failed to deter the Russian invasion of Ukraine in 2022. Though Putin received private warnings from the United States and other Western governments about the political and economic consequences of invading, the West's weak response to Russia's invasion of Georgia in 2008 and Ukraine in 2014 provided ample evidence to Putin that threats in 2022, too, were empty. Furthermore, Putin (incorrectly) expected Ukrainian citizens to welcome his army with open arms, which would lead Ukrainian forces to wither under Russian attack. This misguided assessment of Ukraine's will to fight further undermined the deterrent threat. But the balance of capabilities—Russian power set against weak Ukraine—was an objective reality that undermined hope of deterring Putin's decision to invade. As tanks rolled across the frontier in February 2022, Ukraine did not have the military power (or Western military support) to alter Putin's calculus.

A different balance of power more in favor of Ukraine might have changed Putin's calculus. Imagine, for instance, if NATO in 2014 had delivered to Ukraine the weapons they delivered after 2022. Or what if Ukraine had joined NATO in 2008 or 1998 when Russia did not have the military means nor a leader in place with the impulse to try to stop membership? A stronger Ukraine in NATO could have deterred Putin from invading in 2022.

Regimes

Capabilities shape decisions about war and peace but do not determine them. Today, the United States has the capability to invade Canada, but no one is worried about an American president deciding to invade, occupy, and annex Saskatchewan. Germany and Japan today are much more powerful than they were at the end of World War II, but their weaker neighbors are not worried about being attacked as they were in the last century. Amazingly, Lithuanian leaders have welcomed the permanent stationing of five thousand German soldiers on their soil even though this same neighbor ravaged the Baltic country just a few decades ago. The ability to invade does not automatically lead to war. Other factors shaping the ability and willingness to wage war matter too.

Regime type is one of those factors. As a tendency in international politics, democracies are less likely to go to war with each other than with autocracies; the correlation of peace between democracies is a strong one. Power interacts with regime type too: the correlation of conflict between *powerful* autocracies and *powerful* democracies is also robust. To think of extreme cases, the powerful and democratic United States is not threatened by weak autocracies like Tajikistan or Equatorial Guinea. Nor, for that matter, is Ukraine. But regime type can play an independent role in fueling conflict that is not solely derivative of power. Dictatorships in weaker countries can be threatening to democracies, as American anxieties over the theocracies in Afghanistan and Iran show. And democracy in small countries can threaten even the most powerful autocracies, as China's anxieties about democratic Taiwan prove.

In this vein, changes in regime types have influenced dynamics in Ukraine-Russia relations over the last three decades. In the 1990s, the political systems in both Ukraine and Russia were considered by most to be unconsolidated democracies. In fact, democratization in the Russian Republic in the final days of the Soviet Union helped Ukraine secure its sovereignty and post-Soviet independence. In the final years of the Soviet period, Russia's leading democratic movement, Democratic Russia, considered the democratic forces in Ukraine as their allies, not their enemies. Throughout the 1990s, the leaders of both Russia's democracy and Ukraine's democracy sought integration and closer relations with the democratic West. The security interests of these two new democracies were aligned. There was no specter of war between Ukraine and Russia.

In the first two decades of the 21st century, Ukraine democratized further, albeit in fits and starts, while Russia under Putin became more autocratic. Key moments of democratic breakthrough in Ukraine—the Orange Revolution in 2004–2005 and the Revolution of Dignity in 2013–2014—especially exacerbated tensions between the two countries.[4] To remember the obvious counterfactual, if there was no Revolution of Dignity overthrowing Ukraine's corrupt and increasingly autocratic president Viktor Yanukovych, there would have been no Russian invasion and annexation of Ukraine in 2014. In parallel, tensions between Russia and the wider democratic world rose as Putin sought to undermine democracy in numerous Western countries with even sharper methods, setting the stage for hostilities not seen since the height of the Cold War.

Personalized Dictatorship. Throughout this period, the Russian political regime grew increasingly autocratic under Vladimir Putin as well. Admittedly, this makes it difficult to untangle whether it was the regime type or the individual Russian leader that was driving these tensions. But what is clear is that as Russia became more autocratic, that political system gave Putin more influence over decision-making, making his personal role in starting this war even more apparent.

Not all autocracies are alike and therefore not all dictatorships behave the same way in international politics. Russia's specific form of authoritarianism matters too. It has evolved into a classic personalist dictatorship with overwhelming power concentrated in Putin's hands. In Putin's Russia, power is exercised largely through informal, noninstitutionalized personal relationships: for members of the political elite, their power, influence, and wealth are derived not from their formal position in the Russian political system but rather from one's direct personal relationship with Putin. It is no wonder that nearly everyone thought to be in Putin's inner circle today have relations that stretch back decades, some as far back as Putin's childhood in Leningrad, or his career as a Committee for State Security (KGB) officer, or even his time in the St. Petersburg mayor's office in the early 1990s.

These loyalists have not earned Putin's confidence, let alone trust, by telling him unpleasant hard truths. Like the sycophants that surround most personalist dictators, they have maintained their privileged positions by telling Putin the things he wants to hear. Surrounded by these yes-men and unconstrained by independent political parties, economic interest groups, free media, or robust civil society, Putin now rules from an echo chamber that is increasingly isolated from reality. Misled by his top advisors about the likelihood of quick victory in Ukraine, Putin's personalist dictatorship denied him critical information that could have slowed the march to war.

Even if they disagreed with Putin's decision to launch an ill-advised war against Ukraine in 2022, Russian political elites had no incentive to express their true preferences. Putin's main source of political control is his power to direct the vast inflow of natural resource rents to those individuals who implemented his policy preferences. This, along with a trove of compromising material on elites compiled over decades, provides Putin with an extraordinary blackmail power over government officials and oligarchs who might be tempted to challenge him.

To defect from Putin's coalition (whether before or after the decision was taken to launch the war) would have been highly risky, or even suicidal, with minimal chance of success. His assassination of Yevgeny Prigozhin in 2023, once a Putin loyalist in charge of a vital instrument of Russian power, the mercenary Wagner Group, sent a powerful signal to elites about the costs of defection, echoing earlier coercive acts from Putin such as the killing of Alexander Litvinenko in 2006 and the 2003 jailing for a decade of Russia's richest businessman, Mikhail Khodorkovsky.

Though Russia's power asymmetry was significant and its personalist autocracy nearly unchecked domestically, these two factors alone did not make war inevitable in 2022. A different leader, controlling these same power capabilities and empowered by this same regime type still could have made a different choice about invading Ukraine in 2022. To understand why Russia decided to launch this invasion, we must add a third factor—its leader, Vladimir Putin.

Leaders

Putin was an accidental president. Boris Yeltsin and his inner circle chose Putin to be prime minister in 1999, acting president on January 1, 2000, and their candidate for president in the March 2000 elections. Yeltsin's goal was to preserve the political and economic system in place at the time, not destroy it. At the time, Yeltsin's entourage (Yeltsin himself was quite incapacitated) was worried about the resurgence of an alternative group of elites winning power. This group of challengers centered around communist-friendly prime minister Yevgeny Primakov and Moscow mayor Yury Luzhkov. Putin was considered the best candidate within their circles to defeat these challengers—and he did.

Back then, Putin did not have firm views on many issues. Today, he wants his followers at home and abroad to believe that he resisted the collapse of the Soviet Union, criticized neoliberal economic ideas, and championed conservative values. By 2000, however, he had spent a whole decade working for Russian leaders who worked to destroy the Soviet Union, implemented neoliberal economic reforms, and embraced liberal values.[5] In his first years in power, Putin continued market reforms, including a 13% flat income tax, lower corporate taxes, and conservative fiscal and monetary policies. Initially, he also continued Yeltsin's pro-Western orientation regarding foreign policy, especially after the September 11, 2001, terrorist attacks against the United States, which united Putin and President George W. Bush in their common fight against terrorism. But this would soon change.

What Putin Fears Most: Democracy. In fact, Putin has held one firm view from the very beginning of his political career—a disdain for checks and balances on his power. Almost immediately, he began rolling back independent pockets of political power, starting first with television companies, then oligarchs, and later governors. The 2004 presidential election was much less free and fair than the 2000 contest and was characterized by widespread electoral fraud. By the end of the decade, the debate was over: Russia was a dictatorship, though scholars continued to debate what kind of dictatorship.

But it is not just the idea of a democratic Russia that threatens Putin. It is also the prospect of democratic neighbors, especially Slavic neighbors, that threaten his control and sense of security. Since his earliest days in power, Putin has consistently sought for Russia a privileged and uncontested sphere of influence in the post-Soviet region. In Putin's thinking, Russia, as a great power, has the right to influence and even veto the sovereign political decisions—both foreign and domestic—of its neighbors. The authority to quash any policies that might counter

Russia's interest is the privilege Putin demands. But he also demands exclusivity of such privilege: Russia can be the only great power with free reign to pursue its interests unhindered in the region. Having independent democratic neighbors who make their own decisions is obviously incompatible with Putin's vision: it is hard for him to pull puppet strings from the Kremlin when the puppets have a mind of their own and refuse to dance at his command. It is thus little wonder that he has lashed out with intense—even emotional—hostility whenever democracy has advanced in the region.

Throughout the early 2000s, a series of popular uprisings that would come to be labeled the "color revolutions" swept aside corrupt leaders in several postcommunist countries near Russia, replacing them with new leaders whose foreign policies were generally oriented toward the democratic West. Haunted by the alleged specter of American-led regime change, Putin perceived the 2003 Rose Revolution in Georgia as a threat to his legitimacy at home and a new effort by the United States to peel away Moscow's partners.

Hoping to install a loyal puppet in Kyiv the following year, Putin intervened in the presidential election in Ukraine that triggered the Orange Revolution. Going so far as to actively campaign with his preferred candidate, Viktor Yanukovych, Putin showed his willingness to determine the outcome of that election by any means necessary. Alas, his machinations were thwarted by the Ukrainian people, who had other ideas about how their leaders should be chosen. Putin saw the Orange Revolution in Ukraine in 2004 as an even greater threat than the Rose Revolution in Georgia, in part because Ukraine was a more powerful country and in part because the practice of democracy in a Slavic country undermined Putin's own argument at home that Slavs have a cultural proclivity for a strong leader and powerful autocratic state. If democratic protests could topple corrupt strongmen in Russia's neighboring countries, why could the contagion not spread to Russia?

Regrettably, the Orange Revolution did not produce the democratic consolidation that its leaders aspired to achieve. In 2010, Putin's corrupt Ukrainian puppet, Yanukovych, won the election as president and the defeated incumbent Viktor Yushchenko voluntarily handed over power, a hallmark of peaceful democratic transitions. But with Moscow's man now ruling in Kyiv, Ukraine didn't seem all that threatening to Russia anymore.

The following year, however, the Arab Spring exploded, toppling autocrats initially through mass peaceful demonstrations that rattled Putin. The shocks continued: in late 2011, a falsified parliamentary election in Russia and Putin's announcement that he planned to run for a third presidential term the following spring sparked mass mobilization against Putin and his regime, the greatest threat to his power ever. Putin framed this mobilization as an American plot to challenge his rule and regime—a coup attempt funded and orchestrated by the administration of President Barack Obama. Putin eventually employed even more draconian and repressive methods to quell this democratic challenge to his autocratic rule. One of the popular leaders of the democratic movement, Boris Nemtsov, was murdered in 2015, followed by the 2020 poisoning and 2021 jailing of another popular leader of this movement, Alexey Navalny (who ultimately died, most likely as the result of state-sanctioned murder, in prison in February 2024). But the threat was now well-defined for Putin and his regime: "fifth column traitors" (otherwise known as democratic activists) and their Western allies posed the greatest threat to Putin's power.

Only two years after the Arab Spring and Bolotnaya protests—the name given to the peaceful demonstrations in Russia against Putin in 2011–2012—Ukrainians took to the streets in the fall of 2013, this time to protest Yanukovych's decision to not sign an association with the European Union. In February 2014 (most likely with prodding from the Kremlin), Yanukovych authorized the use of force against the protestors, but the tactic failed, compelling Putin's puppet to flee Ukraine and allowing a new moment of democratic renewal in Ukraine.

Putin was infuriated. For in their refusal to become subservient vassals to the Kremlin, the Ukrainian people proved again with their protests that they saw their future aligned with the democratic West, not autocratic Russia. Both to retaliate against and to weaken the new pro-democracy and pro-Western government in Ukraine, Putin annexed Crimea and supported with money and soldiers a secessionist rebellion in the Donbas region of eastern Ukraine. Throughout this period, Russia also directed its full nonmilitary arsenal against the government in Kyiv, waging a multidomain political, economic, social, and information "hybrid war" in the hopes of toppling the democratically elected Ukrainian government.

Thanks to the resilience of the Ukrainian people, Putin's efforts to neuter Ukrainian democracy have mostly failed for the last two decades. They failed in 2004 when the Orange Revolution prevented Putin from installing his preferred president of Ukraine. They failed in 2014 when the Revolution of Dignity prevented the corrupt Yanukovych from shackling Ukraine's political and economic future with Russia's. And from 2014 onward, they failed to destabilize and topple Kyiv's democratic government, even in the face of a Russian-manufactured-and-funded civil war. But the threat to Putin of Ukrainian democracy remained. Growing impatient and encouraged by his sycophants, Putin finally came to believe that he had only one strategy left to solve his Ukraine problem once and for all: full-scale invasion to achieve regime change and subordination.

What Putin Believes in Most and Understands Least: Identity. Putin's deep-seated hatred of democracy is not the only idea that led him to the fateful decision to invade in 2022. Also important are his views about Ukraine and Ukrainians. Put bluntly, Putin believes that Ukrainians are just Russians with accents and that the state of Ukraine is an artificial construct that should not exist.

Putin does not try to hide these views. In 2008 at the NATO summit in Bucharest, Putin told President Bush, "You have to understand, George, that Ukraine is not even a country. Part of its territory is in Eastern Europe and the greater part was given to us."[6] Putin blames not only the West but also the Bolsheviks for "creating" the idea and reality of a sovereign Ukrainian state. In his 2021 essay "On the Historical Unity of Russians and Ukrainians," he characterizes the 1924 Soviet constitution that created the Ukrainian Soviet Socialist Republic as an equal republic of the USSR as "a time bomb which exploded the moment the safety mechanism provided by the leading role of the [Communist Party] was gone [in 1991]." Tellingly, Putin asserted that this "time bomb" of Ukrainian sovereignty that Lenin and Stalin created threatened the very "foundation of our [Russian] statehood."[7] In Putin's reading, not only does Ukraine lack the right to exist as a sovereign state but its independence threatens Russia's very existence.

Even more dangerous than Putin's view about the illegitimacy of an independent Ukrainian state are Putin's beliefs about the Ukrainian nation, which he considers no less artificial and illegitimate. In adopting the Soviet (and Russian imperial) narrative of Ukrainians as Slavic "little brothers" to Russians, Putin denies Ukrainians the right to exist as anything other than in reference to Russia. Putin concludes his 2021 article with the following:

> Our spiritual, human and civilizational ties formed for centuries and have their origins in the same sources, they have been hardened by common trials, achievements and victories. Our kinship has been transmitted from generation to generation. It is in the hearts and the memory of people living in modern Russia and Ukraine, in the blood ties that unite millions of our families. Together we have always been and will be many times stronger and more successful. For we are one people.[8]

These views on the artificiality of Ukrainian statehood and identity were not merely cynical propaganda to justify chess moves in a realist game of great-power politics; they are deeply held and internalized beliefs that Putin holds. He has spoken on such themes repeatedly before and during the war, including in his February 21, 2022, speech explaining the reasoning behind his full-scale invasion: "Since time immemorial, the people living in the south-west of what has historically been Russian land have called themselves Russians and Orthodox Christians. . . . Modern Ukraine was entirely created by Russia or, to be more precise, by Bolshevik, Communist Russia . . . by separating, severing what is historically Russian land."[9]

Not only did these views justify in Putin's mind the legitimacy of his invasion but they also shaped his expectations for what would happen after the invasion. Russian soldiers would be welcomed by their Slavic brethren in Ukraine, and fellow Orthodox Christians would celebrate the reunification with their historic homeland, Russia. It was a costly mistake: in denying the existence of an independent Ukrainian state and nation, Putin severely underestimated the strength of Ukraine's national identity and the willingness of its citizens to fight and die to defend their *true* homeland.

Through the Looking Glass: Putin's "Nazi" Obsession. Though he denied the existence of a distinct Ukrainian nationality, Putin's beliefs about who exactly he *was* fighting were no less consequential in motivating his war. Who, in Putin's mind, was the enemy that must be eliminated? Here again, his grotesque views on identity, history, and memory are a perversion with deadly—even genocidal—consequences.

In explaining his decision to invade Ukraine, Putin asserted that one of his central aims was "denazification"—that is the overthrow of the Ukrainian government headed by the democratically elected President Volodymyr Zelensky. Casting his war as a noble continuation of the Soviet Union's struggle against Hitler, Putin addressed the Ukrainian armed forces directly in his February 24, 2022, speech justifying the invasion: "Your fathers, grandfathers and great-grandfathers did not fight the Nazi occupiers and did not defend our common Motherland to allow today's neo-Nazis to seize power in Ukraine. You swore the oath of allegiance to the Ukrainian people and not to the junta, the people's adversary which is plundering Ukraine and humiliating the Ukrainian people."[10]

Two years after the start of his invasion, Putin has not abandoned the ideas that fueled his original war objectives: unite Ukrainians and Russians as one Slavic nation, demilitarize, and "denazify" Ukraine. Russia's former president and current member of the Russian Security Council, Dmitry Medvedev, was even more blunt in describing the eliminationist goals of the invasion, stating on his Telegram channel that

The existence of Ukraine is deadly for Ukrainians . . . no matter how much they aspire to the mythical European Union and NATO. When choosing between eternal war and inevitable death and life, the absolute majority of Ukrainians (except for a minimal number of sick nationalists) will eventually choose life. They will realize that life in a big common state, which they do not love much now, is better than death. Their death and the death of their loved ones. And the sooner Ukrainians realize this, the better.[11]

Putin played an essential role in starting this war; the ideas animating his decision to invade were unique, downright unusual, and decidedly deadly. A different Russian leader motivated by different ideas could have responded differently. In fact, we do not have to be too creative to think of a plausible counterfactual. Imagine if the pro-democratic and pro-Western first deputy prime minister Boris Nemtsov had been elected president in 2000. He was Yeltsin's heir apparent until the 1998 financial crisis toppled Nemtsov's liberal government. The Russian political system would not have become so autocratic, and Russia would not have tried to undermine Ukraine's democracy—not in 2004, not in 2014, and not in 2022.

Alternative Explanations

Our explanation for Russia's 2022 invasion of Ukraine is a complex, multifaceted one. The twisted interaction of structural preconditions, domestic politics, and individuals and their beliefs makes for a complicated causal explanation.[12] There are simpler—but flawed—theories. Two are most prominent: Russia's reaction to NATO expansion and Russian imperialism.

NATO Expansion. In a provocative 2014 *Foreign Affairs* article titled "Why the Ukraine Crisis is the West's Fault: The Liberal Delusions That Provoked Putin," John Mearsheimer placed blame for Russia's 2014 invasion of Ukraine squarely on the West's shoulders. "The United States and its European allies," Mearsheimer wrote, "share most of the responsibility for the crisis. The taproot of the trouble is NATO enlargement, the central element of a larger strategy to move Ukraine out of Russia's orbit and integrate it into the West."[13] After a selective narration of the history of NATO expansion that confirms his realist priors and denies any Ukrainian agency in his story, Mearsheimer asserts that the Revolution of Dignity was in fact a "Washington-backed . . . coup" that forced Putin's hand.[14] To achieve a stable peace in Eastern Europe, he argues, "the United States and its allies should publicly rule out NATO's expansion into both Georgia and Ukraine."[15]

Mearsheimer has since doubled down on the "NATO is to blame" argument to explain the 2022 invasion. Nearly four months after the invasion started, he still argued,

> The United States is principally responsible for causing the Ukraine crisis. . . . Specifically, I am talking about America's obsession with bringing Ukraine into NATO and making it a Western bulwark on Russia's border. The Biden administration was unwilling to eliminate that threat through diplomacy and indeed in 2021 recommitted the United States to bringing Ukraine into NATO. Putin responded by invading Ukraine on February 24th of this year.[16]

Mearsheimer's argument and its implications are simple, straightforward, and easy to understand. NATO expansion was threatening to Russia; Russia had no choice but to invade Ukraine in 2014 and again in 2022 to prevent further expansion. To work, however, this explanation has to ignore a lot of history and much of what Putin himself has said about his motivations for invading Ukraine. In Mearsheimer's telling, NATO expansion—pushed relentlessly by Washington— was a consistent and growing source of tension between Russia and the West over the last thirty years. In truth, antagonism between Russia and the West— including over NATO—was a *variable,* not a growing constant, one whose variation bears little temporal relation to Russia's hostile actions toward Ukraine.

The change in Putin's own rhetoric around NATO across his two decades in power is striking. During a 2000 visit to London, he suggested that Russia might join NATO someday:

> Why not? Why not. . . . I do not rule out such a possibility . . . in the case that Russia's interests will be reckoned with, if it will be an equal partner. Russia is a part of European culture, and I do not consider my own country in isolation from Europe. . . . Therefore, it is with difficulty that I imagine NATO as an enemy.[17]

Why would Putin want to join an alliance allegedly threatening Russia?

Putin struck a similarly sanguine tone during a November 2001 visit to the United States, telling an interviewer that "Russia acknowledges the role of NATO in the world of today, Russia is prepared to expand its cooperation with this organization. And if we change the quality of the relationship, if we change the format of the relationship between Russia and NATO, then I think NATO enlargement will cease to be an issue—will no longer be a relevant issue."[18] Asked directly about the admission to NATO of the former Soviet republics of Estonia, Latvia, and Lithuania, Putin in the same interview struck a tone that would be inconceivable today: "We of course are not in a position to tell people what to do. We cannot forbid people to make certain choices if they want to increase the security of their nations in a particular way."

One might be tempted to suggest that the Baltics never held the same strategic significance as Ukraine and thus did not present the same redline as Ukraine's membership in NATO. But Putin's red line over Ukrainian membership did not exist early in his rule. During a May 2002 press conference with Ukrainian president Leonid Kuchma, Putin noted, "I am absolutely convinced that Ukraine will not shy away from the processes of expanding interaction with NATO and the Western allies as a whole. Ukraine has its own relations with NATO; there is the Ukraine-NATO Council. At the end of the day, the decision is to be taken by NATO and Ukraine. It is a matter for those two partners."[19]

If NATO expansion throughout the first two decades of the 21st century was the continuous driver of ever-increasing hostility between Russia and the West, we should not have seen these early expressions of acceptance, nor later instances of cooperative engagement. Yet cooperation is precisely what transpired. While attending the 2010 NATO summit in Lisbon, then-president Medvedev declared, the "period of distance in our relations and claims against each other is over now. We view the future with optimism and will work on developing relations between Russia and NATO in all areas . . . [as they progress toward] a full-fledged partnership."[20] At that summit, he even floated the possibility of Russia-NATO cooperation on missile defense. According to those who were in the room—including one of the authors of this chapter—complaints about NATO expansion never arose.[21]

These episodes of substantive Russia-NATO cooperation *during* the process of NATO's eastward expansion highlight the flaw in the argument that NATO expansion caused Russia to invade Ukraine in 2014 (and again in 2022). Mearsheimer and others promoting this explanation identify the statement issued at the 2008 NATO summit in Bucharest—that both Ukraine and Georgia would one day become NATO members at an unspecified date—as *the* unforgivable sin that made war over Ukraine inevitable. If this were true, why would Russia's cooperation with NATO expand in 2010 under President Medvedev? And if the 2008 declaration was so decisive, why did it take Russia a full six years to invade Ukraine? Timing matters, especially when it doesn't add up.

To this point, Ukraine in early 2014 was nowhere closer to joining NATO than it had been in 2008 or at any other point in its post-Soviet history. From 2010 until December 2014, Ukraine maintained an official policy of nonalignment: the government was prohibited under Ukrainian law from pursuing NATO membership. The Ukrainian parliament revoked this nonaligned policy only in December 2014, nearly ten months *after* Russia had invaded Crimea and the Donbas. How could Ukrainian NATO membership have caused Russia's invasion in February 2014 at a time when neither Kyiv, Washington, nor Brussels were heading in that direction?

The same must be said about the lead-up to the February 2022 invasion. In 2022, there was no imminent "threat" of NATO membership for Ukraine. Just the opposite: NATO leaders, including President Biden, were continually pushing that decision far into the future. During their first White House bilateral meeting in 2021, Biden made clear to Zelensky that NATO membership was not a subject for serious discussion. Ukraine in early 2021 did not begin "moving rapidly toward joining NATO," as Mearsheimer incorrectly claims.[22] By invading Georgia in 2008 and occupying parts of its territory, Putin had stopped all momentum for Georgian membership in 2008. By both annexing Crimea and keeping the Donbas conflict smoldering and alive, Putin did the same thing to Ukraine in 2014. He did not need to invade Ukraine (again) in 2022 to prevent NATO expansion because NATO expansion was not happening.

Perpetual Imperialism. A more compelling alternative theory to our explanation is Russian imperialism. This explanation is believed widely in Ukraine, the Baltic states, and Poland for understandable reasons, given their long history as objects of Moscow's imperial desires. Russian culture is inherently imperial, so the argument goes. Like regime type, this factor only becomes salient when interacting with power: when Russia has the power to do so, Russia invades its neighbors in all directions, including Ukraine. Interregnums interrupt these imperial proclivities when Russia or the Soviet Union has been weak as in 1917, 1941, and 1991. But they do not last. This innate, imperial impulse kicks in when Moscow has the power to invade other countries, irrespective of regime type or leader in the Kremlin. That's what we witnessed in 2022, according to this argument.

The long arc of Russian history provides ample data to support this hypothesis. For several centuries, Russia expanded relentlessly. The country long wore the title of Russian *Empire* with pride. Putin most certainly tapped into this imperial tradition to justify his 2022 invasion of Ukraine, almost as if Russia had an obligation to fulfill its imperial mandate and honor its imperial traditions. Putin openly cultivates comparisons between himself and former tsars of the Russian Empire. This explanation warns that Russian impulses to conquer and devour other countries will not stop in Ukraine. Indeed, Putin himself famously said that

"Russia's borders do not end anywhere," a phrase that subsequently appeared on a billboard in downtown Moscow in January 2024.[23] Other Russian leaders, including most brazenly former president Dmitry Medvedev, have openly advocated for the recreation of the Russian Empire's old borders, which would include the Baltic states, Poland, and Finland.

Putin most certainly has resurrected and nurtured these Russian imperial attitudes from the past to justify his invasion of Ukraine and sustain public support for the war. That he can do so easily and successfully underscores that such imperial ideas and culture do exist in Russian society. Since the war began, these impulses have exploded in public commentary about the war. Putin's propagandists on television and social media now openly advocate imperial ideas.

This theory, however, has its limits. First, it implies that this war was inevitable, no matter who was in power in the Kremlin and what kind of regime type ruled Russia. This argument must ignore a lot of history to be sustained. In 1991, Russia was not acting imperially towards Ukraine—just the opposite. If not for Yeltsin's desire to destroy the Soviet empire, Ukraine might have not ever gained its independence. Yeltsin was just as Russian as Putin. In addition, not all Russians think alike today and their preferences for things like democracy and imperialism have varied over time. Even today there are pockets of Russians who oppose the war, resisting their alleged imperial genes. To be sure, even some Russian opposition leaders have occasionally expressed ideas that are bigoted, racist, and sometimes downright imperial. But to suggest that they all share Putin's commitment to imperial expansion is inaccurate. The same cultural and historical variable cannot explain two different outcomes, either in Russian behavior abroad or in Russian attitudes about Russian wars. To explain this variation, other variables must be added to the equation, factors such as power, regimes, and individuals.

Conclusion

In this chapter, we have argued that the changing balance of power, Russia's form of personalist autocracy, and Putin (and Putinism) are individually insufficient but jointly necessary and sufficient conditions to explain the causes of Russia's war against Ukraine. This multifaceted explanation is more compelling and empirically supported than more simplistic explanations that NATO expansion or Russian imperialism caused this war. The former explanation fails to account for why Russia's attitude and cooperative engagement with NATO—a variable, not a constant—varies temporally in ways that are inconsistent with Moscow's decisions to intervene politically and militarily in Ukraine in 2004, 2014, and 2022.

Conversely, the latter explanation in particular fails to show how imperialism—a supposed constant in Russian culture—accounts for variation in Russia's policies toward Ukraine over the last thirty years. A single constant factor cannot explain variable outcomes. The changing balance of power, consolidating Russian autocracy, and the evolution of Putin's personal beliefs—especially in reaction to the color revolutions and Bolotnaya protests—provide a better fit with the data.

But one piece is missing from our explanation: the precise timing or final precipitant of the war. Specifically, why did Putin choose February 24, 2022, to launch his invasion? Over the last two years, analysts have proposed numerous hypotheses for the proximate precipitants of the Russian invasion of Ukraine in 2022. This speculative list includes the following: (1) Putin's self-imposed isolation during COVID-19 reinforced the dictator's usual echo chamber and intensified his isolation from alternative information sources, leading to highly flawed decision-making; (2) Putin's top intelligence officials misled Putin about the true state of affairs in Ukraine and lied about the success of their efforts to lay the groundwork in Ukraine for invasion; (3) Putin's need to boost his popularity and legitimacy in the lead-up to the 2024 presidential elections led him to launch what he expected to be a quick, victorious war; (4) the May 2021 arrest and treason charges against Ukrainian oligarch and Putin ally Viktor Medvedchuk motivated Putin to act decisively to retain his waning influence in Kyiv; (5) Trump's loss in 2020 took away Putin's hope of negotiating control of Ukraine with Washington; or (6) the disorganized American withdrawal of military forces from Afghanistan in August 2021 convinced Putin that the Biden administration was weak, distracted, and unlikely to intervene on behalf of Ukraine.

Hopefully, future historians will have access to archival materials that can answer this question about precipitants more definitively than we can now. But what is striking about this list, however, is that they all center on the individual beliefs and personal decisions of one man: Vladimir Putin. This is consistent with our argument: individuals and their ideas matter. Just as Putin's long-standing hostility to democracy and his denial of the Ukrainian nation were necessary beliefs that conditioned his choice for war, so too must his personal beliefs on the timing of the war matter in explaining "why now?" The choice for war was his and his alone.

Our explanation of the causes of this war also suggests what factors might shape its end. Putin is an ideologue. His strong ideological convictions compelled him to invade Ukraine in 2022. While Putin remains in power, he is unlikely to change his mind about his goals in this war. If leadership in the Kremlin were to change, the war could end. When that will happen is impossible to predict. Regime change in Russia—more precisely, a transition to democracy—could also end the war. That outcome—a change in the value of one of our variables explaining the causes of this war—is even more unlikely in the short term than a change in leadership. Finally, a change in the balance of power more in favor of Ukraine also could produce an end to this war. If Putin can no longer advance his forces on the battlefield or if his soldiers are forced to retreat due to reduced Russian military capabilities or increasing Ukrainian military capabilities, Putin might be compelled to end his war, either by negotiation or withdrawal.

While he has the means to continue his invasion, however, he will not stop. Of the three factors that combined to cause this war—the balance of power, regimes, and leaders—the balance of power is the most volatile variable of the three in the short term. Today, it remains unclear, especially given America's wavering commitment to help Ukraine win this war, in which direction this variable will change. In the meantime, the rules-based international order and Ukraine's sovereign place in it hangs in the balance.

NOTES

1. Eyre Crowe, quoted in Graham Allison, *Destined for War: Can America and China Escape Thucydides's Trap?* (Boston: Houghton Mifflin Harcourt, 2017), 59.

2. Thomas Graham Jr., "World without Russia?," Carnegie Endowment for International Peace, January 9, 1999, https://carnegieendowment.org/1999/06/09/world-without-russia-pub-285.

3. Michael Kofman, Rob Lee, and Dara Massicot, "Hold, Build, and Strike: A Vision for Rebuilding Ukraine's Advantage in 2024," *War on the Rocks*, January 26, 2024, https://warontherocks.com/2024/01/hold-build-and-strike-a-vision-for-rebuilding-ukraines-advantage-in-2024/.

4. One could even argue that Russia's multifaceted war against Ukraine began in 2004 with Russia's attempt to install Viktor Yanukovych as Ukraine's president, an attack on Ukrainian democracy and sovereignty that precipitated the Orange Revolution.

5. First for St. Petersburg mayor Anatoly Sobchak and then for Yeltsin.

6. Vladimir Putin, quoted in Fiona Hill, "Putin Has the U.S. Right Where He Wants It," *New York Times*, January 24, 2022.

7. Vladimir Putin, "On the Historical Unity of Russians and Ukrainians," Presidential Administration of Russia, July 12, 2021, http://en.kremlin.ru/events/president/news/66181.

8. Putin, "On the Historical Unity of Russians and Ukrainians."

9. Vladimir Putin, "Address by the President of the Russian Federation" (speech, Moscow, February 21, 2022), http://en.kremlin.ru/events/president/news/67828.

10. Vladimir Putin, "Address by the President of the Russian Federation" (speech, Moscow, February 24, 2022), http://en.kremlin.ru/events/president/news/67843.

11. Dmitry Medvedev@medvedev. 2024. "Why Ukraine Is Dangerous for Its Inhabitants," Telegram, January 17, 2024, https://t.me/medvedev_telegram/437.

12. We are fully cognizant of the methodological violations that we are making in using three independent variables to explain one dependent variable.

13. John J. Mearsheimer, "Why the Ukraine Crisis Is the West's Fault: The Liberal Delusions That Provoked Putin," *Foreign Affairs*, August 18, 2014.

14. Mearsheimer, "Why the Ukraine Crisis Is the West's Fault."

15. Mearsheimer, "Why the Ukraine Crisis Is the West's Fault."

16. John J. Mearsheimer, "The Causes and Consequences of the Ukraine War" (lecture, European University Institute, June 16, 2022), https://www.eui.eu/news-hub?id=john-mearsheimers-lecture-on-the-causes-and-consequences-of-the-ukraine-war.

17. David Hoffman, "Putin Says 'Why Not?' to Russia Joining NATO," *Washington Post*, March 6, 2000.

18. "Transcript of Robert Siegel Interview with Vladimir Putin," *NPR*, November 15, 2001, https://legacy.npr.org/news/specials/putin/nprinterview.html.

19. Presidential Administration of Russia, "Press Statement and Answers to Questions at a Joint News Conference with Ukrainian President Leonid Kuchma," press statement, May 17, 2002, http://en.kremlin.ru/events/president/transcripts/21598.

20. Presidential Administration of Russia, "News Conference Following NATO-Russia Council Meeting," news conference, November 20, 2010, http://en.kremlin.ru/events/president/transcripts/9570.

21. For elaboration, see Michael McFaul, "Hard Accounts: Russia's Neighborhood and Missile Defense," in *From Cold War to Hot Peace: An American Ambassador in Putin's Russia* (Boston: Mariner Books, 2018).

22. John J. Mearsheimer, "The Causes and Consequences of the Ukraine Crisis," *National Interest*, June 23, 2022.

23. Vladimir Putin, "Valdai International Discussion Club Meeting" (plenary session, Sochi, October 5, 2023), http://en.kremlin.ru/events/president/news/72444.

Chapter Three

Strategic Fanaticism

Vladimir Putin and Ukraine

Lawrence Freedman

> Fanaticism consists in redoubling your effort when you have forgotten
> your aim.
>
> GEORGE SANTAYANA, *THE LIFE OF REASON*, 1905

The study of strategy is about how individuals and organizations, including states, set objectives and seek to achieve them. The field is broadly defined as being about the relationship of ends to means, and for most purposes in most areas of human affairs, that definition suffices.[1]

The original concept was more narrowly military, referring either to how the art was practiced at the higher levels of command or else what had to be done to get an army to the point of battle, with tactics taking over once battle was joined. The influence of the earlier conceptualizations is still felt, but since World War I, *strategy* has generally referred to the management of the politico-military interface—the role of the armed forces in achieving national objectives set by the government—and that is how it will be used in this paper.[2]

Objectives in Strategy-Making

A common account of good strategy has it starting with clear objectives and then working back to see how these can be achieved. This is misleading since it encourages a view of strategy as a plan with a sequence of steps that can be followed methodically to the desired destination. In practice, strategy starts with the

Sir Lawrence Freedman is Emeritus Professor of War Studies at King's College London. He was the official historian of the Falklands Campaign and served on the UK inquiry into the 2003 Iraq War. His most recent book is *Command: The Politics of Military Operations from Korea to Ukraine*. His Substack is *Comment Is Freed*.

problem at hand and then proceeds through stages, with the options for each stage shaped by those preceding them. Plans rarely work out as intended largely because other actors, allies, and clients, as well as competitors and enemies, do not behave as expected. The relationship between ends and means is in practice dialectical. If means cannot be found to achieve set ends, then the ends will need to be reset.

Objectives are set for both the short term and long term. Those for the short term are about getting to the next stage: they must be realistic to be credible. Those for the long term, looking forward through a number of stages, are more likely to describe the best possible outcome. At times of crisis and war, there are problems setting long-term, ultimate objectives in modest, downbeat terms. This can be bad for morale and discourage mobilization. Governments will rarely admit to seeking anything over than total victory, even if this is combined with a prudent understanding that this may be hard to achieve. Thus, big strategic moves, such as the invasion of another country, will be presented as solving at a stroke otherwise intractable problems, as if the ultimate destination can be reached in one bold leap. If that fails then it becomes necessary to revert to a staged approach. When there is too large a disconnect between short-term and long-term objectives, then belief in the long term will suffer. Unavoidably, strategy starts with the short term but still requires a credible link to the long term. This is where narratives become important. A strategy involves a story about how a conflict can be decided on favorable terms.

The ultimate destination may never be reached. Even if the enemy is defeated as intended militarily, this may not yield the anticipated political end. The conflict may simply move to a new stage requiring fresh strategic moves. This is why strategy is always best considered as a long-running soap opera rather than a three-act play. The episodes are all linked but there are twists and turns in the plotlines and the cast of characters changes over time, but it is all part of the same stream of history.

Structure of the Chapter

We can therefore view a long-running conflict, such as that between Russia and Ukraine, as a staged and dialectical process. In principle, this can go back to the debates with which Putin likes to engage about the early origins of the two states and also the traumas of the 1930s and 1940s. This paper considers the relationship between the two this century, in particular the period since the summer of 2013. It looks at how successive strategic moves set the terms for those that followed. I look at five decisions—in the summer of 2013 to put pressure on Viktor Yanukovych to abandon the association agreement with the EU; to annex Crimea in March 2014; to direct the unrest in the Donbas and Luhansk from April to September 2014; to invade Ukraine on 24 February 2022; to embrace more ambitious objectives and commit more resources in September 2022 in response to the success of the Ukrainian offensive in Kharkiv.

The continuity in Putin's approach—the ultimate objective—has been an underlying desire to bring Ukraine firmly into Russia's sphere of influence, preferably by having a pro-Russian government in power in Kyiv and preventing a move into the Western sphere of influence by joining either the European Union (EU) or North Atlantic Treaty Organization (NATO) or both. This has been in tension with a secondary objective, in play since 2014, which is to fragment Ukraine. The more this was done (starting with the annexation of Crimea), the more Ukraine was likely to look to the West rather than the East. The more territory lost to Russia, the less likely what remains of Ukraine will be ready to comply with Russian wishes, especially when it comes to getting closer to the West.

The Importance of Coercion

Two features of this case are worth noting. First, it is unusual to have such a monopoly on decision-making over such an extended period. In May 2012, Vladimir Putin returned to office after the Dmitry Medvedev interregnum (which also included the war against Georgia). The issue of Ukraine was at the fore thereafter. When Putin describes his decision-making, he rarely implies any extensive consultation. Prior to the full-scale invasion, there was a performative consultation with his security council that was largely designed to show that he was in charge and to belittle his subordinates.[3] The decision to annex Crimea also appears to have been taken by Putin alone, though several people close to him promoted the idea.

The second feature is the central role coercion plays in Russian strategy. This predates Putin but was embraced by Putin as soon as he first became president. A coercive strategy seeks to shape the choices made by the adversary through threats and possibly inducements rather than imposing a choice by acquiring disputed territory or taking control of the adversary state.[4] By the start of our period, economic coercion had become routine for Russia, which often used import bans and extra tariffs and charges to signal displeasure with the overall direction another country was taking. One study showed that Russia adopted such tactics on thirty-nine occasions between 1992 and 1997 and got significant concessions in more than a third of the cases.[5]

The energy sector was central to Russian strategy, both as a source of prosperity and as a tool of foreign policy. The idea that Russia was an "energy superpower" also predates Putin, but once in the presidency, he settled on it as a "big idea." This did not appear as a leap into the unknown. As his advisor Vladislav Surkov put it: "If you have strong legs, you should go into long-jump and not play chess."[6]

The backdrop of high energy prices helped. To make the sector available as an instrument of state policy, the energy companies had to be nationalized, so Gazprom and Rosneft were turned into national champions, their actions governed by politics as much as economics. In a tight market, Russia could offer favors to prized customers and then coerce those considered hostile or ungrateful. By 2007, fifty-five instances of energy blackmail by Russia had been identified.[7] These extended well beyond the former Soviet Union. The coercive elements of Russian strategy continued after the full-scale invasion, not only in the efforts to force Ukraine to capitulate through the strikes on critical infrastructure but also in the attempt to get European supporters to abandon Ukraine by creating an energy crisis. A coercive strategy is normally attempted when a controlling one is not available. It is preferable to be able to take what you want rather than persuade the target to give it to you by threats.

Putting Pressure on Viktor Yanukovych

In the 2004 Ukrainian election, the pro-Russian candidate was Viktor Yanukovych, who came from the Donbas region of eastern Ukraine. Putin supported him with economic inducements and made speeches about the shared heritage of the two countries. The challenge came from opposition leader Viktor Yushchenko. He was almost fatally poisoned (after dining with pro-Russian officials from the Ukrainian security services). Since then, the use of poison against a number of figures deemed hostile by the Kremlin has added credibility to the assumption of Russian culpability in this case.

Though left weakened and disfigured by the poisoning, Yushchenko stayed in the race. The first ballot ended without a clear winner. Yanukovych was declared the victor of the second. Suspicions that the election was rigged led to massive street demonstrations, which came to be known as the Orange Revolution. The Supreme Court of Ukraine, expected to declare the election valid, judged that because of "unlawful" misconduct it was "impossible to declare who won." The court ordered a runoff, which Yushchenko won. Russia's parliament adopted a resolution before the court's ruling that accused the European Union and the Organization for Security and Co-operation in Europe (OSCE) of fomenting unrest in Ukraine.[8] This established a persistent theme in Russian discourse that the real issue was the manipulation of Ukrainian politics and politicians by Western countries and institutions.

As president, Yushchenko struggled with his team, while Putin used Ukraine's dependence to engage the government in stressful negotiations about gas supplies. Disputes on pricing twice saw the Kremlin-controlled Gazprom end gas deliveries to Ukraine, the second time in December 2008, in ways that negatively affected a number of European countries. One key demand was that Kyiv should agree to joint ownership of Naftogaz, Ukraine's state-controlled gas company.

It is clear why Russia wanted to undermine Yushchenko. The complaints about his presidency became standard fare: interfering with Russia's Black Sea Fleet in Sevastopol; supporting Georgia during Russia's military action in August 2008; and seeking NATO membership (raised at the 2008 Bucharest NATO summit). The Russian pressure was rewarded when, helped by the financial crisis, Yushchenko was defeated in the 2010 presidential election by Yanukovych.

Yet Putin also ended up undermining Yanukovych. This was despite him taking the question of NATO membership off the table, renewing Russia's long-term lease on stationing the Black Sea Fleet in Crimea, and passing a new law on the status of the Russian language. He talked about the shared Soviet past without offending Moscow's sensibilities (for example, by not discussing the Holodomor of the 1930s as genocide against Ukrainians). In return, gas prices were reduced by 30%.

Perhaps Putin assumed that the door was now open to push forward with his plans to get Ukraine even closer to the Russian Federation, which meant adhering to his scheme for the Eurasian Customs Union (ECU) in return for discounted energy prices. Yanukovych refused to do this. Nor would he sanction selling controlling shares of Naftogaz to Gazprom. Most importantly, he was prepared to sign a proposed association agreement with the EU at the November 2013 Vilnius summit. He dared not be seen as Putin's puppet, especially if he wanted to win the next presidential election. This was unacceptable to Putin. The choice was binary—either the EU or the ECU (one of the few means available to establish a new multilateral context in which Russian power could be exercised). No compromise formula was allowed.

Yanukovych was personally vulnerable to blackmail because of his highly organized corruption. The key pressure came from the fact that almost a quarter of Ukraine's exports were to Russia. In August 2013, new customs regulations restricted the import of goods from Ukraine, leading immediately to a financial crisis. The economy contracted, foreign reserves were depleted, and total foreign debt rose. There was no obvious way of repaying or rolling over some $10.8 billion of foreign debt.[9]

In November 2013, Yanukovych announced that he would not sign the association agreement with the EU. At once, Putin agreed to buy $15 billion of Ukrainian Eurobonds and reduce the price of Russian natural gas by a third. As Putin met with Yanukovych to agree to the bailout, he declared, "Ukraine is undoubtedly our strategic partner and ally in the full sense of the word."[10]

Even if the association agreement had been signed, there was a long way to go before Ukraine would be ready to join the EU. This was not Russia's last chance to influence Ukraine's choices. By acting as if it was, Putin conspicuously coerced Yanukovych into an unpopular decision.

Annexing Crimea

There was a sharp public reaction to this forced move into the Russian sphere of influence, including mass protests. Putin urged Yanukovych to take a hard line. On January 16, 2014, the government hurriedly passed laws criminalizing the protests. This inflamed the situation, leading to deaths on the streets. Despite a deal brokered by the French, German, Polish, and Russian foreign ministers for a national unity government and new elections, Yanukovych saw no sign that the protests would calm down. On February 22, he fled the country. Even in a system known to be corrupt, Yanukovych was an extreme case. Putin never held him in high regard, as could be seen in the way that he bullied him, which helped to create the conditions for the uprising. There was barely any pretense that Yanukovych was making the key judgments of his own volition.

The anti-Russian movement in Kyiv went down badly in Russophile Crimea. The possibility of annexation was actively studied in the Kremlin and plans were developed. By February 23, as Yanukovych fled, Putin decided to act.[11] As events unfolded, he kept an eye on the larger picture, prepared to hold back should the new Ukrainian government manage to muster a serious response, but it was in disarray and unable to respond.

An important feature of Putin's strategy was his efforts to demonstrate that this was a response to a popular demand, an act of self-determination and not of coercion. On March 4, when asked whether Crimea would join Russia, Putin said no but added that this was a matter for the people of Crimea to decide. Russia would "in no way provoke any such decision and will not breed such sentiments."[12] Yet Russian troops ("little green men" wearing standard uniforms but no mark-

ings) had dragooned Crimean lawmakers into authorizing a referendum on joining Russia. Later Putin spoke of "our soldiers" standing behind "the self-defence
forces of Crimea," making possible "an open, honest and dignified referendum and
help people to express their opinion." On March 16, the referendum provided the
expected overwhelming support for the integration of Crimea into the Russian
Federation. When embracing the decision, Putin spoke of the determination of the
Crimean people to escape from an illegitimate and retrograde government in
Kyiv.[13]

Putin acted as if the situation was truly urgent. He focused on the announced
repeal of the 2012 language law, though within days this move was vetoed by
Ukraine's acting president. Reference was made to the vulnerability of the Sevastopol Naval Base, even though that was covered by a long-term lease. There was
a "wait and see" option, in which he could have asserted Russia's concerns, especially for those in the south and east of the country, and reminded the new government of Russia's importance to Ukraine's economic well-being. In time, a new
government might have sought accommodation. He could have kept his options
open and avoided irrevocable actions.

Two options were eschewed. One was to try to help Yanukovych make a come-
back. Yanukovych could claim to be the legitimate leader and asked Putin to intervene to return him to power. Yet Putin clearly saw him as a busted flush and
went out of his way to prevent him from redeploying to Crimea to develop
resistance to the new regime.[14] Nor did he try to turn Crimea into a "frozen conflict" on South Ossetian or Transnistrian lines. Once detached from Ukraine,
Crimea had to join Russia.

The "Rebellion" in the Donbas

Given the opportunity to take Crimea, which might never arise again, Putin decided that it was better to right what he considered a historic wrong (Nikita
Khrushchev's transfer of the peninsula to Ukraine in 1954).

Yet taking Crimea out of Ukraine meant that the westward move in Ukrainian
politics would be accelerated. Did that mean he was giving up on the rest of
Ukraine, having seized his consolation prize?

There was no chance that a pro-Russian figure would win the May 2014 elections in Ukraine. That option was lost. Instead, Putin appears to have hoped that
the Ukrainian state would disintegrate. He viewed Ukraine as an artificial construct: the western and eastern parts had their own histories. Putin spoke regularly of "Novorossiya," the area north of the Black Sea that had been colonized by

Catherine the Great. There were fanciful suggestions that Poland would seek to acquire the west (these continue). Between the reduced ability to install a pro-Russian president and the possibility of a breakup, Putin could at least hope for paralysis. Denunciations of the new order in Kyiv and the regular allegations of Nazism were combined with demands for a federal structure, which would give the regions a degree of autonomy and ability to block moves toward joining the EU and NATO.

I have examined the story of the "separatist uprisings" in eastern Ukraine during the spring of 2014 elsewhere.[15] Actions in the Donbas were more haphazard than the Crimean takeover. The same model was applied: generating a groundswell of support for a Russian intervention as the condition for further action. The Crimean precedent now shaped what happened in the notionally Russophile parts of Ukraine. It removed a bloc of votes that might have influenced later elections. It set a standard for Russian intervention that encouraged those leading the rebellions while unnerving some who had opposed events in Kyiv but had no desire to be part of Russia.

In the event the demonstrations in Kharkiv and elsewhere did not develop sufficient critical mass to warrant further action. Figures such as militia commander Igor Girkin, who was instrumental in turning what might otherwise have been rowdy protests into violent insurrections, were linked to the Russian security agencies and to figures close to the Kremlin, such as Vladislav Surkov and Putin advisor Sergei Glazyev. But they also had their own ideas. In particular, they aspired to the Crimean precedent and not a new constitutional arrangement in Ukraine. They were also fragmented and often at odds with each other.

After taking over large parts of the Luhansk and Donetsk oblasts in the late spring, they then faced a determined response by the Ukrainian government (which acquired more cohesion and purpose after the May elections that saw Petro Poroshenko become president). At one point it looked like the "separatists" might be defeated. Russia provided more military supplies, although this led in July to the shooting down of a Malaysian airliner in the belief that it was a Ukrainian transport.

Again, there was a "cut losses" strategy that Putin eschewed. Having said that the separatist rebellion had nothing to do with Russia, their defeat could have been lamented as a worthy and spontaneous local uprising that required a humanitarian response. But Putin dared not let people who had apparently rallied to a Russian cause fail spectacularly. Faced with a crisis, he doubled down on his commitment. In August, Russian regular forces moved in and soon gained the upper hand.

Russian forces were soon able to threaten more Ukrainian territory, including the port of Mariupol with the possibility of a land corridor to Crimea. Yet on September 5, an agreement on a cease-fire was reached in Minsk, Belarus. This involved a cease-fire to be monitored by the OSCE. The agreement required the withdrawal of militias and other fighters from the enclaves and promised elections in return for more autonomy for the troubled regions and respect for Russian concerns. Ukraine welcomed this as its combat losses had been heavy and the economy was in free fall. There was no interest in the West in direct military assistance.

In retrospect, Russia was in a better position to win a war with Ukraine at this point than in 2022. While Putin indicated that more territory could have been taken easily, he showed no interest in an occupation that would have meant being stuck with a hostile population and the responsibility for administering and reconstructing the society and economy. Western sanctions were also a factor, especially as the economy was also suffering from a significant decline in the price of oil. It did not need any more disruption in its oil trade and moved to reassure its European customers that it would be a reliable supplier.

Yet the situation was not stable. If the enclaves had been annexed, there would have been a continuing conflict and no negotiated conclusion, with the government of what was left bound to get closer to the West. But without annexation, the territories controlled by the Russian proxies still required subsidies (which grew over time) to avoid internal collapse. The enclaves' leaders were unenthusiastic about the Minsk agreement. They wanted to be part of Russia, and if they had to stand in truly free-and-fair elections, they could well lose. Meanwhile, the Ukrainian government was still pursuing closer ties to the EU. The Deep and Comprehensive Free Trade Agreement between the EU and Ukraine was ratified, although implementation was postponed after Russia threatened tariffs for Ukrainian exports to Russia.

The first Minsk initiative petered out and fighting resumed. Further talks in Minsk in February filled out the details of the previous package. From the start, this was more of a "less-fire" than a "cease-fire." Implementation was complicated by arguments over whether these were measures that would conclude with elections (when the territories would be free of Russian troops and militias), or, as the Russians argued, all pursued in parallel. The enclaves of Donetsk and Luhansk were not self-sufficient, and Ukraine adapted to their loss over time, without ever accepting that this loss should be permanent.

Full-Scale Invasion

There have been numerous analyses of why Putin took the decision to launch a full-scale invasion in February 2022 and why Russian objectives were not achieved, as many expected, in a matter of days.[16] These explanations look at the dependence on Federal Security Service (FSB) subversion, cyberattacks, and direct assaults along multiple axes that were unprepared for Ukrainian resistance and soon stalled, facing serious command and logistical problems. My concern here is with what Putin was hoping to achieve.

The failure to get Minsk implemented as intended left Putin frustrated. The enclaves were in limbo, subsidized by Russia. Any hope that a new Russian-speaking president, Volodymyr Zelensky, who had run as the "peace candidate," would be able to do a deal was soon dashed. Kyiv did not like the idea that Russia would dictate its constitution. Putin concluded that the situation was untenable. Unwilling to withdraw support from the enclaves and with no prospect that the position could be stabilized so long as the government in Kyiv was unwilling to make concessions and was looking for more support from NATO and the EU, Putin decided that the only way out was to change the government. This was reinforced by his long-standing view that Ukraine was an artificial construct with an illegitimate government suppressing Russian-language speakers. This was set out in a tendentious essay written by Putin and published in the summer of 2021.[17]

The creation of the pretext for the invasion followed the pattern of 2014 with an attempt to suggest that Russia was responding to a desperate request for help from a beleaguered population. The choreography involved a decision to recognize the independence of the enclaves on February 21, followed by a contrived incident to demonstrate the danger from Ukraine, and then a request from the Luhansk People's Republic and Donetsk People's Republic for help to which Putin responded positively on the night of February 23, leading to the invasion early the next morning.[18]

As a pretext this worked for moving into Donetsk and Luhansk but not the advance to Kyiv and the attempts to take out Zelensky. The logic of this was that those in the Donbas could never be truly safe until there was a compliant and supine regime installed in Kyiv. Hence the demand for the "demilitarization and denazification" of Ukraine. This view of Ukraine encouraged the arrogant complacency informing the Russian invasion, including the FSB's attempts at subversion.

The potential trade-offs were extreme versions of those evident in 2014. A subservient government in Kyiv would mean demilitarization and neutrality, so no membership in NATO or the EU. The Luhansk and Donetsk People's Republics could be treated as independent entities. But all this was jeopardized by the failure to achieve regime change in the first weeks. Zelensky mobilized Ukrainian society and international support. This meant Russia faced tougher sanctions and Ukraine got more financial and military backing than would otherwise have been the case. It got worse. The war added to the incentives to integrate Ukraine even more into Western institutions, while NATO became even stronger as Sweden and Finland moved to join.

There was an opportunity after March 25, when the Russian Ministry of Defense announced that forces would withdraw from Kyiv and elsewhere and focus on the Donbas. This was a time when serious talks were taking place, and it is possible that Putin believed then (as he has claimed since) that he could achieve through negotiations what could not be achieved through military action, with the enclaves recognized and neutrality promised. That turned out to be a forlorn hope. Ukraine still wanted security guarantees and an end to the occupation. Once the atrocities at Bucha were revealed, all the impetus went after the talks.

September 2022 Reappraisal

After the successful Ukrainian offensive which liberated a substantial amount of territory in early September 2022, there was a major reappraisal in Moscow. This led to the adoption of a new strategy. This was another opportunity to de-escalate the war, although that would have made the failure of the enterprise evident. Putin doubled down, however, responding to hard-line critics who had complained that the war was not being prosecuted with the necessary ruthlessness.

Having resisted for some time, he authorized mass mobilization to address the military's chronic troop shortages. Some 300,000 were called up initially, of which around 120,000 were moved to the front as a matter of urgency. The effect of this decision was that Russian forces could shore up their defenses. Manpower shortages would not force the war to end quickly.

General Sergei Surovikin was appointed as the new commander of the Joint Group of Forces in the Special Military Operation Zone. This was designed to signal a firmer operational grip. He was the choice of the hard-line nationalist faction, including Wagner Group boss Yevgeny Prigozhin (a connection that was later to prove Surovikin's undoing). His approach was largely to improve the land defenses, waiting for fresh units before returning to the offensive in the spring, while concentrating the offensive on attacks on infrastructure.[19]

The attacks on infrastructure were not new, although initially the aim had been to take Ukraine more or less intact. From this point, there was a sense that if Russia could not take Ukraine then it would struggle to survive as a modern industrial state. There was also an immediate coercive attempt. By creating dire conditions for Ukraine through the winter, by means of deliberate and sustained attacks on critical facilities using missiles and "kamikaze drones," the aim was to pose a serious threat to Ukraine's ability to sustain itself. Late in the year, this was close to succeeding with consideration being given to the evacuation of Kyiv.

Most importantly, Putin set in motion the annexation of the four occupied (or more accurately, semi-occupied) oblasts of Donetsk, Luhansk, Kherson, and Zaporizhzhia.[20] Following the Crimean example, referendums were rushed to legitimize the annexations, but under circumstances where they could not begin to be taken seriously, all showing an absurd and uniform majority support not far off 100%.

Now that there was the determination to expand the borders of Russia, the stakes were raised again. As with Crimea, this was an alternative to the lack of a compliant government in Kyiv. Without such a government, however, and with these annexations denied international recognition, this was a recipe for continual instability. In the short term, it made it impossible for Putin to agree to a compromise solution, for now withdrawing troops would mean abandoning part of the Russian Federation.

The fact that Russia did not control all these territories challenged Surovikin's focus on strengthening defenses as the first priority. Putin was reluctant to agree to an evacuation from the city of Kherson, which meant relinquishing more territory, although he accepted the logic in November 2022. By January, Surovikin had been demoted and General Staff Chief Valery Gerasimov had been returned to overall command; Gerasimov immediately resumed the costly "meat grinder" offensives that had marked 2022. This move, and Gerasimov's unimaginative tactics, aggravated tensions with the faction led by Wagner Group owner Yevgeny Prigozhin and General Surovikin, which led eventually to the ill-starred Prigozhin mutiny of June 2023. By the end of the year, Russian forces had only made a limited impression on the line of contact. Meanwhile, Surovikin's defensive work had held up well against the summer Ukrainian offensives.

Conclusion

Bad strategy can take many forms. It normally includes the underestimation of an opponent. It may involve overreliance on some hunch about how others will act, or not thinking through the possible consequences of a course of action, or failing to work out how a good idea can best be implemented. Sometimes the failure is the result not of bad strategy but of unrealistic objectives—what is attempted can never be achieved despite the conviction that there must be a way. The strategist's conceit is to assume that any objective can be reached if available resources are applied with intelligence, imagination, and a steely will, as if every problem has a solution.

Strategic fanaticism takes this one step further: it's a refusal to accept that the problem as framed cannot be solved, a pattern of error that stems from obsession and a readiness to go to extraordinary lengths to satisfy that obsession, even as satisfaction remains elusive. Dictionary definitions of a *fanatic* refer to someone with extreme beliefs that lead them to behave in unreasonable ways. Putin's fixation with Ukraine, almost as soon as he began his second stint as president in 2012, has led to calamitous errors of strategic judgment.

Since 1991 Russians have been reluctant to accept Ukraine as an independent state. This turned, under Putin, into a conviction that Ukraine could only be allowed sovereignty so long as it was deferential to Russia's wishes, accepted a degree of economic integration, and stayed clear of Western institutions. When that could not be guaranteed, it should be dismembered and punished. It might be said that, contrary to the Santayana quote with which this paper opens, Putin did not forget his aim; yet while it was all about denying Ukraine its independence and territorial integrity, the specific objectives shifted and turned, starting with a desire for a compliant president, then aiming for the country's fragmentation while taking Crimea, then insisting on a new constitutional arrangement, and, when that failed to take hold, preparing to impose by force a puppet government in Kyiv, followed by imposed partition.

Following Santayana, as the objectives have proved hard to reach, Putin has redoubled his efforts. With the possible exception of March 2022, following the failure to take Kyiv, the means have become more violent and destructive and the disregard of Ukraine's identity and interests more emphatic. Yet the basic problem remains. Without a compliant government in Kyiv, the situation will remain unstable and, over time, Ukraine will be integrated into NATO and the EU. Russia may hold a chunk of Ukraine, but what they hold is ruined and depopulated. By ensuring that Russia is hated and distrusted by Ukrainians for generations to come, successive moves by Putin have ensured that his ideal end state of a compliant government in Kyiv is now beyond his reach. This would require a further push to take more Ukrainian cities, including Kyiv, and a long-term occupation force to sustain any installed government. For now, at least, this seems to be beyond Russia's capacity.

And this is before we bring into the equation all those costs and consequences that have not been assessed in this paper—the hundreds and thousands of dead, injured, and traumatized; the distortion of the economy; the impact on the well-being of the population; the break with the West and the loss of the European gas market; the dependence on China; and the need to ask favors from North Korea and Iran.

The long view taken in this paper reminds us that strategic decisions are made within streams of history. They are shaped by what went before and, in turn, they shape what comes next. As one stage of a conflict concludes another begins. Some stages can be truly transformational, perhaps because of a decisive military victory or a cease-fire agreement or even a proper peace settlement. But even then the next stage will be dealing with the legacies of what has gone before. History does have its punctuation points, but frequently in conflicts—and certainly in that between Russia and Ukraine—the apparent end points are less conclusive than expected. When the end of this war is discussed, it will only be the end of one stage, especially if it involves partition. For Putin, there can be no lasting peace without a supine government in Kyiv. Equally for Ukraine, it is hard to imagine a lasting peace so long as Putin remains in power.

NOTES

1. The standard definition, involving "ways" as well as ends and means, comes from Arthur Lykke, "Defining Military Strategy," *Military Review* 69, no. 5 (May 1989): 2–8.

2. See Lawrence Freedman, "Strategy: The History of an Idea," in *The New Makers of Modern Strategy: From the Ancient World to the Digital Age*, ed. Hal Brands (Princeton, NJ: Princeton University Press, 2023), 17–40.

3. Paul Kirby, "Ukraine Conflict: Who's in Putin's Inner Circle and Running the War?," *BBC News*, June 24, 2022, https://www.bbc.co.uk/news/world-europe-60573261.

4. The role of coercion in this context is discussed in Andrei Tsygankov, "Vladimir Putin's Last Stand: The Sources of Russia's Ukraine Policy," *Post-Soviet Affairs* 31, no. 4 (February 2015): 279–303; Luigi Scazzieri, "Europe, Russia and the Ukraine Crisis: The Dynamics of Coercion," *Journal of Strategic Studies* 40, no. 3 (January 2017): 392–416; and Andrew S. Bowen, "Coercive Diplomacy and the Donbas: Explaining Russian Strategy in Eastern Ukraine," *Journal of Strategic Studies* 42, nos. 3–4 (December 2017): 312–343.

5. Daniel W. Drezner, *The Sanctions Paradox: Economic Statecraft and International Relations* (Cambridge: Cambridge University Press, 1999), 131–248.

6. Pavel K. Baev, *Russian Energy Policy and Military Power: Putin's Quest for Greatness* (London: Routledge, 2008), 32.

7. Jakob Hedenskog and Robert L. Larsson, *Russian Leverage on the CIS and the Baltic States* (Stockholm: Swedish Defence Research Agency [FOI], 2007).

8. Steven Lee Myers, "Ukrainian Court Orders New Vote for Presidency, Citing Fraud," *New York Times*, December 4, 2004.

9. Then Ukrainian prime minister Mykola Azarov explained: "We made such a decision when it became clear that if we sign the agreement [with the EU], we will face crisis. It was absolutely clear and I can answer for that. So we had nothing left to do but change our mind and find other forms of support for Ukraine." Lawrence Freedman, *Ukraine and the Art of Strategy* (New York: Oxford University Press, 2019), 74. The only alternative would have been a loan from the International Monetary Fund (IMF) that would have required more than Yanukovych could have delivered. Christine Lagarde, head of the IMF, later noted that without a lifeline from Russia "Ukraine was heading nowhere." See Shaun Walker, "Vladimir Putin Offers Ukraine Financial Incentives to Stick with Russia," *The Guardian*, December 18, 2013; and Kenneth Rapoza, "Russia Helped Ukraine, but Now Ukraine Needs More, IMF's Lagarde Says," *Forbes*, April 3, 2014, https://www.forbes.com/sites/kenrapoza/2014/04/03/russia-helped-ukraine-but -now-ukraine-needs-more-imfs-lagarde-says/.

10. Serhii Plokhy, *The Russo-Ukrainian War: The Return of History* (New York: W. W. Norton, 2023), chapter 4.

11. He told senior aides that events had "unfolded in such a manner that we had to start planning how to return Crimea to Russia. We could not leave the region and its people to the whim of fate and the nationalist steamroller." Quoted in Mikhail Zygar, *All the Kremlin's Men: Inside the Court of Vladimir Putin* (London: PublicAffairs, 2016).

12. Presidential Administration of Russia, "Vladimir Putin Answered Journalists' Questions on the Situation in Ukraine," press briefing, March 4, 2014, http://en .kremlin.ru/events/president/news/20366.

13. Vladimir Putin, "Address by President of the Russian Federation" (speech, Moscow, March 18, 2014), http://en.kremlin.ru/events/president/news/20603.

14. Plokhy, *The Russo-Ukrainian War*, 110–111.

15. See Lawrence Freedman, *Command: The Politics of Military Operations from Korea to Ukraine* (London: Allen Lane, 2022), chapter 12.

16. Jack Watling and Nick Reynolds, *Operation Z: The Death Throes of an Imperial Delusion* (London: Royal United Services Institute, April 2022), https://static.rusi.org /special-report-202204-operation-z-web.pdf.

17. Vladimir Putin, "On the Historical Unity of Russians and Ukrainians," Presidential Administration of Russia, July 12, 2021, http://en.kremlin.ru/events/president/news /66181.

18. Vladimir Putin, "Address by the President of the Russian Federation" (speech, Moscow, February 21, 2022), http://en.kremlin.ru/events/president/news/67828; "Transcript: Vladimir Putin's Televised Address on Ukraine," *Bloomberg*, February 24, 2022, https://www.bloomberg.com/news/articles/2022-02-24/full-transcript-vladimir -putin-s-televised-address-to-russia-on-ukraine-feb-24.

19. From Surovikin's first interview as commander: "All measures are taken to build up the combat strength and formations of military units, create additional reserves,

equip defence lines and positions along the entire line of contact, continue attacks with high-precision weapons on military facilities and infrastructure facilities affecting the combat capability of the Ukrainian troops, to reduce the combat capability." See "Statements by the Commander of the United Group of Troops (Forces) in the Area of SVO Sergey Surovikin," *VPK.name*, October 20, 2022, https://vpk.name/en/643342 _statements-by-the-commander-of-the-united-group-of-troops-forces-in-the-area-of-svo -sergey-surovikin.html.

20. Paul Kirby, "Russia to Formally Annex Four More Areas of Ukraine," *BBC News*, September 29, 2022, https://www.bbc.com/news/world-europe-63072113.

Chapter Four

The Failure to Deter

*US Policy toward Ukraine and Russia from the End
of the Cold War until February 24, 2022*

Michael Kimmage

With the sprawling invasion of Ukraine that began on February 24, 2022, the United States has had two notable successes. The first was to deploy intelligence in a way that unsettled the Kremlin, a venture so innovative that it was without precedent in the history of the US intelligence community. By keeping Vladimir Putin off-balance, the White House may have prevented a "false flag" operation—actions staged by Russia and intended to blame the war's outbreak on Ukraine. By impressing on Ukraine and many other countries the likelihood of war months before it broke out, the United States solidified and expedited the response to the invasion when it occurred. Washington's other success was to coordinate financial and military support for Ukraine. From the very start of the war, the United States has been the linchpin of a global coalition stretching across Europe and Asia. This coalition—crucial for Ukraine's many achievements on the battlefield, for its social cohesion, and for its morale—materially strengthened Ukraine in its battle against a powerful and dogged foe.

These successes, impressive as they are, are only part of the story. Regarded from a more critical angle, President Putin's decision to invade on February 24

Michael Kimmage is a professor of history at the Catholic University of America and a senior non-resident fellow at the Center for Strategic and International Studies (CSIS). From 2014 to 2016, he served on the Secretary's Policy Planning Staff at the US Department of State, where he held the Russia/Ukraine portfolio. His latest book is *Collisions: The Origins of the War in Ukraine and the New Global Instability*.

reveals an acute policy failure (or series of failures) for the United States. After World War II, the United States became the security guarantor for Western Europe. Despite never-ending Cold War drama and intrigue—and Soviet invasions of Eastern Europe in 1956 and 1968—there was no war in Europe between 1945 and 1989. For forty-four years, the US maintained a brilliant record of deterrence. After the collapse of the Soviet Union in 1991, the idea of Europe expanded to include the Balkans as well as Central and Eastern Europe, two very imprecise terms of art. A Europe "whole, free, and at peace" grew into the aspirational core of US policy toward a region that encompassed the original NATO countries and the former Soviet Union. Technically a security guarantor only for NATO, the United States faced a NATO that was embedded in a Europe that was evolving. It was this protean Europe that Russia was not deterred from invading in February 2022.

Four intersecting reasons can be adduced for this inability to deter Russia. The first is an ahistorical optimism about Europe: an exaggeration of Europe's genius for peace, for integration, and for the resolution of political differences by nonmilitary means. In the 1990s (and thereafter) this optimism would touch Russia as well. Another reason for failing to deter Russia was the lack of a coherent agenda for Ukraine. Ukraine had to endure a state of unending limbo, which ultimately encouraged Russia's designs on this region of far-reaching strategic importance. A third reason was an aura of listlessness and distraction about the goals set for Ukraine in 2014–2015, which were to make Ukraine a part of Europe's wholeness, its freedom, and its perpetual peace. A diplomatic process commonly known as "Minsk" was constructed to restore regional order but fell well short of the mark. Fourth was the underestimation of Russia. Because Russian capacity and intent were systematically underestimated, economic sanctions or the threat of sanctions became the only means of checking Russia's strategic ambitions in Europe. This aggregation of misjudgments manifested itself in 2014. Eight years later, as war drew near, the first three reasons faded away, but the Kremlin's intent and capacity continued to be underestimated. After the valiant defense of Kyiv and the spectacular Ukrainian advances in the fall of 2022, Russia would be underestimated yet again.

The Promise of European Integration

The Soviet Union's vanishing in 1991 revived Woodrow Wilson's dearest dreams for Europe. One dream was that democratic governance rather than autocratic rule would underpin regional order in Europe, that the drawing together of self-governing European nations might resemble the drawing together of self-governing states after the American Revolution. Resolving disagreements through deliberation would be an advance in civilization, and there would be no better way to advance civilization in Europe, with its Homeric penchant for waging war, than to convince Europeans to replace vendetta and violence with the give-and-take of deliberation, procedure, and law. Another of Wilson's dreams was that ethnic self-determination would define the European state system. Empire would disappear, Wilson imagined, leaving the various nations of Europe free to determine their own destinies. Already in 1919, Wilson was envisioning a postimperial Europe. When life after empire finally came, Europe would be at peace.

After 1991, Europe traced two pleasingly Wilsonian trends. One was the desire of many countries to "join" Europe, which in practice meant entry into the European Union (EU) and the NATO alliance. The United States had initially been hesitant about enlarging NATO: expanding the alliance beyond Germany was first proposed by Poland and the Czech Republic.[1] They had anticipated a will throughout Eastern and Central Europe to incorporate as much "Europe" as could be incorporated. Despite the difficulties of meeting the EU's and NATO's standards, there was a need to transform former Soviet satellites into modern European nations. The other welcome trend (for Washington) was the willingness of Western Europe to open the door to Eastern Europe. Altruism played a role in the push to overcome the horrors of World War II and the tragedy of a Europe marred by Cold War separations. Interests comingled with altruism. Any geopolitical disarray in the East would spill over into Western Europe, and Eastern Europe was an enormous emerging market. European integration, here and there felt as a loss, was predominantly experienced as a step forward, as progress, and as the realization of a better Europe.

For Presidents George H. W. Bush, Bill Clinton, George W. Bush, and Barack Obama, Europe was paving the way. George H. W. Bush could laud his skilled management of Soviet, European, and US interests; he could claim to have freed Europe from the Cold War.[2] Bill Clinton was delighted by the growth of the EU, and he made NATO expansion a signature feature of his presidency. George W. Bush derived his "freedom agenda" from the miracle of peaceful revolution in Europe, which he attributed to Ronald Reagan and his stalwart anti-communism. After the September 11 attacks, Bush projected Europe's break with authoritarianism onto the Middle East: the invasion of Iraq in 2003 was supposed to have been 1989 redux. Although President Obama spoke warmly about a "pivot to Asia," he kept circling back to Europe. For him, Europe was the liberal international order in embryo. By making itself safe for democracy and by giving up on war, Europe was the template for post–Cold War US foreign policy.

Europe's exemplary status and its reputation as a place where swords had been forged into plowshares were never fully deserved. Euro-euphoria hid multiple dilemmas from view, dilemmas that revolved around setting limits to Europe and managing Europe's border with Russia. The European and transatlantic structures that were solidifying in the late 1990s and early 2000s were anything but rationally designed, and, as such, they were not durable. Over time, they would become dangerously haphazard—a mess of wavy, intersecting, and overlapping lines. As the EU and NATO extended into the Balkans, non-NATO, non-EU islands formed to the south of Hungary, to the west of Bulgaria and Romania, to the east of Croatia, and to the north of Greece. Russian troops remained, as they had since 1991, in Moldova, a curious vestige of the Soviet empire. Moscow retained control over Kaliningrad, a non-contiguous bit of Russia that borders Poland and Lithuania. Belarus aligned with Russia, though it was not demonstrably less European than the Baltic republics, while Ukraine became Europe's wild card— less bound to Russia than Belarus but less bound to Europe than Poland. The Iron Curtain, terrible as it was, had been remarkably simple by comparison.

The blissful project of European integration collided with its first obstacle in 2008. That year, Russia invaded Georgia—on Europe's edge or within Europe, depending on the eye of the beholder—and bit off two pieces of territory. A year later, the EU devised the Eastern Partnership (EaP) program of 2009, which addressed Europe where it was most undefined—in the South Caucasus and the westernmost strip of the former Soviet Union. Rather than letting Moldova, Ukraine, Belarus, Armenia, Georgia, and Azerbaijan (the countries singled out for the EaP) float away from Europe and rather than not have a policy toward these six very different countries, the EaP would tie them—lightly—to the European Union. Spurred to a modest degree by geopolitical competition with Russia, the EaP reflected the spirit of post–Cold War Europe. It was exuberantly open-ended: not East against West or North against South, even if these dichotomies could still crop up in 21st-century Europe, but something more fluid. Promising a wide landscape of European integration, the EaP was predicated on a Europe in which big wars were impossible. For this reason, the EaP had no security component whatsoever. It was a legal and commercial initiative.

For the Obama administration, a Europe freed from zero-sum contestation was unlikely to elicit Russian aggression. No European country had the slightest interest in acquiring Russian territory. It was tempting to attribute a similar sense of restraint to Russia's foreign policy. A secure Russia would not endanger the security of others. This Russia would either integrate into Europe or it would be too weak to interfere in European affairs. George W. Bush sought Russia's integration into Europe. Integration plus democratization was the end state of Barack Obama's "reset" with Russia. Ideologically at ease with Putin's authoritarianism, President Donald Trump was likewise convinced that Russia's true place was in Europe and not on China's side. Trump stated the need for partnership with Russia as if it were a transatlantic imperative. Those less certain about Russia's European path might find reassurance in the fact that Russia's economy was roughly the size of Italy's. Russia was a "regional power" in President Obama's words. It could perhaps obstruct outcomes; it could not dictate them. In the 2000s and 2010s, counterterrorism and then an ascendant China were the first-order security threats. A Russia on the periphery of a peaceful Europe fell into a more benign and less interesting category. There was nothing there that had to be deterred.

Ukraine in Limbo

Tinged with optimism about European integration, the EaP harbored an unspoken ambiguity. One year earlier, Ukraine and Georgia had been promised NATO membership. The statements made at the 2008 NATO summit in Bucharest, Romania—where the membership promise was made—were an odd compromise between a White House that sincerely wanted NATO membership for Ukraine and Georgia on the one hand and European countries, France and Germany especially, that prized a working relationship with Russia on the other hand. Maintaining ties entailed some deference to Russia and its notorious dislike of NATO, but the EaP was also (in part) compensation for EU and NATO alliances that were unready to accept Georgia and Ukraine as members. In lieu of direct institutional expansion, affiliation with the European Union, which is all the EaP held out, would be advanced piecemeal. The goals were to preserve consensus within Europe without leaving the field open to Russia's infiltration of the region—and at the same time not intentionally angering Russia. Was the EaP supposed to be hard or soft on Russia? Was it meant to block Russia or to build long-term bridges to Russia? That was the ambiguity.

The noncommittal stance of the EaP harmonized with US strategy vis-à-vis Ukraine, which since 1991 had been a holding pattern. One element of the policy was a general bullishness about Europe and Ukraine's integration into Europe, though in the 1990s the key issue for Washington had not been Ukraine's European path or political reform in Kyiv. It had been Ukraine's possession of nuclear weapons. A viable non-proliferation regime demanded that these weapons be handed over to Russia, to which Kyiv acquiesced. The reward for Ukraine was the Budapest Memorandum on Security Assurances, an agreement to protect Ukraine's sovereignty. Under the umbrella of the Budapest Memorandum, a sovereign Ukraine could be as close to Europe or as close to Russia as it preferred.[3] Ukraine was not being pushed into transatlantic institutions; it was not being formally invited into "the West"; but neither was Ukraine being turned away from Europe or the United States. From 2008 to 2012, the period when the EaP was in its early stages, Dmitry Medvedev was Russia's president. With some squinting, it could appear that Medvedev's Russia was trending in a European and even in a transatlantic direction.

Essential to pre-2014 US policy was a refusal to make any military commitment to Ukraine. For Presidents Clinton, W. Bush, and Obama, Russia was in the foreground: the locus of arms control, the facilitator of US military supply chains in Central Asia during the Afghanistan War, and the intermediary with Iran in the Joint Comprehensive Plan of Action (JCPOA) negotiations and with Syria on controlling chemical weapons. No American president advocated quid pro quo with Russia on Ukraine. None suggested a diminution of Ukrainian sovereignty or an acceptance of a Russian sphere of influence in Ukraine. Yet Russia's outsized regional presence shaped the diplomatic landscape. Ukraine assisted Russia by being in no rush to join NATO before 2014. Unlike Poland and the Czech Republic, Ukraine was agnostic about its geopolitical orientation: not unequivocal about being anchored in Europe and not at all agreed on a Belarus-style alliance with Russia. Practically speaking, Ukraine's in-between status suited the United States. If Ukraine did not have to choose between Russia and the West, the United States could stay on the sidelines, neither capitulating to Russian neo-imperialism (such as it was) nor provoking Moscow unnecessarily. With sufficient strategic patience, the United States could wait for Europe to work its magic on Ukraine and over time on Russia as well.

Strategic patience was a misnomer in context. In the decade between Ukraine's 2004 Orange Revolution and its 2014 Maidan Revolution, the United States was not skillfully navigating the shoals of Central and Eastern European geopolitics. Instead, Washington was abetting two self-reinforcing circumstances—Ukrainian vulnerability and Russian fear. An impoverished country with weak political institutions had only itself to ensure its security. Among 21st-century Europe's most isolated countries (as far as alliances went), Ukraine occupied a place in Europe that has often been a battlefield: the place where Russia and Europe fought over their dividing line in the First World War and the place where the Soviet Union and the Axis powers battled over their dividing line in the Second World War. When Germany lost the war, Western Ukraine was absorbed into the Soviet Union. (Before the war, it had been a part of Poland.) The Soviet Union incorporated Ukraine into the buffer zone it erected between itself and the West in 1945 until 1991 when Ukraine won its independence. By the standards of Central and Eastern European history, the country most likely to become a flashpoint in the 21st century was not Serbia, not Estonia, and not Poland. It was Ukraine.

By overtly favoring a Ukraine that was not subordinate to Russia (as of the Orange Revolution of 2004) and by vaguely favoring a Ukraine in NATO (as of 2008), US policy contributed to Russian anxieties about losing Ukraine. A propaganda version of the Kremlin's worldview rests on the motif of "color revolutions," the claim that the United States builds its global hegemony by destabilizing countries from within, co-opting loyal elites, and then binding countries to an international order run from Washington. The Iraq War was one example of the formula, and Ukraine's Orange Revolution—referred to by Kremlin advisor Gleb Pavlovsky as "our 9/11"—was another.[4] Though there was no CIA plot to overthrow Ukraine's government in 2004, there was a basic transatlantic hope that Ukraine's future would be European, and non-governmental organizations funded by the US government, like the National Endowment for Democracy, actively promoted a Europeanized Ukraine. This hope might merely have been the "spirit of 1989"—eastward the course of European integration. Or it might have flowed from an axiom that was self-evident to 21st-century US and European policymakers: that Ukraine's destiny was for Ukraine and not for Moscow to decide. For many years after 1991, it was hard to regard any of this as especially problematic. Moscow was visibly happy about Ukraine when Viktor Yanukovych became its president in 2010 and was hardly preoccupied by Ukraine in 2011 or 2012.

In November 2013, all of this would abruptly change.

The Failure to Deter through Diplomacy

Between November 2013 and February 2014, Ukraine underwent a revolution. Though slower to take effect, its consequences would be comparable to the assassination of Archduke Franz Ferdinand exactly a hundred years earlier. One consequence was the transformation of Russian foreign policy. Before 2013, Moscow had tolerated degrees of conflict with the West, while safeguarding a widening set of economic and social ties with Europe and the United States. After the Maidan Revolution, Moscow jeopardized these ties in order to exert control over

Ukraine. During Yanukovych's presidency, his pro-Russian posture had forestalled or postponed Putin's confrontation with the West. (Yanukovych's decision not to sign an association agreement with the EU, a climactic moment for the EaP, had been the spark that ignited Ukraine's revolution.) When Yanukovych fled to Russia, in late February 2014, Russia launched its annexation of Crimea. In the ensuing months, it invaded eastern Ukraine. A year later, Russia threw down the gauntlet to the United States in the Middle East, installing its military in Syria. Also, in 2015, Russia initiated its meddling campaign in the 2016 US presidential election. The annexation of Crimea, the move into Syria, and domestic American politics were not isolated data points. They were the new face of Russian foreign policy.

Europe and the United States incompletely grasped the transformations in Moscow. They did not register the Kremlin's mounting radicalism, which preceded Putin's actions in 2014. In 2014 and 2015, Europe and the United States were chasing two vividly incompatible outcomes: the ushering of Ukraine into Europe and the restoration of relations with Russia to some version of the pre-2014 status quo. (In the parlance of US diplomacy, Russia was being given an off-ramp, a chance to turn around and head in the other direction, to get out of Ukraine and back to normalcy.) Europe and the United States had welcomed the Maidan Revolution. It was democratic and overtly pro-European, its protagonists often waving EU flags. Thereafter, US diplomats repeatedly affirmed Ukraine's "Euro-Atlantic integration," a phrase that evoked normative and geopolitical processes as well as the consolidation of transatlantic influence in the region. Ukraine had chosen the West, to which the corollary might be that the West had chosen Ukraine. This the West had undoubtedly done in its rhetoric, and after 2014 the West would be far more intently focused on Ukraine than it had ever been before. But for Ukraine, no security guarantee, not to mention NATO membership, was close to materializing.

The United States reacted more sternly than Europe did to Russia's annexation of Crimea and incursion into eastern Ukraine. Washington levied sanctions on Russia for moves it considered unacceptable, whereas Germany and other European countries held back, still wary of antagonizing a Russia on which Europe depended for its energy supply. When Russian-backed "separatist" forces shot down an airliner with many Europeans on it in July 2014, the European Union signed up with the US sanctions regime. A month later, Russia dropped the pretense of being militarily uninvolved in eastern Ukraine and openly sent in its army, which had a string of battlefield successes. Europe and the United States may not have been pondering deterrence at the time: they were mostly reacting to Russia's

confusing, undeclared, and slow-rolling war on Ukraine. If they were acting diplomatically, as if Russia could be convinced to change gears, nothing Europe and
the United States did in the fall or summer of 2014 hemmed Russia in. Between
2014 and 2016, Russia upped the ante, although Russia's most visible escalation
(after 2015) took place in theaters other than Eastern Europe.

To resolve the crisis in Ukraine, Russia and the West met in Minsk. Negotiated
in the Belarusian capital by Ukraine, Russia, Germany, and France, "Minsk" is an
amalgam of agreements made in September 2014 and February 2015. The transatlantic diplomacy behind "Minsk" admits two rival interpretations. In one,
"Minsk" was the best that the diplomats could do. Germany, France, and the
United States had no appetite for military action in Ukraine: Russia had not ceased
being a nuclear power, and Ukraine was not in NATO. If President Petro Poroshenko, who was elected in May 2014, was suing for peace when he negotiated with
Putin in 2014 and then again in 2015 (which he was), he would have to compromise. The Ukrainian concession would be to eschew any attack on Russian soldiers
in Ukraine, though after 2015 the line of contact was never entirely peaceful. Absent a military lever, the West could ask the Kremlin politely to withdraw its
soldiers from eastern Ukraine and, if possible, from Crimea as well. This would
have been humiliating and ineffective. Better, then, to carry on with the band-aid
of "Minsk," to let the sanctions impose their costs and to see if Putin would lose
interest in military adventurism; thus could "Minsk" be implemented. Russia
might also rid itself of Putin and get back to the sanity of a Europe without war.
Apart from imposing sanctions and then waiting for them to take effect, not much
else was possible.

Another interpretation posits "Minsk" as deterrence, not just as muddling
through, and in this light "Minsk" was a travesty. It did deter Russia from massive
escalation—an invasion of a NATO country or the use of nuclear weapons in
Ukraine or elsewhere, provided Russia was considering these options in 2014 or
2015, which was unlikely. "Minsk" or the sanctions tied to "Minsk" may have de-
flected Russia from its fantasy of "Novorossiya," the reconstitution of an administrative unit from the era of Catherine the Great. Although empirical evidence on
Kremlin decision-making is always spotty at best, a better argument is that Russia was deterred from sweeping across southern Ukraine by a relative lack of local partners and not by Western sanctions. An inhospitable situation on the ground
stopped Russia in its tracks. Confoundingly, "Minsk" was deterrence after the fact,
deterrence as the undoing of extant realities, which Russia had established at the
barrel of a gun. Russia contributed to the false impression that "Minsk" was

deterrence by letting the violence die down along the line of contact in 2015 and by behaving outwardly as if Russia had been deterred in Europe. When it was no longer a war zone, Ukraine vanished from the international headlines. Russia was biding its time, while Western diplomats could congratulate themselves on restoring peace in Europe.

A counterfactual haunts "Minsk" diplomacy. Had Hillary Clinton become president in 2016, and not Donald Trump, US and transatlantic policy toward Russia and Ukraine might have followed another logic. While periodically courting Putin, Trump did little about Ukraine other than to mire Volodymyr Zelensky's presidency in a scandal of Trump's making. Trump did send lethal military assistance to Ukraine—most likely to goad Zelensky into damaging Joe Biden's reputation. Trump clearly wished to lessen the US military presence in Europe, in non-NATO and in NATO Europe. If implementing "Minsk" would involve any sacrifices on the part of the United States, it was better to leave "Minsk" unimplemented. By contrast, a President Hillary Clinton might have experimented with two separate forms of deterrence: the comprehensive arming of Ukraine and the prodding of European partners to do the same; and a sanctions regime that would not be static but would intensify with each month or year if Russia chose not to comply with "Minsk." Perhaps a tougher policy from Washington would have expedited the invasion that Putin carried out in 2022. Perhaps it would have altered Putin's overall calculus and made him think twice about invading.

The historical record and its hard facts tell a grim story about Western policy. From 2015 to 2022, everything about "Minsk" had been contested. For Ukraine, the agreements demanded that Russia first remove its soldiers from Ukraine, after which elections could be held in the East. For Russia, Ukraine needed to give the Donbas autonomous status, after which elections could be held and the Russian soldiers brought home. France, Germany, and the United States did not endorse the Russian view of "Minsk." If at times ambivalent about the Ukrainian view, they were certainly on Ukraine's side. The critical point was the exit of Russian troops from Ukraine, to which Western sanctions had been pegged, and that never happened. The sanctions were maintained without seriously disrupting the Russian economy. Germany went out of its way to normalize relations with Russia after 2015, most conspicuously by signing the Nord Stream 2 pipeline deal, to which the Biden administration gave the green light in 2021. For its first seven or eight months in office, the Biden administration's mantra was a "stable and predictable" relationship with Russia. In June 2021, Presidents Biden and Putin had a cordial meeting in Geneva, "Minsk" having become ancient history by then. Between

2015 and 2021, Putin must have drawn some pointed lessons about the West's true commitment to Ukraine's sovereignty and territorial integrity. He had outwaited the West.

Already twenty-one years in power by 2021, Putin was by then almost seventy years old. Had he been clinging to his wealth and power, had he been enamored of the status quo in and around Russia, Western policy might have worked. Yet Putin was not mellowing with age. Intent on upending the European and perhaps even the global status quo, he would spend 2021 readying Russia for a massive European war. Against this, the West's posture on "Minsk" proved to be almost the opposite of deterrence. In its weakness, its fickleness, and its lack of meaningful implementation, Western policy was an invitation for Putin to go further, which is precisely what he wanted to do.

The Failure to Deter through Sanctions

The final reason Russia would not be deterred in 2022 was the underestimation of Russia. Even in November 2021, at the eleventh hour, discerning the scope of Russian ambition was hard. The Biden administration had been primed to expect war not by any *a priori* realization about Putin's strategic objectives but by high-quality intelligence. For its first ten months in office, the Biden administration had been searching for guardrails—on the premise that Putin could be handled if he was not needlessly antagonized. Informing this misinterpretation of Russian strategy and capacity were three distinct assessments of Russian power: that it might be wielded here and there on Russia's periphery or in Africa or the Middle East but not for a major war in Europe; that Russia would be neither willing nor able to cut itself off from Western economies; and that Russia would not have the social cohesion, the diplomatic acumen, the defense industrial capacity, or the political wherewithal to fight a long war against Ukraine. Raw intelligence—the signs that Putin was heading for war—ate away at some of these assessments in the fall of 2021, and so did intelligence-community predictions that Russia would quickly defeat Ukraine in a rapid and large-scale invasion. Yet the third assessment, which was incorrect, would inform US thinking long after the war had begun.

Russia managed to sow doubt about its intentions, more so with European countries than with the United States. While massing troops near Ukraine and barraging NATO with ultimatums in the winter of 2021–2022, Putin gave the impression that his preparations in the fall of 2021 were probably a bluff (like his preparations in the spring of 2021) and that the troops had been gathered on

Ukraine's borders so Russia could extract concessions from the West. Until the morning of February 24, 2022, most European countries were misled by Putin. Even Ukraine was misled by Putin, including President Volodymyr Zelensky, who could not accept that Russia would wage a sweeping, ruthless war against its neighbor.[5] A common European refrain was that a war in Europe was unthinkable. Washington too was scrambling to catch up with events that only six months earlier had seemed like science fiction. A decade earlier, a military infrastructure could have been put in place to deter Russia from invading Ukraine, had the 2022 war been thinkable back in 2012, when it was far more unthinkable than in 2022. Instead, military aid had to be rushed to Ukraine in the frantic weeks before the invasion. Though it would help to save Ukraine, it would not hinder Russia from occupying some 17% of Ukrainian territory by 2024, from destroying much of Ukraine's infrastructure, and from devastating the country's economy.

It could be that Putin thought Biden was bluffing about Ukraine. Had Putin had a crystal ball, had he been aware of the extraordinary support the United States and other countries would supply Ukraine, he might have rethought his approach and decided not to invade. Biden could have signaled the US military commitment to Ukraine more aggressively, proving to Putin that the West's reaction in 2022 would run along military lines, that it would increase over time, and that it would be for the long haul. Two theses suggest that this might not have made a notable difference. One is Putin's (probable) assessment of the West, which is more nuanced than the narrative of decadence and decline so common in Russian media. Putin, who is not dismissive of the West's military superiority to Russia, assumes that the West cares less about Ukraine than Russia does—or than he does. The weight of past precedent, of the West's distraction after 2015, of its lack of follow-through, is not something that Biden could have quickly overcome in 2021. The other thesis is that many of the factors driving Putin's decision to invade were not especially US-centric. They were specific to Ukraine, to its disobedience (as Putin construed it), to the impression, in Moscow, that time was running out, and to the conviction that if Ukraine were not forcibly rejoined to Russia it would float free and forever fall into Europe.

As Putin's invasion loomed, the West placed its emphasis on sanctions. In the 1990s, Russia revived its economy through trade and investment with the West. Despite vowing to modernize Russia through research and development, Putin heightened Russia's dependence on the sale of fossil fuels, and Europe was among Russia's best markets for gas and oil. Sitting at the center of the global financial system, the United States has unique powers over other countries. Perhaps Putin could gain territory in Ukraine, but by doing so Russia would lose access to Western markets, to Western investment, and by extension to Western technology. Putin invaded regardless. The inefficacy of sanctions can be explained in various ways. One is that Putin did not really care. He was going to restore Russia to the role it deserved to play in Ukraine and the world—at any economic price. Another explanation is that Putin understood the Russian economy better than Western policymakers did. Russia had enough access to non-Western markets to compensate for the severing of Russia's economy from the West and the severing of Western economies from Russia. A third explanation is that the break with the West was not an opportunity cost of the war. It was a reason to opt for war. A geopolitical divorce would free Russia at long last from Western influence, Russia having devolved by 2021 into an anti-Western dictatorship, and it would remove the West's best source of leverage over Russia, which was its economic might.

The underestimation of Russia would persist. A few weeks in, the war was often characterized as Russia's strategic blunder. This framing spoke to the horror of Russia's unprovoked invasion. More precisely, the motif of strategic blunder was a judgment on the limitations of Russian power. Russia stood no chance of winning a war of attrition in which Ukraine was motivated to fight and in which Ukraine had the support of the world's wealthiest and most technologically advanced countries. Geared for war, Putin's authoritarian system was brittle, and by straining Russian society the war might break it. From these deductions came the phrase that captured the US position in 2022. Russia itself would not be attacked; Russia would not be defeated; but it would be led to a "strategic failure." Russia's war in Ukraine would be such a setback for Russia, such a dead end, that it would retreat back to Russia, that it would let Ukraine be, and that it would leave Europe alone. During the war's first two years, however, the West did not assemble sufficient deterrent force to make the war a strategic failure for Russia. Nor was Russia, which mobilized its economy for war and found countries willing to give it materiel, standing still. It was, rather, increasing its military capacity, meaning that the deterrent force required to counter Russia in Ukraine would have to be increased as well.

Learning from the Past

By the two-year mark of Russia's invasion, the war had all the markings of an extended conflict. Both Russia and Ukraine had shown themselves to be resilient in the face of a protracted struggle. For the United States, its European and other allies, and for Ukraine, the obvious goal was to ensure a Ukraine that is sovereign, independent, and capable of defending itself. Yet reaching this goal—however and whenever that happens—would be insufficient for the achievement of a stable European order. A sustainable long-term policy for the region would also depend on learning from history and not repeating the mistakes of the past. To this end, policymakers must recognize that security in Europe, and especially in Eastern Europe is destined to be contested; that strategic ambiguity vis-à-vis Ukraine is likely to be more harmful than helpful; that, if at all possible, publicly articulated priorities for Ukraine should be adhered to patiently, meticulously, and resolutely; and that for decades to come Russia is likely to be formidable in the pursuit of its regional objectives. These objectives, which are deeply embedded in Russian and Soviet history, are as follows: a diminishment or elimination (if possible) of the transatlantic axis in European security and the establishment of a "privileged" zone of involvement for Russia, not just in Ukraine but across and around Russia's border with Europe. To succeed in deterring these objectives, US planning and strategy will have to be comprehensive, patient, and shorn of easy optimism, much as US planning and strategy were in the late 1940s, at the outset of the Cold War.

NOTES

1. On the role of Eastern European nations in NATO expansion and on the debate about NATO expansion in Washington, see M. E. Sarotte, *Not One Inch: America, Russia, and the Making of Post–Cold War Stalemate* (New Haven, CT: Yale University Press, 2021), 149–212.

2. Philip Zelikow and Condoleezza Rice, *Germany Unified and Europe Transformed: A Study in Statecraft* (Cambridge, MA: Harvard University Press, 1995).

3. On Ukraine's "return" of its nuclear weapons to Russia, see Steven Pifer, *The Eagle and the Trident: U.S.–Ukraine Relations in Turbulent Times* (Washington, DC: Brookings Institution Press, 2017), 37–76. See also Eugene M. Fishel, *The Moscow Factor: U.S. Policy toward Sovereign Ukraine and the Kremlin* (Cambridge, MA: Harvard University Press, 2022).

4. Gleb Pavlovsky quoted in Serhii Plokhy, *The Russo-Ukrainian War and the Return of History* (New York: W. W. Norton, 2023), 83.

5. On Zelensky's shock at the outbreak of war on February 24, 2022, see Simon Shuster, *The Showman: Inside the Invasion That Shook the World and Made a Leader of Volodymyr Zelensky* (New York: William Morrow, 2024).

Chapter Five

How the War Will End

Anne Applebaum

The Kremlin planned to take Kyiv in three days, the rest of Ukraine in six weeks. Its plan was both military and political. As the Russian army approached Kyiv, Russian special forces would assassinate President Volodymyr Zelensky, remove his team, and eliminate his supporters. Thousands of prominent Ukrainians would be arrested or murdered. Lists of their names were already in circulation before the invasion began.[1] Russian operatives, confident of their success, were already choosing which luxury Kyiv apartments they would confiscate when they took over the Ukrainian capital.[2] RIA Novosti, the Russian state-owned media service, even ran a premature editorial, forty-eight hours after the invasion began, declaring that "a new world is being born before our eyes." Russia "is restoring its unity," the author wrote. "Ukraine will no longer exist."[3]

The editorial was immediately retracted. Two days into the war, it was already clear that Kyiv would not fall so easily. Nevertheless, the language RIA Novosti used is important to remember, as are the assassination plans, the arrest lists, and the Federal Security Service's real estate ambitions. Any conversation about how the Russia-Ukraine War will end has to begin with an accurate assessment of why it began. Why did Russian president Vladimir Putin invade Ukraine? What did he want to achieve? Unless we understand the answers to those

Anne Applebaum is a Pulitzer Prize–winning historian, a staff writer at *The Atlantic*, and a senior fellow at the Agora Institute and the Johns Hopkins School of Advanced International Studies.

questions, we won't understand what would persuade him, or his successors, to go home.

Dispelling the Myth

So accustomed are American analysts to seeing themselves at the center of every story that many have long imagined that Western foreign policy choices, and Western decisions, are central to the centuries-long power struggle between Russia and Ukraine. This powerful, potent argument takes several different forms. The case for the centrality of American decisions was made most clearly and most prominently by the international relations theorist John Mearsheimer, whose 2014 *Foreign Affairs* article, "Why the Ukraine Crisis Is the West's Fault," is still widely cited and was even promoted by the Russian foreign ministry in February 2022.[4] But versions of this thesis have also been proposed by Jack Matlock, US ambassador to Moscow at the end of the Soviet era, who described NATO expansion as a "profound strategic blunder."[5] Kevin Roberts, the current president of the Heritage Foundation, has blamed "our saber-rattling about Ukraine entering NATO" for the war.[6] And Noam Chomsky has said that the "US and Britain" have "refused" peace negotiations in Ukraine.[7] A long list of extremist pundits, led by Tucker Carlson, has used the same language. This group of critics, who come from the right, the left, and the very center of the foreign policy establishment, is united by their belief that the origins of the current crisis lie in the 1990s—when the Western leaders of NATO decided to admit the nations of Central Europe and the Baltic states—and in the NATO summit of 2008—when the Western powers discussed the admission of Ukraine, declared an aspiration to admit Ukraine, but then blocked Ukraine from joining NATO indefinitely.

Most are also united by their tacit acceptance of the Russian argument that Ukraine is not a real country and does not have a right to sovereignty. Chomsky says this clearly: "Ukraine is not a free actor; they're dependent on what the US determines." Mearsheimer refers to Ukrainian democracy not as something the Ukrainians created but as the product of "Western social engineering." Finally, most of the "America is at fault" clique are either uninterested in the ideological motivations of Vladimir Putin, don't take them seriously, or (in the case of the extremist far right) agree with them. In March 2022, for example, Mearsheimer dismissed the idea that Putin's "aim is to create a greater Russia or the reincarnation of the Soviet Union" and said he believed "the Russians are too smart to get involved in an occupation of Ukraine.[8]

And yet—seven months before the war began, in July 2021, Putin put forward a very clear road map of his intentions in Ukraine, complete with an extensive historical justification. In an essay titled "On the Historical Unity of Russians and Ukrainians," he declared: "Russians and Ukrainians were one people—a single whole." He continued: "These words were not driven by some short-term considerations or prompted by the current political context. It is what I have said on numerous occasions and what I firmly believe."[9]

Most of the rest of the essay was devoted to the history of the region, going back to the early Middle Ages. Putin disputed Ukraine's account of its own history and its long struggle for independence, and he concluded with the idea that "modern Ukraine is entirely the product of the Soviet era." Repeatedly referring to the elected leaders of Ukraine as "neo-Nazis," and therefore as illegitimate, the essay seemed to be calling not exactly for the resurrection of the Soviet Union, but rather for the resurrection of a Russian empire. Since then, his language has varied. Sometimes Putin seems to envision a future for Ukraine as a puppet state, run directly or indirectly by Russia. Sometimes he seems to imagine Ukraine simply becoming a province of Russia. Either way, he does not envision a Ukraine that retains its own sovereignty, let alone its democratic system or a freely elected government. He and others repeatedly refer to Ukraine as an "anti-Russia," a state that *only exists to undermine Russia*. By definition, any negotiation with an "anti-Russia" is impossible: Russia will have to destroy Ukraine altogether.

From the beginning, the Russians were also conscious that the destruction of Ukraine, a large European state with extensive international contacts and links, would destroy a whole series of European and international treaties and norms as well. Among the many international accords the Russians would need to break were the United Nations Charter, which protects the territorial integrity of states, and the Helsinki Accords, which recognized the postwar borders of Europe. They would have to discard the Budapest Memorandum, signed by the United States, the United Kingdom, Russia, and Ukraine in 1994, which specifically guaranteed Ukraine's borders and Ukraine's sovereignty in exchange for the Ukrainian agreement to give up nuclear weapons. The Russian regime understood very well that the reestablishment of a Russian imperial state would immediately put Russia at odds with the interlocking web of treaties and agreements that had kept the peace in Europe since 1945, especially since 1989. Again, they were very clear about this intention. "This is not about Ukraine at all, but the world order," said Sergey Lavrov, the Russian foreign minister, soon after the war began: "The current crisis is a fateful, epoch-making moment in modern history. It reflects the battle over what the world order will look like."[10]

Lavrov's statement and Putin's 2021 essay are linked: they reveal a Russia that intends to occupy or control Ukraine and intends to break treaties, accords, and diplomatic relationships in order to do it. More to the point, they reveal a Russian elite that believes smashing Ukraine and smashing treaties will alter forever a world that they perceive to be dominated by the wealthy democracies, especially the United States. This nihilism is reflected directly in the systematic brutality of Russian troops on the ground.

Certainly, a Russia that was only interested in halting NATO expansion would not have tortured small-town mayors and village leaders like Viktor Maruynak, the mayor of Stara Zburjivka, a small town in Kherson province. Maruynak was arrested in March 2022 and kept blindfolded and handcuffed for three days. He was beaten, stripped naked, deprived of food and drink. Russian soldiers tied wires to his thumbs and then delivered electric shocks using the battery of a field telephone. According to one witness, soldiers described this torture, used during the Soviet invasion of Afghanistan and Russia's wars in Chechnya, as "making a call to Putin."[11] This was not unusual. According to the Ukrainian government, mayors, deputy mayors, and other local leaders from a majority of the Kherson region's forty-nine municipalities were arrested or kidnapped. After the liberation of parts of Kharkiv province in the autumn of 2023, police found evidence of twenty-five torture chambers.[12] Just as the Red Army in 1945 sought to decapitate the leadership of Poland, Hungary, or eastern Germany, so did the Russian army hope to repress the Ukrainian population in 2022.

Political leaders were a priority, but civic leaders were victimized too. Anyone who had been a volunteer, anyone who ran a charity, or anyone who merely helped distribute food and medicine after distribution systems started to break down was a potential target. The Reckoning Project, a team of journalists and researchers who are documenting Russian crimes in Ukraine, has collected many examples of people who were arrested simply for showing any initiative at all. Perhaps because their own country discourages this kind of behavior, the Russian soldiers treated all forms of volunteerism and civic engagement as hostile. In an admittedly sloppy, inconsistent way, the Russians also pressured teachers and school directors, sometimes demanding that they stop teaching Ukrainian history and literature or that they remove all references to Ukraine from their schools. Students of Soviet history will recognize this behavior from the past. In the 1940s, the Soviet occupation regimes also sought to change the nature of Central European societies by altering education and culture as well. The modern Russian army appears, albeit inconsistently, to be operating from the same playbook.[13]

Toward this end, the occupiers have repeatedly demonstrated their intention to eliminate not only the Ukrainian state but also Ukrainian identity and culture. They have forced thousands of Ukrainians to give up their passports and adopt Russian nationality if they want to receive pension payments or keep their jobs. They have deliberately targeted Ukrainian cultural sites, such as destroying a museum dedicated to the Ukrainian poet and philosopher Hryhorii Skovoroda, which was located in a village containing no military targets at all.[14] After flattening the city of Mariupol and killing tens of thousands of people, the Russians began resettling the city with Russians and other non-Ukrainians in order to change the city's national and ethnic profile. Migrant workers and others from depressed regions of Russia have been offered favorable mortgages and other inducements to move to Mariupol. At the same time, the remaining Ukrainians have been deported.[15]

In what will be long remembered as the worst crime of this war, the Russians have also kidnapped children. The International Court of Justice has already issued a warrant to arrest President Putin and Maria Alekseyeva Lvova-Belova, the Russian children's rights commissioner, for overseeing the "unlawful abduction" of thousands of Ukrainian children.[16] Some were lured into summer camps and never allowed to return home. Others were taken from orphanages and other institutions, placed into new families, and told they would now become Russians, not Ukrainians. Like the other human rights violations and war crimes the Russians have carried out in Ukraine, this coordinated, well-planned campaign, reveals again the nature of this occupation. This is not a war of self-defense, nor is it merely a war over the location of the border. This is rather an attempt to eliminate Ukrainians, physically and culturally, to bring up their children as Russians, and to replace Ukraine as a state.

At the same time, this ideological war is a bid to rewrite the rules of the postwar world. The Russians want to show they can bring back, with impunity, cruel forms of repression and occupation familiar to historians of the 20th century. For all of those reasons, this is not a war that can end, or at least not permanently, through a simple negotiation. This war will end either when the Russians win and replace the Ukrainian president with a puppet dictator, as they have wanted to do from the beginning, or it will end when the Russians, like colonial powers of the past, decide that the price they are paying for this project has become too high and go home.

Off-Ramps vs. Defeat

The expression *off-ramp* has a pleasing physicality, evoking a thing that can be constructed out of concrete and steel. But the expression is used in Ukraine metaphorically, referring to a deal that could persuade Vladimir Putin to halt his invasion. Some believe that such an off-ramp could easily be built if only diplomats were willing to make the effort,[17] or if only the White House weren't so bellicose.[18] But there is no evidence that Putin wants to negotiate, that he wants to stop fighting, or that he has ever wanted to stop fighting. According to Western officials who have periodic conversations with their Russian counterparts, he and his team have repeatedly turned down proposals for dialogue.

Nor is there any evidence that Putin wants to partition Ukraine, keeping only the territories he currently occupies and allowing the rest to prosper, as North Korea treated South Korea after 1953, a solution that some have proposed. Because Russian troops are tired and because Russian losses have been so high, it is possible that, at some point, the Russians will decide to negotiate a temporary cease-fire. They have made a similar decision in the past: in 2014 the Russians ended their conquest of eastern Ukraine. But then they used the subsequent six years to rearm and regroup. Until the Russians have given up on their imperial dream, no lasting peace is possible. And to date, they have not done so.

On the contrary, Putin's goal appears to remain the same as it was in February 2022: the destruction of Ukraine—all of Ukraine. He also appears to believe that if he waits long enough, support for Ukraine will decrease and political divisions in the United States and Europe will halt aid. He may be hoping for the minority of Republicans in Congress to block money for Ukraine, or for the pro-Russian far right to win elections in Germany and France. He may be waiting for Donald Trump to become the next American president. Indeed, it is likely that he will do what he can to help all of these things happen, through information campaigns and, in some cases, overt and covert funding as well.

Two years into the war, the Russians are not moderating their language about Europe either. Despite very heavy losses of men and equipment, Putin's allies and propagandists are still talking about how, once they achieve this goal, they will expand their empire further. Dmitry Medvedev, Russia's former president, has described the Baltic States as "our" provinces and has written that they "soiled themselves" over Russia's invasion of Ukraine.[19] Medvedev also published an eight-thousand-word article calling Poland Russia's "historical enemy" and threatening Poles with the loss of their state too.[20] The message was perfectly clear: *We in-*

vaded Poland before, and we can do it again. A hint at how they might be planning further operations lies in the recruitment drive that is already beginning in the occupied territories. The Russians plan to use the newly conquered population of eastern Ukraine as cannon fodder in their continued war. If they occupy the rest of Ukraine, they will treat the rest of the Ukrainian population in the same way. Ukraine will become the source of new soldiers and new funding for a future European war.

Perhaps Putin will be unable to achieve all of this; perhaps Russia is too weak. But he will certainly try. And while he is trying, Russia will be a very dangerous enemy. European and American leaders have spent many years refusing to believe that Putin could possibly want a permanent European war. The very idea seems nonsensical to a political class that thinks of economic progress and prosperity as the most important goal. But the same idea may seem eminently plausible to the Russian president, and no wonder: Putin spent a memorable part of his life as a KGB officer, representing the interests of the Soviet empire in Dresden. He remembers when eastern Germany was ruled by Moscow. If it could be so once, then why not again?

Once again, the stark truth is that this war will only end for good when Russia wins—or when Russia's neo-imperial dream finally dies. This is not impossible: colonial regimes have retreated in the past. Just as the French decided in 1962 that Algeria could become independent of France, just as the British accepted in 1921 that Ireland was no longer part of the United Kingdom, just as the Soviet Union gave up on the idea that Afghanistan could become a communist satellite state, the Russians must conclude that Ukraine is not Russia. Not only do they need to stop fighting but the Kremlin, the elite, and the business community must conclude that the war was a terrible mistake as well, one that can never be repeated. The Russian public must eventually come to agree too. It is not possible to say, in advance, what that decision will look like. But we will recognize this change when it happens. After it does, the conflict is over, and then it will be possible to negotiate a final settlement and the final shape of the borders.

How We Can Help

To reach that endgame, we need to adjust our thinking. First, we need to understand, more deeply than we have done so far, that we have entered a new era of great-power conflict. The Russians already know this and have already made the transition to a full-scale war economy. Forty percent of Russia's 2024 state budget[21]—a conservative estimate—will be spent on defense and security expenditures, representing about 6% of Russia's GDP, a level not seen for decades.[22] Neither the United States nor its European allies have made anything like this shift, and we started from a low base. Jack Watling of the Royal United Services Institute told me that, at the beginning of the war, the ammunition that the United Kingdom produced in a year was enough to supply the Ukrainian army for twenty hours. Although the situation has improved as production has slowly cranked up all over the democratic world, we are not moving fast enough.

Secondly, we need to start helping the Ukrainians fight this war as if we were fighting it, altering our slow decision-making process to match the urgency of the moment. Ukraine received the weapons for its summer fighting very late, giving the Russians time to build minefields and tank traps—why? Training by NATO forces for Ukrainian soldiers has in some cases been rushed and incomplete— why? There is still time to reverse these mistakes. The breakthrough technologies that Ukrainian leaders have requested, which include tools to gain air superiority and better wage electronic warfare, should be taken seriously now, not next year.

But the path to end this war does not only lead through the battlefield. We need to start thinking not only about *helping Ukraine* but about *defeating Russia*—or, if you prefer different language, *persuading Russia to leave by any means possible*. If Russia is already fighting America and America's allies on multiple fronts, through political funding, influence campaigns, and its links to other autocracies and terrorist organizations, then the United States and Europe need to fight back on multiple fronts too. We should outcompete Russia for the scarce commodities needed to build weapons, block the software updates that they need to run their defense factories, and look for ways to sabotage their production facilities. Russia used fewer weapons and less ammunition in 2023 than it did in 2022.[23] Our task should be to ensure that 2024 and the years thereafter are worse.

The West has already sanctioned Russia and put export controls on electronics and many other components necessary for the Russian defense ministry. Paradoxically, there may now be too many of these sanctions, which are difficult to keep track of and enforce, especially when materials go through third or fourth countries. Instead, we should target the most important supply chains, depriving the Russians of the specific machine tools and raw materials that they need to make the most sophisticated weapons. At the start of the war, the United States and its allies froze Russia's foreign-currency deposits. The assets of many Russian oligarchs were frozen too, in the hope that this would make them more inclined to resist the war. With some exceptions, it did not. Now it's time to take those assets and give them to Ukraine. We need to demonstrate that our commitment to the principle of Russian reparations for Ukraine is real.

But some of our money is needed too. Spending it now will produce savings down the line, and not only because we can prevent a catastrophe in Ukraine. By learning how to fight Russia, a sophisticated autocracy with global ambitions, we will be better prepared for later, larger conflicts, if there is ever a broader struggle with China or Iran. More importantly, by defeating Russia, we might be able to stop those larger conflicts before they begin. The goal in Ukraine should be to end Russia's brutish invasion—and to deter others from launching another one somewhere else.

The benefits, to Ukraine, Europe, and the Russians as well, would be immense. A true defeat could force the reckoning that should have happened in the 1990s, the moment when the Soviet Union broke up but Russia retained all of the trappings and baubles of the Soviet empire—its United Nations seat, its embassies, and its diplomatic service—at the expense of the other former Soviet republics. The year 1991 was the moment when Russians should have realized the folly of Moscow's imperial overreach, when they should have figured out why so many of their neighbors hate and fear them. But the Russian public learned no such lesson. Within a decade, Putin, brimming with grievances, had convinced many of them that the West and the rest of the world owed them something and that further conquests were justified.

A military loss could create a real opening for national self-examination or a major change, as it so often has done in Russia's past. Only failure can persuade the Russians themselves to question the sense and purpose of a colonial ideology that has repeatedly impoverished and ruined their own economy and society, as well as those of their neighbors, for decades. Yet another frozen conflict, yet another temporary holding pattern, yet another face-saving compromise will not end the pattern of Russian aggression or bring permanent peace.

NOTES

1. Erika Kinetz, "'We Will Find You': Russians Hunt Down Ukrainians on Lists," *PBS Frontline*, December 21, 2022, https://www.pbs.org/wgbh/frontline/article/russians-hunt-down-ukrainians-on-lists/.

2. Greg Miller and Catherine Belton, "Russia's Spies Misread Ukraine and Misled Kremlin as War Loomed," *Washington Post*, August 19, 2022.

3. Petr Akopov, "The Arrival of Russia and a New World" [Наступление России и нового мира], *RIA Novosti*, February 26, 2022, https://web.archive.org/web/2022022605 1154/https://ria.ru/20220226/rossiya-1775162336.html.

4. John J. Mearsheimer, "Why the Ukraine Crisis Is the West's Fault," *Foreign Affairs*, August 18, 2014, https://www.foreignaffairs.com/articles/russia-fsu/2014-08-18 /why-ukraine-crisis-west-s-fault.

5. Jack F. Matlock, Jr., "I Was There: NATO and the Origins of the Ukraine Crisis," *Responsible Statecraft*, February 15, 2022, https://responsiblestatecraft.org/2022/02/15 /the-origins-of-the-ukraine-crisis-and-how-conflict-can-be-avoided/.

6. Lulu Garcia-Navarro, "Inside the Heritage Foundation's Plans for 'Institutional-izing Trumpism,'" *New York Times Magazine*, January 21, 2024.

7. Ido Vock, "Noam Chomsky: Russia Is Fighting More Humanely than the US Did in Iraq," *New Statesman*, April 29, 2023, https://www.newstatesman.com/the-weekend -interview/2023/04/noam-chomsky-interview-ukraine-free-actor-united-states -determines.

8. Isaac Chotiner, "Why John Mearsheimer Blames the U.S. for the Crisis in Ukraine," *New Yorker*, March 1, 2022.

9. Vladimir Putin, "On the Historical Unity of Russians and Ukrainians," Presiden-tial Administration of Russia, July 12, 2021, http://en.kremlin.ru/events/president/news /66181.

10. "Lavrov Said, That He Had Hope for Compromise in Negotiations with Ukraine" [Лавров заявил, что есть надежда на компромисс в переговорах с Украиной], *TASS*, March 16, 2022, https://tass.ru/politika/14085133. This was not the first time that the rulers of the Kremlin had tried to shake up the international order by imposing a new political system on their neighbors. In 1945, Joseph Stalin told the Yugoslav Communist Milovan Djilas that the Second World War had not been a conflict over land or borders but rather a clash of political ideas. The victors, he said, would not merely liberate Nazi-occupied territories but would bring their own political order too: "Whoever occupies a territory imposes on it his own social system. Everyone imposes his own system as far as his army has power to do so. It cannot be otherwise." Quoted in Milovan Djilas, *Conversations with Stalin* (New York: Penguin, 2014).

11. This material comes from the Reckoning Project and was originally printed in *The Atlantic*. See Anne Applebaum and Nataliya Gumenyuk, "'They Didn't Understand Anything, but Just Spoiled People's Lives,'" *The Atlantic*, February 14, 2023, https:// www.theatlantic.com/ideas/archive/2023/02/russia-ukraine-war-potemkin-occupation -murder-torture/672841/.

12. This paragraph is from Applebaum and Gumenyuk, "'They Didn't Understand Anything.'"

13. See Anne Applebaum, *Iron Curtain: The Crushing of Eastern Europe, 1944–1956* (New York: Anchor Books, 2012).

14. Tim Lister, Olga Voitovych, and Kostan Nechyporenko, "Ukrainian Cultural Landmarks Suffer Fresh Blows as Another Museum Is Hit," *CNN*, May 10, 2022, https://www.cnn.com/style/article/ukraine-culture-destroyed-skovoroda-museum/index .html.

15. Ukrainian World Congress, "Russia Plans to Artificially Resettle Its Citizens to Mariupol," August 30, 2023, https://www.ukrainianworldcongress.org/russia-plans-to-artificially-resettle-its-citizens-to-mariupol/.

16. International Criminal Court, "Situation in Ukraine: ICC Judges Issue Arrest Warrants against Vladimir Vladimirovich Putin and Maria Alekseyevna Lvova-Belova," press release, March 17, 2023, https://www.icc-cpi.int/news/situation-ukraine-icc-judges-issue-arrest-warrants-against-vladimir-vladimirovich-putin-and.

17. Richard Wilcox, "A New Diplomatic Off-Ramp for Russia," *Politico*, March 16, 2022, https://www.politico.com/news/magazine/2022/03/16/austria-offer-model-ukraine-nato-00017537.

18. New York Times Editorial Board, "The War in Ukraine Is Getting Complicated, and America Isn't Ready," *New York Times*, May 19, 2022.

19. Joshua Askew, "Ex Russian PM Dmitry Medvedev Claims Baltic Countries Belong to Russia," *Euronews*, May 17, 2023, https://www.euronews.com/2023/05/17/russias-dmitry-medvedev-claims-baltic-countries-belong-to-russia.

20. "Putin Ally Warns 'Enemy' Poland: You Risk Losing Your Statehood," *Reuters*, November 2, 2023, https://www.reuters.com/world/europe/putin-ally-warns-enemy-poland-you-risk-losing-your-statehood-2023-11-02/.

21. Reuters, "Putin Approves Big Military Spending Hikes for Russia's Budget," *Reuters*, November 27, 2023, https://www.reuters.com/world/europe/putin-approves-big-military-spending-hikes-russias-budget-2023-11-27/.

22. Pavel Luzin and Alexandra Prokopenko, "Russia's 2024 Budget Shows It's Planning for a Long War in Ukraine," *Carnegie Politika*, November 10, 2023, https://carnegieendowment.org/politika/90753.

23. Anne Applebaum, "The West Must Defeat Russia," *The Atlantic*, November 10, 2023.

PART II / The Conflict

Chapter Six

The Russia-Ukraine War

Military Operations and Battlefield Dynamics

Michael Kofman

The Russia-Ukraine War, currently in its third year, with little sign of abating, is the largest conventional armed conflict in Europe since World War II. Although the war aims and scope of the Russian invasion broadly tracked with prewar assumptions, the interaction between Russian and Ukrainian forces during the opening phase of the war did not align with prewar expectations in terms of Russia's force employment, the concept of operations, the conduct of its initial strike, and the absence of a Russian air superiority campaign, as well as the defense that Ukraine mustered. After the first month of intense combat, the course of the war began to align with historic patterns of large-scale conventional wars, featuring prolonged periods of positional fighting, offensives and counteroffensives, sieges in urban terrain, phases dominated by high levels of attrition, and operations to break through a prepared defense. Although Russia was expected to win relatively quickly but did not do so, overall this war does not fall outside historical trends or expected patterns for large-scale conventional wars.[1]

Despite the technological innovations employed—from new types of drones to Starlink terminals used for battlefield communication—the Russia-Ukraine War continues to reinforce the importance of several traditional battlefield dynamics

Michael Kofman is a senior fellow in the Russia and Eurasia Program at the Carnegie Endowment for International Peace. Previously he served as director of the Russia Studies Program at the Center for Naval Analyses, where he conducted research on the capabilities, strategy, and military thought of the Russian Armed Forces.

and well-established concepts in military operations. The first is the importance of mass and ability to employ forces at scale, which becomes more difficult over time as the quality of the force diminishes and its equipment is attrited. Concentration and dispersal remain challenges in this war, with technological developments driving forces toward dispersal on the defense and making it difficult to concentrate on the offense. Second, the criticality of firepower and attaining a fires advantage over an opponent in order to inflict attrition, shock, and suppression has proved particularly important as the Russian and Ukrainian militaries, from a force structure and doctrine perspective, were organized around the employment of land-based fires (both being successors to the Soviet army, which was oriented around decisive employment of artillery). The third is the process of mobilization and reconstitution by which a society is able to sustain a prolonged conventional war, and also that which turns such wars into contests of endurance between national systems. Fourth, this war reinforces that military strategy remains political in nature, where political considerations and assumptions often tend to reign supreme over military logic and a rationalized view of war that often stems from military sciences.[2]

This war also illustrates that capabilities tend to have their greatest impact when first introduced at scale but then drive cycles of adaptation and eventual deployment of counters. There are no silver bullets or game changers, although some capabilities can affect the course of an operation by providing a temporary advantage. What mattered most over time was resilience, adaptation, and effective force employment. The war has been broadly fought with traditional 20th-century conventional capabilities, which were enhanced or supplemented (but not replaced or substituted) by novel systems, new forms of communication, and reconnaissance.[3] In essence, new capabilities and technologies operated alongside established systems rather than rendering them obsolete, as both sides engaged in cycles of adaptation and iterative learning from each other. It is also worth noting that over time the battlefield dynamics were inherently shaped by defense industrial capacity and the ability to mass-produce ammunition, repair equipment, and deploy new types of systems, such as drones, on a large scale.

Finally, the course of the war demonstrates the importance of understanding contingency and human agency in history. The clearer this history becomes, the more evident it is that the outcomes of key battles, especially early on, were not overdetermined.[4] How forces are employed, the introduction of new technologies or tactics, the decisions of commanders and political leaders, along with chance, played a significant role beyond the base correlations of manpower or firepower on the battlefield. This was truer in the earlier phases than during the overall course of the war, however. Strategic factors such as manpower, materiel, money, and mobilization capacity cast a long shadow over the arc of a conflict. As a war becomes more of a marathon and less a race, the material enablers or constraints, state capacity to translate resources into military potential, and other considerations start to become deterministic. Hence any analysis must engage with the inherent tension between the contingency of individual battles or decisions and the structural variables at play. A caveat: there is still a great deal we do not know about this war, including the specifics of individual battles; this chapter represents an early attempt at answering some of those questions based on what is known but over time will need to be refined and corrected as better evidence emerges.

A Tale of Two Wars: The Initial Period vs. the Long War

There are two ways of looking at the war: one that separates it into the initial and then follow-on period of war, or another as a series of phases that periodize it based on the operations conducted and shifts in initiative. This chapter will include both, tying them together in terms of the main factors that proved the most salient or decisive in shaping battlefield dynamics. The first lens positions the war as two war periods: the initial Russian invasion, which failed to achieve its objectives, and everything else that followed. From this perspective, the Russia-Ukraine War consists of a "special military operation," in which Russian forces attempted to conduct a *coup de main* by decapitating Ukraine's leadership, isolating Ukrainian forces, and rapidly occupying the country. This operation can be periodized to February 24–March 25, 2022, by which point Russian forces are already withdrawing from Kyiv and beginning to redeploy for a more conventional campaign in Ukraine's eastern Donbas region.[5]

The first period of the war can be judged as deciding whether Ukraine would retain its sovereign status and identity as an independent nation, and the course of the battles in that period stemmed in large part from Russian political assumptions going into the war as well as Ukrainian assumptions in advance of the invasion. The Russian assumptions were that Ukraine could easily be paralyzed and overtaken without the need to plan for a prolonged conflict; the Ukrainian assumptions were that there would be no Russian invasion or that at worst a Russian military operation would focus on Ukraine's Donbas region rather than an occupation of the entire country. What follows, then, is the "long war," a traditional, conventional conflict whose overall aim is to determine the geographic boundaries of that state and its economic viability. While Moscow seeks to destroy

Ukraine as a state, its minimal war aims are focused on the Donbas, securing "annexed" territory, and undermining Ukraine's economic potential rather than seeking to install a pro-Russian government in the capital and occupy the country. Moscow seeks to impose its will on Ukraine, but the goals pursued after March 2022 appear revised down from installing a pro-Russian regime and occupying most of the country.

Consequently, the first period of the war is characterized by a Russian effort privileging speed, simultaneity, and shock, which interacted with a Ukrainian mobile defense and positional defense fixed around urban terrain. Many of the battles during the first month of the war were meeting engagements, as Russian forces attacked along numerous axes of advance and Ukrainian forces scrambled to deploy and defend. This intense maneuver phase is not atypical at the start of a conventional war. It then transitioned to a series of campaigns that were broadly defined by set-piece battles, attritional fighting, telegraphed offensives against prepared defenses, and localized counterattacks.

Similarly, an intense period of air combat then led to a degree of mutual air denial as both air forces found ways over time of contributing to tactical engagements or through long-range strike campaigns. Alongside the ground war, a series of skirmishes were fought for control of the Black Sea over the course of 2022 and 2023, determining access to Ukraine's economically vital ports. Here Russia's Black Sea Fleet first held the initiative by enforcing a blockade but over time lost it, finding itself displaced from the northwestern parts of the Black Sea and increasingly hunted by Ukraine's missile strikes when docked in port. The efforts on land and at sea were loosely coordinated, proving to be complementary theaters of war more than integrated efforts. The importance of both was expressed by the father of the Soviet navy, Admiral Sergei Gorshkov, who once wrote that "armies win the war, but navies determine the peace." The outcome of the contest for the Black Sea may therefore prove the most significant factor in how the war ends and in determining Ukraine's economic viability. It may also prove a significant source of leverage for one side versus the other in future negotiations.

Periodizing Military Operations

A periodization of the war based on the operations conducted yields roughly six distinct phases. These are the initial invasion of February 24–March 25, 2022, the battle for the Donbas of March 25–August 31, Ukrainian offensives between September and November of 2022, the Russian winter offensives between December 2022 and April 2023, Ukraine's offensive between June and September of

2023, and the follow-on period during which Russia had retaken the strategic initiative from October 2023 through the winter of 2024. This chapter will subsequently explore these periods, but it is useful to lay out first what ties them together: in essence, the arc of the war, from the perspective of military operations and battlefield dynamics.

After the initial Russian invasion failed, the Russian military faced a structural deficit of manpower. This is because it invaded with a peacetime force structure that depended on, but had not conducted, mobilization and had no plan for prolonged sustainment or how to replace major combat losses. Russian forces compensated for this deficit with a significant advantage in firepower, which enabled progress, but that advantage dwindled over time. Ukraine had mobilized first, filling its manning tables and expanding its brigades, which then had manpower to hold trenches or defend cities but lacked munitions. Hence it faced the inverse problem: After the introduction of Western artillery and precision-strike capabilities, Russia's fires advantage declined, and more importantly Russian forces fired through their ammunition reserves. In the first year of the war, Russia lacked mass but had firepower, whereas the opposite was the case for Ukraine. Ukraine was able to take advantage of an important asymmetry during the fall of 2022, when, after months of attrition, Russian forces lacked manpower and had exhausted their offensive potential.

Mobilization in the fall of 2022 stabilized Russian lines, and Ukraine no longer enjoyed a decisive advantage in manpower, fires, or the capacity to employ forces. However, for much of 2023 Russia had to ration artillery, finding itself with mass but lacking a fires advantage. Consequently, it was successful in mounting a prepared defense but unsuccessful in prosecuting offensives because the force at its base required a combination of mass and fires as the key ingredients in how it operates. Ukraine similarly found itself without a decisive advantage in either manpower or fires in 2023 but with the daunting task of having to pursue a set-piece battle against a prepared defense. This interaction between availability of mass and fires is an important factor in success or failure of operations throughout the war.

No less important was force employment: what the force made of the means it had available. Both sides struggled with employing forces at scale, albeit at first for different reasons. The Russian military took heavy losses in the initial invasion, dramatically degrading its force quality, command capacity, and ability to operate doctrinally. Russian units couldn't put the pieces back together because the pieces weren't there, and hence regressed to fighting largely as small packets of either mechanized units or dismounted infantry. Over time the Russian army could re-place quantities of manpower and materiel but not regenerate the loss of quality to enable larger-scale operations or greater complexity in how forces were used. This challenge was compounded by growing defenses on both sides, making it dif-ficult to concentrate the force on the offense. Ukraine's military was oriented around defense in depth and mobile defense from the outset and was centered on brigade structures without higher command echelons (division, corps, army) and thus lacked the experience, command, and logistical layers necessary to employ forces offensively on a larger scale. Brigades did (and still do) much of the plan-ning, integrated horizontally. There were operational command layers above them, but day to day they were not tying the fight together. Force employment constraints and issues stemming from lack of organizational capacity were com-pounded by significant losses among officers and noncommissioned officers in the Ukrainian military during the first year of fighting.

Consequently, by 2023 both Russia and Ukraine maintained hundreds of thou-sands of troops along a 1,000-kilometer line of contact but with a circumscribed capacity to conduct offensive operations. This meant in practice that both sides tended to pursue smaller offensive operations, spaced along the broad front, and that major offensives were executed as a series of smaller-scale tactical actions. In 2023, Russian forces restored mass but suffered shell hunger, and they could not establish significant advantages in fires. Ukraine, on the other hand, struggled to establish a localized advantage or, even more importantly, to exploit breaches in order to turn them into breakthroughs. Hence both sides could make incre-mental gains at high cost, but the tactical situation was often stalemated such that neither side could achieve its objectives in offensive operations during 2023. The lack of relative advantage in mass and fires, combined with a significantly constrained capacity for force employment, offers the better causal explanation for the outcomes observed. This situation will not necessarily continue through 2024, as Russia increasingly holds advantages in manpower, equipment, and ammunition.

Prepared defense remained a major impediment to the successful employment of maneuver warfare. Historically, this is neither a surprising nor an inconsistent finding when reflecting on past conventional wars in which such operations were conducted. Drones, both for reconnaissance and strike, made it even more difficult to mass forces for offensives or to achieve any element of surprise. Land warfare generally favors the defender because it is easier to defend than to attack, but in this context, military technology and tactics further exacerbated this historical tendency. The net effect was an increased cost for offensive action, a reduction in the element of surprise or shock achieved from maneuver-centered operations, and a strong shift toward destruction-based warfare whose leading characteristic is attrition. Both sides struggled with the aforementioned fundamental issues in terms of force quality, being able to organize large-scale operations, and either a deficit of manpower or a deficit of firepower, each of which made it difficult to attain a decisive advantage.

Examining the Initial Invasion

The initial Russian campaign proved to be the reconciliation of an unworkable concept of operations, which did not anticipate or plan to engage an organized and sustained Ukrainian defense, pitted against a Ukrainian defensive effort, across several fronts, which also did not anticipate the invasion or its likely vectors of attack. In short, the outcome was highly contingent. Russia's initial invasion was a heavily leveraged and risky operation, premised on the assumption that a long war could be avoided if its forces executed a *coup de main*. The underlying political assumption was that the invasion would prove complementary to an extensive subversion campaign and that Russian intelligence had established the necessary conditions for its success.[6] Hence, the unconventional warfare component failed first, and subsequently the conventional invasion that hinged on it quickly became unglued.

Russian forces proved vulnerable as they were organized into long columns, tied to roads, and trying to meet tight timetables in an effort to rapidly advance into the country. The overall force was brittle, heavily supplemented by auxiliaries mobilized from the Luhansk and Donetsk People's Republics (LDNR) and national guard (Rosgvardia) units and deployed with formations that were at best optimized for a local war of short duration. The plan's central premise was that Ukrainian leadership could be paralyzed, deployed Ukrainian forces quickly fixed and isolated, and the Russian military would shift to an occupation phase. Much hinged on the ability of the Russian airborne to rapidly insert themselves into the Ukrainian capital, and the eastern and central grouping of forces being able to fully encircle it, thereby removing the Ukrainian government or severing its linkages to the rest of the state. Both the encirclement effort and the rapid insertion effort failed. Similarly, Russian forces tried to bypass major cities in an effort to isolate and blockade them, akin to US "thunder runs" from the 2003 invasion of Iraq, but found themselves engaged by Ukrainian brigades and supporting volunteer units. The diffusion of the Russian invasion meant that small leading elements of battalion tactical groups could be outmatched by Ukrainian units that had organized fire support and could make use of the country's depth to mount an effective mobile defense.

Russian forces advanced rapidly into Ukrainian territory but did not control it, and Moscow was unable to achieve its political objectives at the outset of the war. From an operational perspective, the initial invasion did not reflect how the Russian military trains and organizes to fight in larger-scale combat operations. It featured a very different command-and-control structure, dividing forces into five groupings of forces, with the air support similarly split, and no unity of effort. Spread across different axes, Russian forces were unable to mass, and tied to roads, they did not deploy as combined arms formations in the field. Their support and fires elements often lagged far behind advancing mechanized units. Advancing columns spread into competing directions, increasing the burden on logistics and making it difficult to maintain command and control. Several of the formations were led by the Rosgvardia and riot police, who assumed they would be stabilizing cities rather than facing combat. At this point, a veritable mountain of evidence supports the view that the Russian military was attempting to execute something similar to the seizure of Crimea in 2014, but on a much larger scale, rather than planning for an intense and costly battle with Ukraine's armed forces.[7]

That said, Ukraine's military scrambled from garrisons in the last twenty-four hours before the Russian assault. Ukraine's intelligence had not assessed the invasion as imminent until the last moments, and the political leadership held firmly to the position that all-out war was unlikely, preventing mobilization until the final week in the run-up to the war.[8] Ukraine's ready formations were largely concentrated in the Donbas, leaving the capital almost completely undefended. An eleventh-hour sortie, ordered by Ukraine's commander in chief, saved the armed forces from catastrophic losses during the initial Russian strike on February 24, but these units had to hastily meet advancing Russian formations rather than man a prepared defense.[9] Ukrainian brigades benefited from an influx of volunteers, auxiliaries, and a mixture of forces that stalled the Russian advance as regular formations mobilized and deployed to mount a defense.

Much of the Ukrainian force was operating independently, defending sectors, and coordinating horizontally between units. This is where Ukraine's advantage in initiative, junior leadership, and tactical adaptation paid off over the inculcated rigidity of Russian command and control. The Russian invasion sought to make rapid advances, supported by infiltrators, which confused the picture inside Ukraine, making it difficult to manage. Hence there were numerous friendly-fire incidents, as different defending forces lacked rules of engagement and were unsure who controlled what. Western weapons, such as anti-tank guided missiles, proved useful in stalling the Russian advances, but the key factor during this period was Ukraine's artillery and its ability to concentrate fires against individual Russian units.[10] Western intelligence also played a role from the very first hours of the war in providing situational awareness and resilient communications to higher echelons, though it remains unclear how much of a factor this was in aiding the defense nationwide.

The plans and objectives were also kept secret from the Russian troops until the final days, which meant that readiness issues were unresolved, maintenance was unaddressed, and Russian forces were psychologically unprepared for such a campaign. This led to significant losses of armored fighting vehicles during the first days of the invasion due to maintenance issues rather than combat. The problem was particularly acute as the Russian military was based around a partial mobilization model, which meant that readiness and maintenance levels were likely to be padded throughout the force to begin with. Research and fieldwork over the past two years has established that the critical factor in the Russian invasion was less the quality of Russian forces, or intangibles, and more how the force was structured, organized, and employed.[11] The latter stemmed from the supremacy of political decision-making over sound military logic or rational force employment.[12] When the "special military operation" failed, Russia's war effort suffered from a strategic misalignment between Russian political objectives and military means. But some of the key battles were quite close, and the invasion could have also gone the other way if Ukraine's political or military leadership had made a different set of choices during the early days of the war.

The Russian Air Campaign

One of the more surprising and confounding areas of performance during the Russian invasion was the weak, or at times seemingly missing, Russian air force.[13] The initial strike campaign did not appear to generate the sortie rate or missile expenditure anticipated, while much of Ukraine's critical infrastructure was left intact because it was not targeted. The overall execution of the Russian strike campaign was also subject to the peculiar political assumptions and constraints that governed the Russian invasion, leading to poor force employment, a divided air force supporting regional groupings of forces, and a campaign that would struggle to provide support if Ukraine's air defense had managed to disperse and survive the first set of strikes. First, it is important to note that the entire concept behind the Russian operation was incompatible with a prolonged air campaign to attain air superiority. Ukraine was not only the largest country in Europe (not including Russia) but possessed an extensive array of ground-based, radar-guided air defense systems. The overall number of air defense units, much of it legacy capability inherited from the Soviet Union, exceeds that of many countries in Europe combined. Campaigns against much easier targets, such as Iraq or Yugoslavia, suggest that it would have taken several months with the outcome uncertain.

Given Russian assumptions, which drove the military strategy, a prolonged air campaign was not only incompatible in terms of timelines; it was also likely judged to be unnecessary. An air superiority campaign would eliminate the element of surprise for the ground-force invasion, which in turn meant that Ukraine could have months to mobilize resistance or fortify population centers. The United States or other countries would then have time to attempt an intervention or significantly arm Ukrainian forces. Russia's invasion was premised on being able to catch Ukraine relatively unprepared, and it is difficult to see how that could have been accomplished with weeks or months of preparatory strikes. The central organizing Russian assumption was that Ukraine would collapse quickly and that a demonstrative strike campaign, a cheaper version of "shock and awe," would be sufficient to achieve this.

The Russian Aerospace Forces focused on suppression of Ukrainian air defense, ground support, offensive counter-air, and massed long-range strikes.[14] There was a unified strike campaign integrating missile strikes from a diverse array of platforms (air, land, and sea), and Russian forces did strike many of the known Ukrainian air defense sites. Russian airstrikes were supported by electronic warfare to suppress Ukrainian early warning and fire-control radars during the initial strike campaign, and it appears that these air defenses were suppressed during the first few days of action. Many of the units were dispersing and deploying during this time. The strikes were far less effective than the Russian military likely hoped, however, and Ukrainian air defense managed to disperse in the hours leading up to the Russian campaign, which dramatically reduced its impact.

Russia's air force was effective in air-to-air engagements against the Ukrainian air force, which was qualitatively and quantitatively outmatched, but it couldn't execute dynamic targeting against Ukrainian air defense and was unable to provide ground support once Ukraine's air defense systems came online. The air campaign revealed that the Russian air force, despite improvements observed in Syria during their 2015 intervention, was still largely incapable of planning and executing composite air operations on a larger scale.[15] Russia's air force had few experienced pilots, a limited park of precision-guided munitions, and was saddled with large numbers of dated platforms like Su-25 attack aircraft, whose mission profile had become obsolete thirty years ago (much the same can be said of the American A-10). The initial performance, though, was less a technical issue; rather it was driven by the organizational limitations, that is, the "software" of the Russian military, which lacked the capacity and experience for conducting complex air operations of this type and therefore hinged its hopes on a successful initial set of strikes.

Doctrinal and force-quality factors were also critical to understanding Russian airpower performance and placing it into the right context. The Russian armed forces were not organized around the strategic employment of airpower, displacing most fires into land-based systems, and the Russian Aerospace Forces had never previously conducted a campaign of this type against a network of ground-based air defenses. The priority for Russian airpower was not destruction of enemy air defense, or offensive counter-air, because NATO force structure lacks ground-based air defenses in the first place, and NATO airpower has significant overmatch over Russian tactical aviation. Russian Aerospace Forces were focused on air defense, long-range strike, and ground support to the extent they could provide it given the technical limitations of their platforms. This mission usually fell to combat helicopters, which could engage in dynamic targeting.

The Russian air force had neither the historical experience nor the training or mission requirements to conduct a campaign of this type at scale. Doctrinally, the Russian military had overinvested in the idea that precision strikes could achieve decisive effects early on in a conflict, including cognitive impact, shock, and paralysis, leading to surrender and a loss of cohesion for the opposing force.[16] Much of the Russian thinking on military strategy prior to the war shifted toward destruction of an opponent's economic and military potential at depth and disaggregation of their war effort, which was heavily predicated on the ability to employ long-range strike and nonkinetic capabilities.[17] The core tenets of Russian military strategy shifted planning away from strategic ground offensives, or the need for a high density of forces to hold terrain, and into an enthusiastic embrace of precision-strike systems that were meant to achieve decisive effects on a fragmented battlefield.[18]

Over time the Russian Aerospace Forces began to claw back relevance. First, through a series of strike campaigns employing cruise missiles and long-range drones acquired from Iran. These had some effect but ultimately lacked strategic impact. Neither air force could provide effective ground support, with both sides resorting to firing unguided rockets from behind the forward line of troops, a highly ineffective tactic. Russian combat helicopters proved much more relevant to the fighting in 2023, countering Ukrainian mechanized advances during the summer offensive, which proved vulnerable due to a lack of supporting short-range air defense. Over time the Russian air force began to deploy glide-bomb kits, which allowed it to conduct standoff strike missions across the front. Ukraine's air force steadily modified aircraft to employ Western precision-guided munitions: first, HARM anti-radiation (anti-radar) missiles, then guided bombs (JDAMs), and eventually delivering air-launched cruise missiles. These led to successful strikes against high-value targets such as bridges, headquarters, and the Russian Black Sea Fleet itself.

The Naval Campaign

Initially the Russian fleet took control of the Black Sea, conducted long-range strikes with sea-launched cruise missiles, and deployed amphibious assault ships with embarked naval infantry to threaten an amphibious assault against Odesa. This forced Ukraine to keep units in reserve during the Russian invasion to hedge against such a contingency. Ukraine also mined the access to Odesa, along with the beaches. Russian forces were unable to advance past Mykolaiv; there was thus no place to make a landing that could link up with the ground campaign, and the sea conditions were unsuitable for an amphibious landing. The fleet therefore focused on imposing an outer blockade but quickly grew vulnerable to Ukraine's anti-ship coastal defense cruise missiles. The loss of the *Moskva*, the flagship of the Black Sea Fleet, was a major symbolic blow and forced the fleet to retreat. A series of skirmishes over Snake Island, off Ukraine's coast, further pushed Russian forces out of a position to effectively blockade commercial traffic to Odesa as Ukrainian special forces gained control of the island.

The Russian navy shifted to imposing a blockade-in-being, essentially threatening ship traffic but without actively enforcing a blockade. This was less an issue while Russia and Ukraine were part of a series of arrangements governing maritime exports, such as the grain deal, but Moscow withdrew from the agreements in 2023. Over the course of the year, Ukraine steadily established a transit corridor, challenged the blockade, and began to resume commercial shipping. Strikes with drones and cruise missiles forced the Russian navy to rebase its larger combatants to the eastern part of the sea, in Novorossiysk. Over time, Ukrainian units would raid Russian-occupied gas platforms in the Black Sea, steadily eating away at Russian control and situational awareness. Ukrainian uncrewed surface vehicles began to gain greater range, threatening Russian ships coming out of port in and around Crimea. The Russian Black Sea Fleet found itself increasingly cornered, fighting a defensive battle, without much combat utility beyond resupply missions and launching missile strikes, which could be conducted by other parts of the force. The fleet lost several vessels from strikes in port or dry dock as well as a number of landing ship tank amphibious ships. Subsequently, Russia lost the initiative in the Black Sea in 2023, and Ukraine was increasingly able to effect sea denial, if not sea control, in the northwestern part of it by the end of the war's second year.

The Battle for the Donbas (Donets River Offensive)

After their defeat around Kyiv, Kharkiv, and Mykolaiv in the south, Russian forces regrouped and redeployed. The focus of this operation was on Ukraine's Donbas region, although at this stage the Russian military had lost a significant percentage of its initial force quality and equipment during the failed invasion. The Russian military initially invaded with approximately 150,000 personnel, but about a third of this force included mobilized units from the occupied LDNR and Rosgvardia units intended for the occupation phase. Having been mauled in the first month of fighting, the Russian army lacked manpower. The Russian land forces were optimized around a partial mobilization model, which left them operating typically at 70%–90% readiness. Over time, the readiness was reduced, which led to fewer and fewer soldiers manning formations. It was also an army staffed by conscripts in key support roles, on an annual rotation. These were legally prohibited from being employed outside of wartime conditions. In essence, two-thirds of the force was unavailable for combat operations, so the force generation potential of the Russian military was quite small in peacetime.

As a result of these constraints, Russian brigades of 3,500–4,000 men in practice could generate no more than 2 battalion tactical groups, consisting of perhaps 600 men each.[19] The invasion force consisted of approximately 130 such battalion tactical groups of varying sizes. Having revised the force structure over time by cutting infantry and reducing readiness to save costs, the Russian leadership made choices that would greatly impact their force's combat effectiveness in Ukraine. Russian units were stacked with artillery, armor, and supporting elements such as electronic warfare or communication systems, but they lacked infantry and were logistically heavy to support. What that meant in practice is that they would struggle to fight for cities, operate off roads where supporting infantry was necessary, or hold and control large tracts of terrain, which is exactly what the conditions in Ukraine required. It was subsequently difficult for Russian forces to engage in combined arms maneuver because they were desperately short on the principal combat arm required: infantry. This type of force generation—battalion tactical groups—was doctrinally intended for local wars of much smaller scale and employment for relatively short duration, where the organic logistics assigned to the unit might be sufficient for three- to ten-day deployments. The overall Russian force structure proved ill-suited for the war, especially in terms of the types of formations employed, which were brittle and difficult to employ if the initial operation failed.

Despite that failure, and the force's self-evident inability to conduct operations across such broad fronts with so little manpower, the Russian political leadership refused to conduct mobilization until seven months into the war (September 2022). Instead of fixing manpower, the Russian military offset its deficit in personnel with an artillery fire advantage of approximately 12:1 over Ukrainian forces.[20] They fired an average of 20,000 shells per day during this period and likely averaged 15,000 over the course of 2022. Ukrainian forces were outmatched in fires and low on ammunition. At this stage, Western military assistance became a deciding factor, as a panoply of Western artillery and High Mobility Artillery Rocket System (HIMARS) long-range precision-strike systems entered the war.[21] Most importantly, Western ammunition enabled Ukraine to sustain defensive fire. Brutal battles, in urban environments like Mariupol and Sievierodonetsk, exhausted the Russian offensive in the Donbas. Although Russia's sieges of Mariupol and Sievierodonetsk were ultimately successful, Russia was forced to rely on mobilized personnel from LDNR for those battles, and that strategy was unsustainable. The decisive factor in the Russian campaign in 2022 was artillery firepower, but Russian forces had lost the ability to operate at significant scale given the deterioration in quality and losses among maneuver units. It was also apparent that they struggled doctrinally to adapt to the forces available to them, which no longer had sufficient personnel to staff battalion tactical groups, and were attempting to use unit fragments as though they were complete battalions.

Ukraine's Offensives in the Fall of 2022 (Kherson and Kharkiv)

In September 2022, Ukraine launched two major offensives of its own. In 2022, attrition worked to Ukraine's advantage. The Kherson operation was the primary offensive, where Russian forces were arrayed in defensive lines, whereas the Kharkiv operation was designed to take advantage of Russia's degraded and unbalanced force posture along the front. The Russian military had to choose between defending Kherson and reinforcing Kharkiv, and it chose Kherson, taking on significant risk in Kharkiv. When the war began, Ukraine had mobilized and substantially expanded its armed forces. Its military grew several times in size. Conversely, Russia was trying to stabilize a front stretching more than 1,600 kilometers with a depleted force and a patchwork of auxiliary units. In Kharkiv, Russian forces were a sparsely manned line, employing LDNR and Rosgvardia units. The bulk of the regular army forces were remnants of the western military district, in some places existing at 25% strength with low morale due to losses and desertions.[22] Variation in the force degraded interoperability, which compounded the depletion problem. Morale was also a factor, with units suffering from non-combat losses of soldiers who refused to continue serving under contract.

Ukrainian forces broke through at Kharkiv, leading to a Russian rout, but the Russian airborne held in Kherson. The initial Ukrainian offensive in September failed to achieve a breakthrough. The geometry of the battlefield was highly favorable to Ukraine, with Russian units separated from their supplies by the Dnipro River. Months of HIMARS strikes reduced the Russian ground lines of communications to one bridge across the Kakhovka Dam and a network of ferries. Russian forces contained a renewed Ukrainian offensive in October, but they were compelled to retreat in order to preserve the force, as the costly battle strongly favored Ukraine. Russian units had no hope of counterattack and were in an increasingly precarious position even if Ukrainian forces could not achieve a breakthrough. Russian strategy changed to a primarily defensive one, reducing the frontage they had to defend and fortifying along the front while trying to execute a large-scale strike campaign against Ukrainian infrastructure. The expanded strike campaign, which unfolded through the winter of 2023, was better organized and planned than prior Russian efforts, but it failed to degrade Ukraine's electricity grid enough to achieve Russian objectives.

Kherson was an early indicator that even with Western systems and advantages in precision strike, it would prove very difficult to break through a prepared defense. Russian morale was not so low as to easily give up defensive lines and prepared positions. The Russian airborne was ultimately able to withdraw from Kherson in detail, with much of their equipment. Russian leadership ordered a partial mobilization, calling up 300,000 men in September in a shambolic process, but one that eventually served to stabilize Russian lines and refill their depleted manning tables. The defeat at Kharkiv liberated thousands of square kilometers, but it did not lead to a cascade collapse of the front. This success led to outsized expectations that the war might prove short and that it could be repeated under very different conditions elsewhere. At this stage, Russian forces were in dire need of reconstitution over the winter, but the Ukrainian army, despite being advantaged overall, was also not in a condition to keep pressing.

Russia's Winter Offensive and the Battle for Bakhmut, 2023

The Russian military tried to retake the initiative, first by attempting to fix Ukrainian forces around Bakhmut. Russian airborne redeployed there, in support of the Wagner Group, and so did Ukrainian units who had fought in Kherson. Bakhmut was a relative sideshow to the war and strategically unimportant, but the winter fighting propelled it to become a centerpiece battle. It was further imbued with political symbolism as the bellwether in a contest of will between the two countries. Bakhmut was a battle both for the city and for a much larger front around it on its southern and northern flanks. The Wagner Group was not especially effective, despite being mythologized as such. Its main advantages were that the Russian airborne covered its flanks to prevent counterattacks, that it was granted access to convicts from the Russian prison system to use as expendable assault infantry, and most importantly, that Russian forces enjoyed a fires advantage of 5:1 for much of the battle. The centrality of fires is what led the group's leader, Yevgeny Prigozhin, to constantly complain about having insufficient artillery ammunition, despite receiving more supplies than any other Russian grouping of forces at the time.

Ukraine's strategy was characterized by a "not one inch" mentality, unwilling to cede ground even if the defensive terrain behind Bakhmut was much more favorable than defending the city itself. This "hold at all costs" approach had clear downsides and at times led Ukrainian leadership to reinforce failure rather than success. Having succeeded in attriting Russian forces over the summer, the military pursued the same strategy in 2023, but the conditions had now changed significantly in terms of Russian manpower availability and capacity to replace losses. Russian forces were leveraging expendable troops while reconstituting the rest of the force and entrenching across a broad front in Ukraine. Ukraine enjoyed a favorable loss ratio over Russia of up to 1:4 in total casualties during the nine-month battle, but the Russian troops fighting under the Wagner Group were likely 70% convicts.[23] Bakhmut pitted Ukraine's more-experienced soldiers against Russia's more-expendable formations. Ukraine lost the city in May and has not been able to retake it, although both sides claimed victory in the battle on the basis of the losses inflicted. For Russian forces, Bakhmut was at best a Pyrrhic victory, which did not lead to any breakthroughs, but dragging out the battle would have knock-on effects on Ukraine's offensive later in 2023.

In late January 2023, the Russian military launched its own winter offensive, which consisted of five localized offensives trying to pressure Ukrainian forces along a broad front. This effort proved unsuccessful because the Russian forces lacked a fires advantage and didn't have sufficient enablers to breach minefields; its force quality had deteriorated to such an extent that Russia could not coordinate attacks in larger formations. Many of the attacks were undertaken by company- or platoon-sized units, which were defeated. Russian forces had restored mass but could not employ forces at scale and had to ration artillery support. This was primarily not the result of HIMARS strikes but because Russian forces were spendthrift in 2022 with their volume of fire and burned through their ammunition reserves. This forced a change in tactics to conserve ammunition, and the Russian military began to employ drones for counterbattery fire on a large scale, along with precision-guided munitions.

Ukraine's Offensive, Summer–Fall 2023

After Russia's failed winter offensive, Ukraine sought to seize the initiative and deal a major blow to Russian forces in the southern part of the country. The theory of victory was premised on Ukrainian forces breaking through to the Sea of Azov, then holding at risk Russia's positions in Crimea, which could grant significant leverage in negotiations. This was at least the West's objective in resourcing the offensive. Ukraine sought war termination on favorable terms and the battlefield leverage to achieve it. The United States and a coalition of Western countries established a crash train-and-equip program for Ukrainian forces. The West trained and equipped nine brigades for the offensive, while Ukraine would field additional brigades from the armed forces, national guard, and territorial defense troops.

Ukraine's military split its forces and fires along three axes, Bakhmut, Velyka Novosilka, and Tokmak, in hopes of pinning down Russian forces and preventing redeployment between the different fronts. Essentially, there were three offensives, one of which was the main effort. Russian forces anticipated the main effort at Orikhiv, where they had concentrated their defenses. In 2023, Russian force density was much higher relative to terrain held, and Russian engineering brigades prepared extensive lines of defenses, with deep minefields, bunkers, and cemented trenches. In the south, along the Orikhiv-Tokmak axis, the Russian military had multiple defensive lines and held the high ground. Ukraine faced an established defense, a high force-density-to-terrain ratio, and unfavorable geometry. There were hopes that the initial breaching operation would lead to shock and a retreat of the forward Russian lines, especially with the added capability provided by Western equipment. However, the initial Ukrainian breaching effort in June failed. Newly trained Ukrainian units made common mistakes with respect to planning, coordinating artillery fire with assaults, orienting at night, and employing breaching equipment and in a few cases had engaged in unfortunate friendly-fire incidents.[24]

Ukraine's offensive suffered from some of the same challenges the Russian forces faced in the winter. Ukraine's brigades could not scale force employment on the offense. This meant that a brigade-level attack was in practice two reinforced companies advancing, backed by artillery. Ukraine was deploying combat power onto the battlefield in small packets, unable to coordinate and support formations at a larger scale. The overall artillery advantage Ukraine enjoyed amounted to relative parity, and the difficulty in sequencing meant that the forces could not achieve shock or suppression. Western equipment had superior survivability but was hardly a game changer. More experienced units, without Western equipment, performed better in both offensive and defensive tasks, demonstrating that experience and leadership figured prominently in combat effectiveness. This reinforced the overall battlefield dynamic: it was less about the capabilities of specific systems or platforms themselves and more about the quantity and how these systems were being employed by the force. Without proper support or enablers to overcome defenses, even the best Western equipment was rendered ineffective or unemployable in the context of the fight.

The Ukrainian military changed tactics, emphasizing dismounted infantry assault, which reduced losses and preserved equipment but did not result in a breakthrough. There was a point during the offensive when Ukraine had a fires advantage and had a prospect of making another attempt at a major breakthrough, but Ukraine exhausted its offensive capacity by October without reaching its minimal objectives. In September, Russia rotated in airborne regiments as reserves and launched its own offensive in Avdiivka in October. The Russian offensive in Avdiivka also failed to achieve a breakthrough but initiated another grinding battle that would drag on into the winter, leading to the city's fall in February 2024. Russian forces lost a significant amount of armored fighting vehicles attempting a double envelopment, but they too struggled against a prepared defense and lacked the enablers to breach minefields successfully. By this point in the war, first-person view drones had moved to the forefront of tactical engagements and began to deny mobility during the day. This battle was a microcosm of an observed dynamic throughout the war: when armored assaults failed, both sides switched to dismounted infantry tactics and tried to establish localized fires superiority because they were unable to break through by employing mechanized formations. Over time, the scale of action was further reduced to assault groups of eleven to sixteen men, being delivered by two to three armored fighting vehicles directly onto an enemy position, who would then have to assault and hold it for the duration of the day.

Ukraine's summer offensive failed in large part because the attacking force enjoyed no advantage in firepower, did not have the requisite enablers to overcome a well-prepared defense, and could not scale force employment to exploit breaches in the Russian lines. There was also no adjustment in military strategy when the initial breaching effort did not succeed, and the offensive continued to be split along three axes, even though none of them showed a significant likelihood of breakthrough. These decisions were likely made at the political level, reducing the military's ability to redeploy forces from Bakhmut to the main effort, which was not showing progress. The offensive culminated when the force ran out of assault-capable infantry and the supply of artillery ammunition from Western countries began to dwindle. The battlefield dynamics in 2022–2023 suggest that despite the growing prevalence of uncrewed systems and increasing use of tactical strike drones, the capacity that mattered the most was the availability of artillery ammunition and infantry capable of sustaining offensive action.

Conclusion

The Russia-Ukraine War is ultimately not a war that defied expectations but rather in most cases validated them. Although the initial invasion constituted a surprising and unworkable concept of operations, resulting in a failed Russian attempt at a *coup de main*, the long war that followed hewed closely to historical patterns of large-scale protracted wars. Throughout the war both sides struggled with combining mass and firepower in order to achieve a decisive advantage. Beyond material and manpower resources, the deciding factor was often force employment, and therefore force quality remained an important variable. Both forces struggled with the cycle of reconstitution and regeneration of combat power, able to replace quantity but not substitute for quality lost during the early phases of the war. The course of the conflict was therefore unsurprisingly a seesaw of offensives, counteroffensives, sieges, and prolonged periods of attritional fighting between two militaries with sufficient staying power to sustain the fight.

This war also raises questions on how best to integrate intangibles or soft factors into military analysis. Morale was a tactical enabler, promoting unit cohesion, but not a decisive factor in the war and hardly a constant for either side. Focusing on the tangibles, what can be quantified alone, is insufficient. Weighing intangibles, which are difficult to assess, however, can easily lead to preferences or magical thinking being substituted for defensible military analysis. The chief determinants of outcomes were not morale but capacity for force employment, chiefly organizational capacity, experience, ability to adapt and innovate, and the quality of leadership. Experienced units consistently performed better independent of their equipment. Once key parts of a force were lost, it was difficult to adjust and quickly recover since the pieces could no longer doctrinally be put together the same way.

Similarly, technology proved important but represented only one aspect of what provided advantage or offset it on the battlefield. Drones enabled or enhanced existing capabilities and facilitated new tactics and strike options, but they did not replace legacy systems. These new or novel technologies did not lead to breakthroughs or significant changes in territorial control between the forces as they proliferated on the battlefield. Despite the steady deployment of new and more capable Western weapon systems, the advantages they offered on the battlefield were at times fleeting, leading to adaptation and counters from the Russian side. In hindsight, they were tactically significant, and even at times operationally impactful, but strategically indecisive when compared with the larger factors of manpower, materiel, and defense industrial capacity. Ukraine mobilized first, Russia second, and the West did not sufficiently mobilize its production capacity in a timely manner during the first year of the war.

This had a structural effect on the course of the conflict, constraining Ukraine's options by the end of 2023, leaving Russia with a growing advantage in manpower, equipment, and ammunition in 2024. While Ukraine, and the West, retain options to rebuild Ukraine's advantage, if these trends are not addressed, a conflict that began so dismally for Moscow might still lead to Ukraine being forced to negotiate an end to the war from a position of weakness.

NOTES

1. See Stephen Biddle, "Back in the Trenches," *Foreign Affairs*, August 10, 2023, https://www.foreignaffairs.com/ukraine/back-trenches-technology-warfare; Stephen Biddle "How Russia Stopped Ukraine's Momentum," *Foreign Affairs*, January 29, 2024, https://www.foreignaffairs.com/ukraine/how-russia-stopped-ukraines-momentum.

2. The following views are based on the author's findings from two years of fieldwork in Ukraine, including numerous interviews with Ukrainian troops, officers, and senior officials, along with data-gathering efforts over the course of four trips from 2022 to 2023.

3. See Stacie Pettyjohn, *Evolution Not Revolution* (Washington, DC: Center for a New American Security, February 8, 2024), https://www.cnas.org/publications/reports /evolution-not-revolution; Jeffrey Edmonds and Samuel Bendett, *Russia's Use of Uncrewed Systems in Ukraine* (Clarendon, VA: CNA, March 2023), https://www.cna.org/reports/2023 /05/russias-use-of-drones-in-ukraine. The author also has a forthcoming report with Rob Lee on the use of first-person view tactical drones and their impact on the war.

4. See, for example, writing on the critical Battle of Hostomel Airport during the first hours of the war. Liam Collins, Michael Kofman, and John Spencer, "The Battle of Hostomel Airport: A Key Moment in Russia's Defeat in Kyiv," *War on the Rocks,* August 10, 2023, https://warontherocks.com/2023/08/the-battle-of-hostomel-airport-a -key-moment-in-russias-defeat-in-kyiv/.

5. Some periodize it to March 29, but this is incorrect. The first announcement made that Russian forces were shifting to a Donbas-centered campaign was by Colonel General Sergey Rudskoy, the chief of the General Staff's Main Operational Directorate. This statement was largely repeated on March 29, 2022, by Sergei Shoigu, the minister of defense, using similar language. Russian forces had already begun withdrawing by March 25.

6. See Jack Watling, Oleksandr V. Danylyuk, and Nick Reynolds, *Preliminary Lessons from Russia's Unconventional Operations during the Russo-Ukrainian War, February 2022–2023* (London: Royal United Services Institute, March 2023), https://www.rusi.org/explore -our-research/publications/special-resources/preliminary-lessons-russias-unconventional -operations-during-russo-ukrainian-war-february-2022.

7. For comparison, see earlier analysis of the Russian seizure of Crimea in Michael Kofman et al., *Lessons from Russia's Operations in Crimea and Eastern Ukraine* (Santa Monica, CA: RAND Corporation, 2017), https://www.rand.org/pubs/research_reports /RR1498.html.

8. Based on author interviews in Kyiv, 2022–2023, including with senior military and intelligence officials.

9. Alya Shandra, "Syrskyi In, Zaluzhny Out: What Our Army Sources Expect from Ukraine's Army Reshuffle," *Euromaidan Press*, February 10, 2024, https://euromaidan press.com/2024/02/10/syrskyi-in-zaluzhnyi-out-what-to-expect-from-ukraines-army -reshuffle/.

10. See Mykhaylo Zabrodskyi et al., *Preliminary Lessons in Conventional Warfighting from Russia's Invasion of Ukraine: February–July 2022* (London: Royal United Services Institute, November 2022), https://www.rusi.org/explore-our-research/publications /special-resources/preliminary-lessons-conventional-warfighting-russias-invasion -ukraine-february-july-2022.

11. Zabrodskyi et al., *Preliminary Lessons in Conventional Warfighting.*

12. Jeff Edmonds, "Start with the Political: Explaining Russia's Bungled Invasion of Ukraine," *War on the Rocks*, April 28, 2022, https://warontherocks.com/2022/04/start -with-the-political-explaining-russias-bungled-invasion-of-ukraine/.

13. See Justin Bronk, *The Mysterious Case of the Missing Russian Air Force* (London: Royal United Services Institute, February 2022), https://www.rusi.org/explore-our-research/publications/commentary/mysterious-case-missing-russian-air-force.

14. For a good overview of this campaign, see Justin Bronk, *Russian Combat Air Strengths and Limitations: Lessons from Ukraine* (Clarendon, VA: CNA, April 2023), https://www.cna.org/reports/2023/04/Russian-Combat-Air-Strengths-and-Limitations.pdf.

15. Bronk, *Russian Combat Air Strengths and Limitations*; see also Anton Lavrov, *The Russian Air Campaign in Syria* (Clarendon, VA: CNA, June 2018), https://www.cna.org/reports/2018/06/COP-2018-U-017903-Final.pdf.

16. Sam Cranny-Evans and Sidharth Kaushal, *The Intellectual Failures behind Russia's Bungled Invasion* (London: Royal United Services Institute, April 2022), https://www.rusi.org/explore-our-research/publications/commentary/intellectual-failures-behind-russias-bungled-invasion.

17. See Michael Kofman et al., *Russian Military Strategy: Core Tenets and Operational Concepts* (Clarendon, VA: CNA, August 2021), 55–72. See also Michael Kofman et al., *Russian Strategy for Escalation Management: Evolution of Key Concepts* (Clarendon, VA: CNA, April 2020), 53–66, https://www.cna.org/reports/2020/04/DRM-2019-U-022455-1Rev.pdf.

18. See Kofman et al., *Russian Military Strategy*.

19. Michael Kofman and Rob Lee, "Not Built for Purpose: The Russian Military's Ill-Fated Force Design," *War on the Rocks,* June 2, 2022, https://warontherocks.com/2022/06/not-built-for-purpose-the-russian-militarys-ill-fated-force-design/.

20. See Jack Watling and Nick Reynolds, *Ukraine at War: Paving the Road from Survival to Victory* (London: Royal United Services Institute, July 2022), https://www.rusi.org/explore-our-research/publications/special-resources/ukraine-war-paving-road-survival-victory.

21. Adapted from Franz-Stefan Gady and Michael Kofman, "Making Attrition Work: A Viable Theory of Victory for Ukraine," *Survival* 66, no. 1 (February 2024): 7–24.

22. Mari Saito, Maria Tsvetkova, and Anton Zverev, "Abandoned Russian Base Holds Secret of Retreat in Ukraine," *Reuters,* October 26, 2022, https://www.reuters.com/investigates/special-report/ukraine-crisis-russia-base/.

23. Based on fieldwork and interviews in Bakhmut during the battle, February–March 2023, and follow-up interviews in July and November of 2023. Units reported attrition ratios ranging between 1:3 and 1:5, with 1:5 typically against Wagner convict units and 1:3 against regular Russian formations or more experienced Wagner personnel. The overall consensus was a 1:4 attrition ratio over the course of the battle among a range of individuals in different echelons/units.

24. See Michael Kofman and Rob Lee, "Perseverance and Adaptation: Ukraine's Counteroffensive at Three Months," *War on the Rocks*, September 4, 2023, https://warontherocks.com/2023/09/perseverance-and-adaptation-ukraines-counteroffensive-at-three-months/.

Chapter Seven

Russian Military Resilience and Adaptation

Implications for the War in Ukraine and Beyond

Dara Massicot

Two weeks before Russia invaded Ukraine in February 2022, British defence secretary Ben Wallace flew to Moscow for crisis talks. According to Wallace, when he warned his counterpart not to invade Ukraine, Russian defense minister Sergei Shoigu shrugged off his warning and said, "We can suffer like no one else."[1] This statement is more than an offhand comment or prewar bravado. It reflects a commonly held belief in the Russian military that Russian soldiers are more resilient and more able than their enemies to withstand the hardship and exhaustion of war. Two years into the war, despite poor morale, absent or abusive commanders, difficult living conditions, and staggering casualties, Russian forces continued to wage their high-intensity war against Ukraine. The bleak circumstances of the deployed Russian forces had not led to mass desertions or mutinies, nor had they impeded Russia's ability to sustain attacks on Ukrainian forces.

What role does resilience play in the Russian military's ability to withstand setbacks and continue to execute its high pace of combat missions? This chapter considers the sources, methods, and operational implications of resilience in the

Dara Massicot is a senior fellow in the Russia and Eurasia Program at the Carnegie Endowment for International Peace. Her research focuses on defense and security issues in Russia, with an emphasis on Russian military capabilities, defense reform, and the ongoing war in Ukraine. Prior to joining Carnegie, Massicot was a senior policy researcher at the RAND Corporation and a senior analyst for Russian military capabilities at the Department of Defense.

Russian military at war, in particular, the role that Russian military culture, history, and training play in creating a unique form of combat resilience.

Russian forces deployed in Ukraine meet their own criteria for resilience: the ability to perform complex tasks in dangerous conditions. While its military is not a healthy force by many metrics, Russia's training, military culture, and history contribute to its forces' combat resilience by desensitizing soldiers to casualties and poor conditions and emphasizing holding positions at great costs. There have been a few periods in the war when resilience faltered: in the opening months of the war and during the collapse of the Kharkiv front in August 2022. The conditions that undermined resilience in those circumstances—mostly understrength units, materiel shortfalls, and being operationally surprised by Ukrainian forces—have not been present since the summer of 2023. Russian authorities also have various tools to enforce compliance with orders and prevent large-scale desertions when resilience falters, such as the use of barrier troops, detention centers, and harsh discipline. In wartime, Russian resilience is strained, but it seems to be holding. Russian military personnel receive very few postcombat decompression supports, however, and problems such as mental health disorders and substance abuse are likely to emerge in years to come.

Defining Resilience: Comparing US and Russian Military Concepts

Resilience in combat is defined differently by country. While both the US and Russian militaries seek the creation of resilient and combat-ready personnel, they approach this issue in different ways, and with different results. For example, in the US military, "resilience" is often defined in the context of mental health and the ability to overcome adversity either in combat conditions or in a personal capacity. In Russia, however, there is no direct translation of the word "resilience" in military parlance. For the Russian military, concepts of resilience are often framed in the context of "combat stability" or "psychological-moral readiness," and these concepts are almost exclusively tied to the ability to execute specific combat tasks under challenging conditions.

In the US military, resilience is defined slightly differently by service, but surveyed definitions of resilience share a common theme of facing adverse situations and growing from setbacks, whether as an individual, as a military unit, or as a leader. High levels of resilience contribute not only to readiness in a military or professional context but also to personal success. Resilience training in the US military focuses on resilience as a process that can be learned and maintained, rather than an ability innate to some individuals and not others. Resilience is discussed holistically, and wellness in all aspects of an individual's life—work, personal life, and mental and physical wellness—contributes to resilience.[2]

The US Army's Directorate of Prevention, Resilience and Readiness defines resilience as "the ability to persevere, adapt, and grow in dynamic or stressful environments."[3] The US Army's *Field Manual 7-22* defines resilience in a similar way: "resilience is the ability to face and cope with adversity, adapt to change, recover and learn from a setback, and grow from an experience."[4] Resilience is a quality that can be enhanced at an individual level to optimize performance. For a unit, enhancing resilience can build cohesion and increase combat effectiveness.[5]

Resilience training is offered in a few ways in the US Army—one method is a ten-day training course called the Master Resilience Training Course. In recent years, the army has created "Ready and Resilient" performance centers that offer training and education to units and individuals alike.[6] More commonly, resilience is a component of US Army training exercises. The inclusion of realistic training exercises that simulate common combat stressors, combined with after-action discussions, is a common way to build resilience in the army, and predeployment resilience training is required for all combat deployments longer than ninety days.[7] To make soldiers resilient, this training emphasizes setting realistic expectations, identifying triggers in combat, learning stress-management techniques, and using supports and resources if needed. Veteran soldiers take the course with inexperienced soldiers and share stories as part of the learning process. The training asks personnel to acknowledge that stressful or life-threatening situations will arise and teaches them tools to cope. Resilience training also teaches the importance of unit cohesion ("battle buddies") and "trust in your leaders and knowing they are thinking about your welfare and survival."[8] Resilience exists along a spectrum spanning predeployment, combat conditions, and postdeployment reintegration.

The US Air Force also has a "Spectrum of Resilience" for airmen and its guardians that focuses on care at different levels: the individual (effective stress management and ensuring health and wellness); family and friends; peer social and support groups in the military; and for those that need it, clinical and medical health supports. The US Air Force enumerates four types of resilience: mental, physical, social, and spiritual.[9] The US Navy and the Marine Corps define resilience as "the process of preparing for, recovering from, and adjusting to life in the face of stress, adversity, trauma, or tragedy."[10] Each service has its own Combat and Operational Stress Control (COSC) program, which is designed to prevent, identify, and intervene if necessary when combat and operational stress is detected on deployment or in garrison.[11] In the Marine Corps, for example, COSC identifies a spectrum of stress responses that range from "green" (a Marine showing adaptive coping and wellness), "yellow" (a Marine showing usually mild and transient distress impairment), "orange" (a Marine showing more severe or persistent distress with lasting evidence such as personality changes), to "red" (a Marine considered "ill" from stress injuries that are not healing without intervention).[12]

How Does the Russian Military Define Resilience?

Like the US military, the Russian military considers highly resilient personnel to be better at coping with combat challenges and overcoming adverse or extreme situations. The Russian approach to defining and nurturing resilience is different from the US military's approach in that it focuses on psychological fitness and readiness to efficiently execute combat tasks. Russian concepts of resilience and adaptability are tied to military service and combat conditions, with comparatively little attention paid to reintegration or decompression after a combat deployment.

First, the term most often used in Russia to describe what the US military refers to as resilience is Боевая устойчивость, or "combat stability." Combat stability is composed of many factors that allow a Russian unit to complete its assigned combat mission under difficult circumstances—and psychological readiness is an important part.[13]

In the Russian military, mental resilience of service personnel is often described as морально-психологическая готовность, or "moral-psychological readiness." High psychological readiness, along with physical readiness, means that a soldier is ready to execute combat tasks under difficult circumstances.[14] For military leaders, psychological readiness is associated with the ability to "reasonably assess and predict the situation and make the right decision in combat," initiative, and the will to win.[15] Other traits that are regularly included in concepts of combat resilience include courage and heroism (often incorporating historical examples from World War II), and spiritual and moral readiness to defend the Russian Fatherland.[16]

Modern Russian training to improve resilience and psychological readiness has consisted of three broad themes since the 1990s: first, devotion to Russia ("the Fatherland") and loyalty to the military and other servicemen; second, the specific psychological training of professionals to execute combat tasks under difficult conditions;[17] and third, the "ability to withstand any information and psychological influence of the enemy."[18]

Since 2015, training programs to build resilience have focused on the following conditions: clarifying the goals of Russian state defense policy to military personnel (Russia's role in the world and the military's role in that vision); creating realistic combat stressors in training; psychological self-regulation; ideological cohesion and political unit cohesion; the work of political officers for military discipline; and "high moral, cultural, and spiritual values."[19]

In particular, four building blocks are present in Russian resilience training: first, the "motivational foundation" (cause of war, strategic situation for Russia, international humanitarian law, etc.); second, training that includes elements of surprise, fear, danger, and risk; third, active and independent combat skills (education and self-regulation skills); and finally, "moral political unity of worldview and beliefs" to build unit cohesion.[20] Personnel are taught by political officers, and recommended slogans include "a close-knit military team is the basis of combat readiness," "the strength of a military team is in friendship and mutual assistance," "strong friendship and discipline are the basis of victory."[21] Anecdotes from some Russian soldiers inside occupied Ukraine suggest that only some of them viewed this political training as mandatory, and for them it was not serious.[22]

In the Russian military, "psychological training" is a system of activities designed to "ensure [the soldiers'] psychological readiness for active and effective actions on the battlefield and resistance to the influence of modern means of struggle."[23] Psychological readiness can be increased in the following ways, according to Russian military theorists: more exposure to realistic combat experiences in training; real-world deployments; more patriotic education and patriotism; motivation to improve professionalism; and finally, the role of love and how it can amplify feelings of duty to the nation and to peers in service.[24]

In the years prior to the invasion of Ukraine, political officers were reintroduced to military exercises, and their roles in these scripted events offer some clues as to what their combat roles have been inside occupied Ukraine. For example, within Russia's Zapad-2021 exercise was a small exercise called Cohesion-2021, which focused on restoring soldiers to psychological readiness in combat, counteracting "negative information and psychological influence," and assessing the resilience of personnel under simulated combat conditions.[25] Another defensive application to Russian psychological training is intended to "protect against negative information" from enemy forces.[26] In this area, during exercises and training events, military psychologists in the Western Military District in the two years before the invasion of Ukraine worked on tasks like "stabilizing the sociopolitical situation" and dispelling rumors within a garrison or deployment site.[27]

Measuring Resilience

In the Russian military, moral-psychological readiness is one of multiple factors for measuring combat proficiency.[28] The Russian military uses psychological testing to ensure soldier reliability—defined as the ability to regulate emotions while continuing to function or achieve combat tasks and resistance to stress.[29] According to Russian military strategists, all military personnel have been required since 2015 to undergo professional psychological evaluation for "neuropsychic stability" upon their intake to professional contract service.[30] Testing criteria included emotional regulation and the ability to function under stress

Individual psychological readiness scores were intended to give Russian commanders an understanding of which soldiers are more resilient than others and could therefore take on more difficult combat tasks. These scores were to be aggregated into one score at the unit level to create a "moral-psychological factor" for units. Initial attempts to evaluate the force more broadly were patchy and lacked methodological rigor; they might even yield inaccurate results, according to Russian strategists S. V. Goncharov and O. G. Zayets.[31] The authors argued that if no system was in place to systematically measure the impact of combat stressors on individual soldiers, unit commanders to General Staff planners would not understand how their soldiers react to combat stress.

In 2020, a "regional center of psychological work" was established in the Western Military District and was charged with four tasks: (1) screening prospective and current soldiers for mental illness and "deviant behaviors" that would make them unfit for service, (2) organizing psychological training and preventing destructive behavior, (3) clinical psychological support of personnel and their families, and (4) implementing a system of psychological testing and monitoring of service personnel.[32] In the months prior to Russia's invasion, this group surveyed and observed junior officers and determined that the "insufficient psychological literacy of junior command staff does not allow them to effectively build individual and group work with subordinates."[33] Although some Russian strategists advocated for a more rigorous and automated mechanism to capture and analyze the moral-psychological factors of personnel, no system had been implemented on the eve of Russia's invasion of Ukraine.[34]

Russian strategists often note that how a soldier or civilian responds to stress in peacetime is not the same as in wartime conditions, with the latter being difficult to assess prior to combat. Goncharov and Zayets proposed measuring two sets of factors to measure psychological readiness: one for steady-state psychological readiness and another for wartime psychological readiness. The wartime assessment factors proposed were derived from expert surveys of around five hundred ground-forces commanding officers and professional enlisted personnel in the mid-2010s. Their proposed indicators of wartime psychological readiness are as follows:

- personal significance of the ongoing armed struggle;
- faith in their military leaders and direct commanders;
- antagonism or hatred of the enemy;
- confidence in their superiority (or victory) over the enemy;
- general well-being; and
- understanding upcoming actions in battle.[35]

At the outset of the invasion in 2022 and during the months that followed, many of these indicators almost certainly declined for Russian troops, with the exception of antagonism or hatred of the enemy. By late 2023, confidence in the military's superiority over the enemy had increased, as did understanding upcoming actions in battle as the dynamics of the war shifted to positional warfare.

"Social-political factors" contribute to military personnel's resilience but are not related to combat conditions. On the eve of Russia's invasion of Ukraine, the top three "social-political factors" identified by Russian military theorists Goncharov and B. B. Ostroverkhii were unit leadership quality and command decisions, Russian society's perception of soldiers and the level of social protection for soldiers, and whether military-political work in the unit was effective in mentally preparing soldiers.[36] As discussed below, the Russian government has taken steps to address many of these factors.

The Role of Military Culture and Military History

Resilience had been studied since the 1800s by tsarist-era military psychologists, who focused on issues such as "the moral resilience of troops."[37] By the early Soviet period, this term had been replaced by "political-moral state" as a new communist political ideology was introduced into the Red Army. The Soviet military and post-Soviet Russian military frequently used historical lessons and training courses on patriotic values to encourage "moral-political" and psychological readiness. Historical references often focus on courage, lore of certain commanders, and famous battles, with the most frequent references coming from World War II (known as the Great Patriotic War in Russia). These references skew heavily toward personal sacrifice, difficult fighting conditions, tales of valor, and absorbing extensive casualties. Such references and lessons occur across an individual's period of service, and senior commanders are expected to be conversant in military history and particularly in instances of bravery and sacrifice.[38] An older example—a famous Alexander Suvorov quote—"Die yourself, but save your comrade," is still taught.[39] In particular, Joseph Stalin's famous order, "Not one step back!"—which meant holding positions at all costs—has been used in materials provided to Russian soldiers inside occupied Ukraine since 2022.[40] Echoes of the Soviet past still reverberate in modern times. Russian military regulations discuss the importance of holding positions under attack.[41] In the war in Ukraine, Russia has also reinstituted blocking forces (barrier troops or counter-retreat forces), allegedly with orders to shoot those who desert or give up their positions.[42]

In 2019, Russia reestablished the Military-Political Directorate of the Armed Forces to increase psychological readiness and resilience within the troops. Political officers (referred to as *zampolit* during the Soviet era) were also reintroduced into all Russian units. The Military-Political Directorate's leadership noted that they would base their curriculum "on the experiences of Russian and Soviet militaries, wars, and military conflicts, in which our warriors demonstrated the highest moral-political qualities of the defenders of the Motherland."[43] Its main responsibilities, according to the Russian Ministry of Defense, are the moral-political and psychological state of forces, order and military discipline, developing the service member's ideology, and creating close-knit military teams capable of conducting missions in any environment and under any conditions.[44]

Russian Combat Resilience during the War in Ukraine, 2022–2024

How have the Russian concepts of resilience and training programs contributed to combat resilience during the war in Ukraine? Prewar understanding of factors that contribute to resilience has influenced the policy choices that the Russian government has made since 2022. For example, as noted above, Russian sociologists identified which nonmilitary factors could undermine resilience (legal status and social protections for the soldiers, Russian citizens' views of the war, and the degree of political work and control of the information space). The Russian government has taken direct actions in all of these areas by increasing benefits and linking the war tightly to the iconography and historical weight of World War II in order to ensure broader (if passive) support among the Russian population and to bolster support and resilience within the military.[45] Political officers are present at each echelon of units to monitor soldiers and interrogate them if they falter inside occupied Ukraine, according to recovered Russian personnel rosters.[46] Since 2022, Russia has banned many Western media and social media platforms in an effort to limit outside influences or information on how the war is progressing, and public debate of many military topics (such as casualties or operational setbacks) has been criminalized.

Other prewar factors that contribute to resilience, according to some Russian strategists, remain largely intact as of early 2024, such as personal belief in the conflict, hatred of the enemy, and confidence in superiority over the enemy.[47] Russian media and social media are full of examples of Russian soldiers expressing antagonism toward or hatred of Ukrainians, as well as a continued belief in their own superiority. These comments often take an imperialistic tone and sometimes are accompanied by ethnic slurs against Ukrainians. Today, Russian officials and Russian soldiers largely believe that they are fighting aspects of NATO power in Ukraine. The Russian Orthodox Church is supportive of the war. As mobilization has led to an increase in ammunition, manpower, and scaling-up of key equipment such as drones, Russian soldiers as of 2023 and early 2024 are likely to be feeling more confident about the war's trajectory, in a way that they were not in 2022 amid repeated Russian setbacks and retreats.

Despite severe casualties, poor field conditions, and commanders of varying quality, Russian soldiers mostly continue to endure their circumstances inside occupied Ukraine. Russian forces are executing operations despite absent or abusive commanders and the challenging nature of the fight. During the disastrous opening months of the war in 2022, some units abandoned equipment and positions while on the offensive, yet these units would later reconstitute and be redeployed to other parts of the front. Russian forces during the Prigozhin rebellion of June 2023 did not desert or halt their combat operations despite an armored column advancing on Moscow, the takeover of the war's military headquarters in Rostov, and the detention of one of the war's deputy commanders, General Sergei Surovikin. Desertions as of early 2024 have been growing, but they still constitute only a small percentage of overall combat strength inside Ukraine.[48] There have been no mass refusals of orders or cascading refusals along the front lines, even during the collapse of the Kharkiv front in 2022.

The quality of the Russian force's resilience training has changed since September 2022. Much of the prewar force was lost before Russia declared a partial mobilization of three hundred thousand troops and began introducing foreign fighters, former mercenaries, and convicts into the force. Initially, Russian convicts were recruited with the opportunity to "earn" their freedom after six to eighteen months of combat service, while all other Russian personnel are deployed to Ukraine indefinitely (or "until the end of the special military operation" per presidential decree).[49] These convicts have experience coping with dangerous and difficult physical circumstances, which makes them uniquely resilient, although not in a way that would be considered positive or reinforcing to cohesion. Convicts are said to create persistent challenges with poor discipline and drug use on deployment. The Kremlin has since altered its inmate recruiting policy to make service terms indefinite, to match the regular Army's current status.[50]

Challenges to Russian Resilience in Ukraine

Although Russian forces in the aggregate remain resilient according to the Russian definition of the term, resilience is strained in several critical areas that will have long-term implications for the forces, even if these problems are being managed with draconian measures in the short term.

Russian military psychologists and sociologists have identified the following factors that undermine combat performance at war, and nearly all of these have been undermined by Russia's conduct of the war in Ukraine:

> *General combat factors:* Threat to life and physical harm, wounds, contusions, injuries, death of loved ones and colleagues, demonstration of death and human suffering, prolonged intense activity, sudden and unexpected changes, features of the weapons used;
>
> *Situational combat factors:* Volume and ratio of losses of the parties, isolation, intensity of combat operations; and
>
> *Factors of psychological battle stress:* Danger, suddenness, unexpectedness, novelty, lack of time and information, losses, discomfort, participation in violence, and conflicting commands or strong interference.[51]

Other enemy actions that are believed to undermine Russian personnel readiness in combat are enemy fire or strikes, problems with physical security for Russian personnel, poor decision-making regarding logistics and combat support, poor fire support, and lack of coordination with other combat units.[52] Russian forces have encountered many of these issues in Ukraine since 2022.

For example, the Russian soldiers' faith in senior commanders is low, but it is important to understand that their faith in commanders was never high to begin with. Trust and respect-based command relationships are a recent phenomenon in the Russian military, as a result of defense reforms initiated in 2009.[53] This cultural shift did not appear to take hold throughout the military, however, particularly among the most senior officer ranks. In the immediate aftermath of the invasion, as the initial invasion plan fell apart, some of the old methods of command styles quickly returned, such as secrecy, absenteeism, and physical abuse.

The first six months of the war delivered multiple serious shocks in rapid succession to Russia's prewar army of professional enlisted soldiers and officers, which undermined resilience and led to a small number of resignations and some units abandoning their equipment during early offensives. First, this group experienced the shock that they would be going to war and that their commanders had deceived them.[54] Second, Ukrainian forces resisted fiercely when Russian planners assumed that they would not. Third, many Russian units were damaged or destroyed while also discovering how quickly their officers became either indifferent or brutal, particularly in the north, where fighting was the most difficult. Finally, some were surprised by the state of their equipment: either not maintained as it should have been or not working at all. Russia had not yet closed the legal loopholes that allowed for resignation, and during this period, a small percentage of personnel resigned, often asserting moral opposition to the war or alleging breach of contract.[55] While not all these resignations were honored by local commanding officers, some were. Resignations also occurred in clusters within units.[56] Many of these shocks faded over time and became less relevant by 2023, as Russian society realized it was at war and Russian mobilization produced more men and weapons; new replacements have entered the war with different expectations.

A great deal of compelled behavior from Russian authorities hides problems with resilience and the will to fight inside occupied Ukraine. Russian personnel serving in Ukraine cannot voluntarily leave unless they commit a crime, reach maximum age, or are injured or killed. Since the early months of the war, Russia has created barrier units that are reportedly intended to capture or shoot deserters, as well as detention centers (including windowless rooms or basements) for deserters and those who refuse to fight inside occupied Ukraine. Some soldiers there have been beaten by their guards.[57] At these detention centers, it is rumored that a combination of Russian intelligence officers, political officers, and other groups interrogate and punish these personnel until they return to the front. It is unclear what percentage of these soldiers are returned home to Russia to enter the court-martial system, where even then, their sentences are often commuted and they are returned to the front.[58]

To cope with their circumstances, some soldiers self-medicate with alcohol and in some cases illegal drugs (often methamphetamines or "bath salts").[59] While the pervasiveness of this trend is difficult to quantify, illegal substance use has increased with the introduction of Russian prisoners into the ranks. Some Russian personnel refuse to fight.[60] Videos of discipline problems within Russian units show commanders attacking subordinates, firing weapons at or near them, digging open pits to hold unruly personnel (often mobilized personnel or those recruited from Russian prisons), or putting those who refuse to fight into cellars.[61] These examples are indicative of discipline problems and challenges to resilience, but they do not give a sense of the pervasiveness across the front.

On the whole, Russian positions have not capsized due to poor morale or lack of resilience, even as units are likely underperforming as a result of prolonged exposure and stress and lack of rotations. There is one notable exception: the Russian collapse in the Kharkiv area in August 2022. In the weeks prior, Russia sent units from the Kharkiv area to reinforce the south, where Ukrainian forces were trying to liberate Kherson. This action left northern units exposed and understrength. Defensive lines were too thin, Russia had not yet dug in, and the units were significantly undermanned (some at 50%–60% strength, according to recovered personnel rosters).[62] When Ukrainian forces attacked, the forces were unprepared, understaffed, and could not communicate well with their command, which had been struck by missiles. As a result, units broke, and their personnel fled chaotically, returning to Russia proper or to occupied areas to the south.

Conclusions

Can Russia's deployed forces in Ukraine be considered resilient? According to how the Russian military defines the concept—executing combat tasks under difficult conditions—they are. Despite poor conditions, severe casualties, and multiple reconstituted units staffed with a deteriorating quality of personnel, Russian forces in the aggregate continue to execute their missions. Over time, there has been a reduction in efficiency, most likely as a result of prolonged exposure to combat stress, reduced force quality over time, and infrequent rotations. Russian soldier resilience had only had one large-scale failure in 2022, when Russian lines collapsed near Kharkiv. That event was caused by understrength units, poorly prepared positions, and operational surprise. The factors challenging Russian resilience have dissipated since early 2023, as Russia's manpower and materiel advantages have grown due to mobilization, the construction of defensive belts, and the faltering of Western military assistance to Ukraine in the fall of 2023.

Since 2022, the Kremlin has taken measures to shore up important contributing factors to resilience according to the logic of their prewar understanding: increasing financial and social benefits for soldiers, linking the war to World War II for prestige and support, and suppressing negative information or sources of negative information about the war, among many other steps. It has also created multiple layers of detention or punishment inside occupied Ukraine for those who try to desert their posts or refuse their orders, suggesting that resilience is not universal and that tensions are somewhat masked by Russia's "stop loss" personnel policies.

Much of the Russian forces' combat resilience strategy is remarkably short-term, with little thought given to long-term well-being or retention of personnel. The long-term costs of this war to the soldiers fighting it have not yet been revealed. The resilience demonstrated by Russian forces that keeps them in their positions under difficult combat conditions—either voluntarily or by force—may be harmful to them and to Russia more broadly in the long term. Russian soldiers receive little mental health support or decompression and reintegration support after a combat deployment. PTSD and other mental health disorders are likely to be prevalent in this group when they are released from service after the active phase of the war concludes, as was the case in previous conflicts.[63] It remains to be seen how Russian veterans will be treated by society upon their return, but early anecdotes suggest that the civilian population may be wary.[64]

What does all this mean for the rest of the war in Ukraine and perhaps even for NATO's security? Russia may conclude that its resilience is a contributing factor in outlasting Ukraine and the combined efforts of the West, and that its ways of war are working. The Russian military understands and copes with suffering and sacrifice in a very particular way, because of its history, past wars, training, and military culture. These factors create a unique form of resilience to poor conditions and even poor treatment by their own commanders.

Efforts to deter the Russian military by punishment or to compel an end to the war by punishment—through sanctions and casualties in particular—may not be the most effective strategies against a country absorbing high casualties in the way it is doing, with few political repercussions (or suppressed political repercussions) at home. How Russian society views its soldiers at war, how soldiers understand how they are viewed, and the implications of these conditions for domestic stability are important factors in resilience and the will to fight, and should also be considered. A strategy for Ukraine centered on attrition or punishment has thus far proved insufficient against an adversary willing to absorb upwards of three hundred and fifty thousand casualties of varying severity and losses of thirteen thousand pieces of equipment over the past two years.[65] Russian leaders remain willing to pay high costs in personnel and equipment for modest gains and do not appear all that concerned about challenges to domestic stability.

A more effective strategy would be one centered around denial, based on observed Russian patterns. In the past two years, Russian forces have responded to denied or degraded areas of operation by modifying tactics and relocating away from the threat. They have made these changes in response to Ukrainian air defenses, precision-strike capabilities, defensive positions, and strikes on Black Sea Fleet assets. A strategy focused on denial could be centered on the following concepts: deterring or degrading future Russian ground offensives using prepared Ukrainian positions, provision of long-range strike weapons that can target Russian regeneration capacity or strike capacity, additional air defenses, and counter-drone technology. In the past two years, the Kremlin has been willing to lose infantry and other personnel on the ground in order to save platforms; in their thinking, it is the platforms that are more challenging to replace. A reassessment of what deters Russia from war, or compels it to end a war, is needed, while keeping the Russian form of resilience in mind.

NOTES

1. Shane Harris et al., "Road to War: U.S. Struggled to Convince Allies, and Zelensky, of Risk of Invasion," *Washington Post*, August 16, 2022, https://www.washingtonpost.com/national-security/interactive/2022/ukraine-road-to-war/.

2. Lisa S. Meredith et al., *Promoting Psychological Resilience in the U.S. Military* (Santa Monica, CA: RAND Corporation, 2011), https://www.rand.org/pubs/monographs/MG996.html.

3. Directorate of Prevention, Resilience and Readiness, Office of the Deputy Chief of Staff, US Army, "Army Resilience Directorate," accessed February 15, 2024, https://www.armyresilience.army.mil/ard/R2-home.html.

4. Research Transition Office, Walter Reed Army Institute of Research, "Pre-Deployment Resilience Training for Soldiers," July 2023, https://media.defense.gov/2023/Jul/17/2003260980/-1/-1/1/dcrt-pre-deployment-resilience-training-for-soldiers-wrair-v3-aug21-for-distro.pdf. The definition of resilience is adapted from US Army *Field Manual 7-22*.

5. Directorate of Prevention, Resilience and Readiness, "Army Resilience Directorate."

6. Directorate of Prevention, Resilience and Readiness, Office of the Deputy Chief of Staff, US Army, "ARD: R2 Performance Centers," accessed February 15, 2024, https://www.armyresilience.army.mil/ard/R2/R2-Performance-center.html.

7. Research Transition Office, "Pre-Deployment Resilience Training for Soldiers."

8. Research Transition Office, "Pre-Deployment Resilience Training for Soldiers."

9. Department of the Air Force Integrated Resilience, US Air Force, "Resilience," accessed February 15, 2024, https://www.resilience.af.mil/Resilience/.

10. US Marine Corps, "Combat and Operational Stress Control," December 20, 2010, https://www.fitness.marines.mil/Portals/211/Docs/Spiritual%20Fitness /MCRP%206-11C%20%20Combat%20and%20Operational%20Stress%20Control.pdf; US Marine Corps, "Spiritual Fitness," accessed February 15, 2024, https://www.fitness .marines.mil/Resilience/Spiritual-Fitness/.

11. US Marine Corps, "Combat and Operational Stress Control."

12. US Marine Corps, "Combat and Operational Stress Control."

13. V. B. Zarudnitsky, "Factors for Achieving Victory in Future Military Conflicts" [Факторы достижения победы в военных конфликтах будущего], *Voennaya Mysl'*, no. 8 (August 2021): 34–37. The Russian Ministry of Defense defines combat stability as follows: "A state of force groupings . . . that allows them to maintain combat effectiveness and realize their inherent combat capabilities to ensure the guaranteed completion of the assigned combat mission in conditions of active opposition. It depends on the composition of the group of forces, their combat readiness, and combat ability, as well as survivability of control systems and forces and means that comprehensively ensure that they carry out the combat mission." Russian Ministry of Defense, "Combat Stability" [Боевая Устойчивость], accessed February 15, 2024, https:// archive.ph/OKSVq#selection-711.0-711.467.

14. V. T. Dotsenko, "Psychological Readiness of Military Personnel: Problems and Ways of Formation" [Психологическая готовность военнослужащих: проблемы и пути формирования], *Voennaya Mysl'*, no. 1 (January 2019); L. V. Peven, "Law of the Primary Importance of the Spiritual Element for Victory in Battle" [Закон Главенствующего Значения Духовного Элемента Для Победы В Бою], *Voenno-istoricheskii zhurnal*, no. 4 (April 30, 2023): 66–79.

15. Dotsenko, "Psychological Readiness of Military Personnel"; Zarudnitsky, "Factors for Achieving Victory in Future Military Conflicts."

16. Dotsenko, "Psychological Readiness of Military Personnel."

17. "Moral Preparedness and Psychological Ability of Military Servicemen for Combat Operations" [Моральная Готовность И Психологическая Способность Военнослужащих К Боевым Действиям], *VVS Sevodnya*, nos. 15–16 (July 2006): 14.

18. E. I. Fedak and D. A. Federin, "Adaptation Potential of Moral, Political, and Psychological Readiness of Military Personnel" [Адаптационный Потенциал Морально-Политической И Психологической Готовности Военнослужащих], *Morskoi Sbornik*, no. 9 (2021).

19. Fedak and Federin, "Adaptation Potential of Moral, Political, and Psychological Readiness of Military Personnel."

20. Fedak and Federin, "Adaptation Potential of Moral, Political, and Psychological Readiness of Military Personnel."

21. Elena Loskutnikova, "A Friendly Team Is the Basis of Combat Readiness" [Дружный Коллектив—Основа Боеготовности], *Suvorovskii Natisk*, no. 6 (2023).

22. In a booklet issued to soldiers, the Russian authorities denounce the army's "shameful" retreat from Kherson and urge a return to "Stalinist methods." Lilia

Yapparova, "'Not a Single Step Back!,'" *Meduza*, April 5, 2023, https://meduza.io/en/feature/2023/04/05/not-a-single-step-back.

23. Dotsenko, "Psychological Readiness of Military Personnel."

24. Dotsenko, "Psychological Readiness of Military Personnel."

25. Anton Garkavenko and Olga Vinokurova, "Military Psychologists Are Called Upon to Ensure Psychological Readiness" [Обеспечить Психологическую Готовность Призваны Военные Психологи], *Na strazhe Rodiny*, no. 50 (2021).

26. Evgenia Sedenkova, "High Morale Is the Key to Success in Battle," *Krasnaya Zvezda*, no. 95 (2021).

27. Sedenkova, "High Morale Is the Key to Success in Battle."

28. Maria Matrynova, "Psychological Support" [Психологическое Сопровождение], *Kaspiets*, no. 11 (March 2020), https://dlib.eastview.com/browse/doc/61142992. The broader prewar definition of psychological work with military personnel is "a system of coordinated, purposeful measures in the interests of the life of the troops, to maintain the psychological stability of personnel for tasks and preserve the mental health of military personnel, their families, and civilian personnel of the armed forces more broadly."

29. Anika Binnendijk et al., *Russian Military Personnel Policy and Proficiency: Reforms and Trends, 1991–2021* (Santa Monica, CA: RAND Corporation, 2023), 105; Russian Ministry of Defense, "Psychologists of the Baltic Fleet Are Preparing Servicemembers for Participation in the Parade for the 76th Anniversary of Victory in the Great Patriotic War," April 25, 2021.

30. S. V. Goncharov and O. G. Zayets, "Assessment and Recognition of the Moral and Psychological Factor during Decision-Making by Commanders Using Automated Systems of Command and Control" [Оценка и учет морально-психологического фактора при принятии командирами решений с использованием автоматизированных средств управления войсками], *Voennaya Mysl'*, no. 8 (2015).

31. Goncharov and Zayets, "Assessment and Recognition of the Moral and Psychological Factor." Goncharov and Zayets noted that the process to measure "moral and psychological factors" under combat conditions lacked implementation in many units and was reliant on individual commanders to collect and record and report this information and relied on others to self-assess their own readiness.

32. Garkavenko and Vinokurova, "Military Psychologists Are Called Upon to Ensure Psychological Readiness."

33. Garkavenko and Vinokurova, "Military Psychologists Are Called Upon to Ensure Psychological Readiness."

34. S. V. Goncharov and B. B. Ostroverkhii, "Assessment and Accounting by the Commander of a Formation (Military Unit) of the Socio-Political Situation in the Area of Upcoming Hostilities" [Оценка И Учет Командиром Соединения (Воинской Части) Социально-Политической Обстановки В Районе Предстоящих Боевых Действий], *Voennaya Mysl'*, no. 8 (August 2021). Goncharov suggested that moral-psychological factors should be assessed by three criteria: motivations (moral-political), emotional-volitional (psychological factors), and operational.

35. Goncharov and Zayets, "Assessment and Recognition of the Moral and Psychological Factor."

36. Goncharov and Ostroverkhii, "Assessment and Accounting by the Commander of a Formation."

37. S. V. Goncharov, "Retrospective of Research into the Role of the Moral Factor in War" [Ретроспектива исследований роли морального фактора в войне], *Voennaya Mysl'*, no. 5 (2013).

38. Binnendijk et al., *Russian Military Personnel Policy and Proficiency.*

39. Elena Loskutnikova, "A Friendly Team Is the Basis of Combat Readiness."

40. Yapparova, "'Not a Single Step Back!'"

41. Alexander Vedenin, "Building Resilience" [Формируя Стойкость], *Ural'skie Voennye Vesti*, no. 29 (2021). Well-defended positions are described as having available fires and senior military commanders taking action to strengthen the defense, in the telling of a Russian ground-forces battalion commander.

42. Pjotr Sauer, "Russian Soldiers Say Commanders Used 'Barrier Troops' to Stop Them Retreating," *The Guardian*, March 27, 2023, https://www.theguardian.com/world/2023/mar/27/russian-soldiers-commanders-used-barrier-troops-stop-retreating.

43. Natalia Val'khanskaya, "Main Military-Political Directorate of the AF RF Celebrates Centennial" [Главное военно-политическое управление ВС РФ отмечает столетие], *Zvezda TV*, May 15, 2019, https://tvzvezda.ru/news/2019515136-l1Bh2.html.

44. Ministry of Defense of the Russian Federation, "Main Military-Political Directorate of the Armed Forces of the Russian Federation" [Главное военно-политическое управление Вооруженных сил Российской Федерации], 2019.

45. Yapparova, "'Not a Single Step Back!'"

46. Main Intelligence Directorate of the Ministry of Defense of Ukraine, "List of Personnel of the 20th Guards Motorized Rifle Division of the Armed Forces of the Russian Federation" [Список особового складу 20-ї гвардійської мотострілецької дивізії ЗС РФ], March 2, 2022, https://gur.gov.ua/content/spysok-osobovoho-skladu-20yi-hvardiiskoi-motostriletsikoi-dyvizii-zs-rf.html.

47. Goncharov and Zayets, "Assessment and Recognition of the Moral and Psychological Factor."

48. Maxim Litavrin and Sergey Golubev, "Evading > Refusing > Fleeing. A Year of Mobilization in Russia through Trials and Verdicts," *Mediazona*, September 21, 2023, https://en.zona.media/article/2023/09/21/awolornotawol.

49. Zoya Sheftalovich, "Full Text of Putin's Mobilization Decree—Translated," *Politico Europe*, September 21, 2022, https://www.politico.eu/article/text-vladimir-putin-mobilization-decree-war-ukraine-russia/.

50. Andrei Krasno, "'Muting the Horrors': Experts Warn of Addiction Crisis as Russian Soldiers Return from Ukraine," *Radio Free Europe / Radio Liberty*, June 18, 2023, https://www.rferl.org/a/russia-soldiers-addiction-ukraine-war-alcohol-drugs/32464317.html.

51. Fedak and Federin, "Adaptation Potential of Moral, Political, and Psychological Readiness of Military Personnel."

52. Goncharov and Zayets, "Assessment and Recognition of the Moral and Psychological Factor."

53. Binnendijk et al., *Russian Military Personnel Policy and Proficiency*.

54. Dara Massicot, "What Russia Got Wrong," *Foreign Affairs*, February 8, 2023.

55. Timofei Rozhanskiy, "Why Russian Soldiers Are Refusing to Fight in the War in Ukraine," *Radio Free Europe / Radio Liberty*, July 20, 2022, https://www.rferl.org/a /russian-soldiers-ukraine-refuse-fight/31952117.html; "'We Have No Idea Who We're Fighting For': How Russia Threatens Contract Soldiers Who Refuse to Fight in Ukraine," *Meduza*, May 16, 2022, https://meduza.io/en/feature/2022/05/16/we-have-no -idea-who-we-re-fighting-for.

56. Anton Troinovsky and Marc Santora, "Growing Evidence of a Military Disaster on the Donets Pierces a Pro-Russian Bubble," *New York Times*, May 15, 2022.

57. Yapparova, "'Not a Single Step Back!'"; "'They Told Us Nobody's Going to Take Us Home': Russian Soldiers Held Captive in Luhansk Region for Refusing to Fight in Ukraine," *Meduza,* July 22, 2022, https://meduza.io/en/feature/2022/07/22/they-told-us -nobody-s-going-to-take-us-home; "'I Go to War in My Sleep': Russia Is Failing to Provide PTSD Support for Soldiers Returning from Ukraine; Psychiatrists Expect Disaster," *Meduza*, January 26, 2023, https://meduza.io/en/feature/2023/01/27/i-go-to -war-in-my-sleep.

58. Anna Pavlova, "When Soldiers Say No: Hundreds of Russian Servicemen Face Trial in Defiance of Ukraine Deployment, Mediazona Study Reveals," *Mediazona*, April 11, 2023, https://en.zona.media/article/2023/04/11/500.

59. Krasno, "'Muting the Horrors.'"

60. Erika Kinetz, "'You'll Die in This Pit': Takeaways from Secret Recordings of Russian Soldiers in Ukraine," *AP News*, November 26, 2023, https://apnews.com/article /ukraine-war-russian-soldiers-intercepted-audio-takeaways-10ab4b2f14ed59436523e800 dea2e57a.

61. Carl Schreck, "'Simply Medieval': Russian Soldiers Held in Pits and Cellars for Refusing to Fight in Ukraine," *Radio Free Europe / Radio Liberty*, July 16, 2023, https:// www.rferl.org/a/russian-soldiers-punished-refusing-fight-ukraine/32505035.html.

62. Mari Saito, Maria Tsvetkova, and Anton Zverev, "Abandoned Russian Base Holds Secret of Retreat in Ukraine," *Reuters*, October 26, 2022, https://www.reuters .com/investigates/special-report/ukraine-crisis-russia-base/.

63. Dara Massicot, "Dara Massicot Believes That Russia Faces Twin Personnel Crises in Its Armed Forces," *Economist*, May 31, 2023, https://www.economist.com/by -invitation/2023/05/31/dara-massicot-believes-that-russia-faces-twin-personnel-crises-in -its-armed-forces.

64. Paul Goble, "Returning Veterans of War in Ukraine Greater Threat to Russia than Afgantsy Ever Were," Jamestown Foundation, January 19, 2024, https://jamestown .org/program/returning-veterans-of-war-in-ukraine-greater-threat-to-russia-than -afgantsy-ever-were/.

65. "Attack on Europe: Documenting Russian Equipment Losses during the Russian Invasion of Ukraine," *Oryx* (blog), February 24, 2022, https://www.oryxspioenkop.com /2022/02/attack-on-europe-documenting-equipment.html; "Russia's Losses in the War with Ukraine: Mediazona's Summary," *Mediazona*, accessed on December 15, 2023, https://zona.media/casualties.

Chapter Eight

Planning for the Worst

The Russia-Ukraine "Tiger Team"

Alexander Bick

C risis management is notoriously reactive, as leaders struggle to assess, weigh, and shape rapidly unfolding events. But not always. The unprecedented warning provided by US intelligence agencies in the fall of 2021 concerning Russia's preparations to launch a full-scale invasion of Ukraine created an equally unprecedented opportunity. Much has already been written about the steps that the Biden administration took to publicly expose Russia's designs, rally allies and partners, impose sanctions, and ramp up military and financial support to Ukraine—steps that proved critical to Kyiv's initial success repelling Russian forces and thwarting President Vladimir Putin's grandest ambitions.[1] Behind these steps lay arguably one of the most consequential contingency planning efforts in recent memory. This chapter tells the story, drawing on my experience leading the "Tiger Team" charged with developing the playbook that guided the US response.[2] It is both a first cut at history and a case study in national security crisis management. My aim is to complement our understanding of the substance of US policy with a deeper appreciation for the process. A luxury in good times, the ability to anticipate and rigorously plan for future crises will only

Alexander Bick is associate professor of the practice at the University of Virginia's Batten School of Leadership and Public Policy. He served in the Biden administration as director for strategic planning at the National Security Council and as a senior advisor and member of the Secretary's Policy Planning Staff at the US Department of State.

become more important in the years ahead, as the United States confronts an increasingly contested and uncertain strategic landscape.

Policy Context

President Joe Biden came into office on January 20, 2021, vowing to stand up to Putin, restore a bipartisan consensus on US policy toward Russia, and repair the damage done by the previous administration to US relationships around the world, including with Ukraine.[3] The new administration had two urgent priorities with respect to Russia. The first was to extend the New START Treaty, both as a means to reinforce existing arms control and to create a basis for potential further cooperation. The second was to hold Russia accountable for a sequence of malign actions that had gone unanswered.[4] Foremost among these was Russia's interference in the 2020 US elections, but equally urgent were responses to the SolarWinds hack, the chemical poisoning of Russian opposition leader Alexei Navalny, and indications that Russia had paid bounties to the Taliban to kill US service members in Afghanistan.[5] There would be no reset; instead, the aim was to restore deterrence while ensuring that the US response was sufficiently calibrated to avoid initiating a new escalatory cycle. This was accompanied by an invitation to Putin to attend a summit later that year.

The goal of establishing a more "stable and predictable" bilateral relationship was tested in April, when Russia massed tens of thousands of troops along Ukraine's border. While calling for Russia to pull back its forces, the administration calculated that engaging Putin would help ease tensions and might create opportunities to address some long-standing irritants. The Geneva summit on June 16, 2021, appeared to validate this approach: a businesslike meeting with Putin resulted in commitments to restore or establish dialogues on strategic stability and cybersecurity. Over the following months, as these dialogues got underway, Putin withdrew the bulk of Russian forces from Ukraine's border. Back in Washington, the administration quietly launched a Russia policy review to build out the strategy. As National Security Council spokeswoman Emily Horne would later put it, "At that point, there was no reason to believe that Russia was on the precipice of a major invasion."[6]

That assessment changed rapidly in the fall, when intelligence came in indicating that Russia was planning a large-scale, multipronged assault aimed at replacing the government in Kyiv. At a meeting in the Oval Office in October 2021, Chairman of the Joint Chiefs of Staff Mark Milley presented a sobering assessment of the scale of Russia's ambitions and the consequences for Ukraine.[7] Over the next several weeks, the administration worked to develop a fuller intelligence picture and erect the main pillars of a new strategy to "deter and dissuade" Putin from enacting this plan. Biden decided to declassify sensitive intelligence to help rally US allies and dispatched Central Intelligence Agency Director William J. Burns to Moscow to warn Putin that the consequences of a new invasion would be severe. Given Putin's quasi-messianic conviction that Ukraine rightfully belonged to Russia, as well as Biden's fondness for saying that "superpowers don't bluff," it was imperative the US government be prepared to deliver on this threat.[8]

Origins of the Tiger Team

From the beginning, it was clear that a full-scale Russian invasion of Ukraine would have major strategic consequences for the United States. At this time I was serving in the strategic planning directorate at the National Security Council (NSC), an office created in the George W. Bush administration to help lead interagency planning and provide independent advice to the national security advisor.[9] In mid-November, my colleague Rebecca Lissner and I began drafting a memorandum to Jake Sullivan that laid out several potential scenarios for Ukraine, identified the most pressing strategic questions we would need to answer in each scenario, and recommended the NSC either lead or commission a dedicated contingency planning exercise.[10] On receipt of the memo, Sullivan agreed immediately. He also shared a note he had received several days earlier from John Hyten, vice chairman of the Joint Chiefs of Staff, recommending that the NSC conduct a "pre-mortem" exercise to imagine what the administration would say from the podium following a Russian invasion and help clarify the steps we should be taking now.[11]

In my experience, dedicated interagency contingency planning—as opposed to one-off discussions of "risks and opportunities" or long-term operational and strategic planning—is rare.[12] The press of regular business, opportunity costs against existing policy work, and ingrained institutional resistance, especially at the State Department, all conspire against making the necessary investments in time and personnel. This case was different.

Partly this was due to the quality of the intelligence. But it also reflected the priorities and experience of Biden's national security team. In an interview with *Politico*, Sullivan would later recount a conversation with his deputy, Jon Finer, in November 2021 about a scene in the film *Austin Powers* in which a steamroller inches toward a man at the far side of the room. The man stands frozen, shouting "No!" as the steamroller inexorably approaches. "I said I was determined that we were not going to be that guy—just waiting for the steamroller to roll over Ukraine,"

Sullivan said. "We were going to act."[13] He explicitly linked this determination to his earlier experience working on Ukraine. As has been widely reported, multiple senior officials, including Sullivan and Finer, served in the Obama administration in 2014, when Russia's "little green men" appeared in Crimea, taking the Ukrainian government and the United States by surprise and creating a damaging *fait accompli* on the ground. Having been outplayed by Putin in that case, there was a strong and shared conviction not to repeat the same mistake.[14]

Another important factor was Afghanistan. Extensive interagency planning was done over the spring of 2021 to make sure the United States was prepared in the event Biden made the decision to withdraw all remaining US forces. An after-action review by the State Department later noted that this planning considered a range of possible contingencies, including a significant deterioration of the security environment that would have required the complete closure of the US embassy.[15] However, the administration failed to anticipate or adequately plan for a worst-case scenario in which the Taliban seized Kabul *before* the US withdrawal. The resulting crisis in August convinced many senior officials of the necessity to incorporate more creative analytic exercises and simulations in crisis planning, and to more rigorously evaluate the implications of low-probability, high-impact events.[16]

At the conclusion of a Principals Committee meeting just before the Thanksgiving holiday, Sullivan announced that the White House would establish an interagency group to think through the full range of actions we would take if Russia chose to invade Ukraine. The goal was to ensure we were fully prepared, even while preventing an invasion remained the primary focus of the administration's work. Sullivan promised to come back to the Principals on the structure of the group. Over the break I reached out to several colleagues with deep experience in crisis management and planning, as well as to the Policy Planning Staff at the State Department and officials at the Joint Staff. Based on these conversations, I prepared a short proposal to convene an NSC-led planning cell with representatives from all the major national security agencies. By the time I returned to the office on November 29, Sullivan had already settled on a model: he wanted a "Tiger Team," and he asked me to lead it.

Tiger Teams are most commonly associated with the Department of Defense, which has used small, cross-functional teams of experts to address a variety of policy and operational challenges at least since the 1960s. Indeed, my one experience with a Tiger Team was at the Pentagon during the Obama administration, when Colin Kahl, then a professor at Georgetown University but previously deputy assistant secretary of defense for the Middle East, was asked to assemble an interagency group to devise strategic options in the wake of the Islamic State's blitzkrieg across western Iraq and eastern Syria in the summer of 2014. However, it is in the field of engineering that Tiger Teams are most common and with which they are most closely associated. A 1964 article in an aerospace journal defined a Tiger Team as "a team of undomesticated and uninhibited technical specialists, selected for their experience, energy, and imagination, and assigned to track down relentlessly every possible source of failure in a spacecraft subsystem or simulation."[17] By far the most famous example was the team of engineers assembled by Gene Kranz in April 1970 to avert a potential catastrophe on the Apollo 13 mission, when one of its oxygen tanks exploded in mid-flight, some two hundred thousand miles from earth.[18] Kranz did not use the term itself, and his team differed in important respects from a traditional Tiger Team. But the high stakes, intense time pressure, and Kranz's methodical, information-driven approach to problem-solving have since become inseparable from the model itself.

My primary concern was to ensure that the new team would have the latitude to be nimble and creative, while at the same time being sufficiently plugged-in to agency leadership to have consistent and timely access to the information we needed to plan. Three factors made this possible. First, in assembling the team I reached out directly to agency leadership, in most cases the chief of staff, to explain what we were trying to accomplish and solicit their support to identify candidates, each of whom I asked be dedicated to the effort full time. This improved agency buy-in, set the team apart from the regular policy process, and helped mitigate (but not resolve) concerns within the agencies that the team would circumvent normal lines of authority. Second, I made clear to NSC colleagues, especially those responsible for Russia and Ukraine policy, that they would have full visibility on the Tiger Team's work and that we would otherwise stay out of their way. Finally, Sullivan invited me to attend the daily meeting on Russia and Ukraine he had been holding in his West Wing office since early November, and both he and Finer made the Tiger Team a standing item on the agenda for Deputies and Principals Committee meetings.[19] This ensured policy connectivity and enabled us to elevate issues for decision as planning or events required. It also sent a strong signal to the agencies to accelerate their own planning.

Planning for the Worst

The first meeting of the Tiger Team took place in early December 2021 in a secure room at the Eisenhower Executive Office Building. We were roughly ten people: myself; my NSC Russia directorate colleague David Shimer, who would play an indispensable role driving the team's work and drafting the playbook; and one representative each from the Departments of State, Treasury, and Defense, the United States Agency for International Development (USAID), and the Directorate of National Intelligence. By agreement, the Joint Staff delegated two individuals, one responsible for planning and the other for current operations. The Departments of Energy and Homeland Security joined subsequently.[20] Since I asked for individuals, not positions, seniority varied—several team members were front-office staffers, others were drawn from the Russia or Ukraine teams in their respective agencies. Some came from planning offices. The delegate from State, for example, was a member of the Policy Planning Staff and a foreign service officer who had served in both Moscow and Kyiv.

I laid out our mandate: to think through every possible dimension of the US response and produce a "break glass" playbook to guide it. Our goal was to complete this task before Christmas, if at all possible. There was no need to participate in the ongoing parlor game to figure out whether Putin would invade. This should be taken as a given and our work proceed from there. I stressed that the group would need to operate as a team and that members would be expected to contribute freely based on their expertise, rather than holding to building-cleared talking points. We agreed to meet three times per week by secure teleconference.

The first order of business was to make sure that we were all on the same page concerning the scenario itself. Would we focus on the worst case or on what we judged most likely? I was still unconvinced that Putin would risk a multipronged assault, including on Kyiv, that would leave his forces outnumbered and exposed, so initially I favored the latter approach. But a consensus quickly formed within the group that we should plan for the worst. This was more faithful to the available intelligence, and we agreed it would be much easier to scale back a more robust US response plan than it would be to try to ratchet up the response if we were caught flat-footed. Events would later prove this to be the right choice, as our scenario almost perfectly anticipated Russia's military operation on February 24, 2022. It also had significant implications for the way we thought about our options that wouldn't become clear until much later.

Another urgent task was to articulate a list of strategic objectives to guide our plans. Naturally, high-level policy documents on Russia and Ukraine from earlier in the administration had neither foreseen nor developed objectives specific to a full-scale invasion scenario. To develop a coherent plan, we needed the equivalent of "commander's intent." The closest thing we had was a list of objectives the Joint Staff had developed for Chairman Milley that he shared with the president during the Oval Office meeting in October. In a later interview, Milley recounted these as: (1) avoid a kinetic conflict between the US military and NATO with Russia, (2) contain the war inside the geographic boundaries of Ukraine, (3) strengthen and maintain NATO unity, and (4) empower Ukraine and give it the means to fight.[21] Using these as a starting point, the team developed a more comprehensive list that encompassed our broader diplomatic, humanitarian, and other objectives, including to ensure that Ukraine emerged from the war as a democratic, independent, and sovereign state. This list was reviewed and approved by the Deputies Committee and would guide planning going forward.

We also had to get a handle on planning that was already underway in various parts of the government. By this time, Treasury had developed detailed sanctions options and begun socializing them with the European Union, as well as the United Kingdom, Canada, and Japan.[22] Here, the substance of operational and contingency planning was effectively the same. By contrast, contingency planning was significantly less mature at the Departments of State and Defense, where the early focus was on convincing allies of the veracity of US intelligence assessments and building a coalition. At Energy, Homeland Security, and USAID, the implications of a full-scale Russian invasion were only beginning to come into focus, and contingency planning had not yet begun. We immediately tasked out more than a dozen papers—on military support, force posture, diplomatic engagement, homeland defense, humanitarian assistance, and other topics. We then established a regular rhythm of briefings within the team that enabled us to cover each topic sequentially, bringing in technical experts from the corresponding department or agency when required. Where plans already existed, we "caught the fish as they swam by," incorporating these into a single, comprehensive document that could help us see how the pieces fit together, identify gaps, and begin to think through policy choreography.[23] Where plans or intelligence assessments didn't exist, we pressed the agencies to produce them. This approach allowed us to catalyze and integrate contingency planning; it also helped us expedite decisions on questions that had not yet been considered in the regular policy process, or where a lack of clear guidance stymied progress.

This effort paid dividends. In December, USAID began planning to deploy a Disaster Assistance Response Team (DART) to Ukraine and to pre-position humanitarian supplies in Dubai.[24] The State Department developed or refined detailed contingency plans, not only for US embassies in Kyiv and Moscow but also to isolate Russia at the United Nations, rally international support for Ukraine, and suspend, modify, or maintain cooperation with Russia on issues where we had continued to engage, including strategic stability, cybersecurity, Iran's nuclear program, and the Arctic. To reassure US allies, the Pentagon deployed additional US military forces to Europe and began planning for the establishment of new NATO battalion battle groups in Bulgaria, Hungary, Romania, and Slovakia. The Department of Homeland Security accelerated engagement with the private sector on the potential for retaliatory Russian cyberattacks.[25]

Perhaps the most consequential line of effort related to military support. Over the fall, the administration was trying to balance two contradictory objectives— to ensure that Ukraine had the capabilities to defend itself, while avoiding any steps that might increase the likelihood of an invasion or affix blame on the United States. As Colin Kahl, then under secretary of defense for policy, later put it, "we didn't want to inadvertently speed up the Russian clock, incentivize Putin, or give him a pretext to make a decision he had not made. Us leaning too far forward could create dynamics either within the alliance or as we were trying to build world opinion against the Russians that made us look like we were the provocateurs."[26] Despite this, the president decided to approve the second Presidential Drawdown of $200 million in military support for Ukraine, but only after speaking to Putin on December 7—and without the accompanying public announcement that would later become routine.[27]

The Defense Department, which had been delivering lethal support to Ukraine since 2017, was well positioned to sustain or even increase military assistance if Russia launched a more limited incursion in eastern Ukraine. However, surging lethal support into a contested battlespace—where Russia had established air superiority and replaced the government in Kyiv—was a completely different problem. This scenario raised a thicket of operational, diplomatic, and legal questions. To answer them, and following preliminary work and outreach by the Tiger Team, the NSC established a small group to assess options to support a potential Ukrainian insurgency.[28] This work would ultimately position the United States to rapidly ramp up assistance once Russia's invasion had begun; it also served (alongside the threat of sanctions) as an important component of the administration's deterrent messaging to Russia.

By Christmas these plans were beginning to mature and we had a draft of the full playbook. At a Principals Committee meeting several days earlier, Sullivan had announced that the NSC would organize a series of table-top exercises in the new year to run through an invasion scenario, consider permutations, and identify the strengths and weaknesses of our plans. At this point the work of the Tiger Team turned to organizing these exercises, revising the playbook, and preparing agency leadership to participate. No one expected to get much of a holiday; I managed an appearance at home on Christmas Eve and was back in the office on December 27.

Table-top exercises can take many forms, but in general they inhabit a middle ground between a full simulation and an informal, structured conversation; the core objective is to clarify roles and responsibilities and improve leaders' readiness to perform their duties in a crisis. In this case, we chose to focus on the main scenario in the playbook, with shorter portions of the exercise dedicated to alternative and branch scenarios. The first table-top was held at the Deputies level, the second for Principals, both in early January.[29] A senior intelligence officer for Russia served as the facilitator, offering "injects" and encouraging participants to stay "in role" as much as possible. The exercises began with an intelligence briefing that mirrored the scenario we had developed, allowing the leadership of each agency to imagine themselves in the moments following a Russian invasion and enact the steps their agencies would take.

The exercises were revealing in several ways. First, they exposed sequencing and timing deficiencies that still needed to be overcome if we wanted to be ready to execute a comprehensive response on "Day 1." This was especially important with respect to sanctions. By this time the sanctions packages themselves were approaching completion, but it became clear that we weren't yet prepared either to impose costs on Russia immediately or to demonstrate from the outset that we had additional measures at the ready. Both were required to fulfill the strategy that Deputy National Security Advisor for International Economics Daleep Singh referred to as "start high, stay high."[30] We came to a similar conclusion about the need for further preparations to ensure new NATO deployments could be executed swiftly. And since the scenario envisaged that airstrikes on targets in Kyiv during the first phase of Russia's military operation would shut down commercial air traffic and impede other modes of transportation, the exercise led us to conclude that waiting until this point to relocate US government personnel would be too risky—we needed to draw down Embassy Kyiv in advance. We also needed to sharpen the message to US citizens in Ukraine, in line with the department's "no double standard" principle.[31]

Second, the examination of alternative scenarios short of a large-scale, multi-pronged Russian invasion prompted a vital discussion on thresholds. Would our response be the same across all scenarios, or calibrated? Would a smaller-scale invasion lead some of our allies and partners to rethink their own actions, and, if so, would we proceed along the main lines of our economic and military response without them? Could we meaningfully distinguish a smaller-scale operation from the early phases of a large-scale one, recognizing that Russia had sufficient capabilities along Ukraine's border to scale-up over time—as it had done in 2014? Lengthy debate on these questions contributed to a decision that our approach would be binary, not calibrated: any invasion, irrespective of scale, would trigger a tough US response.[32]

Finally, in the initial design we built in a "hot wash" to provide everyone an opportunity to step back, not only to evaluate the approach as a whole but also to think through broader strategic implications. There was consensus, for example, that Russia's overreach would present opportunities, including to strengthen the NATO alliance and enhance deterrence vis-à-vis China. We also recognized the potential to help Europe radically reduce its dependence on Russian gas and hasten its transition to clean energy. And we considered the risk that the US and allied response to Russia's actions could deepen Moscow's dependence on Beijing, encouraging their strategic partnership and potentially threatening the dominance of the dollar. To keep these issues in focus, the State Department's Office of Policy Planning was asked to develop them into a paper on global risks and opportunities. This work would inform the administration's approach and later serve as the basis for a major speech by Secretary of State Antony Blinken on Russia's "strategic failure" delivered in Helsinki, Finland, NATO's newest member.[33]

In all these respects, the table-top exercises identified gaps and catalyzed further planning work. What I had imagined would be a capstone to our efforts instead proved to accelerate them.

The playbook was revised over the following weeks and approved by the president in the second week of February. Its subsequent circulation as a Cabinet memorandum meant that officials across the US government had a comprehensive picture of the US response plan and their respective roles within that plan two weeks before the first Russian tank crossed the Ukrainian border.[34] Having completed its task, the Tiger Team was formally disbanded. Sullivan would restore the team a month later, after the invasion began. This second iteration was led by NSC staffers Paul Brister and David Shimer, who were given a fresh mandate to plan for a range of potential emerging contingencies, including a refugee crisis, a Russian attack on NATO territory, and Russian use of chemical, biological, or nuclear weapons.[35] These efforts continued to pay dividends over the following months—including, for example, when in mid-November missile fragments fell in Poland, sparking concerns across the NATO alliance.[36]

Lessons Learned

No two crises are the same, and the unique circumstances that led to the creation of the Russia-Ukraine Tiger Team and shaped much of its work make it difficult to draw lessons that will be broadly applicable. Especially unusual was the accuracy, detail, and advance warning on Russia's plans and intentions provided by the US intelligence community. It is hard to think of an international security crisis on this scale for which the United States had as much time to prepare. Since the war in Ukraine is ongoing, and its outcome remains uncertain, it is also difficult to assess the ultimate success or failure of the US response and thus of the underlying planning. Nevertheless, the fact that contingency plans were quickly put into operation, along with the scale of the planning effort, make the Tiger Team an important case study.

Several points stand out. First, leadership matters. Critical to the success of the Tiger Team was strong and sustained senior-level support, in this case from the national security advisor. Sullivan immediately grasped the value a dedicated contingency planning effort would add, empowered me to assemble and lead the team, made sure that Cabinet officials lent it their support, devoted significant time in the Principals Committee and to the table-top exercises, and leveraged the power of Cabinet memoranda to codify and disseminate the final plans. A commensurate outcome would have been impossible without his leadership.

A second factor that contributed to the Tiger Team's success was its formal separation from the regular interagency policy process—along with clarity that the two processes would run in parallel. This arrangement enabled the group to focus and systematically work through a future scenario, without being encumbered by or interfering with the main policy effort. It freed the team to be more creative and adaptive. It enabled us to foresee challenges and requirements that had not yet arisen. And it provided a vehicle to explore and develop ideas that otherwise would have languished as agency leadership prioritized near-term demands.

This was not without friction: creating a team that reported directly to the national security advisor and in some cases submitted proposals directly to the Deputies Committee circumvented multiple layers within the bureaucracy. While this dramatically enhanced the speed at which we could move, it had the unintended effect of occasionally rankling deputy assistant and assistant secretaries who felt cut out of the process.

Third, the Tiger Team underscored just how labor-intensive planning can be. Broadly speaking, the team helped lay the foundation for a policy that remains in place today. In a narrower sense, however, more than two months of planning bought the administration less than a week of predetermined policy implementation. Almost immediately, key assumptions that undergirded the team's work failed, and we were off script. Still, those days were essential.[37] Rather than building the play in real time, key enablers were already in place, allies and partners were on board, and agency leadership could focus on making adjustments where required. We had also considered the larger strategic picture well in advance, rendering unnecessary a debate on first principles that would have slowed decision-making. Indeed, the breathtaking speed at which international affairs were reordered in the days following February 24 was at least partly a consequence of the fact that both the United States and Russia were implementing plans that had been months in the making.[38] This was very different from the US withdrawal from Afghanistan the preceding August, when the Taliban's seizure of Kabul required the administration to rapidly rework, and in some cases reverse, core decisions.

Fourth, the planning effort offers a note of caution for those who are confident in our ability to predict future events. Public debate has focused on the failure of multiple experts, political-risk firms, and even superforecasters to correctly assess that Putin would decide to invade.[39] Our problem was different. The intelligence community has rightly been commended for its success in warning about Russia's military plans and intentions, an achievement that has boosted its global reputation, especially following the damaging failure in Afghanistan.[40] In devising our planning scenario, the Tiger Team got the scale, geography, and timing of Russia's military operations almost exactly right. But we were wrong on almost everything else. We overestimated the Russian military, underestimated Ukraine's capabilities and resolve, and failed to anticipate the extent to which fear and public revulsion would reshape European politics in favor of tougher response options, some of which seemed out of reach only days before.[41] To be sure, there was disagreement both within the Tiger Team and across the administration on these assessments, with the strongest critique coming from those with the most recent experience in Russia and Ukraine. It was our good fortune that, in each case, events surprised us to the upside. But this should not obscure the significant gaps between the world we planned for and the world that came into being after February 24.

This had important implications. Since we underestimated Europe's response, especially with respect to cutting Russia off from SWIFT and freezing its sovereign assets, we almost immediately stepped further up the escalation ladder with Russia than our initial plans had anticipated. In hindsight, many have concluded that Putin does not have the appetite for a war with NATO, and therefore that the risk of escalation was low. But this was by no means clear at the time and could still be proved wrong.[42] Similarly, the dismal performance of Russian forces and Ukraine's success on the battlefield defied intelligence predictions of a rapid Russian military victory.[43] Corresponding plans—to assist the evacuation of Ukrainian officials, help establish a government in exile, and potentially support a Ukrainian insurgency—no longer met the moment, or needed to be revised. These examples serve as an important reminder that even a methodical, intelligence-driven planning process will err in significant ways.

Finally, and following from this, it is clear that we devoted far more resources and attention to determining what Russia would do than we did to rigorously evaluating the aftermath. While planning for the worst-case invasion scenario proved extremely prescient, our pessimism concerning the outcome on the battle-field over the following weeks may have inadvertently encouraged us to embrace a more modest set of objectives than was warranted. Alongside a short-term response plan, we might have benefited from taking a longer view from the outset that considered multiple potential post-invasion scenarios, including ones more favorable to Ukraine. Had we done so, we might have identified additional options to support Kyiv's early counteroffensives, before Russia was able to dig in. And we might have had a head start on thinking through the implications of a drawn-out conventional war, including the impact on global food security, the need to ramp up the US defense industrial base, and the potential that Russia would turn to Iran and North Korea to meet its own military inventory deficits.[44]

Conclusion

We can of course never know what would have happened had US intelligence not detected what Russia was up to or if the administration had squandered the opportunity to plan. Ukraine might have been erased as a sovereign, independent state, emboldening Russia and creating a major crisis for the other former Soviet republics and NATO.[45] The Tiger Team—and the larger planning effort of which it was a catalyst and part—helped to avert a disaster. Timely US intelligence and military support were critical, including in the successful defense of Kyiv.[46] Months of diplomatic consultations enabled the United States to build a broad coalition and isolate Russia globally, while the swift imposition of tough economic sanctions and export controls (at least temporarily) collapsed the ruble and diminished

Russia's ability to project power, probably for years to come.[47] Dogged efforts to shore up European energy supplies and blunt Russia's cyber capabilities denied Moscow two of its favored coercive instruments. And while the initial effort to deter Russia from launching the invasion did not succeed, Biden's vow to defend "every inch" of NATO territory—a vow backed by the deployment of significant new capabilities and more than twenty-thousand additional US troops—has thus far prevented the war from metastasizing into an even more dangerous confrontation between Russia and NATO.

Only time will tell whether these accomplishments endure and cohere into a successful policy response over the long term. The failure of Ukraine's summer 2023 counteroffensive, faltering political support in the United States and Europe, and Russia's growing confidence all present major challenges—challenges that should be the focus of tomorrow's plans.

ACKNOWLEDGMENTS

I would like to thank Peter Andreoli, Matan Chorev, Peter Feaver, David Holmes, Colin Kahl, Ciara Knudsen, Rebecca Lissner, Jon Massicot, Phyllis Parker, and David Shimer for reading and commenting on an early draft of this chapter. Neither their comments nor the chapter itself reflect the official view of the US government. All remaining errors are of course my own.

NOTES

1. See, for example, Shane Harris et al., "Road to War: U.S. Struggled to Convince Allies, and Zelensky, of Risk of Invasion," *Washington Post*, August 16, 2022; Erin Banco et al., "'Something Was Badly Wrong': When Washington Realized Russia Was Actually Invading Ukraine," *Politico*, February 24, 2023; and Susan Glasser, "Trial by Combat: Jake Sullivan and the White House's Battle to Keep Ukraine in the Fight," *New Yorker*, October 9, 2023.

2. Ellen Nakashima and Ashley Parker, "Inside the White House Preparations for a Russian Invasion," *Washington Post*, February 14, 2022.

3. Joseph R. Biden, "Why America Must Lead Again: Rescuing American Foreign Policy after Trump," *Foreign Affairs*, January 23, 2020.

4. US Department of State, "On the Extension of the New START Treaty with the Russian Federation," press release, February 3, 2021, https://www.state.gov/on-the -extension-of-the-new-start-treaty-with-the-russian-federation/.

5. Trevor Hunnicutt, Arshad Mohammed, and Andrew Osborn, "U.S. Imposes Wide Array of Sanctions on Russia for 'Malign' Actions," *Reuters*, April 15, 2021,

https://www.reuters.com/world/middle-east/us-imposes-wide-array-sanctions-russia
-malign-actions-2021-04-15/.

6. Harris et al., "Road to War."

7. Interview with Mark Milley in Banco et al., "'Something Was Badly Wrong.'"

8. Vladimir Putin, "On the Historical Unity of Russians and Ukrainians," Presidential Administration of Russia, July 12, 2021, http://en.kremlin.ru/events/president/news/66181.

9. Peter Feaver and William Inboden, "A Strategic Planning Cell on National Security at the White House," in *Avoiding Trivia: The Role of Strategic Planning in American Foreign Policy*, ed. Daniel W. Drezner (Washington, DC: Brookings Institution Press, 2009), 98–109.

10. Kathleen Carroll, "A Tiger Team Plans for the War in Ukraine," Carnegie Corporation of New York, July 14, 2023, https://www.carnegie.org/our-work/article/how-scholarship-can-inform-foreign-policy-better-outcomes/.

11. Gary Klein, "Performing a Project Premortem," *Harvard Business Review*, September 2007, https://hbr.org/2007/09/performing-a-project-premortem.

12. Examples of interagency planning over the past two decades include State and Defense Department planning for the invasion of Iraq in 2002, NSC-led planning for the Iraq surge in 2006, and contingency planning efforts related to Iran, North Korea, and Syria during the Obama administration. Ironically, the last of these—which focused on preparing for the "day after" the anticipated fall of President Bashar al-Assad—convinced many US officials that contingency planning above all represented a waste of time and resources.

13. Interview with Jake Sullivan in Blanco et al., "'Something Was Badly Wrong.'"

14. Jonathan Guyer, "What Biden Learned the Last Time Putin Invaded Ukraine," *Vox*, February 7, 2022, https://www.vox.com/2022/2/7/22916942/biden-lessons-russia-2014-invasion-ukraine-crimea.

15. US Department of State, *After Action Review on Afghanistan: January 2020–August 2021*, March 2022, https://www.state.gov/wp-content/uploads/2023/06/State-AAR-AFG.pdf.

16. The White House, *U.S. Withdrawal from Afghanistan*, April 6, 2023, https://www.whitehouse.gov/wp-content/uploads/2023/04/US-Withdrawal-from-Afghanistan.pdf.

17. J. R. Dempsey et al., "Program Management in Design and Development," in *Proceedings of the Third Annual Aerospace Reliability and Maintainability Conference* (New York: Society of Automotive Engineers, 1964), 7, 8.

18. Gene Kranz, *Failure Is Not an Option: Mission Control from Mercury to Apollo 13 and Beyond* (New York: Simon and Schuster, 2009), 308–339. It is perhaps worth noting that in his description of the early moments of the Apollo 13 crisis, Kranz immediately reached for a military analogy: "I had heard of the fog of battle, but I had never experienced it until now." Kranz, *Failure Is Not an Option*, 312.

19. Interview with Jake Sullivan in Banco et al., "'Something Was Badly Wrong.'"

20. The Departments of Energy and Homeland Security joined subsequently.

21. Harris et al., "Road to War."

22. Interview with Victoria Nuland in Banco et al., "'Something Was Badly Wrong.'"

23. Philip Zelikow, "To Regain Policy Competence: The Software of American Public Problem-Solving," *Texas National Security Review* 2, no. 4 (September 2019): 110–127.

24. Interview with James Hope in Banco et al., "'Something Was Badly Wrong'"; see also United States Agency for International Development, "USAID Deploys a Disaster Assistance Response Team to Respond to Humanitarian Needs in Ukraine," press release, February 24, 2022, https://www.usaid.gov/news-information/press -releases/feb-24-2022-usaid-deploys-disaster-assistance-response-team-respond -humanitarian-needs-ukraine.

25. US Department of Homeland Security, "DHS Designated as the Lead Federal Agency to Respond to Russia-Related Impacts to the United States," press release, February 24, 2022, https://www.dhs.gov/news/2022/02/24/dhs-designated-lead-federal -agency-respond-russia-related-impacts-united-states.

26. Interview with Colin Kahl in Banco et al., "'Something Was Badly Wrong.'"

27. Christina L. Arabia, Andrew S. Bowen, and Cory Welt, *U.S. Security Assistance to Ukraine*, Congressional Research Service Report IF12040 (Washington, DC: Office of Congressional Information and Publishing, January 2024), https://crsreports .congress.gov/product/pdf/IF/IF12040.

28. David Ignatius, "The Biden Administration Weighs Backing Ukraine Insurgents If Russia Invades," *Washington Post*, December 19, 2021.

29. A third table-top exercise was held in February to review the final playbook.

30. Interview with Daleep Singh in Banco et al., "'Something Was Badly Wrong.'"

31. The White House, "Press Briefing by Press Secretary Jen Psaki and National Security Advisor Jake Sullivan," press briefing, February 11, 2022, https://www.white house.gov/briefing-room/press-briefings/2022/02/11/press-briefing-by-press-secretary -jen-psaki-and-national-security-advisor-jake-sullivan-february-11-2022/.

32. President Biden was subsequently criticized for stating that actions short of a full-scale invasion likely would prompt debate among allies over the appropriate response. See Kevin Liptak, "Biden Predicts Russia 'Will Move In' to Ukraine, but Says 'Minor Incursion' May Prompt Discussion over Consequences," *CNN*, January 19, 2022.

33. Antony J. Blinken, "Russia's Strategic Failure and Ukraine's Secure Future" (speech, Helsinki, June 2, 2023), https://www.state.gov/russias-strategic-failure-and -ukraines-secure-future/.

34. Interview with Derek Chollet in Banco et al., "'Something Was Badly Wrong.'"

35. David Sanger et al., "U.S. Makes Contingency Plans in Case Russia Uses Its Most Powerful Weapons," *New York Times*, March 23, 2022, https://www.nytimes.com /2022/03/23/us/politics/biden-russia-nuclear-weapons.html.

36. Mark Strzelecki, "Unconfirmed Report of Russian Missiles Hitting Polish Village Sparks Worries across NATO," *Reuters*, November 15, 2022, https://www.reuters .com/world/europe/explosion-kills-two-poland-near-ukraine-border-2022-11-15/.

37. This lends further support to Dwight Eisenhower's famous dictum that "plans are nothing; planning is everything."

38. The French diplomat Pascal Confavreux described this as "a feeling of acceleration of history." Interview in Banco et al., "'Something Was Badly Wrong.'"

39. "Post-Mortem: Lessons Learned in Superforecasting Russia's Invasion of Ukraine," Good Judgment, March 2022, https://goodjudgment.com/wp-content/uploads /2022/03/1570-Post-Mortem-v2.pdf; see also Peter Scoblic and Philip Tetlock, "Fumbling the Crystal Ball: Policymakers Can't Afford to Spurn the Science of Prediction," *Foreign Affairs*, December 16, 2022, https://www.foreignaffairs.com/world/fumbling -crystal-ball.

40. Vivian Salama and Warren Strobel, "Four U.S. Intelligence Agencies Produced Extensive Reports on Afghanistan, but All Failed to Predict Kabul's Rapid Collapse," *Wall Street Journal*, October 28, 2021.

41. The White House, "Joint Statement on Further Restrictive Economic Measures," press release, February 26, 2022, https://www.whitehouse.gov/briefing-room/statements -releases/2022/02/26/joint-statement-on-further-restrictive-economic-measures/.

42. Austin Carson, "The Missing Escalation in Ukraine: In Defense of the West's Go-Slow Approach," *Foreign Affairs*, September 14, 2023, https://www.foreignaffairs .com/eastern-europe-caucasus/missing-escalation-ukraine.

43. Glasser, "Trial by Combat."

44. Michael Shear and David Sanger, "White House Says North Korea Providing Russia with Ballistic Missiles," *New York Times*, January 4, 2024.

45. Hal Brands, "Ukraine and the Contingency of Global Order: What If the War Had Gone Differently—or Takes a Sudden Turn?," *Foreign Affairs*, February 14, 2023, https://www.foreignaffairs.com/ukraine/ukraine-and-contingency-global-order.

46. Paul Sonne et al., "Battle for Kyiv: Ukrainian Valor, Russian Blunders Combined to Save the Capital," *Washington Post*, August 24, 2022.

47. "Ukraine Update," UK Defence Intelligence, December 30, 2023.

Chapter Nine

US Strategy in Ukraine

Kori Schake

The Biden administration's objective in the war was clear, consistent, and repeatedly conveyed publicly: to assist Ukraine in preventing the success of the Russian invasion without provoking Russia to expand the war beyond Ukraine—and especially without drawing the United States directly in. Minimizing the risks of escalation while providing direct assistance and orchestrating the international political, economic, and military effort in support of Ukraine has been Biden administration policy for the first two years of the war.

Responding to the invasion on February 24, President Joe Biden made absolutely clear the limits of US interest:

> Although we provided over $650 million in defensive assistance to Ukraine just this year—this last year, let me say it again: Our forces are not and will not be engaged in the conflict with Russia in Ukraine. Our forces are not going to Europe to fight in Ukraine but to defend our NATO Allies and reassure those Allies in the east.[1]

Kori Schake leads the foreign and defense policy team at the American Enterprise Institute. She has previously held jobs in the Departments of State and Defense, the National Security Council, and on the 2008 McCain presidential campaign, and taught at the Johns Hopkins School of Advanced International Studies, the University of Maryland, West Point, Stanford University, and in the Department of War Studies at King's College London.

He further conveyed the vulnerability of US support by engaging in an extended peroration about shielding Americans from any increase in energy costs.

The administration was also clear about Russian intentions; as President Biden said, Russia "seeks to obliterate Ukraine and subjugate its people."[2] The asymmetry of Russia fighting an unlimited war and Ukraine being wholly reliant on US support while the United States placed stringent limitations on its contribution to Ukraine's desperate effort to preserve its country was a significant strategic advantage for Russia.

Biden administration policy was principally concerned about limiting American risk, not maximizing Ukraine's ability to restore its people's security and the country's territorial integrity. And the administration was not wrong to have ruthlessly assessed US interests and devised a strategy consistent with the limits of those interests. The particular strategy they devised was to provide extensive but limited support to Ukraine for as long as it takes.

Problems have arisen, though, because while warfare is not static, this strategy is. And as the war has ground on, Biden administration strategy has come up against its limitations: battlefield stalemate, fraying domestic support in countries aiding Ukraine, discouragement by Ukraine of its prospects, Russia's mobilization of international support and growing conviction that if it perseveres it will attain its objectives. These are all the result of the costs and temporal consequences of the Biden strategy.

Antebellum

Strategy is a theory of the case: what is happening, what interests are engaged, what tools and resources are available to affect what is happening, the timing and sequencing of activity to attain policy objectives. It is best utilized as a verb, not a noun. As Lawrence Freedman argues, rather than *having* a strategy, policymakers are most successful when *practicing* strategy, constantly evaluating its prospects in light of events and rebalancing its elements.[3]

The Biden national security strategy was outlined admirably and unusually early by the administration in March of 2021. Biden's strategy envisioned "building back better at home and reinvigorating our leadership abroad."[4] It viewed democracy under siege, China as the paramount threat, but acknowledged "both Beijing and Moscow have invested heavily in efforts meant to check U.S. strengths and prevent us from defending our interests and allies."[5] It committed to the idea that "diplomacy, development, and economic statecraft would be the leading elements of

American foreign policy."[6] Like most National Security Strategy (NSS) reports, it is long on encomiate pronouncements ("we will make smart and disciplined choices") and devoid of the budgetary constraint that actually determines strategy.

The main geopolitical thrusts of Biden national security strategy were China as the pacing threat, and "mini-détentes" with other problematic countries.[7] Neither Russia nor Iran nor North Korea have taken the deal, however. And despite the administration's claim that "a powerful military matched to the security environment is a decisive American advantage," the administration's evaluation of sufficiency is so wildly out of synch with bipartisan views in Congress that the legislative branch added $25 billion to the administration's first defense budget and $45 billion to the second.[8] Factoring in inflation, Biden actually cut defense spending in his first two budget proposals.[9]

The Department of Defense (DOD) cajoled the term "integrated deterrence" into the Biden administration's official 2022 National Security Strategy as a way to "combine our strengths to achieve maximum effect in deterring acts of aggression."[10] It entails "the seamless combination of capabilities to convince potential adversaries that the costs of their hostile activities outweigh their benefits."[11] How this differs from regular deterrence was never clear, nor, despite its popularity in DOD rhetoric, does the concept appear to have affected administration policy.

So in advance of Russia's invasion, the administration had developed a defensible intellectual construct to guide policy, albeit one that was somewhat freighted by affectatious baubles like "integrated deterrence." But the implementation of their policy—that is, their strategy—had a fundamental vulnerability, which was their hostility to international trade.

The administration made a number of good moves to reinforce and expand allied cooperation in defense, and created a common front with allies on punitive economic actions (for example, sanctions on semiconductors). But it obdurately refused to provide what allies were begging for: a positive vision that would help countries to reduce their economic reliance on China. That would have required openness to significant trade deals, which the administration ideologically opposes as contravening "foreign policy for the middle class."[12] The approach actually increased reliance on the military elements of their strategy, a problem compounded by underfunding and questions about US credibility and competence in the aftermath of withdrawal from Afghanistan.

President Biden's description of his administration's actions in the run-up to the 2022 Russian invasion was:

We warned the world what Putin was planning. Even some in Ukraine didn't believe we were—what we had—our intelligence community found. We made sure NATO was prepared to deter any aggression against any member state. We pursued intense diplomacy with Russia, seeking to avert this terrible war. And when Russian bombs began to fall, we did not hesitate to act.[13]

And as early as March of 2022, Pentagon officials were declaring US policy toward Ukraine a stunning success of integrated deterrence for preventing Russia from attacking a NATO country.[14]

The administration evidently anticipated a potential Russian invasion of Ukraine as early as March of 2021, when the Russians held large-scale exercises. It also made numerous private attempts to deter Russia's invasion, including a proposed United States–Russia summit and meetings with CIA Director William J. Burns in Moscow in November 2021 and Secretary Antony Blinken in January 2021 in Geneva.[15] So even by its own admission, administration efforts to deter the Russian invasion failed.

The Strategy

The administration's strategy once Russia did invade Ukraine was comprised of five main elements: disclosing intelligence information, rallying international support, imposing economic sanctions, isolating Russia diplomatically, and providing military assistance to Ukraine.

Info Wars. The most novel element of the administration's strategy was the way it declassified, shared with allies, and revealed to Russia its information on their activities, thus publicizing in advance of action what Russia was preparing. While strategic use of information both true and false is a traditional element of war, in the decades before the Ukraine war, the United States had been abysmal at political warfare, fumbling to determine how a free and open society could shield its domestic space from adversary incursion, pious and clumsy about how to weaponize knowledge of adversary plans and actions.

The administration believed it delayed the Russian invasion by several weeks, prevented a potential Russian false flag effort, and deflated threats of chemical and nuclear weapons. At a minimum, it did valuably warn Ukraine, facilitate allied cohesion, and affect global public attitudes about Russia.[16] Parenthetically, it also restored confidence in US intelligence assessments, strengthening an important component of US policies.

But there was a second side to the coin, which is what our adversaries learned about us. The most consequential piece of intelligence about the US war effort wasn't extracted from the shadows, but revealed by the Biden administration itself: the United States was overweeningly concerned about Russian escalation.

President Biden and his national security advisor repeatedly defended the limitations of US support to Ukraine by saying they didn't want to start World War III.[17] Especially early in the war, the White House conveyed publicly to Russia the limits of US interests in Ukraine's defense by emphasizing that America would not take actions to precipitate conflict with Russia.

Perhaps picking up on those anxieties, Russia periodically hinted at nuclear use in the conduct of the war, deployed tactical nuclear weapons to Belarus, and exercised their release procedures. Nuclear threats also figured in Russia's declaration of Ukrainian provinces in and beyond their control as Russian territory in order to extend deterrence of US support to those areas.

The concern's sway over policy was especially striking since the administration didn't give much credence to Russian nuclear threats. The director of national intelligence, Avril Haines, and director of central intelligence, William Burns, concluded and publicly testified that Russia's threats were designed to intimidate the United States rather than presage actual use.[18]

Russia's nuclear threats did not prevent US support for Ukraine, but they ensured no involvement in Ukraine of US troops, substantially delayed decisions on delivery of types and quantities of US equipment, and prevented the use of US weapons to strike Russian territory.

So the positive impact of political warfare was counterbalanced by the United States projecting its limiting fear of Russian escalation.

The Biden administration did an excellent job orchestrating international condemnation when Russia once again raised the specter of nuclear use in February 2023.[19] That may suggest the administration had realized that conveying its anxiety increased the value of Russian threats. If so, it would reposition the United States advantageously in the event that Russia's fortunes and forces in Ukraine crumble and the likelihood of Russian nuclear use goes considerably up.

Team Sports. The deft diplomacy that countered Russian nuclear threats with condemnation by two major nuclear countries not supporting Ukraine was of a piece with much good work to create broad international participation and supportive involvement from international institutions. The Biden administration orchestrated condemnation of the invasion in international organizations (the United Nations, the Group of Seven advanced economies, the G20, the European

Union, the International Criminal Court, and NATO) while leading vigorous bilateral efforts.

Initial results were sweepingly impressive, with 90 countries sponsoring and 141 countries (of 193) voting in the UN General Assembly to condemn Russia's invasion; only Belarus, North Korea, Eritrea, Syria, and Russia voted against the resolution.[20] Countries beyond Europe—Japan, Australia, Singapore—were mainstays of the diplomatic, sanctions, and even weapons provision. President Biden went to Europe within a month to stand shoulder to shoulder with NATO allies and encourage the people of Ukraine. NATO acted swiftly and decisively to activate forces and provide commanders authority to enact the common defense. And while Russia's aggression (rather than adroit diplomacy) precipitated Sweden and Finland's decision to join NATO, bringing an end to hundreds of years of neutrality was a strong signal of NATO's value and confidence in American leadership (although the Biden administration's inability for such an extended time to bring about Turkish acceptance somewhat attenuated the message). The administration organized a worldwide effort involving fifty countries to identify war materials and financial support that could be provided to Ukraine and did the hard diplomatic work of persuading countries to provide it even when it left the United States and other countries short for their own security needs.

None of those diplomatic achievements would have been possible without the Biden administration's determination to assist Ukraine and enormous efforts to bring countries together and deliver significant institutional action. None of this would have been attempted if Donald Trump had won the 2020 presidential election. In addition to providing essential international support to Ukraine, the Biden administration strengthened the United States by demonstrating what America—and no other country—is capable of.

The administration was quick to trumpet its commitment. Secretaries Blinken and Austin went to Kyiv in late April 2022 to convey "America's stalwart support for the Ukrainian government and Ukrainian people, including through our significant assistance to Ukraine's security, governance, economic and humanitarian needs."[21] But the Biden administration also pressed Ukraine to negotiate an end to the war from its inception: during this trip, Secretary Blinken emphasized "renewed support for Ukraine's efforts to end the Russian aggression through diplomacy and dialogue" and argued that "our continued support will strengthen Ukraine's hand on the battlefield and at the negotiating table."[22]

The NATO summit perfectly illustrated the inherent contradictions in the administration's policy: although the United States committed to placing more US forces in Europe to reassure NATO allies, it refused to consider Ukrainian prospects for NATO membership.[23] Emphasizing the depth of the US commitment to NATO allies unfortunately highlights the extent to which Ukraine exists outside that state of grace. In lieu of any encouragement for Ukraine in terms of ascending to the alliance's collective defense, the Biden administration increased its monetary assistance to the country and began emphasizing the longevity of its assistance commitments.[24]

Diplomatic efforts began losing altitude: the September 2023 G20 summit, chaired by India, declined to condemn Russia; Turkey denied passage to British minesweeping ships intended to clear Russian mines from the Black Sea; for precious months, Hungary's support for Russia prevented European Union assistance to Ukraine; and Slovakia elected a government similarly inclined toward Russia. Even Poland, the most stalwart supporter of Ukraine, experienced protests against Ukraine joining the EU. Countries of the global south understandably worried about food prices and the vast differential in Western countries' concern about war in Ukraine versus wars elsewhere. And within the coalition supporting Ukraine—including Ukraine itself—domestic politics began reasserting themselves and diffusing focus. Nowhere was that truer or of greater significance than in the United States, where the president advanced supplemental funding legislation to Congress to aid Ukraine, but—as of early 2024—could not muster the votes to pass it.

Russia also began gaining international cooperation: North Korea and Iran were supplying it with ammunition and drones, China began shipping non-lethal supplies, trade routes for Western products were diverting through Central Asian countries to indirectly supply Russia. Collusion was significant enough to cause concern about an axis of authoritarian powers operating together in Europe and the Middle East.

Still, the diplomatic element of the Biden administration's strategy strikingly succeeded in delivering international institutions and broad international support for Ukraine, even if isolation of Russia began eroding and sustaining support was increasingly difficult.

Where's the Kaboom? The administration also used the time provided by the early intelligence releases to build consensus on expansive economic sanctions targeting the Russian financial, energy, and transportation sectors, along with overseas holdings of the state and individuals and export controls to limit technology access. As the president said, "We're going to impair their ability to compete in a high-tech 21st-century economy."[25] The Biden administration also clearly believed economic sanctions would cripple Russia. Speaking in Warsaw, the president said "these economic sanctions are a new kind of economic statecraft with the power to inflict damage that rivals military might."[26] He underscored the point in the press conference:

> Q: And—and with that—with his ambitions, you're confident that these devastating sanctions are going to be as devastating as Russian missiles and bullets and tanks?
>
> THE PRESIDENT: Yes. Russian bullets, missiles, and tanks in Ukraine. Yes, I am.
>
> Q: Thank you, President Biden. If sanctions cannot stop President Putin, what penalty can?
>
> THE PRESIDENT: I didn't say sanctions couldn't stop him.[27]

The G7 was the institutional lever for implementing sanctions. This strategy drew the support of a surprising breadth of countries beyond Europe, including Singapore. The main cost of Russia sanctions has been paid by European countries, which to their great credit European governments shouldered, aggressively reducing their dependence on Russian energy imports. But despite several rounds of sanctions and Western companies' efforts to voluntarily enact their own penalties to deny products and redirect supply chains, economic levers failed to significantly impede the Russian war effort.

Capable work by Russia's central bank, the avoidance of compliance by numerous countries (including China, India, Turkey, North Korea, Saudi Arabia, Pakistan, and the United Arab Emirates), the effective use of third-party transshipment through Central Asia, and the massive retooling of the Russian economy to wartime production demonstrated the difficulty of effecting economic damage.[28] The International Monetary Fund concluded that in the war's first year the effect of sanctions was less than half the effect of the 2008 financial crisis on Russia.[29] While Russian energy revenues fell by 24%, trade volumes returned to pre-war levels on diversion to China and India.[30]

So draconian economic sanctions have been much less successful than the strategy anticipated and required.

Politics by Other Means. The military elements of Biden administration strategy were both the most expansive and problematic. Expansive because of the sheer magnitude of military equipment provided, and problematic because these efforts revealed the difficulty of reconciling the US's two fundamental policy goals: assisting Ukraine while ensuring Russia did not expand or escalate the war.

On the day Russia invaded Ukraine, the United States announced the deployment of seven thousand US troops to Europe. The following day, the Supreme Allied Commander Europe (SACEUR) activated the NATO Response Force and the United States authorized $350 million in assistance for Ukraine, drawing down from DOD stocks.[31] Thus began a steady drumbeat of increasing military assistance to Ukraine and reassurance of US allies that has continued throughout the war. This effort had the effect of reinforcing the extent to which the United States is committed to NATO allies but not to Ukraine, thereby encouraging Sweden and Finland to join NATO but cementing Biden administration opposition to any encouragement of Ukraine's NATO aspirations.

DOD created the Ukraine Defense Contact Group in April of 2022. The UDCG met monthly at Ramstein Air Base in Germany to hear from Ukraine what military support was needed, identify which countries among the coalition had it, negotiate what of it they were willing to provide, and work the logistics of delivery to Ukraine. By its second meeting, forty countries participated; by the third meeting there were fifty.

The president committed to aid Ukraine "as long as it takes."[32] But an enduring commitment to provide support is not the same as providing Ukraine with the support it needs to achieve its objective: driving Russia out of Ukraine's internationally recognized territory. As Phillips O'Brien points out, US military provisions have been systems of limited range and defensive purpose.[33]

The contradiction in US policy between supporting Ukraine and preventing Russian escalation produced a repetitive cycle of Ukraine pleading for systems Washington denied, allies (particularly the United Kingdom) moving forward without the United States, the Biden administration bowing to public criticism and international pressure and slowly relenting, providing the systems months and even years later than when they would have been most effective.[34] That was the pattern for delivery of HIMARS rockets, Abrams tanks, F-16 aircraft, cluster munitions, and ATACMS rockets. Insult was added to injury when Pentagon officials defended their hesitance by saying the Ukrainians didn't need these particular systems, couldn't learn to operate them in time to affect the war's outcome, or that it wasn't the best use of available funds.[35]

It took until the eleventh presidential security assistance package for the United States to send High Mobility Artillery Rocket Systems (HIMARS).[36] The tank debate was also particularly illustrative of the Biden self-image of stalwart support clashing with his actual tentativeness. Ukraine pled for tanks. The United States finally relented and agreed to provide them in late January 2023, with President

Biden justifying the move by saying "they [the Ukrainians] need to be able to counter Russia's evolving tactics and strategy on the battlefield in the very near term."[37] Despite acknowledging the urgency of the situation, the Biden administration debated this decision for months and initially planned to deliver the tanks a year later.[38]

In terms of F-16s, the Biden administration had to be pushed by allies: the administration initially insisted fighter aircraft weren't relevant to the war, then that pilots couldn't be trained in such a compressed period of time, then that fighter planes were too expensive. Finally, in March 2023, it agreed that partner nations could deliver F-16s to Ukraine. In May of that year, it announced that the United States would participate in training pilots to fly those F-16s, only after being shamed by allies who had already agreed to contribute aircraft. Along the way, the Biden administration publicly assured the Russians that "these F-16s will not be relevant to the upcoming counter offensive."[39]

The consequences of delay in delivering weapons and ammunition were most tragically and visually evident in Russian construction of defenses in late 2022 and early 2023. Satellite photography reveals Russian minefields and entrenchments establishing defense in depth beyond the range of Ukrainian forces during the six months between when Ukraine asked for tanks, and when the United States agreed.[40] And America only agreed after it was clear Germany would not provide its tanks unless the United States also did—so sending the corrosive message that the United States was trying to get allies to take risks of retaliation that we were not willing to bear ourselves.

With the failure of the fall 2023 Ukrainian offensive to produce a dramatic breakthrough of Russian defenses, grim resignation set in in the West, with an expectation that the war would drag on at least until 2025 and that weapons-providing countries would run out of support to give. Despite that conclusion, the Biden administration did not commit either the funding or the effort to revivify the industrial base of the United States or its allies. Ukraine's armorers and financial supporters now had domestic fronts of opposition and bare weapons cupboards, the gruesome arithmetic of casualties and population size between Russia and Ukraine had become significant, and even Ukraine's president—the symbol of the country's heroic resistance—had difficulty getting political traction in Washington.

Stalemate on the eastern front and the US policy restrictions on using weapons to target Russia resulted in Ukraine shifting emphasis to Crimea, engaging in acts of sabotage against Russia, further developing its domestic defense industry, and hoping for a technological breakthrough that would restore mobility on the battlefields.[41] These conditions would place even more weight on the policy decision, driven by fear of escalation, to allow Russian territory to be a sanctuary in which US weapons are not employed.[42]

Fixing the Deficiencies

The Biden administration might have done three things better:

- enlisted the president in repeatedly making a public case for why it's in American interests for Ukraine to win and explaining how the price of the venture matches the value;
- expended the political and economic capital to dramatically and quickly increase weapons production and delivery;
- recognized that it is Russia that should be most concerned about escalation, not the United States, and adopted tactics that asserted the conviction.

President Biden asked an enormity of the American people—fifty-four tranches of military assistance to Ukraine, totaling $45 billion, through the end of 2023—without expending his political capital to make the case about why that is in American interests or where this commitment fits among our priorities.[43]

And it was a major problem that the president's rhetoric far outstripped his policy. Ukrainians should be forgiven their frustration at the chasm between President Biden categorically stating that Putin "must be stopped" and his administration's hesitancy at taking action to accomplish that end. When Russia launched its most expansive air raid of the war on Ukraine in January 2024, the White House contented itself with issuing a public statement condemning congressional delays in providing aid. That condemnation was justified, but a White House statement was a poor means of achieving either the halting of Russian devastation of Ukraine or congressional passage of additional aid.

Nor did the administration move fast enough to repair the glaring vulnerability that aid to Ukraine has exposed, which is the shortfall of weapons and munitions in allied inventories. Concerns by defense ministries—including the Pentagon—that weapons ought not be provided to Ukraine because they are in short supply for our own needs would be much more persuasive if those inventories were anywhere near adequate for our needs. The pace of utilization by Russia and Ukraine magnifies the inadequacy of our stockpiles, but does not significantly exacerbate it: every Western military, including America's, would run out of necessary firepower in weeks were we fighting a war even of the Russia-Ukraine level of intensity, much less a war in which we had to traverse the vast Pacific Ocean to defend a small island near the enemy's mainland.

Money and policy can solve this problem. The defense industry would love to have multiyear contracts that make it economically viable to build factories and train a workforce. Military services would love budgets that do not require them to exclude funding in the hopes that Congress will override the administration's political direction on the topline for defense. Allies would love to see regulatory restrictions on co-production relaxed, and that will be essential to produce the quantity of weapons and ammunition they need to contribute meaningfully to co-alition warfare. Yet as of early 2024, there were only faint signs the administration was willing to commit the resources to make its strategy executable.

Most consequential for Ukraine, however, would be a conceptual shift in which the United States became less concerned about escalation than the country—Russia—that would lose its war of aggression even more quickly should it draw Washington and its allies into direct participation. Deterrence is fundamentally about competitive risk-taking, and America continued to be hemmed in by adversaries less risk-averse than it was, even when Washington had a much wider margin for error given its strength.

Conclusion

President Biden's strategy had the enormous benefit of incurring no American casualties. It also showcased American leadership in upholding international order and mobilizing international coalitions, demonstrated the expansive reach and economic dominance of the United States and its allies, conveyed the engineering and operational excellence of Western military equipment, was cost-effective in terms of the destruction imposed on an adversary military, and reinforced the commitment by NATO allies to their common defense. And unquestionably, without the crescendo of effort undertaken by the Biden administration, Ukraine would have lost its war and been extinguished as a nation.

Nonetheless, by early 2024 the Biden administration found itself in a similar position strategically to the Bush administration in 2005: having committed enormous resources to a war effort that was not succeeding and probably could not attain success on the current trajectory, the government remained intellectually unwilling to adopt approaches that might produce a better outcome. And as in

George W. Bush's Iraq War, Joe Biden's presidential administration was now inseparably tied to the war in Ukraine: should the effort fail, it would look of a piece with the disastrous denouement of American involvement in Afghanistan.

The main deficiency of Biden administration strategy was their obduracy in repeating mistakes. They often treated strategy as a noun rather than a verb. And in warfare, adaptability to changing circumstances is often the difference between success and failure. The administration started strong, using information adroitly, developing a bazooka of economic sanctions, orchestrating broad international and institutional support, and providing a cornucopia of military equipment to Ukraine.

But it persisted in errors that conveyed the tentativeness at the core of US policy long after the conditions that justified concern had abated, and it was slow to redress gaping vulnerabilities like the paucity of military stockpiles that impair not only Ukrainian war efforts but also America's. Thus, the longer Russia's war in Ukraine went on, the less the administration's static assessment of the war as a strategic failure for Russia matched events and the worse Biden administration strategy wore.

What the Biden administration ought to have done that it did not is adjust its strategy over time to tighten the noose around Russia until Putin lost on the battlefield, reconsidered the value of continuing to destroy Ukraine, or was driven from power in Russia. The United States ought to have provided weapons of greater ferocity sooner, allowing Ukraine to retaliate in kind to Russian attacks. Instead of conveying American reticence, this would have given Russia cause to fear that its actions would provoke greater support for Ukraine. Furthermore, the administration should have made it clear that additional attacks on civilian targets will provoke a short timeline for Ukraine's admission into NATO with the territory under its control and commitment to eventual reunification. Finally, Russia should be aware that if they use a nuclear weapon, the United States and allies will hunt down everyone involved in the decision and execution and either kill them or see them in the Hague. The administration should also issue appeals to the Russian people not to support a genocidal war.

The Biden administration continues to believe Russia has suffered a strategic failure in Ukraine, although the longer the war drags on, the more difficult it is to avoid seeing Russia's territorial gains, casualty tolerance, and ability to persevere despite Western sanctions. The war has also exposed the paucity of Western weaponry production, fissures in Western solidarity, and the convergence of authoritarian support, indifference, and hostility from the Global South. The longer the war continues, the more strategic timidity rather than strategic resolve appears as the defining feature of US involvement.

NOTES

1. Joseph R. Biden, "Remarks by President Biden on Russia's Unprovoked and Unjustified Attack on Ukraine" (speech, Washington, DC, February 24, 2022), https://www.whitehouse.gov/briefing-room/speeches-remarks/2022/02/24/remarks-by -president-biden-on-russias-unprovoked-and-unjustified-attack-on-ukraine/.

2. The White House, "Statement from President Joe Biden on Russia's Aerial Assault on Ukraine," press release, December 29, 2023, https://www.whitehouse.gov/briefing -room/statements-releases/2023/12/29/statement-from-president-joe-biden-on-russias -aerial-assault-on-ukraine/.

3. Lawrence Freedman, *Strategy: A History* (Oxford: Oxford University Press, 2013).

4. The White House, *Interim National Security Strategic Guidance*, March 3, 2021, 6, https://www.whitehouse.gov/wp-content/uploads/2021/03/NSC-1v2.pdf.

5. The White House, *Interim National Security Strategic Guidance*, 8.

6. The White House, *Interim National Security Strategic Guidance*, 14.

7. Hal Brands, "Biden's Foreign Policy Vision Is Officially Dead," *Bloomberg*, October 29, 2023, https://www.bloomberg.com/opinion/articles/2023-10-29/israel -hamas-latest-biden-s-foreign-policy-vision-is-officially-dead.

8. Leo Shane III and Joe Gould, "Congress Passes Defense Policy Bill with Budget Boost, Military Justice Reforms," *Defense News*, December 15, 2021, https://www .defensenews.com/news/pentagon-congress/2021/12/15/congress-passes-defense-policy -bill-with-budget-boost-military-justice-reforms/; Connor O'Brien and Lee Hudson, "House, Senate Negotiators Agree to Add $45B to Biden's Defense Budget," *Politico*, November 30, 2022, https://www.politico.com/news/2022/11/30/house-senate -negotiators-45b-biden-defense-budget-00071367.

9. Elaine McCusker, "Joe Biden's Aspirational Defense Budget," *The Hill*, March 28, 2023, https://thehill.com/opinion/national-security/3922015-joe-bidens-aspirational -defense-budget/.

10. The White House, *The National Security Strategy of the United States*, October 12, 2022, 20, https://www.whitehouse.gov/wp-content/uploads/2022/10/Biden-Harris -Administrations-National-Security-Strategy-10.2022.pdf.

11. The White House, *National Security Strategy*, 22. Illustrative of the extent to which the Department of Defense and not the Biden White House takes ownership of the concept, Google searches produce only defense-related sites and references.

12. Jake Sullivan, "Remarks by National Security Advisor Jake Sullivan on Renew- ing American Economic Leadership at the Brookings Institution" (speech, Washington, DC, April 27, 2023), https://www.whitehouse.gov/briefing-room/speeches-remarks/2023 /04/27/remarks-by-national-security-advisor-jake-sullivan-on-renewing-american -economic-leadership-at-the-brookings-institution/.

13. Joseph R. Biden, "Remarks by President Biden on Supporting Ukraine, Defending Democratic Values, and Taking Action to Address Global Challenges | Vilnius, Lithuania" (speech, Vilnius, July 12, 2023), https://www.whitehouse.gov/briefing-room /speeches-remarks/2023/07/12/remarks-by-president-biden-on-supporting-ukraine -defending-democratic-values-and-taking-action-to-address-global-challenges-vilnius -lithuania/.

14. A senior DOD official was quoted as saying, "I don't think there's any doubt that the model of integrated deterrence comes out smelling pretty good from this." See Greg Jaffe and Dan Lamothe, "Russia's Failures in Ukraine Imbue Pentagon with Newfound Confidence," *Washington Post*, March 26, 2022.

15. Erin Banco et al., " 'Something Was Badly Wrong': When Washington Realized Russia Was Actually Invading Ukraine," *Politico*, February 24, 2023, https://www .politico.com/news/magazine/2023/02/24/russia-ukraine-war-oral-history-00083757.

16. Ken Dilanian et al., "In a Break with the Past, U.S. Is Using Intel to Fight an Info War with Russia, Even When the Intel Isn't Rock Solid," *NBC News*, April 6, 2022, https://www.nbcnews.com/politics/national-security/us-using-declassified-intel-fight -info-war-russia-even-intel-isnt-rock-rcna23014.

17. Joe Biden quoted in Steven Nelson, " 'That's Called World War III': Biden Defends Decision Not to Send Jets to Ukraine," *New York Post*, March 11, 2022; Aaron Blake, "Why Biden and the White House Keep Talking about World War III," *Washington Post,* March 17, 2022.

18. Avril Haines and William Burns quoted in Peter Schroeder, "The Real Russian Nuclear Threat," *Foreign Affairs*, December 20, 2023.

19. Kiran Sharma, "Quad Slams Nuclear Threats as 'Inadmissible' in India Huddle," *Nikkei Asia*, March 3, 2023, https://asia.nikkei.com/Politics/International-relations /Quad-slams-nuclear-threats-as-inadmissible-in-India-huddle.

20. "General Assembly Resolution Demands End to Russian Offensive in Ukraine," *UN News*, March 2, 2022, https://news.un.org/en/story/2022/03/1113152.

21. US Department of Defense, *Russian War in Ukraine Timeline*, last modified February 23, 2024, https://www.defense.gov/Spotlights/Support-for-Ukraine/Timeline/.

22. US Department of State, "Secretary Blinken and Secretary Austin's Travel to Ukraine" (readout, April 25, 2022), https://www.state.gov/secretary-blinken-and -secretary-austins-travel-to-ukraine/.

23. Jim Garamone, "Biden Announces Changes in U.S. Force Posture in Europe," *DOD News,* June 29, 2022, https://www.defense.gov/News/News-Stories/Article/Article /3078087/biden-announces-changes-in-us-force-posture-in-europe/.

24. See, for example, US Department of Defense, "$1.1 Billion in Additional Security Assistance for Ukraine," press release, September 28, 2022, https://www .defense.gov/News/Releases/Release/Article/3173378/11-billion-in-additional-security -assistance-for-ukraine/.

25. Biden, "Remarks by President Biden on Russia's Unprovoked and Unjustified Attack on Ukraine."

26. Joseph R. Biden, "Remarks by President Biden on the United Efforts of the Free World to Support the People of Ukraine" (speech, Warsaw, March 26, 2022), https://

www.whitehouse.gov/briefing-room/speeches-remarks/2022/03/26/remarks-by
-president-biden-on-the-united-efforts-of-the-free-world-to-support-the-people-of
-ukraine/.

27. Biden, "Remarks by President Biden on Russia's Unprovoked and Unjustified
Attack on Ukraine."

28. Daphne Psaledakis, Simon Lewis, and Timothy Gardner, "US Issues Sweeping
Sanctions Targeting Russia over Ukraine War," *Reuters*, December 12, 2023, https://
www.reuters.com/world/us/us-issues-sweeping-sanctions-targeting-russia-over-ukraine
-war-2023-12-12/.

29. Rebecca M. Nelson, *The Economic Impact of Russia Sanctions*, Congressional
Research Service Report IF12092 (Washington, DC: Office of Congressional Information
and Publishing, December 2022), https://crsreports.congress.gov/product/pdf/IF/IF12092.

30. Vladimir Soldatkin and Darya Korsunskaya, "Russia's Oil and Gas Budget
Revenue Down 24% in 2023," *Reuters*, January 11, 2024, https://www.reuters.com
/business/energy/russias-oil-gas-budget-revenue-down-24-2023-2024-01-11/; Darren
Anderson and Daniel Crook, "The Big Leak: How Trade Sanctions on Russia are
Failing" (Singapore: Hinrich Foundation, 2023), https://www.hinrichfoundation.com
/research/wp/trade-and-geopolitics/how-trade-sanctions-on-russia-are-failing/.

31. US Department of Defense, *Russian War in Ukraine Timeline*.

32. Biden, "Remarks by President Biden on Supporting Ukraine, Defending Demo-
cratic Values, and Taking Action to Address Global Challenges | Vilnius, Lithuania."

33. Phillips P. O'Brien, "Does Biden Want Ukraine to Win?", *Wall Street Journal*,
January 1, 2024, https://www.wsj.com/articles/does-biden-want-ukraine-to-win-deal
-russia-war-crimea-military-aid-630dbe60.

34. Valery Zaluzhny, "Ukraine's Commander-in-Chief on the Breakthrough He
Needs to Beat Russia," *Economist*, November 1, 2023, https://www.economist.com
/europe/2023/11/01/ukraines-commander-in-chief-on-the-breakthrough-he-needs-to-beat
-russia; Phillips P. O'Brien and Edward Stringer, "America's Unconvincing Reasons for
Denying F-16s to Ukraine," *The Atlantic*, May 11, 2023, https://www.theatlantic.com
/ideas/archive/2023/05/ukraine-military-f-16-aircraft/674022/.

35. Dan Lamothe, "Congress Presses Pentagon on Biden's Reluctance to Give
Ukraine F-16s," *Washington Post*, February 28, 2023, https://www.washingtonpost.com
/national-security/2023/02/28/republicans-ukraine-biden-pentagon/.

36. US Department of Defense, "$700 Million in Additional Security Assistance for
Ukraine," press release, June 1, 2022, https://www.defense.gov/News/Releases/Release
/Article/3049472/700-million-in-additional-security-assistance-for-ukraine/.

37. David Vergun, "Biden Announces Abrams Tanks to Be Delivered to Ukraine,"
DOD News, January 25, 2023, https://www.defense.gov/News/News-Stories/Article
/Article/3277910/biden-announces-abrams-tanks-to-be-delivered-to-ukraine/.

38. C. Todd Lopez, "Ukrainians to Get U.S. Tanks by Fall," *DOD News*, March 21,
2023, https://www.defense.gov/News/News-Stories/Article/Article/3336826/ukrainians
-to-get-us-tanks-by-fall/.

39. C. Todd Lopez, "F-16 Training, Aircraft, to Fill Ukraine's Mid-Term, Long-Term
Defense Needs," *DOD News*, May 23, 2023, https://www.defense.gov/News/News

-Stories/Article/Article/3405085/f-16-training-aircraft-to-fill-ukraines-mid-term-long
-term-defense-needs/.

40. Brady Africk, "Ukraine Maps Show the Price of Allies' Hesitation," *Washington Post*, July 31, 2023.

41. Zaluzhny, "Ukraine's Commander-in-Chief on the Breakthrough He Needs to Beat Russia."

42. O'Brien, "Does Biden Want Ukraine to Win?"

43. US Department of Defense, "Fact Sheet on U.S. Security Assistance to Ukraine," press release, December 27, 2023, https://media.defense.gov/2023/Dec/27/2003366049/-1/-1/1/UKRAINE-FACT-SHEET-27-DEC.PDF; Christina L. Arabia, Andrew S. Bowen, and Cory Welt, *U.S. Security Assistance to Ukraine*, Congressional Research Service Report IF12040 (Washington, DC: Office of Congressional Information and Publishing, January 2024), https://crsreports.congress.gov/product/pdf/IF/IF12040.

Chapter Ten

Nuclear Lessons and Dilemmas from the War in Ukraine

Francis J. Gavin

After Russia's brutal attack on Ukraine, what have we learned about the role of nuclear weapons—both in the war and in world politics writ large?

Since the end of the Cold War, nuclear weapons have operated as a ubiquitous, powerful presence shaping world politics, all while, ironically, remaining largely invisible, rarely discussed or even thought about.[1] These fearsome weapons constrained the actions of key players, often without them being fully aware of it. These powerful effects occurred despite thermonuclear weapons never being used in combat and being largely irrelevant to most aspects of contemporary international relations. Indeed, the leading nuclear power, the United States, took important steps in recent decades to decrease the salience of the bomb, both in world politics and its own grand strategy. This is one reason why the dramatic reappearance of nuclear politics during the Russia-Ukraine war has been so unsettling and jarring.

Russia's invasion of Ukraine, and the nuclear threats that followed, returned nuclear weapons to the forefront of global politics for the first time since the Cold War ended—and arguably, since the days of crises in the late 1950s and early 1960s. Understandably, many analysts and policymakers have revisited the decades-long ideological and geopolitical competition between the Soviet Union and the United

Francis J. Gavin is the Giovanni Agnelli Distinguished Professor and the director of the Henry A. Kissinger Center for Global Affairs at the Johns Hopkins School of Advanced International Studies.

States to see if it holds lessons or instructions for our current age, while others have highlighted how different current circumstances are from the past. As the war progresses, we are beginning to have a better, if incomplete, sense of the role nuclear strategy and statecraft have and will continue to play, both in this war and world politics writ large. With great power political tensions increasing, such crises may become more common.

The Inscrutability of Nuclear Crises

It is important to highlight how little we actually know both about nuclear dynamics in general and their role in the Russia-Ukraine War, and how much of what follows are, at best, educated guesses. Nuclear crises are difficult to evaluate, for several reasons.

First, how should we define a nuclear crisis?[2] The broadest definition would be a dispute of some sort involving at least one country possessing the bomb. Many international relations databases accept this standard. The problem, of course, is that nuclear states may have all sorts of confrontations where neither the stakes nor the circumstances make the chance of nuclear use seem at all plausible. A narrower definition is a conflict between nuclear states that has a real chance of escalating to nuclear use. But how does one make that assessment of nuclear risk? Some examples are easy: President John F. Kennedy's demand that the Soviet Union remove nuclear-tipped missiles from Cuba in October 1962 begot a frightening crisis where all the participants believed the danger of nuclear war was considerable. Clear examples like that, however, are rare. If NATO forces invaded Russia, that would likely generate pressures on Russia to respond with nuclear weapons. But American and Russian military forces are not in direct combat, nor is the current war, save for occasional sabotage efforts, being fought on Russian soil; rather, it is a proxy war, with one side providing aid to the adversary of the nuclear power, similar to Russia and China's support of North Vietnam (1960s–1970s) or the United States' support of the mujahideen in Afghanistan (1980s).

This leads to a second challenge: nuclear use is largely binary. You either detonate nuclear weapons in a conflict or you don't. This is different than most instruments of state power, such as sanctions, cyberattacks, or conventional war, where you can increase or decrease the intensity easily. It is true that there is a range of nuclear use, from a demonstration shot to a full-scale thermonuclear war, but the line between nuclear use and nonuse is seen as quite stark and presumably the barrier to cross it is very high. We don't know exactly where that bar is beforehand, however. In Russia's case, its doctrine states that it might use nuclear weapons if weapons of mass destruction were used against it or if the existence of the state was in jeopardy, a high standard. On the other hand, on several occasions Russia's leadership appeared to threaten nuclear use if circumstances far below a threat to state survival occurred.

A third challenge emerges from the first two: there exist powerful incentives to bluff, or, to use a less polite word, to lie about your intentions surrounding nuclear weapons. This is not necessarily true in other elements of state strategy and statecraft, where lying is often punished. In a crisis without nuclear weapons, for example, both sides can make rough assessments about which side will have the upper hand if a war breaks out, calculating their capabilities and interests. If tanks are what matter on the battlefield, and one side has fifty, and the other has one hundred and fifty, the side with the smaller arsenal is only going to push their claims so far given that there is a good chance they could lose if the dispute came to blows. With nuclear weapons, however, what matters is less how many you have and more your willingness to use them. In other words, it is resolve—a far less objective or measurable characteristic—rather than capabilities or even interest that matters, though both capabilities and interest feed into resolve in ways that are hard to calculate beforehand. This generates perverse incentives. Responsible states and leaders recognize that nuclear use is abhorrent and that making nuclear threats is irresponsible. Irresponsible (or simply weaker) states and leaders, however, could exploit their adversary's sense of responsibility by making bold threats of nuclear use. The more responsible side might back down, even if they have greater power and the more righteous cause, in order to avoid a nuclear detonation.

The fourth issue also highlights another way in which nuclear decision-making is different from other forms of statecraft: the decision to use the bomb is uniquely concentrated in one person's hands, the leader of the state. This is true in Vladimir Putin's Russia as well as the United States, where the president retains sole authority to launch the bomb. There are important historical and strategic reasons that nuclear decision-making has evolved this way—it was by no means inevitable—but it has important consequences for how we evaluate the chance of nuclear use. While there may be informal norms or implicit safeguards to limit the leader, the key variable for nuclear use is who the decision-maker is and what their priorities, history, temperament, and inclinations are. More than most elements of statecraft and strategy, understanding nuclear decision-making and nuclear deterrence requires an assessment of psychology, both individual and collective, a category that is notoriously difficult to measure and quantify *a priori*.

This leads to the final challenge: we lack powerful tools to predict the likelihood of nuclear use. Nuclear weapons were detonated against adversaries in war only twice: when the United States bombed Hiroshima and Nagasaki within a week of each other, in August 1945. They have not been used since. During a potential crisis, it can be difficult to make probabilistic claims about whether or not an adversary will use nuclear weapons and under what circumstances, since the database of past events is close to empty. Analysts make a variety of claims about the likelihood of escalation, often quite confidently, but these assessments are rarely better than educated guesses based on deductive logic rather than empirical claims. Many of the theories that often underpin our current strategies are quite old, generated some time ago—the 1950s and 1960s. They are primarily informed by the Cold War rivalry between the Soviet Union and the United States. Those Cold War theories and strategies emerged from and dealt with a world much different than the one we face today, one where a full-scale strategic thermonuclear surprise attack—a "bolt from the blue"—was the greatest fear, and the murderous, totalitarian behavior of Hitler's Germany and Stalin's Russia was in living memory. Few of these theories we use today have been updated since, despite our contemporary world looking nothing like the one nuclear strategists such as Thomas Schelling, Albert Wohlstetter, and Herman Kahn confronted.

The same is true of *ex post* assessments about deterrence. People argue, for example, that nuclear deterrence succeeded during the Cold War because it prevented the Soviet Union from invading Western Europe. That may be true. Perhaps, however, the Soviet Union never intended to attack, or was dissuaded from doing so for reasons that had nothing to do with the nuclear weapons. It is very hard to make concrete, conclusive claims about why something did *not* happen.

Consider, for example, the story about the Biden administration picking up signals that the Russians were considering using nuclear weapons in September 2022, and the administration's stern warnings that if the Russians moved forward, they would pay a terrible if unspecified price. Were the Russians deterred by America's threats? Or were they deterred by other sources, such as China's rather remarkable and quite public warnings against nuclear use? Or, knowing that the United States would pick up and react to evidence of preparing for nuclear use, could the Russians have been bluffing in order to get America's attention and achieve a political end? There is no way of knowing: even Putin may not have been sure and might have wanted to see how things played out. This makes such crises especially unsettling. As Janice Gross Stein points out, "There is good evidence that leaders not only do not know the preferences of their adversary as conditions change, at times they may also not know their *own* preferences."[3]

The correct reaction to the dangers and uncertainty surrounding nuclear crises and possible nuclear war is both seriousness and epistemological humility. Given the consequences, nuclear threats cannot simply be ignored, but given the nature of nuclear dynamics, they should not necessarily be taken at face value. Figuring out how to respond requires balance, sensitivity, and a willingness to update one's preconceptions. Unfortunately, that has not been how many analysts have responded to nuclear dynamics surrounding the war, instead viewing America and Russia's behavior as validating their previous assumptions. It is like the tale of Goldilocks: some believe the United States' response has been too hot, risking Russia's nuclear use, whereas others say it has been too cold, taking Russia's threats too seriously and unnecessarily limiting its response. If the war ends and there is no nuclear use, some will say that Russia was bluffing the whole time, and that there was never a real threat. If at some point in the future nuclear weapons are used, others will see the reasons for use were always obvious, in clear sight, and inevitable. In other words, we appear to be right until we are not, and most of our assessments emerge from our prior theories of world politics and nuclear dynamics. This blinds us to an important factor—nuclear use (or nonuse) may come when we least expect it or emerge from unexpected, previously unanalyzed paths. Few, for example, foresaw Yevgeny Prigozhin and the Wagner Group's June 2023 revolt or anticipated how it would play out. Politics often unfolds in nonlinear and surprising ways and from hidden causal paths that are only recognized after the fact.

The same is true, by the way, of what the world and the conflict might look like the day after nuclear use. Imagine the Russians used battlefield nuclear weapons in their war against Ukraine. What would be the consequences? The best we can do is speculate.

One can conjure up a scenario where the world reacts in horror to Russian nuclear use and, fearing further nuclear escalations, demands the conflict end, forcing Ukraine to the negotiating table—all to Russia's advantage. Such a world might highlight the value of nuclear threats and nuclear use, reversing the decades-long trend to minimize the role nuclear weapons play in world politics. Just as plausibly, however, one can also imagine a scenario where—by using nuclear weapons against Ukraine—Russia loses all remaining global support, including from China, whose implicit backing and economic aid is almost required for Russia to continue its efforts. Russia might not only find itself completely isolated.

The United States and the West might feel the constraints have been removed and respond with devastating cyber, conventional, and other non-nuclear capabilities against Russia that cripple its war effort. Segments of Russian society or even its elite might move against the regime. Seeing Russia punished for its nuclear use might send a powerful signal to the world, causing the global community to double down on its efforts to reduce the salience of nuclear weapons in global affairs.

Quite frustratingly, nuclear politics, even more than most elements of statecraft and strategy, is marked by deep uncertainty. Amongst many of the terrifying dilemmas of nuclear weapons, there is little we can say with great confidence. We aren't really sure what defines a nuclear crisis or how best to assess nuclear threats or escalatory pressures until after the event we are trying to avoid—nuclear use—takes place, and even then, our assessment would likely be speculative. We aren't even sure what the consequences of nuclear use on the battlefield might be. Given the extraordinary threat of nuclear weapons, however, hard choices about nuclear statecraft and strategy still must be made, even if they are based on little more than guesswork.

Statecraft and strategy, however, demand that choices be made, even/especially in the face of danger and uncertainty. How should we assess how American leaders performed, and what are the lessons from nuclear strategy and statecraft moving forward?

Nuclear Lessons?

Perhaps the most important if obvious lesson is that nuclear dynamics should be assessed within the context of the larger interests and goals of the states involved. In other words, both the nuclear dynamics of Russia's war on Ukraine and the United States' response must be analyzed in terms of what each side wanted to achieve and sought to avoid. One can plausibly suggest that in February 2022, Russia sought to conquer Ukraine at a low cost, and in the process, weaken and divide NATO while increasing its own comparative prestige and power. The United States sought to deter Russia from invading. After that strategy failed, it attempted to support Ukraine's defense without getting involved in a direct military conflict with Russia while maintaining cohesion with its European allies.

Despite (or even because of) the fact that American leaders faced such deep uncertainty about the future, difficult choices had to be made in February 2022 and beyond, and risks and rewards balanced. For many analysts, several years into the war, these decisions are easily criticized. Russia continues its murderous assault on a blameless sovereign nation, with no sign of stopping. It has successfully worked around Western sanctions and has mobilized for a longer war while receiving explicit or implicit support from a variety of states, especially in the global south. The war has brought China and Russia closer together, as well as increased the contributions and coordination from Iran and North Korea. Meanwhile, the military support from the United States and other Western countries often came slowly, haphazardly, or in an uncoordinated fashion, sometimes because stockpiles were low, other times because the supplier was concerned about the escalatory consequences of providing certain kinds of weapons. As the war settles into an ugly attrition battle and other international crises pull attention away, political support for Ukraine has waned in Western countries.

There is another way of viewing the ongoing conflict. Imagine that if you had told American policymakers in February 2022 that Russia's invasion would be largely blunted, that the country would suffer enormous and previously unimaginable losses in men and material, with Ukraine remaining a sovereign state fighting beyond anyone's expectations. Further, imagine that you had told those same policymakers that Russia's long-term demographic, economic, technological, and even military prospects were now quite bleak as a direct consequence of the war with Ukraine. In all likelihood, decision-makers in Western capitals would have been surprised. Now imagine they were told that this would happen while NATO simultaneously maintained cohesion, increased its military capabilities and expanded to include Finland and Sweden. Imagine, too, that the United States had contributed to severely degrading a rival at low cost, demonstrated extraordinary intelligence capabilities while testing and honing military capabilities that might be useful in other contingencies (such as a war with China), and became the most important global player in oil and gas markets. And that all of this happened without drawing the United States or NATO into direct conflict with Russia or with Russia using nuclear weapons. It is likely this scenario would have been on the highly optimistic range for many people in February 2022.

These divergent assessments highlight the difference between the *ex ante* world of the decision-maker, marked by great uncertainty, risk, and competing interests—including domestic politics, the Middle East, and the demands of countering an aggressive, rising China—and the *ex post* world of the critic, who often only assesses how things came out without interrogating counterfactuals that resulted in a different, and often far worse, world. Arguably, the positive outcomes are all the more remarkable, as they emerged in the shadow of persistent Russian nuclear threats, some implicit, others explicit, which drove at least some analysts to urge greater caution and even appeasement.

Beyond this larger point about assessing nuclear dynamics through the lens of political goals and interests, at least four other elements of nuclear dynamics have emerged from the conflict, while two remaining issues are less clear.

First, inter-conflict deterrence and stability appeared to settle in early. During the first days of the war, it was expected that both nuclear powers, Russia and the United States, would have to move slowly and uncertainly in regard to each other's nuclear posture, since each side's red lines were unclear. Dangerous missteps, many assumed, could easily lead to unexpected crisis and dangerous, even nuclear, confrontation. Many analysts were guided by their notions of inadvertent escalation, a powerful framework developed during the Cold War but largely based on certain views about how the July 1914 crisis led to the First World War. Nuclear use might occur, it was suggested, not because anyone planned to use the bomb, but because the fog of war, political misperception, and the operational mix of conventional and nuclear capabilities might lead to irresistible pressures. In reality, the United States and Russia appeared to roughly identify each other's red lines early, on and interwar deterrence has been remarkably stable. Even when crises or accidents emerged, neither side appeared eager to escalate against the other. On both sides, nuclear forces and operations appeared to be quite separate, and protected, from conventional operations. The Biden administration also updated its analysis of what Russia's red lines were—too slowly for some, to be sure—increasing its military support over time as it appeared Russia's red lines were neither as red, nor as close, as they originally believed. This was best demonstrated in its measured release of particular weapons systems over time—high-mobility artillery systems of various ranges, Patriot missiles, and advanced armored vehicles, for example. There even appeared to be impressive levels of direct and indirect government communication on nuclear questions. As Janice Gross Stein reveals, much of this came from an intentional American strategy of escalation management, which she labels "learning by doing": taking incremental steps, pausing to assess whether a critical threshold had been reached, then moving again.[4]

Second and relatedly, nuclear threats made by the Russians appeared to have limited utility. There was a healthy scholarly debate during the Cold War about the effectiveness of what has been labelled nuclear brinkmanship. Could making nuclear threats help a state achieve political ends that were otherwise out of reach? Soviet premier Nikita Khrushchev deployed nuclear threats during the crises over the status of West Berlin between 1958 and 1961. Looking over the evidence, these threats were hollow, though they were taken quite seriously at the time. American president Richard Nixon also used nuclear threats, sometimes half-heartedly, to achieve certain political ends, both during the Vietnam War and the 1973 war in the Middle East. In neither case was brinkmanship successful, though at least in the case of Khrushchev and Berlin, it gave leaders in the West pause. In some ways, this is unsurprising. Given the consequences of nuclear use and fears of escalation from a single use to a larger thermonuclear war, any nuclear threat, no matter how irresponsible, must be evaluated and assessed in a serious manner. That said, it is obvious to all that nuclear threats are more likely than not to be bluffs. Vladimir Putin and some in his inner and outer circles issued nuclear warnings not seen since the Cold War. While the Biden administration publicly condemned Russian threats and privately issued warnings, it did not appear to reverse any policy decision in the face of the threats. In other words, it does not appear that Russia was rewarded with concessions despite making irresponsible statements. That said, the administration likely limited its range of responses *ex ante* to preclude a nuclear crisis. It is interesting to reflect upon what the United States would have done in a counterfactual world where Russia did not possess nuclear weapons.[5]

Third, the strategic nuclear balance has not appeared to play a significant role in this crisis. Nuclear scholars have long argued over whether or not strategic nuclear superiority conveys advantages in a crisis, and if so, how one would measure both nuclear primacy and its consequences.[6] Indeed, in an important 2006 article, Daryl Press and Keir Lieber suggested that the United States possessed a meaningful first strike capability versus Russia,[7] while Matthew Kroenig has argued that nuclear primacy carries significant benefits for its possessor.[8] No doubt Russia's strategic forces have improved quite a bit since 2006, and the United States is also engaged in a significant and expensive modernization of its own forces. Yet throughout the crisis, few have seemed to note (let alone analyze) what the actual strategic balance is and whether it has affected decision-making in either Moscow or Washington, DC. Arguably, this is because the conflict remains a proxy war; if American or NATO forces were directly involved in fighting Russian forces on their soil, perhaps the strategic balance would come into play. Still, it is notable how little discussion there has been over the state, readiness, and size of the two largest nuclear powers' forces. Indeed, there was some effort to continue strategic arms control limitations either formally or informally.

Fourth, the war has not, as of yet, appeared to generate increases in global proliferation pressures or the viability of the nuclear non-proliferation regime. There was reason in February 2022 to think it might. Ukraine had foresworn its access to weapons left behind by the former Soviet Union after the latter's collapse in exchange for weak security guarantees. Ukraine's actual access to these weapons was uncertain and contested, but there is a belief in some corners that it had near-nuclear status. If Ukraine had acquired these weapons, a powerful argument could be made that Russia would have been deterred from invading.

It might be argued that the key lesson for any state that was facing security threats from a nuclear neighbor that did not want to accede to pressure and coercion was that it had to make a choice. Either it could enter a tight, binding security alliance with the United States—similar to NATO—or it could develop its own nuclear weapons. States such as Vietnam, facing a nuclear China, or the Arab Gulf states, concerned about Iran's nascent nuclear program, would either seek a tight alliance or their own nuclear weapons. Even those states under America's nuclear security umbrella, like South Korea and Japan, might feel that they needed their own nuclear weapons to offset the credibility concerns behind United States security guarantees.

One could also imagine a concern about the wider Nuclear Non-Proliferation Treaty regime. The regime has always been vexed by an obvious inequality between the states that possess nuclear weapons and those that have foresworn them. There are a variety of reasons that states abjure nuclear weapons, but one is the promise that nuclear weapons states won't exploit their unfair advantage to coerce and commit aggression against non-nuclear states. In other words, the non-nuclear states may expect the rest of the world, including and especially the nuclear weapons states, to respond vigorously to protect them from coercion and reverse any aggression from a nuclear-armed state. That Russia felt able to invade Ukraine and escape punishment and even censure from many parts of the world, including nuclear weapons states like China, India, and even Israel, had to give states without nuclear weapons pause.

While it is still early, proliferation pressures do not seem considerably stronger than they were before the crisis. The United States worked to strengthen and deepen its nuclear cooperation with South Korea, which appears to have lessened proliferation pressures there for the time being. Before the October 7, 2023, Hamas attack on Israel, the United States was working on a complex deal with Saudi Arabia that might have provided strong security guarantees. Interestingly, it appears that states that do face intense security challenges prefer to benefit from the United States extending its nuclear deterrence as opposed to developing their own atomic weapons. Proliferation dynamics could obviously change, especially if Ukraine loses the war and the United States does little to prevent the loss. Looking at a map, however, most of the world is free from sharp geopolitical pressures, and where those pressures exist, the states involved either possess the bomb, like South Asia, or are enmeshed in America's nuclear umbrella.

What has been less clear?

One issue is whether or not a nuclear environment made the war more or less likely, and once war began, whether nuclear use was more or less likely. During the Cold War, strategist Glenn Snyder posited the concept of the stability-instability paradox.[9] Snyder highlighted a dilemma: if the strategic balance between two nuclear powers in a conflict is stable (or in other words, both sides are mutually vulnerable), then matters at the sub-strategic levels will be more uncertain and potentially violent. In other words, if nuclear arsenals of the two competing players cancel each other out, then they do not have to worry about a conventional war, or even the use of battlefield nuclear weapons, escalating to a strategic exchange.

The international relations scholar Robert Jervis challenged this framing, arguing it relied on an unrealistic certainty about how each side would respond in a crisis.[10] Jervis claimed that there was enough uncertainty in how each side would respond, enough incentive to manipulate risk in ways that would heighten this uncertainty, and enough pathways to inadvertent escalation to actually deter conflict between nuclear powers at lower levels.

Scholar Colin Kahl, who served as US under secretary of defense for policy between April 2021 and September 2023, has noted that it is unclear what counts for uncertainties in the stability-instability paradox.[11] Both Russia and the United States sought to achieve their interests without triggering a nuclear war. Russia had more at stake in the conflict, whereas the United States (and its allies) had greater conventional capabilities. To Kahl, this meant Russia was more likely to manipulate the risk inherent in the conflict by making nuclear threats, whereas the burden on the United States was to manage risks. To accomplish the latter, the Biden administration, controversially, said that while it would help Ukraine, it would not risk World War III while doing so, though it would risk World War III to defend NATO territory. The administration would also call out and condemn Russian nuclear threats and convey that nuclear use would beget a consequential response.

As discussed earlier, Russia's threats appeared to have limited effects, and the pathways and likelihood of inadvertent escalation were less likely than many scholars in the Jervis vein predicted. That said, it is hard to know what to make of Russia's nuclear threats. Did Putin's nuclear red lines evolve over time? Was Russia dissuaded by United States threats of catastrophic consequences if it used nuclear weapons? Or was it the public statements by third parties like India and, most surprisingly, China, which persuaded Russia to resist? Or was it all a bluff? Could it be that the United States response was *too* cautious, and that it paid too-close heed to Russian threats it never planned to carry out? Is it fair to judge America's reactions in February 2022 when, unlike now, the United States possessed little actual evidence of how Putin would react to various escalatory moves?

The truth is we can't know. As Janice Gross Stein contends, even the cautious and arguably successful "learning by doing" strategy can ultimately fail, since policymakers using "an incremental strategy may cross an adversary's threshold of escalation without knowing they are doing so."[12] Or we could be lulled into focusing on the wrong threats: a recent commentary suggested that focusing on Russia's battlefield use may blind US analysts to a potentially more likely and certainly more terrifying atomic attack on NATO itself.[13]

This leads to a larger unknown: How might the crisis affect another geopolitical hotspot where two nuclear powers might square off, the Taiwan Strait? There are two ways of looking at this.[14] On the one hand, China might interpret the Biden administration's clear statement that it sought to avoid a direct military clash with Russia and put a premium on reducing nuclear risk as a sign of weakness. China's leaders might reason that the same logic would apply if they were to invade Taiwan: the United States might provide military aid and support—arguably a harder task when it comes to an island nation—but would not intervene with its own military forces. In other words, the United States would be deterred from a conventional military response by China's nuclear forces.

On the other hand, China probably can't help but notice how poorly a job Russia's previously esteemed military forces did trying to accomplish the far easier mission of invading a contiguous land power. President Xi Jinping's purge of his Strategic Rocket Forces, apparently due to concerns about widespread corruption, may also indicate that China is not ready for major combat. China has also presumably noticed how impressive US intelligence capabilities were, and how much risk it was willing to take by providing military capabilities that decimated Russia's forces. Furthermore, President Joseph Biden has made it clear he sees the Taiwan scenario differently than Russia's war with Ukraine, and so Beijing should not count on the United States standing aside in a Taiwan conflict. It is also important to note that for whatever other reckless, aggressive actions China has taken in recent years, it has come out strongly against nuclear use by Russia; one could have imagined China saying nothing, or issuing private warnings instead of public statements.

How have nuclear dynamics affected the war in Ukraine? The answers are, unfortunately, murky and even unknowable. Nuclear weapons remain a terrible, catastrophic threat; their particular characteristics induce what some people might consider undue caution while at the same time incentivizing irresponsible geopolitical behavior. It is hard to say much *ex ante*, except to disregard anyone who makes strong claims in one direction or another: that Russia would never use nuclear weapons or that the United States has already pushed too hard and made the risk of nuclear war far too high. The past two years reveals the answer lies frustratingly in between those two extremes and is likely to remain there.

NOTES

1. Francis J. Gavin, *Nuclear Weapons and American Grand Strategy* (Washington, DC: Brookings Institution Press, 2020).

2. For an overview, see Mark S. Bell and Julia MacDonald, "How to Think about Nuclear Crises," *Texas National Security Review* 2, no. 2 (February 2019): 40–65, http://tnsr.org/wp-content/uploads/2019/03/TNSR-Journal-Vol-2-Issue-2-Bell-and-Macdonald.pdf; for the ensuing debate, see Brendan Rittenhouse Green and Austin Long's argument (as well as Bell and Macdonald's reply) in Green et al., "Contrasting Views on How to Code a Nuclear Crisis," *Texas National Security Review* 2, no. 4 (August 2019): 130–139, https://tnsr.org/wp-content/uploads/2019/10/Correspondence_TNSR-Vol-2-Issue-4.pdf.

3. Janice Gross Stein, "Escalation Management in Ukraine: 'Learning by Doing' in Response to 'The Threat that Leaves Something to Chance,'" *Texas National Security Review* 6, no. 3 (Summer 2023): 29–50, https://tnsr.org/2023/06/escalation-management-in-ukraine-learning-by-doing-in-response-to-the-threat-that-leaves-something-to-chance/.

4. Stein, "Escalation Management in Ukraine."

5. The obvious answer might be that the United States would have felt less constrained, provided more lethal aid, and perhaps considered intervening more directly. On the other hand, would the United States have cared as much about the behavior of a non-nuclear Russia toward a country where few core American interests were engaged, especially given that NATO likely possessed powerful enough forces to prevent incursions beyond Ukraine?

6. Todd S. Sescher and Matthew Furhmann, *Nuclear Weapons and Coercive Diplomacy* (Cambridge, UK: Cambridge University Press, 2017).

7. Daryl Press and Keir Lieber, "The End of MAD? The Nuclear Dimension of U.S. Primacy," *International Security* 30, no. 4 (Spring 2006): 7–44, https://www.belfercenter.org/sites/default/files/legacy/files/is3004_advanceproof_lieberandpress.pdf.

8. Matthew Kroenig, "Nuclear Superiority and the Balance of Resolve: Explaining Nuclear Crisis Outcomes," *International Organization* 67, no. 1 (Winter 2013): 141–171.

9. Glenn Synder, *The Balance of Power and the Balance of Terror* (Chandler, 1965).

10. Robert Jervis, *The Meaning of the Nuclear Revolution* (Ithaca, NY: Cornell University Press, 1989).

11. Colin Kahl, "The Stability-Instability Paradox: Managing Nuclear Escalation Risks in Ukraine," CISAC Stanford, video, published November 8, 2023, https://www .youtube.com/watch?v=4OsTLN7A1sw

12. Stein, "Escalation Management in Ukraine."

13. Peter Schroeder, "The Real Russian Threat: The West is Worried about the Wrong Escalation Risks," *Foreign Affairs*, December 20, 2023, https://www.foreignaffairs .com/ukraine/real-russian-nuclear-threat.

14. For an excellent overview, see Hal Brands, "Welcome to the New Era of Nuclear Brinkmanship," *Bloomberg Opinion*, August 27, 2023, https://www.bloomberg.com /opinion/articles/2023-08-27/how-nuclear-threats-not-weapons-have-shaped-the-war-in -ukraine.

Chapter Eleven

Fallacies of Strategic Thinking in the Ukraine War

Thomas G. Mahnken and Joshua Baker

Ever since the outbreak of the Ukraine War in February 2022, observers have mined the conflict for insights into the changing character of war. The fact that the conflict has unfolded in ways that defied expectations highlights the challenges associated with measuring military power. As Phillips O'Brien noted, "the entire shape of the war is very different from what experts had imagined."[1] Instead of the lighting war that many expected, Russia's invasion of Ukraine was, according to O'Brien, "chaotic and slow." Whereas many assumed that Ukrainian forces would be quickly routed, they instead fought with an intensity, determination, and effectiveness that surprised many in the West, let alone Vladimir Putin and Russian military leaders. The purpose of this chapter is to use the Ukraine War and predictions regarding its character, course, and outcome to explore an enduring set of challenges that soldiers, statesmen, and scholars face as they attempt to understand a war both in prospect and as it unfolds. It is organized into four parts, proceeding chronologically, examining (1) prewar assertions of the rationality of war and of Vladimir Putin, (2) prewar and early wartime assessments of the military balance between Russia and Ukraine, (3) fallacies of interaction and adaptation

Thomas G. Mahnken is a professor of the practice with the Merrill Center for Strategic Studies at the Johns Hopkins School of Advanced International Studies and the president and CEO of the Center for Strategic and Budgetary Assessments. Joshua Baker is a recent graduate of the Johns Hopkins School of Advanced International Studies, where he concentrated in security, strategy, statecraft, and international economics.

during the course of the war, and (4) more recent wishful thinking about the termination of the war.

Fallacies of Rationality

Before assessing the quality of strategic thought on the Ukraine War itself, it is useful to go back to the months leading up to the Russian invasion of February 24, 2022. During this period we encounter three fallacies: one about the rationality of war and two about the rationality of Vladimir Putin as an adversary. The first, the *Fallacy of the Irrationality of War*, is an expression of the belief that the use of force flows from the breakdown of policy rather than serving as its extension. This view, which is widespread in the United States and in Western societies more broadly, holds that wars occur due to irrational behavior or accident rather than through an assessment of risk and reward on the part of the belligerents. At its heart, it represents a denial of the fact that some aims are important enough to use force to achieve and that force can serve as an instrument of policy.

In the months leading up to the Russian invasion of Ukraine, there was plenty of wishful thinking that such a war would be irrational. Writing in November 2021, Jeff Hawn argued that Russia wasn't about to attack Ukraine because occupying its neighbor "would be expensive, dangerous, and pointless." To the contrary, he blamed the "reckless behavior" of Western governments in vowing to defend Ukraine's territorial sovereignty for increased tensions. At no point in the article did he mention the name "Vladimir Putin."[2] Before war broke out, journalist David Ignatius described diplomatic talks between the United States and Russia as being plagued with "nonstarter" proposals which left little "wiggle room" for diplomacy to do its work.[3] Such a description probably led readers to think that war between Ukraine and Russia was the result of diplomatic failure rather than the next evolution of Russian policy.

Contrary to such wishful thinking, Putin saw the use of force against Ukraine as a rational option. He made it clear in public statements long before launching the war that he saw Ukraine's statehood as illegitimate and claimed that Ukraine was an integral part of Russia. Members of Putin's inner circle expressed similar sentiment in the lead-up to the invasion. Former prime minister Dmitry Medvedev on numerous occasions had described Russians and Ukrainians as one people, disregarding Ukraine's independent identity from Russia. Sergey Lavrov, Russia's foreign minister, went so far as to describe former Soviet republics as "orphans," insinuating that Moscow intended to exert control over its neighbors. Putin, therefore, was not seeking a diplomatic solution over Ukraine, but had already decided to further subvert Ukrainian independence and identity by any means necessary.[4]

If the Fallacy of the Irrationality of War is ultimately a philosophical statement about the disutility of force to achieve political aims, then the *Fallacy of the Irrational Adversary* represents a tendency to dismiss adversaries whose decision-making calculus differs from our own as "irrational." At its core, it represents a lack of strategic empathy—the ability to understand a situation from the perspective of another. Strategic empathy involves an understanding of both the motives of an adversary as well as the myriad conditions that influence their decision-making. To the contrary, too often observers fall prey to analogous thinking, assuming that an adversary will behave as they have done in the past or that they will make the same rational calculations as we do.[5] The United States has failed the test of strategy empathy repeatedly, characterizing such adversaries as Saddam Hussein, Slobodan Milošević, and the three generations of the Kim family who have ruled North Korea as insane or irrational rather than seeking an understanding of their decision-making.

In July 2021, Putin published a five-thousand-word essay offering insight into his world view and understanding of history. In this piece, Putin rejected Ukrainian independence and described Russians and Ukrainians as "one people." Additionally, he blamed poor Russo-Ukrainian relations on Western "agents." Most important, Putin revealed his true intentions by hinting that Russia ought to annex additional territory from Ukraine. He boldly claimed that he was "becoming more and more convinced of this: Kyiv simply does not need the Donbas."[6] But instead of taking Putin at his word, it appears that most analysts simply dismissed his rationale as illogical.

In the lead-up to Russia's invasion of Ukraine, there was a tendency among some observers to portray Putin as "completely bonkers" or "stark raving mad," even speculating that he might have become unhinged due to pandemic isolation or illness.[7] Indeed, leaders such as British Prime Minister Boris Johnson and French President Emmanuel Macron publicly cast doubt on Putin's rationality. In fact, under Putin's leadership Russia had already established a track record of using force to achieve policy goals in situations where Western observers predicted he would not, including in Georgia in 2008, Ukraine in 2014, and in Syria during 2015.[8]

Similarly, a number of observers took the buildup of Russian forces on Ukraine's border to be a bluff or even a cry for attention rather than a serious military threat. As Samuel Cranny-Evans testified before the British Parliament on February 8, 2022:

In terms of the present build-up, there is a lot of evidence to suggest that it is more about opening a dialogue between Russia and the US. There are obviously Russia's security concerns on Ukraine, but we know that a much bigger frustration for the Kremlin is the way in which it feels left out of some of the global discussions, whether that is right or wrong. That is not to excuse them, but my perception is that, for the Kremlin, this is much more about having a conversation with the big players around the table than it is about Ukraine.[9]

The fraternal twin of the Fallacy of the Irrational Adversary, the *Fallacy of the Hyper-Rational Adversary*, was also present in prewar assessments of Putin's behavior. This fallacy is based upon the belief that adversaries carefully calculate their actions based upon a universal logic. Such a fallacy lies at the heart of much deterrence theory, as well as some approaches to strategic bombing theory.[10] Like its fraternal twin, the Fallacy of the Irrational Adversary, it represents a failure to embrace strategic empathy. In this case, however, observers substitute a mechanistic rationality for an understanding of an individual leader's frame of reference.

A number of scholars embraced such a view of Vladimir Putin in the lead-up to his invasion of Ukraine. As Dmitri Trenin wrote in *Foreign Affairs* in December 2021, "Despite the Western media's predilection for depicting Putin as reckless, he is, in fact cautious and calculating, particularly when it comes to the use of force. Putin is not risk-averse—operations in Chechnya, Crimea, and Syria are proof of that—but in his mind, the benefit must outweigh the cost. He won't invade Ukraine simply because of its leaders' Western orientations."[11]

Putin is neither irrational nor someone who calculates mechanically according to a universal logic. Rather he, like other leaders, acts according to his own view of world events, which is based upon his own incomplete and imperfect sources of information. He made the case for conquering Ukraine long before acting on it and has continued to articulate a historical case for Russia's invasion of Ukraine.[12] One doesn't need to agree with Putin's stilted view of history to acknowledge the fact that it influences his behavior. In the end, however, the failure to empathize with Putin led observers to dismiss or misinterpret his actions in the lead-up to Russia's attack on Ukraine.

Fallacies of Assessment

A second set of mis-assessments took hold in the hours and days following Russia's attack on Ukraine. These flowed from the pervasive challenges associated with assessing military balances, particularly in peacetime.[13] Absent the test of war, a violent struggle between belligerents, it is difficult to accurately weigh the military balance. Observers tend to measure that which can be quantified while downplaying or ignoring those vital dimensions of military power that defy quantification such as leadership, will, competence, and ability to adapt under fire. Similarly, they may draw inapt analogies to the past behavior of the belligerents or import assumptions from one situation to another. As a post-mortem of prewar wargames conducted by the RAND Corporation showed, even though the Russian military possessed many of the advantages posited in simulations conducted before the war, such as "abundant time to prepare its plans and forces for the attack, freedom to choose when and how the war would begin, the ability to operate from Belarusian territory, and an absence of competing security demands that would limit its ability to shift forces from elsewhere in Russia to participate in the operation," it nonetheless squandered them. Moreover, "Designing an operation based on the optimistic assumption that a lightning attack would overwhelm a weak Ukrainian defense opened the door to a catastrophic Russian failure when the defenders turned out to be far more determined than expected."[14]

Scholars speculating on the shape of a prospective campaign in Ukraine tended to both overestimate Russian military capabilities and underestimate those of Ukraine. For example, writing on the eve of the Russian invasion, Michael Kofman and Jeffrey Edmonds envisioned an air campaign that would feature "hundreds of bombers as well as ground-launched cruise and ballistic missiles." On the other side of the ledger, they argued that "Ukrainian air defenses are in short supply, and they would be unlikely to provide effective cover for most of the country's ground troops. They would be quickly overwhelmed."[15]

Overestimation of the Russians was paired with underestimation of the Ukrainians. As Kofman and Edmonds put it:

> The Ukrainian military has substantially improved since 2014, thanks to Western assistance, and it has gained combat experience from the war in the Donbas. But the experience is largely limited to trench warfare and artillery skirmishes. Kyiv is still ill prepared for a renewed Russian invasion of this scale. Ukraine's military is generally understaffed and has limited familiarity with warfare designed to surprise and disrupt enemies. Its armed forces are composed of thousands of conscripts with limited experience. Russian battalion tactical groups, by contrast, are filled with more skilled, contract servicemen. Ukraine's air force is dated and stands no chance against its Russian counterpart.[16]

Both analysts also assumed that the Ukrainian forces would be unable to mount an "active defense" in a country as vast as Ukraine. In the likely event that the country was quickly overwhelmed, Kofman and Edmonds suggested that it could adopt "guerrilla warfare" tactics or, as a last resort, retreat into urban areas and draw Russian units into a costly urban warfare campaign.

The *Fallacy of Overestimation* is the embodiment of worst-case thinking. It flows from giving too much weight to an adversary's strengths and one's own weaknesses. It often features (consciously or unconsciously) in military thinking, where it is codified in "worst-case planning." Similarly, intelligence assessments that seek to avoid strategic surprise can emphasize an adversary's strengths and one's own weaknesses. Although the Fallacy of Overestimation may sometimes be prudent, it causes statesmen and strategists to discard viable strategic options.[17] For example, the overestimation of Russian military capabilities on the brink of Moscow's attack on Kyiv yielded an unwarranted sense of fatalism that led policymakers to neglect preparing for the possibility that a Russian attack would not lead to a quick, decisive victory over Ukraine.

This tendency to overestimate Russian military capabilities persisted both before and during the early phases of the war. Writing in January 2022, Samuel Charap and Scott Boston of the RAND Corporation argued that "Russia has the ability to carry out a large-scale joint offensive operation involving tens of thousands of personnel, thousands of armored vehicles, and hundreds of combat aircraft. . . . Ukrainian forces would begin the conflict nearly surrounded from the very start."[18] Similarly, Jack Detsch predicted that Russian missile salvoes "would turn the skies above Kyiv, Ukraine, into an effective no-go zone: using short-range missiles to knock out Ukraine's runways, airports, and fighters on the ground."[19]

Writing on the eve of the war, Robert Kagan also predicted disaster: "A final word about Ukraine: It will likely cease to exist as an independent entity. . . . After Russia installs a government, expect Ukraine's new Moscow-directed rulers to seek the eventual legal incorporation of Ukraine into Russia."[20] Others similarly argued that a Russian invasion would inevitably lead to the collapse of the Ukrainian military, leading to an insurgency against Russian occupation.[21] The belief that the conquest of Ukraine was a *fait accompli* not only spawned a sort of script writing, described further below, but also blinded observers to the possibility that Ukraine's war with Russia might become a protracted one and delayed efforts to assist the Ukrainian government.

Within the Kremlin, Putin and his generals similarly overestimated the capabilities of their armed forces. As Roger N. McDermott noted, "Putin's flawed decision-making likely resulted not only from badly crafted intelligence—especially from the FSB—but also from his largely successful *previous* experience of using military force."[22] Additionally, Russia's General Staff vested considerable confidence in the capabilities of their intelligence services and armed forces, thus believing any war with Ukraine would be short. As such, Putin and his military commanders "created an invasion plan that was riddled with false assumptions, arbitrary political guidance, and planning errors that departed from key Russian military principles."[23]

Soon after the initial invasion began, however, the Russian situation began to deteriorate rapidly. Russian advances into Ukraine met stiffer than expected resistance. The invasion force slowed, creating miles-long traffic jams on Ukrainian roadways, which meant that Russian artillery was often beyond range of Ukrainian batteries, even while Ukrainian guns could range the forward Russian positions. The Russians found themselves facing the challenge of resupply. Moreover, attacks throughout the depth of Russian forces advancing on Kyiv made the Russians reluctant to push forward electronic warfare and air defense systems out of fear that they would likely be destroyed or captured by Ukrainian forces. This had two consequences: the suppression of Ukrainian air defenses and communications capabilities lasted only for the first week of the invasion.[24]

Assessments of Ukraine's armed forces that underplayed their effectiveness likely flowed from a number of sources. Overall, observers paid much more attention to the Russian side of the balance than to Ukraine. Moreover, to the extent that they did consider Ukraine's military capabilities, it is unclear how heavily US training of and assistance to Ukrainian forces in the lead-up to the Russian attack weighed in assessments of the military balance. Although Ukrainian forces had seen combat in eastern Ukraine since 2014, such experience was of limited value in assessing their effectiveness against a large-scale Russian invasion.

As the Russian invasion failed, analysts tended to emphasize Russian military incompetence as the sole or main reason why Putin failed to achieve his objectives.[25] Such explanations not only led to false conclusions, but also detracted from the fact that the Ukrainian military fought with a level of intensity, determination, and professionalism that was not widely expected prior to the outbreak of the war. Even some Ukrainian commanders were shocked by their own troops' determination to continue to fight and defend Mariupol despite impending encirclement.[26] By the summer of 2023, Ukrainian forces had driven Russian troops back from roughly half of the territory they had seized since the invasion began. As a result, the Ukrainian military appeared far more powerful and the Russian military appeared far weaker than prewar expectations.[27]

The course of the initial phase of the war caused observers to overcorrect their prewar overestimation of Russian forces and underestimation of the Ukrainians. Instead, there was an unwarranted overemphasis on Russian failures and Ukrainian successes. Despite a poor track record overall, in some cases Russian forces demonstrated their ability to conduct complex operations. During their retreat from Kherson in November 2022, for example, the Russians succeeded in withdrawing two army-sized groupings from the right bank of the Dnipro River, including an estimated 42,370 troops, 253 tanks, 400 armored personnel carriers of various type, and several thousand wheeled vehicles, all to fight another day. Such a task is no small feat and demonstrated a level of competence within the Russian military.[28] In addition, the Russian military demonstrated its ability to innovate and adapt, albeit at a high cost. In early 2022, Russia began to deploy large elements of the Wagner mercenary group around Bakhmut and throughout eastern Ukraine. In these areas, Wagner operatives and conscripts engaged in human wave assaults against prepared Ukrainian defenses. Although such tactics may seem archaic, they were not launched out of desperation, but instead because they allowed Russian commanders to identify weaknesses in Ukrainian defenses to be exploited later. They also helped to identify strong points in Ukrainian defenses, thus revealing their positions to inevitable Russian counterbattery fires.[29]

Disregarding Russia's ability to adapt and innovate in the war led to unrealistic expectations for Ukraine in future operations. Previous Ukrainian successes at Kyiv, Kharkiv, and Kherson encouraged expectations that the next Ukrainian offensive—one equipped with Western hardware such as Leopard tanks and armored Bradley Fighting Vehicles—would break through Russian defenses or sever Russia's land bridge to Crimea.[30] In fact, despite achieving some limited successes, Ukraine's summer offensive failed to achieve the breakthrough that many Western observers had hoped for. The breakthrough Ukraine desired was still possible, but as Stephen Biddle noted, any Ukrainian success predicated on the belief that Russian forces remain "ill prepared . . . logistically unsupported," and composed of troops who were "unmotivated and unwilling to defend their positions" was not.[31]

Fallacies of Interaction

The Russian military has evolved since its invasion of Ukraine, just as Ukrainian armed forces had in the years following the annexation of Crimea in 2014 and have continued to do in the face of Russian attack. This is yet another reminder that war is an interactive endeavor. And yet, as the initial campaigns of the Ukraine War unfolded, both belligerents and observers fell prey to fallacies of interaction and adaptation.

One common fallacy of interaction is the *Fallacy of the Silver Bullet*. This flows from the mistaken belief that some instrument of war holds the master key to sound policy and strategy. It is based upon the premise that some new way of war has rendered previous approaches obsolete. By contrast, how belligerents combine technology with innovative doctrine and organization and how they adapt to their adversary have historically proven more important than the advent of new weapons themselves.[32]

Past generations of strategic theorists saw the advent of strategic bombing in the 1920s and 1930s as the key to preventing war, just as some nuclear theorists believed that in the nuclear age deterrence had replaced warfighting as the central purpose of military organization. In the lead-up to and early phases of the Ukraine War, a number of analysts viewed cyber operations as a silver bullet that would lead to a decisive strategic result for Russia. As Kofman and Edmonds wrote, "In addition to relying on traditional firepower, a Russian operation would be supported by electronic warfare. . . . Ukrainian commanders could suddenly find it impossible to use established channels to coordinate their responses to Russia's invasion, forcing them to use less secure means of communication."[33] Similarly, they argued that "achieving information dominance during a conflict is a cornerstone of Russian military strategy, and Moscow could also use its cyber-capabilities to engage in psychological warfare."

Although a full accounting of the effectiveness will take time, there is nonetheless little evidence that Russian cyber operations produced strategic effects, such as diminishing the Ukrainians' will to resist.[34] The minimal effect of cyber operations in the Ukraine War appears to have been the result of three complementary developments. First, in some cases there was an overestimation of just what Russian cyber operations could accomplish. Second, it appears that Russian forces did not conduct cyber operations to the fullest extent possible because they hoped to capture Ukraine intact and wanted to be able to use its infrastructure for their own purposes. Third, Ukrainians and others took actions to defend themselves against Russian cyberattacks, further diminishing their effectiveness. Although the Russian military did launch an attack on the Viasat satellite communication network, for example, such an attack had a negligible effect on Ukrainian operations both because the attack was quickly countered and because Ukrainian forces were not dependent upon it for command and control.[35]

Another common fallacy of interaction is the *Fallacy of Script Writing.* This fallacy consists of the notion that one side in a conflict can dictate the other side's choices. It represents a denial of the agency of the adversary and a refusal to consider the impact of interaction.

It seems clear that Russian decision-makers engaged in script writing in planning the invasion of Ukraine. It appears, for example, that Russia's theory of victory was predicated upon Moscow's ability to destabilize and disorganize Ukraine internally, which would in turn incapacitate the Ukrainian government, disable military command and control, undermine public confidence in the government, and minimize aid from international partners. The Russian theory of victory rested upon Moscow's ability to gain the support of Ukrainian elites for the invasion. As a result, the Russian military anticipated encountering little sustained, organized resistance.[36] In assessing the prewar situation, Russian planners appear to have seen what they wanted to see and disregarded evidence that suggested that most Ukrainians would view Russians as occupiers rather than liberators.[37]

Many military experts fell prey to their own version of the Fallacy of Script Writing, arguing that there was literally nothing that Ukraine could do to prevent a Russian victory, including the provision of Western military assistance to Kyiv. In an essay tellingly titled "The West's Weapons Won't Make Any Difference to Ukraine," Samuel Charap and Scott Boston argued,

> In short, the military balance between Russia and Ukraine is so lopsided in Moscow's favor that any assistance Washington might provide in coming weeks would be largely irrelevant in determining the outcome of a conflict should it begin. Russia's advantages in capacity, capability, and geography combine to pose insurmountable challenges for Ukrainian forces tasked with defending their country. The argument for aid—changing the course of the war—thus does not hold water.[38]

Such an argument denied Ukraine agency in the conflict.

We should be glad that Russian decision-makers fell prey to script writing. As a result, what could have been a short war has become a protracted one. Of course, such an outcome wasn't inevitable. Had Russian forces quickly seized Hostomel Airport, as they had planned, and driven quickly on to Kyiv, the result might have been different. Similarly, had Ukrainian President Volodymyr Zelensky lost his nerve and fled Ukraine, or had Russian forces killed or captured him, then today's conversation about the Ukraine War would be much different.

Fallacies of War Termination

The initial Russian campaign having failed to deliver a quick, decisive victory, and the 2023 Ukrainian counteroffensive having similarly failed to deliver a decisive result, has led both sides to engage in a war of attrition. Accordingly, observers have paid growing attention to the process of terminating the war.

The *Fallacy of Decisive Victory* is based upon the false dichotomy between absolute, decisive victory and failure. Put another way, it is a reflection of the belief that, contrary to Carl von Clausewitz's counsel, the results of war *are* final. Because we are uncomfortable with war, we like to think we can wish it away. However, as Margaret MacMillan writes,

> When the war in Ukraine finally comes to an end, as all wars do, Ukraine and its supporters may well hope for an overwhelming victory and the fall of the Putin regime. Yet if Russia is left in turmoil, bitter and isolated, with many of its leaders and people blaming others for its failures, as so many Germans did in those interwar decades, then the end of one war could simply lay the groundwork for another.[39]

The Fallacy of the Decisive Victory can be seen in forecasts that either Moscow or Kyiv will win an overwhelming victory that will end the conflict decisively. As discussed throughout this chapter, commentators and analysts alike thought Russia would make quick work of Ukraine through overwhelming firepower and maneuver warfare. When that outcome failed to materialize, commentators made the mistake of assuming that once Ukraine was equipped with Western equipment, Ukrainian forces could achieve a quick victory over Russia. Ukrainian successes during the Kharkiv and Kherson offensives seemed to support such a possibility, which led many in the West to place "undue emphasis" on the outcome of Ukraine's summer 2023 offensive.[40]

Although that offensive yielded some minor victories (including on the Black Sea), it failed to achieve a decisive breakthrough. Russia's utilization of "deep defense," at least for the time being, appears too much for Ukrainian forces to handle. Additionally, Russia's transition to a "deep defense" also signals Moscow's intent to prepare for a long war, one in which Russia's frontline troops seem to be well resourced and more willing to defend their positions.[41] It is therefore essential that Ukraine, along with its Western backers, prepare for a long war, one that closely resembles the great wars of the 20th century. Like the Ukraine War, such conflicts were rooted in ideology and fueled by nationalist desires. For his part, Putin continues to deny the existence of a Ukrainian state and shows no interest in meeting Ukraine earnestly at the negotiating table. Ukraine, on the other hand, appears equally unwavering in its commitment to fight on and unwilling to negotiate with Putin. The conflict, therefore, reminds us that, absent the total overthrow of an adversary, wars end through a combination of battlefield success and political negotiation: how far one army is able to go militarily influences how much that country's government can demand politically. The Ukraine War, therefore, has yet to run its course, meaning that more fighting is to be expected.

Conclusion

A central argument of this chapter is that an awareness of the pitfalls that soldiers, statesmen, and scholars frequently fall prey to is a useful starting point to formulating and implementing sound strategy. In particular, the analytical track record of the Ukraine War serves as a sharp reminder that understanding the features of a future war from the perspective of peace is difficult. Indeed, it is one of the most fundamental challenges that members of the military profession face, and one of the things that separates the military profession from other occupations. The late Sir Michael Howard likened the challenge facing peacetime military planners to that of a ship's crew attempting to navigate by dead reckoning through a thick fog of peace.[42] We should study where assessments went wrong but also realize that there are limits to predicting *a priori* the course and outcome of wars.

A key dimension of this challenge has to do with the unknowable response of an adversary to the firing of the first shot. Military overseers, Howard asserted, must "guess whether the first shock of battle will steel the enemy's resolve and stiffen his resistance, or whether, like a Bologna flask, it will shatter as soon as its surface is scratched."[43] The violent interaction of belligerents, infused with a mixture of rationality, passion, and chance, is a central characteristic of war, yet understanding that interaction—let alone predicting it in advance—is exceedingly difficult. The Ukraine War was shaped decisively not just by Russian missteps in the early phases of the war, but also by heroic Ukrainian resistance. Had things gone differently, had Russian forces proven to be more competent or even just luckier and had Ukrainian resistance been less pronounced, then the resulting war would have unfolded much differently, and we would be drawing different lessons from it.

Second, although predicting the features of a future war from the perspective of peace is challenging, the onset of war does not clarify everything. To the contrary: understanding the character of an ongoing conflict is itself difficult. As Clausewitz famously wrote, "The first, the supreme, the most far-reaching act of judgment that the statesman and commander have to make is to establish by that test the kind of war on which they are embarking; neither mistaking it for, nor trying to turn it into, something that is alien to its nature."[44] The course of the war has witnessed both overestimation and underestimation of the capabilities of both Russian and Ukrainian forces.

Third, and relatedly, learning the lessons of war is difficult, and learning the lessons of an ongoing war, replete with incomplete and inaccurate information, is even more challenging. It is particularly difficult to learn the right lessons rather than just reinforcing preconceived notions.

Finally, the determinants of success in long wars are different from those in short wars. Whereas surprise, new ways of war, and operational virtuosity loom large in short conflicts, victory in protracted conflicts often hinges on other factors. Sound strategy and operational art are always at a premium, but success or failure in protracted wars often hinges on one side's ability to out-produce the other, maintain its societal cohesion while undermining that of its adversary, and gather and nurture a coalition while disrupting that of the enemy. As we look forward to the end of the Ukraine War, considerations such as these will play a more prominent role than those that framed assessments of the military balance between Russia and Ukraine before the outbreak of the war.

NOTES

1. Phillips P. O'Brien, "The War That Defied Expectations: What Ukraine Revealed About Military Power," *Foreign Affairs*, July 27, 2023, https://www.foreignaffairs.com /ukraine/war-defied-expectations.

2. Jeff Hawn, "Russia Isn't About to Attack Ukraine: Moscow Occupying Its Neighbor Would Be Expensive, Dangerous, and Pointless," *Foreign Policy*, November 17, 2021, https://foreignpolicy.com/2021/11/17/russia-isnt-about-to-attack-ukraine/.

3. David Ignatius, "As the U.S. and Russia Debate Ukraine, It's Hard to See Wiggle Room," *Washington Post*, January 11, 2022.

4. Jack Watling and Nick Reynolds, *The Plot to Destroy Ukraine* (London: Royal United Services Institute, February 2022), 4, https://www.rusi.org/explore-our-research /publications/special-resources/plot-destroy-ukraine.

5. Claire Yorke, "Is Empathy a Strategic Imperative? A Review Essay," *Journal of Strategic Studies* 46, no. 5 (2023): 1082–1102, https://doi.org/10.1080/01402390.2022.2152800.

6. Vladimir Putin, "On the Historical Unity of Russians and Ukrainians," Presidential Administration of Russia, July 12, 2021, http://en.kremlin.ru/events/president/news/66181.

7. David Von Drehle, "Putin is Reading from Stalin's Playbook. Here's How the West Should Handle Him," *Washington Post*, February 22, 2022, https://www.washingtonpost.com/opinions/2022/02/22/russia-ukraine-putin-goes-stalin-crazy/.

8. Cited in Roseanne W. McManus, "Perhaps Putin Thinks Acting Crazy Is a Good Strategy. My Research Says Otherwise," *Washington Post*, March 6, 2022, https://www.washingtonpost.com/politics/2022/03/06/putin-unstable/.

9. Defence Select Committee of the Parliament of the United Kingdom, *Oral Evidence: Russia-Ukraine Crisis, HC 1064*, February 8, 2022, https://committees.parliament.uk/oralevidence/3411/pdf/.

10. See, for example, Robert A. Pape, *Bombing to Win: Air Power and Coercion in War* (Ithaca, NY: Cornell University Press, 1996).

11. Dmitri Trenin, "What Putin Really Wants in Ukraine," *Foreign Affairs*, December 28, 2021, https://www.foreignaffairs.com/articles/russia-fsu/2021-12-28/what-putin-really-wants-ukraine.

12. Yaroslav Trofimov, "How Putin's Obsession with History Led Him to Start a War," *Wall Street Journal*, February 11, 2024.

13. For examples from previous wars, see Thomas G. Mahnken, *Technology and the American Way of War Since 1945* (New York: Columbia University Press, 2008), 168–169, 196–197, 206–207.

14. Gian Gentile et al., *Revisiting RAND's Russia Wargames after the Invasion of Ukraine: Summary and Implications* (Santa Monica: RAND Corporation, 2023), 6, https://www.rand.org/pubs/research_reports/RRA2031-1.html.

15. Michael Kofman and Jeffrey Edmonds, "Russia's Shock and Awe," *Foreign Affairs*, February 22, 2022, https://www.foreignaffairs.com/articles/ukraine/2022-02-21/russias-shock-and-awe.

16. Kofman and Edmonds, "Russia's Shock and Awe."

17. The Fallacy of Underestimation is the fraternal twin of the Fallacy of Overestimation. It flows from giving too much weight to an adversary's weaknesses and one's own strengths. Whereas the Fallacy of Overestimation most often resides among military planners, its fraternal twin most often resides among civilian policymakers. Whereas the Fallacy of Overestimation makes decision-makers discard viable strategic options, the Fallacy of Underestimation makes them believe they have options that they do not in fact have.

18. Samuel Charap and Scott Boston, "U.S. Military Aid to Ukraine: A Silver Bullet?," *RAND Blog*, January 21, 2022, https://www.rand.org/pubs/commentary/2022/01/us-military-aid-to-ukraine-a-silver-bullet.html.

19. Jack Detsch, " 'They're So Destructive': Russian Missiles Could Dominate Ukraine's Skies," *Foreign Policy*, January 20, 2022, https://foreignpolicy.com/2022/01/20/russia-missiles-ukraine-biden/.

20. Robert Kagan, "What We Can Expect after Putin's Conquest of Ukraine," *Washington Post*, February 21, 2022.

21. Stephen Fidler, "How Might the War in Ukraine End? Five Factors Will Shape the Outcome," *Wall Street Journal*, March 2022.

22. Roger N. McDermott, *Did Russia's General Staff Miss Warnings of a Hard Campaign in Ukraine?* (London: Royal United Services Institute, May 2022), https://www.rusi.org/explore-our-research/publications/commentary/did-russias-general-staff-miss-warnings-hard-campaign-ukraine.

23. Dara Massicot, "What Russia Got Wrong," *Foreign Affairs*, February 8, 2023, https://www.foreignaffairs.com/ukraine/what-russia-got-wrong-moscow-failures-in-ukraine-dara-massicot.

24. Jack Watling and Nick Reynolds, *Operation Z: The Death Throes of an Imperial Delusion* (London: Royal United Services Institute, April 2022), 2, 3, 4, https://www.rusi.org/explore-our-research/publications/special-resources/operation-z-death-throes-imperial-delusion.

25. Watling and Reynolds, *Operation Z*, 2, 3, 4.

26. Watling and Reynolds, *Operation Z*.

27. O'Brien, "The War That Defied Expectations."

28. Sergio Miller, "Russia's Withdrawal from Kherson," *WavellRoom*, January 6, 2023, https://wavellroom.com/2023/01/06/russias-withdrawal-from-kherson/.

29. Jack Watling and Nick Reynolds, *Meatgrinder: Russian Tactics in the Second Year of Its Invasion of Ukraine* (London: Royal United Services Institute, May 2023), 5, https://www.rusi.org/explore-our-research/publications/special-resources/meatgrinder-russian-tactics-second-year-its-invasion-ukraine.

30. Stephen Biddle, "How Russia Stopped Ukraine's Momentum: A Deep Defense Is Hard to Beat," *Foreign Affairs*, January 29, 2024, https://www.foreignaffairs.com/ukraine/how-russia-stopped-ukraines-momentum.

31. Biddle, "How Russia Stopped Ukraine's Momentum."

32. Stephen Biddle, "Back in the Trenches," *Foreign Affairs*, August 10, 2023, https://www.foreignaffairs.com/ukraine/back-trenches-technology-warfare.

33. Kofman and Edmonds, "Russia's Shock and Awe."

34. Matthias Schulze and Mika Kerttunen, "Cyber Operations in Russia's War against Ukraine: Uses, Limitations, and Lessons Learned So Far," *SWP Comment*, no. 23 (April 2023), https://www.swp-berlin.org/publications/products/comments/2023C23_CyberOperations_UkraineWar.pdf.

35. Schulze and Kerttunen, "Cyber Operations in Russia's War Against Ukraine."

36. Jack Watling, Oleksandr V. Danylyuk, and Nick Reynolds, *Preliminary Lessons from Russia's Unconventional Operations During the Russo-Ukrainian War, February 2022–February 2023* (London: Royal United Services Institute, March 2023). Such an approach appears to have been most successful in southern Ukraine, where it contributed to Moscow's territorial gains early in the war.

37. Massicot, "What Russia Got Wrong."

38. Samuel Charap and Scott Boston, "The West's Weapons Won't Make Any Difference to Ukraine," *Foreign Policy*, January 21, 2022, https://foreignpolicy.com/2022/01/21/weapons-ukraine-russia-invasion-military/.

39. Margaret MacMillan, "How Wars Don't End," *Foreign Affairs*, June 12, 2023, https://www.foreignaffairs.com/ukraine/how-wars-dont-end.

40. Michael Kofman and Rob Lee, "Beyond Ukraine's Offensive," *Foreign Affairs*, May 10, 2023, https://www.foreignaffairs.com/ukraine/russia-war-beyond-ukraines-offensive.

41. Biddle, "How Russia Stopped Ukraine's Momentum."

42. Michael Howard, "Military Science in an Age of Peace," *Journal of the Royal United Services Institute* 119, no. 1 (March 1974): 3–11.

43. Carl von Clausewitz, *On War*, ed. and trans. by Michael Howard and Peter Paret (Princeton, NJ: Princeton University Press, 1984), 572.

44. Clausewitz, *On War*, 88–89.

PART III / Global Dimensions and Implications

Chapter Twelve

The Ukraine War and Global Cleavages

Ashley J. Tellis

The Russian invasion of Ukraine, which began in February 2022 and continues to this day, promises to be far more detrimental to the post–Cold War international order than even the awful 9/11 terrorist attacks on the United States and the US invasion of Iraq that ultimately followed. While President George W. Bush's Iraq campaign was launched based on mistaken judgments about Saddam Hussein's weapons of mass destruction, it was nonetheless intended to bolster the international order by preventing the spread of such threats.

In contrast, Vladimir Putin's war against Ukraine represents wanton aggression aimed at the evisceration of an independent state through the forcible annexation of its territory. As such, it violates the fundamental principle enshrined in the United Nations (UN) Charter: that naked force cannot be used to alter territorial boundaries irrespective of the grievances involved, much less eliminate an existing, internationally recognized state. Furthermore, it represents an assault by an authoritarian power against a democracy, however imperfect the latter may be. And—worse—it exemplifies revanchism insofar as Moscow's war is intended to reabsorb Ukraine as part of its ambition to reconstruct the Russian empire that dissolved with the ending of the Cold War.

Ashley J. Tellis is the Tata Chair for Strategic Affairs and a senior fellow at the Carnegie Endowment for International Peace, specializing in international security and US foreign and defense policy with a special focus on Asia and the Indian subcontinent.

Not without reason, then, the dominant view in the West has been that the Russian invasion of Ukraine represents the starkest threat to international order witnessed in the post–Cold War period. Given this judgment, the early expectation within the United States and Europe, and in the political West more generally, was that the international community would stand solidly united in condemning Russia's invasion of Ukraine as a blatant violation of the postwar international regime. The six resolutions that were debated and voted upon in the UN General Assembly (UNGA) from March 2022 to March 2023—all pertaining to different aspects of the Ukraine war—however, told a different and more complicated story.

To be sure, all six resolutions condemning Russian behavior in different ways were supported by substantial majorities. Barring the two resolutions that pertained to suspending Russia from the UN Human Rights Council and the preparations for securing Russian reparations, all the other motions were routinely supported by some 140-odd countries. The states consistently in opposition to all the resolutions were a small coterie of Russian allies.

But what is striking is that a significant number of countries—between 32 and 38—chose to abstain from condemning Russia more or less regularly across all six resolutions, and some 10 to 18 countries did not vote at all, depending on the issue in question. Most of the prominent abstaining countries are located in what is today often—and admittedly problematically—called the "Global South,"[1] with Algeria, China, India, Kazakhstan, Pakistan, and South Africa, being among the more prominent. Many of these states, being postcolonial entities in different ways, are usually deeply concerned about threats to national sovereignty, and hence, their conspicuous reluctance to condemn what to most in the West is flagrant Russian aggression is perplexing, at least in the first instance.

Three Blocs at Odds

The voting record on the Russian invasion of Ukraine in the UNGA does not fully clarify the extent of the current cleavages in the international system. The record of votes is a useful but still incomplete indicator of the anxieties many states have about the current international order, which is viewed as insufficiently responsive to their national aspirations. Thus, although large majorities voted to condemn Russia because it had brazenly crossed an unacceptable line—invading a neighboring state—the disquiet within significant parts of the international community suggests that the Russian invasion of Ukraine has divided the international community into three groups—what G. John Ikenberry has labeled "Three Worlds."[2]

The first group consists of the United States and its closest allies in Europe and Asia, all relatively developed and powerful states that are fully committed to opposing the Russian invasion and are currently involved in different ways in assisting Ukraine's war effort. The collective response of these states to the Russian invasion in Ukraine is *balancing*: internally building up their military capabilities to deal with the long-term threats posed by Russia and its de facto confederates as appropriate but, equally, collaborating among themselves and with Ukraine to assist Kyiv in resisting the Russian onslaught through the provision of arms, intelligence, and military training.[3]

The second group consists of states that have geopolitical affinities with Russia and are generally opposed to the West because they perceive themselves as targets of hostile Western policies—more specifically, hostile US-led Western policies—on a range of issues from strategic competition to human rights. This group includes China and Iran, which even as they have formally abstained from condemning Russia in the UNGA have effectively expressed solidarity with Moscow as a fellow victim of aggressive US policies toward them. Other members in this group include the Democratic People's Republic of Korea (North Korea), Belarus, Eritrea, Syria, Cuba, Nicaragua, and Venezuela. The behavior of this group is functionally *bandwagoning*: whether through tangible actions or merely rhetorical support, they have made common cause with Russia against the West, supporting Moscow's war against Kyiv as a vehicle for their myriad grievances against the wider liberal international order led by the United States.

The third group, the largest of the three blocs currently present in the international system, consists of a large and diverse number of states that are functionally "nonaligned" and whose behavior ranges from active opportunism to passive neutralism. In general, this group includes—but is emphatically not limited to—many of the 30-odd states that have consistently abstained and many of the 10-odd states that have usually not voted on the six UNGA resolutions pertaining to the Ukraine War. It strikingly includes India, which as a result of its neutrality has effectively supported Russia's war; Turkey, a US ally and NATO member; Indonesia, a state that has frequently condemned Russia in the UNGA; as well as other prominent countries such as South Africa, Vietnam, Pakistan, Bangladesh, and Kazakhstan, which usually abstained. In general, the behavior of this third group represents a form of *distancing*: a desire to stay aloof from the conflict by avoiding both a manifest opposition to Russia and an explicit embrace of Moscow.

For all its significance, the threefold cleavage in the international system that has been brought to the fore by the Russian invasion of Ukraine cannot be

considered a structural attribute. It does not describe the systemic distribution
of power as conventionally understood. Membership in at least two of the blocs,
those opposed to the United States—the "axis of resistance"—and those seeking
to escape the rivalry between the West and its opponents, could fluctuate depending on the fate of their constituent regimes and the specific issues that confront
them in their encounters with American (and allied) power. As such, they represent congeries of self-regarding states rather than a real coalition, unlike the US-
led Western political universe that is more enduring in contrast. Consequently, the
currently existing blocs must be treated only as manifestations of the persistent
processes of international politics insofar as they represent mainly "bargaining behavior within a power structure."[4]

This behavior is shaped, initially, by differing visions of international order: the
first vision emphasizes respect for the choices of democratic countries and is
rooted in a liberal understanding of politics both within and outside states; the
second vision emphasizes the primacy of security and is rooted deeply in a realist
conception of politics; and the third vision accepts elements from both the previous frameworks but, being sensitive to power inequalities between states, seeks
to preserve a sanctuary wherein the weaker nations can escape both foreign pressures in their internal affairs as well as the competitive rivalries among the great
powers. In the final analysis, however, these ideational differences intersect with
concrete interests, and therefore, the "membership" of any given state in one
grouping or another depends on how its conceptions about international order in-
teract with its material circumstances.

Colliding Visions of Order

The three different visions of order appear to be at least in tension, if not in
outright collision, at the ideational level. The dominant vision of international order in the West is rooted in liberal internationalism. This worldview recognizes
states as the most important actors but views their security-seeking activities,
though important and primary, as embedded in a larger environment defined by
international society. The presence of both entities—national states and international society—consequently, makes the international system a "society of states."[5]

This society of states is most stable when its order-producing constituents are
governed by consent. The resulting peacefulness within them then carries over
outside their boundaries because their normative and structural features ineluc-
tably shape their foreign conduct as well. A society composed of liberal states is
thus naturally peaceful; although some defensive instruments are necessary to

protect security, the larger tranquility is bolstered by fostering productive international activities such as trade. Because trade creates a web of prosperity, it also generates disincentives for conflict. War in this vision is therefore averted because the constituent states are well-ordered domestically and their security-seeking is embedded in a cooperative quest for expanding prosperity both within and across national boundaries.

Since international society is invariably not composed entirely of democratic states, peaceful interstate relations require either the expansion of democracy abroad or the acceptance of certain minimal rules of international conduct by all, such as the eschewing of aggression and conquest, a norm that in practice is also reinforced by the preservation of a balance of power, especially between liberal and nonliberal states. As a consequence, war becomes an atypical aberration in normal international politics.

Since the end of World War II, this vision of international society nurtured European integration with US support. It began with the creation of Pan-European institutions, such as the North Atlantic Treaty Organization (NATO), which were originally designed to contain Soviet military power but later engendered deepened European integration through the European Union, which made economic management, foreign policy harmonization, and democratic consolidation all integral elements of the European project. After the Cold War, both of these European institutions progressively expanded to include many of the states that were previously under Soviet domination on the assumption that such enlargement could not pose, almost by definition, a threat to any country outside its fold.

When Ukraine, which lies adjacent to Russian borders, sought NATO and EU membership, Russia—because of both its own history and its existence outside of liberal Europe—grew increasingly anxious about the geopolitical dangers to its security. As a result of the Cold War, Russia had long nurtured a jaundiced view of NATO, viewing it as an extension of hegemonic US power directed against itself rather than as the defensive instrument against postwar Soviet expansionism in Europe that it actually was. This perception was strengthened by the reality that the United States is a Janus-faced state: it is undoubtedly liberal in that it upholds rule by consent domestically and promotes its propagation abroad, but it is simultaneously a tenacious practitioner of realpolitik that uses force whenever required to protect its democratic allies and preserve the global primacy that enables it to promote its ideals, defeat the threats to its security, and maintain the international system that serves its interests.

Unlike the Europe encompassed by NATO and the EU, which is self-consciously liberal in its domestic and international politics, and the United States, which is liberal in its domestic politics and its international ambitions but often wields its power abroad in accordance with realist dictates, Russia is and has been for most of its history the embodiment of thorough and undiluted realpolitik. Although many countries outside the "pacific federation"[6] of Western liberal democracies share similarities with the Russian worldview, Russia and China today stand out as great powers that have assimilated machtpolitik in their domestic politics as well as their foreign policy and, as such, have consciously sought to maintain their distance from the liberal universe.

The ideational gulf between Russian realpolitik and Western liberalism regarding international order is thus quite stark. Moscow's vision of order is centered solely on the primacy of security-seeking states. Although other elements such as norms, organizations, and institutions exist in the international system, states matter most of all and they cannot be constrained by liberal solutions such as peaceful conflict resolution or the compulsions of prosperity. The natural condition of the international system, in Russia's experience, has thus always been conflict: because security is scarce in international politics (and is just as scarce domestically as well), Moscow today has sought to immunize itself by erecting a sturdy authoritarianism at home while maintaining large military forces—including a formidable nuclear arsenal—and seeking a controlling influence over its neighbors. Russia, in other words, has sought to neutralize external security threats by taking refuge in imperialism, understood as domination over others, in order to protect its security.

This approach today has been reinvigorated by other factors, including, and especially, Putin's beliefs that Russia has been humiliated by the West after the end of the Cold War and has been forced into accepting arrangements that are against its interests, which must now be corrected; Russia's unique cultural identity as the "chief defender of Christianity and faith in God"[7] in the face of the Western retreat from traditional religiosity, which makes it the natural locus of resistance to liberalism; and Russia's mission as a great power—even if this appellation is denied to it by the West—which consists at the very least of defending the entire "Russian world,"[8] an arena that includes all Slavic states as well as Russian minorities in various borderland countries. These convictions have bolstered the "strategic realism"[9] of Moscow's traditional approach to security—imperial expansion as a means of protecting the core—resulting in repeated security threats, at varying levels of intensity, being levied at its neighbors and beyond. Consequently, while Moscow desires cooperation with others that serves its interests, it has not relinquished the view that interstate competition, understood either as active violence or the perpetual preparation for it, is the norm in international politics.

With such premises, it is not surprising that Russia has viewed NATO's post–Cold War expansion in largely zero-sum terms. When the smaller countries of the Cold War Soviet empire—Bulgaria, Romania, Slovakia, and Slovenia—and three erstwhile Soviet republics—Estonia, Latvia, and Lithuania—joined the US-led military alliance, Moscow's anxieties, however elevated, were kept in check. But the dam burst when NATO contemplated its expansion to eventually include Ukraine. As the then US ambassador to Russia, William J. Burns, cabled from Moscow in 2008, "Ukrainian entry into NATO is the brightest of all redlines for the Russian elite (not just Putin)."[10]

In an effort to avert the denouement finally presented by Putin's invasion, Moscow offered proposals—ever since Boris Yeltsin's presidency—that attempted to protect its interests in Europe. These Russian proposals, which were intended to prevent NATO from expanding right up to its borders, underscored its view that the expansion of Western security (to include that of the former Soviet-controlled states) should not come at the price of increasing Russian insecurity. At the end of the day, the ideas proffered by Moscow failed to persuade both Washington and its European partners, thus leaving open the possibility that Ukraine could secure membership in both NATO and the EU at some point in the future.

That Russia under Putin has sought to foreclose this possibility conclusively through war demonstrates how the liberal and realist conceptions of international order have collided in Ukraine. The liberal internationalism of the West views the expansion of the institutions within its pacific federation as inherently peaceful. It represents the beneficial expansion of democratic peace and exemplifies the freedom of choice that all states have—and which democratic states, especially, have because they are governed by consent—in choosing whom they want to affiliate with. This freedom to choose is the essence of state autonomy and represents an important attribute of sovereignty in the international system. The realist inheritance of the Russian vision, which is intensified by the fears of threats to its identity, culture, and influence, does not, however, permit Moscow to perceive these possibilities benignly. Rather, they are assessed through the prism of power and competition, and because security in its many dimensions is scarce in international politics, they are judged as permanently altering the Eurasian balance of power in ways that fundamentally undermine Russian security.

If Russia was a weak state as it once was after 1991, it might have had to live with the discomfiting reality of reduced security. But because it is no longer as infirm as it once was, it has used its military power—however ineptly as it has done during this campaign—to attempt to eliminate the threat posed by the possibility of NATO appearing at its doorstep. In so doing, it has underlined the realist roots, albeit qualified by cultural elements and Putin's own personality, of its competing vision of international order: all states deserve secure geographic environs, but great powers have distinctive prerogatives that must be respected even if they abridge the security of weaker neighbors. The demand that NATO permanently exclude Ukraine from its expansion plans is thus analogous to the long-standing US effort to prevent any strategic dangers from manifesting themselves in the areas proximate to its homeland. Since Putin still views Russia as emphatically a great power—even if Western perceptions are strikingly different—his actions reflect his belief that Moscow too should enjoy the privileges accruing to all other great powers throughout history.

This view is not Putin's alone. Many countries outside of the liberal West believe that the Ukraine crisis cannot be properly judged, politically and morally, without admitting to the inadvertent consequences of the West's desire to expand the pacific federation in Europe. Threatening the core interests of a great power, in this judgment, made war inevitable. China and South Africa have most transparently levied this charge. But even India, which has carefully refrained from officially supporting this position, accepts its substance for the most part. Thus, even when Russia's nonaligned critics are dismayed by its decision to invade Ukraine, they are sympathetic at least to Moscow's fears of a heightened threat, even though few countries, if any, would buy into Putin's allegation that Ukraine cannot subsist as a legitimate and independent entity because it "has never had stable traditions of real statehood."[11]

In any event, the Ukraine War and the US effort to garner universal condemnation of the Russian invasion has resulted in many countries in the Global South seeking to opt out of what they perceive as a return to new forms of charged rivalries. Unlike the West's liberal internationalism and Russia's culture-inflected realism, those that have sought to remain neutral in this crisis have not articulated a clear statement of their alternative vision of order. They obviously value elements of the liberal project, such as the global trading system and the benefits offered by various multilateral organizations. But as postcolonial states for the most part, they dislike the intrusiveness of the great powers in matters of their domestic politics, a problem that is especially acute for non-democratic or imperfectly democratic countries. Thanks to their histories, however, they are also conscious of the realities of power: while they all seek to protect their security and autonomy in different ways, they recognize that structural inequalities exist in international politics, and great powers, therefore, should not be provoked unnecessarily.

All the same, most of the nonaligned states of the Global South have been unified by three specific concerns. First, they are animated by what is viewed as the hypocrisy of the West, given its own past violations of sovereignty, such as in Kosovo, Iraq, Libya, and Syria. Although the specifics in each case differ—and even though each of these interventions can be defended, however uneasily—they are often concatenated in the consciousness of many nations, which then invariably produces a moral equivalence between the West and Russia where great-power military intervention is concerned.

Second, they are alarmed by the pain inflicted by the food and energy disruptions created by the war and the other travails arising from the US-led sanctions regime that followed. This leads to their all-too-justified fear that global resources will now be plowed, once again, into geopolitical competition, with damaging consequences for the larger development agenda. As a consequence, the poorer countries have placed a

> greater focus on [the war's] disruptive effect on their economies and the consequent need to restore stability, rather than concern with [its] territorial and human rights violations. The immediacy of the painful economic spillover of conflict [has] translated into a position that support[s] a cessation of the war, even if that—as some in the West [have] argued—would play into the hands of Putin.[12]

Third, they are alienated by the failures of global governance institutions, which, because of the inequalities in representation, are judged to be unresponsive to their needs. Whether it be the deadlock in the UN Security Council caused by competing veto-wielding interests, the paralysis of the World Trade Organization's dispute settlement process, or the inability of the Bretton Woods institutions to finance development activities on the scale required, these disappointments are attributed quickly to the inequity in representation in these bodies. This has encouraged the growth of new alternatives—such as the BRICS, the Asian Infrastructure Investment Bank, and the Belt and Road Initiative—as well as calls for the reform of the UN Security Council, which only promises further contestation and possible paralysis.

This dissatisfaction with the existing system has not translated into any real alternative to the liberal international order as an organizing framework for world politics. The old intellectual construct of nonalignment still survives but has lost the animating force it once enjoyed during the Cold War, both as an idea and as a movement. To the degree that there is any replacement that binds the Global South today, it is represented weakly by the new shibboleth of "strategic autonomy" in the context of the rising demand for "polycentrism"[13]—an old Indian idea that dates back to the high tide of the Cold War—which is often colloquially and mistakenly referred to by the term *multipolarity*.

The notion of strategic autonomy, captured by the phraseology of *active nonalignment* (ANA), is viewed as a response to the conflictual conditions of the present time. As Jorge Taiana summarized it:

> The ANA privileges the national interest and does not subordinate it to the interest of any [other great] power. It is not about keeping equidistance in polarized situations. It is about evaluating each decision according to how toward sustainable development with social justice is strengthened. The ANA is not a defensive nor a passive option. It seeks to modify a reality that is not favorable to developing countries. It also provides a link with a group of countries that are increasingly relevant every day, in our own region as well as in Asia and in Africa. And it is a policy that understands that the contingencies of the present do not prevent us from staying the course toward a better future.[14]

While the negative element of resistance to the great powers is thus baked into the idea of strategic autonomy, the positive element consists of a demand for recognition where the preferences of a multiplicity of states are accorded due consideration, even if they are not as powerful as the weightiest actors in the international system.

The term *multipolarity* is often misused by leaders in the Global South to justify their desire to be taken seriously. Often, the countries they represent are not true poles in the conventional sense of the term but merely one of many centers of influence, each of which possesses varying degrees of autonomy. Yet what is really being contested through the use of the term is the traditional idea that a few great powers alone have the privilege of defining the "rules of the game" in an international system that is increasingly fractured, multilayered, and cross-cutting. Through both its negative and positive elements, the Global South is thus rejectionist: it seeks simultaneously to escape the pressures of the competition between the West and Russia (or China), while carving out space to assert its own interests, even as it utilizes the institutions and benefices offered by both sides in the overarching rivalry.

Intersections with National Interests

These distinctive ideational streams do not, however, suffice to position any given nation in either the balancing, bandwagoning, or distancing bloc. Whether a state ends up in one particular group or the other depends on how its vision of global order intersects with its national interest, which is in turn a composite outcome of six variables pertaining to the Ukraine war: (1) regime type, (2) leadership preferences, (3) stakes in the outcome, (4) physical proximity to the conflict, (5) ties to the belligerents, and (6) benefits and costs accruing to the country. The interaction of these variables, against the backdrop of what is still a US-dominated international order, shapes how states conceive of their national interests in the conflict and accordingly positions them in one of the three groupings.

The states that make up the US-led coalition balancing against Russia in the Ukraine War are distinguished most conspicuously by their regime type—an attribute shared also by the bandwagoning bloc opposed to the West. All the states that have actively supported Kyiv in its defense against Russian aggression are democracies. Even the most conspicuous dissident in the coalition, Hungary led by Prime Minister Viktor Orbán, is a parliamentary democracy. The threat posed by an authoritarian regime like Russia is an important animating element for most of the European partners and binds the balancing coalition together.

Because confronting Moscow in the face of long-standing energy dependence served as an inhibiting factor early on for many European countries, the brave decisions taken by political leaders—for example, Giorgia Meloni in Italy, Boris Johnson and now Rishi Sunak in the United Kingdom, Olaf Scholz in Germany, and Mark Rutte in the Netherlands, to cite only a few cases—were crucial to resisting Russia at a time when their countries, among other regional states, were highly dependent on Moscow for energy imports and their populations were particularly vulnerable to economic dislocation. The importance of leadership choices is also demonstrated by an exception that tests the rule: Hungary's Viktor Orbán, in contrast, who has impeded European efforts to support Ukraine and expand NATO.

For all the effects of personalities, however, a nation's stakes in the outcome of the war and its proximity to the conflict bear heavily on its decision to balance against Russia. On these counts, almost all the European partners of the United States recognize that Russian aggression, if unpunished, threatens their collective security as well as their own preservation and autonomy individually. Their physical proximity to the conflict only intensifies these concerns, so it is not surprising that those states closest to the war—the East European nations formerly controlled by Russia—are the biggest champions of aiding Ukrainian resistance even if they are by no means the wealthiest countries in Europe.

The support offered by Washington's Asia-Pacific partners, primarily Japan, South Korea, and Australia, also corroborates the larger proposition that the Russian invasion represents a dangerous threat not only to the security of the political West as a whole but to the larger liberal order underwritten by the United States—which provides important collective goods for the entire international system. Defeating Russian aggression obviously protects European security immediately, but it also provides demonstration effects that could help ward off future threats potentially mounted by China in East Asia.

The states that have bandwagoned with Russia through support for its actions against Ukraine represent a different conception of national interest: one that centers on resistance to the United States and the international order it upholds through varying forms of solidarity with Moscow. The most striking commonality of all the states that form this axis of resistance is their antipathy to liberal politics: they are all deeply authoritarian regimes ruled by dictators—as is evident in China, North Korea, Eritrea, Syria, and Cuba—even though some of them, such as Belarus, Iran, Nicaragua, and Venezuela, have the semblance of electoral democracies. While their regime type naturally puts them in opposition to the US-led liberal order, this resistance is amplified by the choices of their leaders, who view their hold on domestic power as threatened both by the values espoused by Washington and, equally importantly, its policies toward their nations individually.

Thus, China's Xi Jinping views US efforts to support Taiwan and Washington's creation of a balancing coalition in the Indo-Pacific as a direct threat to both the Communist regime in Beijing and its desire to amalgamate the various foreign territories that it claims as its own. Iran's supreme leader, Ali Khamenei, and the theocratic regime he presides over, still views the United States as the "Great Satan," a power that is determined to both prevent Tehran's acquisition of nuclear weapons and contest Iran's claim to regional hegemony. North Korea's strongman, Kim Jong Un, has similar grievances: he views the United States as the singular obstacle to his totalitarian regime, his dream of reunifying the Korean Peninsula under Pyongyang's tutelage, and his ambition to sustain a potent nuclear weapons program. Belarus's president, Alexander Lukashenko, who has relied on Moscow for subsidies and political support to sustain his authoritarianism for nearly three decades, views the US opposition to his fraudulent 2020 reelection as deeply threatening to his power and has since allied even more tightly with Russia's Vladimir Putin.

All four of these states, accordingly, have become strong supporters of Russia's war against Ukraine, in large part because of their competition with the United States. Although Beijing poses as neutral in the conflict, Xi's "no limits" pact with Putin prior to the war served as a critical form of geopolitical support for Moscow. Although China has, in large part because of US pressure, refrained from aiding Russia by transferring military equipment, it has subsidized the latter's war effort through the export of integrated circuits and combat-relevant manufactured goods, such as ball bearings, trucks, and earth moving equipment, as well as through accelerated imports of Russian oil. Iran and North Korea have aided Russia's military operations more directly: Tehran has supplied Russia with large numbers of armed drones, and North Korea has transferred vast quantities of ammunition. Belarus too has aided the Russian war effort through the simple realities of geography: it permitted Moscow to use its territory, which offers the shortest land route to Kyiv, to stage part of the invasion of Ukraine.

The other countries that have bandwagoned with Russia—Eritrea, Syria, Cuba, Nicaragua, and Venezuela—have supported Moscow primarily through diplomatic and symbolic instruments. These are largely weak states whose sympathy for Russia is driven by their individual histories of confrontation with the United States but is intensified by the personal grievances of their leaders, which has led to a strong embrace of Moscow. Thus, for example, Isaias Afwerki, Eritrea's dictator, holds the United States and its allies responsible for siding with Ethiopia in the 1998 war that resulted in his country's humiliating defeat. Syria's Bashar al-Assad was saved entirely by Russia's assistance since the 2011 civil war in his country, thus making his commitment to Vladimir Putin both personal and political. Similarly, Cuban, Nicaraguan, and Venezuelan ties with Russia are long-standing and are intimately linked to the Russian support for their authoritarian regimes over the years—in the case of Cuba, dating back to the Cold War.

All the countries represented in the group of bandwagoning states, thus, have a different but distinctive stake in the outcome of the Ukraine war: although they have no physical proximity to the combat zone and, as such, are not directly threatened in a way that the European allies of the United States are, they do not wish to see Russia, their strategic partner, defeated by Western power at a time when their links to Moscow are important for success in their own confrontations with Washington. Because the latter competitions can be existential for these countries, close ties with Russia, and sometimes among themselves, are essential for their survival (or at least for the survival of their ruling regimes). The close ties that they consequently nurture with Moscow are also in striking contrast to their tenuous links with Kyiv. Because they judge that the costs of a Russian defeat to each of them individually are significant, their support for Russia over Ukraine becomes a logical outcome of their perceived national interests. Where they vary conspicuously is in their capabilities, so the strongest among them—China, Iran, North Korea, and less obviously Belarus—see their aims advanced by tangibly assisting Moscow in this war, while the weaker can only profess verbal support from the sidelines.

The positions taken by the countries in the third group on the Ukraine war, those remaining nonaligned in different degrees, are also shaped significantly by their particular interests. It is difficult to summarize how these interests intersect with the worldviews of each of these nations because their number is large, and they are remarkably diverse as far as their regime types are concerned. But if India, South Africa, Indonesia, Turkey, and Kazakhstan are taken as representatives in this category, they span the gamut from electoral autocracies, such as Kazakhstan, to mutating democracies, such as India and South Africa, to shallow democracies, such as Turkey and Indonesia. Although genuinely liberal democracies with competing power centers and vibrant civil societies also exist in this grouping, many of the most influential states are marked by the presence of charismatic politicians at the helm who exercise outsize influence over their national choices: Prime Minister Narendra Modi in India, President Recep Tayyip Erdoğan in Turkey, and Nursultan Nazarbayev, the former president of Kazakhstan who still yields influence in his country's politics, remain good examples.

With the exception of Turkey, none of these countries are located in close proximity to Ukraine. Consequently, they do not have pressing equities in the war's outcome even though they have all suffered in different ways, with some like India even benefiting, from its disruptions. Obviously, they do not wish to see Ukraine, a sovereign state, annexed through Russian force of arms, but because this outcome is now improbable—in large part because of Western assistance to Kyiv—they have been freed to pursue their own ambitions in ways that do not put them at stark odds with either the West or Russia. In fact, their ties with both Russia and Ukraine, however asymmetrical, allow them to engage both sides in ways that advance their own interests.

India remains a good example of such maneuvering. New Delhi has had longstanding ties with Moscow dating back to the Cold War. It has historically viewed Russia as a special protector of its interests, especially in the UN Security Council, and was traditionally a major buyer of Russian military equipment. Beyond these legacy links, however, India still views Russia as a great power and as a critical element of the multipolar order that India hopes will one day replace US hegemony globally. The Ukraine War has undoubtedly put India's special relationship with Russia to the test. Despite its discomfiture with Putin's invasion—because of the blatant violation of sovereignty it represents—New Delhi has assiduously avoided criticizing Russia openly because preventing a closer affiliation between Moscow and Beijing was important to New Delhi at a time when Sino-Indian relations were increasingly strained. Moreover, India did not want to put at risk the close ties it still enjoyed with the Russian defense-industrial complex. And it gambled—correctly—that Washington would overlook these linkages, as well as the lifeline India has thrown to Moscow through its increased purchases of Russian oil, because of the US interest in collaborating with India against China. New Delhi was thus able to protect its ties with Russia and the United States simultaneously; it has also extended modest support to Ukraine concurrently by offering humanitarian aid, while weakly appealing to Putin to end his war, thus making the dichotomous investments necessary to protect its interests across the board.

South Africa and Indonesia are other examples of countries that have chosen to walk a fine line between Russia and the West in an attempt to protect their specific equities. Pretoria's sympathies for Moscow can be traced to the links the African National Congress (ANC) had to the Soviet Union during the apartheid era, when Moscow provided the liberation movement—the precursor of the current government—with financial and political support as well as arms. South Africa today appears to have reciprocated that support—shaped largely by the ANC's leadership preferences—even though South Africa's economic and cultural links with Russia are minimal. Again, the calculation in Pretoria seems to be that its ambition to play a larger role in representing Africa on the global stage is better advanced by compelling US attention to its ability to maneuver between the rivals than simply satisfying Washington with an open condemnation of Russia. Because the United States is increasingly sensitive to the concerns of the Global South in the context of its own rivalries with Russia and China, South Africa's determination to avoid taking "a very adversarial stance against Russia"[15] is judged by Cyril Ramaphosa's regime as promising greater benefits than costs to South Africa.

Turkey and Kazakhstan also represent similar strategies where the pursuit of self-interest is concerned. Despite being a longtime NATO member, Turkey has declared both the West and Russia to be "equally"[16] reliable and, hence, has engaged both Kyiv and Moscow simultaneously, to the point of selling armed drones to the former and facilitating its wheat shipments abroad while intensely engaging with Putin, with perhaps some sympathy for a country that has also lost an empire. Turkey's maneuvering between the two blocs has been shaped greatly by Erdoğan's own political astuteness as well as his dismay about Turkey's treatment by the EU, leading to a strategy that condemns Russia's belligerence on the one hand but seeks to avoid "imperiling Turkey's close relationship with Moscow or upsetting Turkey's business opportunities with Europe"[17] on the other hand. Ankara's approach to the Ukraine conflict is striking because its policies have not simply reflected NATO and EU preferences. Rather, Erdoğan's desire to preserve Turkey's relations with the West (and Europe particularly) without alienating Russia (and China) excessively has driven him to play a role that seeks to consolidate Turkey's position as a major regional power that can wield influence beyond its immediate borders.

The observed behaviors of the myriad nations in the nonaligned group thus confirm an intense desire to avoid becoming trapped in the ongoing rivalry between the US-led liberal bloc and authoritarian powers that resist it. These states have undoubtedly gained from many of the institutions created as a product of US hegemony in the postwar era. But because they believe that these gains have not yet been sufficient, they have often demanded a reform of the existing system. Many of the countries in this grouping also have substantial international ambitions of their own—ambitions that are better advanced by exploiting the cleavages between the US-dominated bloc and its antagonists rather than simply allying with one or the other. Their complex neutrality on the Ukraine War, then, does not necessarily represent a lack of sympathy for Kyiv's victimization by Moscow but rather a determination to advance their own interests over and above the aims pursued by the combatants and their supporters.

So, What Should the United States Do?

The fact that the Ukraine War has revealed cleavages of the sort visible since February 2022 should not obscure the reality that these differences predate the conflict. The war did not produce these fractures; it merely highlighted them. The splits themselves are simply a product of the success of American hegemony in the postwar period and the liberal international order it has begotten. For that reason, the cleavages are almost inevitable—just as they were during the Cold War. Then as now, the antagonism of some nations toward the United States and its allies, both at the ideational and the power-political levels, created bifurcations that could not be wished away. The existence of such competition also created opportunities for many countries to attempt to escape it even as they sought to exploit it for their own ends. This outcome, too, is natural in an international system populated by self-regarding entities that are differentiated by capability, interests, and distance from the principal protagonists.

Consequently, Washington should not spend too much time fretting about the chasms in the global system. These rifts are durable even if some members in the various groups move across the seams over time. Given these realities, the United States should just double down on protecting its own interests. Because the effort to safeguard—and expand—the pacific federation of democratic states will occasionally require that the United States employ military power, Washington will also be susceptible to charges of hypocrisy and double standards. The United States must not be deterred by such critiques. Although it should—and as a liberal state always will—attempt to accord "a decent respect to the opinions of mankind," as the US Declaration of Independence put it, the exercise of its power cannot, when necessary, be constrained by the complaints of others.

Consequently, the most important task facing Washington in Ukraine today is to ensure the defeat of Russian aggression irrespective of the views of its adversaries and other bystanders. This will require leading by example as it has already done: providing Kyiv with military and financial assistance to ensure that it can recover its lost territories and by so doing signal the West's resistance to any efforts at changing borders through force. Because the next twelve to twenty-four months will be critical to achieving these aims, the United States and its partners cannot let up on their efforts now. Defeating Russia's aggression is an investment not only in protecting European security—an objective that is intrinsically valuable to the United States—but it could also by demonstration serve to deter other similar acts of revisionism that might be contemplated by others, for instance, by China in Asia.

It is unfortunate that the United States lost the opportunity to aid Ukraine more effectively in the early months of the conflict when its own timidity and its defense industrial constraints prevented it from arming Kyiv with the necessary capabilities that might have promised greater success when the Russian offensive was disorganized and ineffective. Today, the costs of overcoming the strong Russian defenses on occupied Ukrainian territory have increased, but this burden only justifies increased support for Ukraine, especially on the part of the European allies. The strengthening of Western solidarity during this war has been impressive, but it must now be focused on meeting Ukraine's more demanding challenges ahead.

This campaign will necessarily take time, but even as it unfolds, the United States should resist calls for a premature negotiation between Ukraine and Russia. Concurrently, it must fix the leaky sanctions regime that has enabled Moscow to sustain its war effort, engaging both its antagonists and the bystanders who have contributed to keeping Russia afloat. Persuading countries in the axis of resistance will undoubtedly be difficult because their strategic interests collide with those of the United States. Convincing neutrals will not be easy either because of their own independent interests, but some progress may be possible on the margins.

In any case, what the United States should *not* do is to reify either the axis of resistance or the nonaligned universe: because there may be states in each group—likely more in the latter than the former—that are susceptible to tacit bargaining, Washington should persist with engaging each of the relevant countries appropriately in the hope of limiting their opposition or their opportunism. China, Turkey, and India stand out as pivotal players in this context. Obviously, success here is not assured, which makes the collective Western investments to support Ukraine all the more important.

While Washington's response to the extant cleavages must minimize their distractibility in the near term, bolstering the liberal international order through the judicious employment of American resources should remain a longer-term strategic objective. Such investments are not a wasteful extravagance, as is sometimes argued in the United States, but rather are essential for the legitimation of American power and primacy in what is still a rivalrous international system.

NOTES

1. Stewart Patrick and Alexandra Huggins, "The Term 'Global South' Is Surging. It Should Be Retired," Carnegie Endowment for International Peace, August 15, 2023, https://carnegieendowment.org/2023/08/15/term-global-south-is-surging.-it-should-be-retired-pub-90376.

2. G. John Ikenberry, "Three Worlds: The West, East and South and the Competition to Shape Global Order," *International Affairs* 100, no. 1 (January 2024): 121–138.

3. C. Todd Lopez, "Allies, Partners Central to U.S. Integrated Deterrence Effort," US Department of Defense, March 1, 2023, https://www.defense.gov/News/News-Stories/Article/Article/3315827/allies-partners-central-to-us-integrated-deterrence-effort/.

4. Robert O. Keohane and Joseph S. Nye Jr., *Power and Interdependence*, 4th ed. (Boston: Longman, 2012), 17.

5. Hedley Bull, *The Anarchical Society: A Study of Order in World Politics*, 3rd ed. (New York: Columbia University Press, 2002).

6. Hans Reiss, ed., *Kant's Political Writings* (Cambridge: Cambridge University Press, 1970), 104.

7. Lilia Shevtsova, "The Maidan and Beyond: The Russia Factor," *Journal of Democracy* 25, no. 3 (July 2014): 74–82.

8. Kari Roberts, "Understanding Putin: The Politics of Identity and Geopolitics in Russian Foreign Policy Discourse," *International Journal* 72, no. 1 (March 2017): 28–55.

9. Scott G. Feinstein and Ellen B. Pirro, "Testing the World Order: Strategic Realism in Russian Foreign Affairs," *International Politics* 58 (2021): 817–834.

10. William J. Burns, *The Back Channel: A Memoir of American Diplomacy and the Case for Its Renewal* (New York: Random House, 2019), 233.

11. Vladimir Putin, "Address by the President of the Russian Federation" (speech, Moscow, February 21, 2022), http://en.kremlin.ru/events/president/news/67828.

12. Chris Alden, "The Global South and Russia's Invasion of Ukraine," *LSE Public Policy Review* 3, no. 1 (September 2023): 1–8, https://ppr.lse.ac.uk/articles/10.31389/lseppr.88. Much of the discussion in these paragraphs about the response of the Global South is based on Alden's excellent essay.

13. Bimla Prasad, "A Fresh Look at India's Foreign Policy," *International Studies* 8, no. 3 (July 1966): 277–299.

14. Jorge Taiana, "Argentina and the Third Position," in *Latin American Foreign Policies in the New World Order: The Active Non-Alignment Option,* eds. Carlos Fortin, Jorge Heine, and Carlos Ominami (London: Anthem Press, 2023), 237.

15. Tim Cocks, "South Africa's Ramaphosa Blames NATO for Russia's War in Ukraine," *Reuters*, March 18, 2022, https://www.reuters.com/world/africa/safricas-ramaphosa-blames-nato-russias-war-ukraine-2022-03-17/.

16. Mansur Mirovalev, "Turkish Neutrality: How Erdogan Manages Ties with Russia, Ukraine amid War," *Al Jazeera*, September 28, 2023, https://www.aljazeera.com/news/2023/9/28/turkish-neutrality-how-erdogan-manages-ties-with-russia-ukraine-amid-war.

17. Brian Michael Jenkins, "Consequences of the War in Ukraine: Two Areas of Contention—Turkey and the Balkans," *RAND Blog*, March 6, 2023, https://www.rand.org/pubs/commentary/2023/03/consequences-of-the-war-in-ukraine-turkey-and-the-balkans.html.

Chapter Thirteen

Putin's Point of No Return

Andrea Kendall-Taylor

In the months after Russia's invasion of Ukraine, once it was clear that Kyiv would sustain its fierce resistance, US policymakers were quick to frame Russia's actions as a strategic failure. Speaking in Warsaw in March 2022, US president Joe Biden established the frame. "Notwithstanding the brutality of Vladimir Putin," he said, "let there be no doubt that this war has already been a strategic failure for Russia."[1] Senior leaders at the State Department and the Pentagon argued the same. Secretary of State Antony Blinken in June 2023 declared, "Putin's war of aggression against Ukraine has been a strategic failure, greatly diminishing Russia's power, its interests, and its influence for years to come."[2] Under Secretary of Defense for Policy Colin Kahl similarly stated, "I can say one thing with confidence, which is, Russia has already suffered a massive strategic failure. That's not going to change."[3] And yet, headed into the third year of the war, the picture had changed. Having blunted Ukraine's 2023 offensive and amid signs of fatiguing Western support for Ukraine, the Kremlin looked confident that things were heading in Moscow's direction.

Andrea Kendall-Taylor is senior fellow and director of the Transatlantic Security Program at the Center for a New American Security (CNAS). She previously served as deputy national intelligence officer for Russia and Eurasia at the National Intelligence Council (NIC) in the Office of the Director of National Intelligence (DNI) and as a senior intelligence analyst at the Central Intelligence Agency (CIA).

Time will tell whether the war ends in a strategic defeat for Moscow. But what is clear is that Putin's decision to invade Ukraine was the point of no return in his long-standing crusade against the West. Since the invasion, Putin has only grown more dogmatic and committed to confrontation, not just with Ukraine but also with the West, with the United States at its center. Although the war is first and foremost about controlling Ukraine and its choices, Putin's ultimate objective is to dismantle NATO once and for all, and in doing so to push the United States out of Europe. That, Putin appears to calculate, would provide the final, fatal blow to the security order in Europe and potentially to the global order he seeks to revise. Although Putin has long harbored these objectives, his invasion of Ukraine hardened his resolve and narrowed Moscow's options. Putin's willingness to accept risk in pursuit of this confrontation has grown over time, and, intent to shape his legacy as a great Russian leader, he is unlikely to leave the difficult task of revising the global order in Russia's favor to a successor.

To this end, Putin is reorienting Russia around the cause of confrontation, first with Ukraine but also with the United States and NATO. He is reshaping society, has put the economy on a wartime footing, and doubled down on partnerships with like-minded partners, especially in China, Iran, and North Korea. These changes will not easily be undone. Confrontation with the West has become the organizing principle of Russia's domestic and foreign policies, and Putin points to Russia's "existential struggle" with the West as the primary justification for his regime and its actions.[4] Even if the fighting in Ukraine subsides or ends, Putin will require confrontation to keep his regime in power. Russia has been changed by its war in Ukraine in ways that ensure that Moscow will remain a challenge so long as Putin is in power, and most likely well beyond his departure.

Russia Reoriented

Since the invasion, Putin has moved Russia in a darker, more totalitarian direction. Even before the war, repression in Russia was on the rise. After more than twenty years in power, Putin had grown more reliant on repression to maintain control—a trend that is common among longtime autocrats, who, after decades in office, become increasingly out of touch with their populations and have few tools other than repression left to ensure their survival in office.[5] But the invasion has led to a significant ratcheting up of these efforts. The Economist Intelligence Unit reported that Russia suffered "the biggest democratic decline of any country in the world" in 2022 as the Kremlin sought to eradicate any source of opposition to it or its war. In the months after the invasion, actions such as a spate of mysterious deaths of businessmen and managers at state-owned firms—many of whom fell from windows—helped to instill fear in and therefore the compliance of the elite. New laws criminalizing the spreading of "false information" about or "discrediting" Russia's military forces and their actions in Ukraine with prison times of up to fifteen years have squelched dissent. Russian courts have strangled civil society, opposition figures have been jailed, and arbitrary arrests and prosecution of citizens who oppose the war or the Kremlin's policies have dampened the potential for organized opposition to the regime.

But as any good autocrat knows, fear and repression alone are an inadequate basis of stability. In his first two terms in office, Putin derived popular support from his ability to cast himself as the leader who delivered high growth and brought an end to the tumult of the 1990s. High oil prices also allowed him to purchase the support of politically important Russians, incentivizing loyalty to the regime. But if by 2022 these pillars of stability were already weakened, the war has further eroded them. Putin's war in Ukraine is constraining Russia's economy, deteriorating living standards for many Russians, and leaving fewer economic resources available to distribute to regime insiders to ensure their continued support. Although repression is effective—research shows that it increases the durability of autocrats who use it[6]—an overreliance on repression carries risk. High levels of repression reduce an autocrat's ability to access good information as people are afraid to pass along unvarnished views, raising the risk of mistakes that can destabilize regimes. An overreliance on repression can also create a basis of discontent that increases the prospects that even small sources of frustration can more quickly spiral out of control.

As a result, Putin has sought to strengthen the ideological foundation of his regime—one that, even if inconsistent, is anchored by a vision of Russia as a distinct civilization in confrontation with the West—as a means to legitimate and therefore safeguard his rule.[7] Such narratives are far from new, but since the invasion, Putin has doubled down on convincing Russians that the West is out to destroy the Russian state. As described by Andrei Kolesnikov, Putin has reframed the "special military operation" in Ukraine into a multidimensional war against the West. As he aptly describes, "Putin's goals in Ukraine are no longer limited to returning Ukraine to Russia but now encompass what has become an existential rematch with the West, in which the Ukraine war is a part of a long, historically significant clash of civilizations. Putin sees himself as completing the mission begun by his historic predecessors, who were always forced to fight Western encroachment."[8]

Although the West may not see itself as being at war with Russia in Ukraine, Putin sees Russia as being at war with the West and the Kremlin is using all levers available to convince Russians of this view. Such narratives fill state-controlled newspapers and TV. But the Kremlin is also intent on indoctrinating younger Russians who rely far less on these information sources, underscoring just how sticky these ideas are likely to be. In short, the Kremlin is militarizing the next generation of Russians and preparing them for long-term confrontation with the West. Elementary school–aged children participate in marching practice, older kids are taught to throw grenades and shoot with real ammunition, and new patriotic youth groups are proliferating—Education Minister Sergei Kravtsov said at the end of 2023 that there are now about ten thousand so-called military-patriotic clubs in Russian schools and colleges, and a quarter-of-a-million people take part in their work.[9]

Online, numerous government-run and promoted groups have sprouted up pushing the idea that Russia is under threat from the United States and NATO. The Russian authorities are even rewriting textbooks that, in addition to perverting the history of Ukraine, are pushing Putin's narrative of historical grievance and laying out an existential battle for the nation's survival. According to a new textbook released in September 2023, "The West became fixated with destabilizing the situation inside Russia. . . . The aim was not even hidden: to dismember Russia and to get control over its resources."[10] Historian of Russian war propaganda Ian Garner describes the Kremlin's pervasive efforts to reshape Russians' views: "in paramilitary youth groups for children, in compulsory training in schools and universities, in the constant diet of films and shows about wars past and present, and in military parades and through conscription, young Russians are being prepared to play out the nation's historically fated role as the savior of humanity."[11]

Not only are Putin's efforts to build the ideological pillar of his regime creating a political foundation for long-term confrontation with the West, but he has put the economy on a wartime footing, making it likely that the Kremlin will have the capacity to pursue it, even if fighting in Ukraine ends. Russian defense spending in 2024 will reach 6% of GDP—the highest it has been since the collapse of the Soviet Union and more than double what it was before the invasion.[12] The real numbers are probably higher if estimates of classified expenditure are included. Factories in Russia producing military equipment are working nonstop,[13] and as the Kremlin continues to benefit from high oil prices and effectively circumvent sanctions, military production has surged. Despite Western sanctions, Russia's missile production is greater now than it was before the invasion[14] and Moscow is building its own domestic capacity to manufacture the Iranian drones that the Kremlin uses to target Ukrainian cities. Ukrainian officials estimate that Russia can produce around one hundred thousand drones per month, whereas Ukraine can only churn out half that amount.[15] Russia is also turning out more tanks now than before the war and producing more ammunition than the United States and Europe. A senior Estonian defense ministry official told the *New York Times* in the fall of 2023 that Russia's current ammunition production was seven times greater than that of the West.

Russia's economy more broadly also continues to defy expectations of collapse. In 2023, Russia's economy grew by 3.1%, and in January 2024, the International Monetary Fund (IMF) upgraded its outlook for 2024, anticipating Russia's economy will grow by 2.6%. To be sure, underlying problems exist. Issues like rising inflation, the government's continued overreliance on oil revenue, the costs of integrating the territories it illegally annexed from Ukraine, and labor shortages—resulting from the large number of Russians that left the country and the movement of workers out of civilian sectors and into defense industries paying higher wages—have the potential to bite. The government's redirection of expenditure to the military and away from social spending may also generate public discontent. But it remains uncertain when and to what extent such dynamics would cause more serious challenges for the Kremlin.

For now, Russia is unlikely to change its foreign policy course as a result of economic pressures. Its leaders have prepared the economy for conflict, and its resilience under harsh Western sanctions suggests Moscow will have the resources to not just sustain the war in Ukraine but rapidly regenerate its military capacity. In January 2024, German defense minister Boris Pistorius warned that the timeline for Russia to regenerate forces is likely to be much shorter than many think. While noting that a Russian attack is not likely "for now," he underscored the view of German experts that "expect [that in] a period of five to eight years this could be possible."[16] Some European allies assess it could be sooner.

What's more, now that the Kremlin has mobilized its defense industrial base, it is unlikely to quickly reverse the changes, even if fighting in Ukraine ends. The war in Ukraine has allowed the Russian state to increase its control over the economy, giving the Kremlin greater influence that it is unlikely to dispense with. Likewise, now that new drone factories are built and lines of production have been created, they will not be quickly shuttered. Many Russians, too, have grown reliant on jobs in war-related industries. Putin has gone through the difficult steps of shifting Russia's economy to a wartime footing and, rather than reverting back, may look for new opportunities to justify its continuation. Alternatively, even if Putin does not seek out conflict, the mobilized capacity he has at his disposal will better enable him to seize on opportunities as he sees them.

Just as the war has become the organizing principle of Russia's domestic policy, so too has Putin reoriented Russian foreign policy around his struggle with the West. Putin in particular has doubled down on relationships with like-minded partners in China, Iran, and North Korea. Given the invasion of Ukraine and the lack of a foreseeable future with the West, the Kremlin realistically had no options other than to deepen partnerships with such actors. Moreover, for Russia, the war in Ukraine remains its top priority and these countries provide critical sources of trade, weapons, and component parts that Moscow needs to sustain the fighting. In 2023, trade between Russia and China topped $240 billion, an increase of 26% from the previous year and a new record for the two countries.[17] China's exports to Russia of machinery and electrical equipment also reached a new all-time high in December of 2023, as China has become the single biggest exporter to Russia.[18] Likewise, Iran has become Russia's top military backer, providing artillery and tank rounds for use in Ukraine, as well as one-way attack drones that Russia uses against Ukrainian cities. Defense cooperation with North Korea has similarly deepened, with North Korea providing an invaluable source of ammunition along with ballistic missiles that Russia has fired on the battlefield in Ukraine.[19]

But even if Russia has deepened relations with these countries opportunistically, the Kremlin also sees them as fellow travelers in its showdown with the West. Moscow sees great utility in cultivating ties with those countries that share a hostility to the status quo and the United States in particular. Moscow understands that by working with these partners, it is less isolated and vulnerable to the foreign policy tools of the United States and its partners. But unlike before the invasion, Russia is all in on cultivating an axis of upheaval to counter the United States and the West. Russia's response to Hamas's October 7 attack on Israel is telling. Russia had a historically important relationship with Israel and long prided itself on being a balancer in the Middle East—the only country that could talk to all sides in a conflict. Yet, in the wake of Hamas's 2023 attack, Russia firmly backed Hamas. Moscow was willing to jettison its role as a balancer and downgrade its relationship with Israel because it sensed an opportunity to discredit the United States in the region. Russia's actions in the Middle East underscore the Kremlin's commitment and sense that now is the time to weaken the United States and break the US-led global order. Its relations with China, Iran, and North Korea amplify these efforts.

A Persistent Problem

The longer that Putin is in power the deeper the roots of these domestic and foreign policy changes will grow. The Kremlin will remain committed to pumping out propaganda painting the West as the enemy and Russia as being under grave threats, the persistence of which will shape longer-term public attitudes and preferences. The longer Putin remains, the more opportunity there will be for the repeated interactions among Moscow, Beijing, Tehran, and Pyongyang that help smooth over the historic distrust present in some of these partnerships and build the scaffolding for more enduring partnerships. Already, Putin is replacing ties to the West through a new dependence on China, creating greater path dependency in that relationship.[20] The longer these dynamics are at play, the more enduring Putin's worldview will be.

Moreover, given Putin's dismantling of institutions, civil society, and other centers of power, the expectation should be that autocracy in Russia will endure after Putin departs. The historical record shows that for all post–Cold War autocrats (except monarchs) in power for twenty years or more, authoritarianism persists past the leader's departure in 76% of cases. When such leaders are also older personalist autocrats, authoritarianism endures—either with the same regime or with the establishment of a new one—92% of the time.[21] Moreover, the same elite often remains in place after longtime leaders leave office—a prospect that would be made more likely if Putin leaves office as a result of his natural death or an elite-led coup.[22] Moreover, since Russia's invasion of Ukraine, Russia's security services, especially the Federal Security Service (the successor to the Soviet Union's Committee for State Security, or KGB), have benefited and grown even more influential. The more Putin relies on repression to maintain stability, the more power he must grant them. The security services—which have long held especially paranoid and hostile views of the United States—are primed to maintain influence beyond Putin. Unless there is significant turnover among the ruling elite when Putin goes, Russia's confrontational posture will endure.

Such continuity in the elite would likely extend to Russia's external relations. Successors who seek to orchestrate change frequently provoke fierce resistance from the "old guard" who have maintained significant control even once a longtime leader departs. New leaders may try and sideline the old guard, but more often than not new leaders who inherit office after a longtime leader dies or in the aftermath of a coup tend to adhere to the previous program. In countries such as Syria and Uzbekistan, for example, the successors of longtime leaders Bashar al-Assad (who inherited office after his father died in office) and Shavkat Mirzi-yoyev (who inherited office from longtime leader Islam Karimov) showed early signs of liberalization like the release of political prisoners, only to fall back on traditionally more-repressive practices. In part for these reasons, research by political scientist Sarah Croco finds that when successors come from the same regime as leaders involved with the initiation of a war, they are likely to continue the conflicts they inherit.[23]

By invading Ukraine, Putin has created prickly problems that will be difficult for future leaders to address, for example, how to end the war including resolving the status of Crimea and the other territories Russia has illegally annexed, wartime reparations, and accountability for war crimes. These issues will make new leaders vulnerable to accusations of capitulating to the West and therefore long complicate Russia's relations with the United States and Europe. Although a new leader could change the tone of Russia's external relations—just as the transition from Putin to Dmitry Medvedev created an opening for US-Russia cooperation that did not exist with Putin as president—the broad contours of Russian foreign policy likely will endure.[24]

Turbulent Times

There will be no turning back for Putin from his confrontation with the West. With ties with the United States and Europe broken, and his resolve to undermine the European and global orders hardened, he is committed to the course. Because Putin has passed his point of no return, Russia is likely to pose greater challenges on NATO's periphery, for NATO itself, and to the global order more broadly as Russian actions catalyze the coalescence of an axis of upheaval bent on rewriting the rules of the international system.

Putin is likely to pursue his confrontation with the West most intensely in Europe and Eurasia. For Moscow, the countries of the former Soviet Union have arguably taken on greater importance since Russia's invasion of Ukraine as the Kremlin seeks to protect its image and role as a great power. Moscow has long judged that to be a great power a country must first be a regional one. Yet Russia's standing in countries such as Moldova, Armenia, and some countries in Central Asia and the Balkans where Russia has historically held sway has been damaged in the wake of its invasion as governments and their citizens have grown more wary of Moscow. Russia's waning influence predates its invasion of Ukraine. Russia had, for example, opted not to respond to regional instability, including in 2010 when Russia did not help its ally Kyrgyzstan control violent unrest.

Now fears of Russian intentions have increased such concerns across the region. Russia's invasion has also reduced the attractiveness of Moscow as a security provider and economic partner and prompted these countries to look to other powers, like the European Union, China, Turkey, and Iran, as increasingly attractive alternatives. Yet Russia is unlikely to quietly accept its deteriorating role. Looking forward, Moscow will seek to uphold its influence making Eurasia a critical focus of Russian efforts to maintain its image as a global power. Russia could, for example, step up efforts to undermine pro-European governments in Moldova and Armenia, raising the risk of instability on NATO's periphery.[25]

Moreover, Russia's declining status in some Eurasian states will raise the stakes of retaining its influence where it remains, especially in Belarus, Serbia, and with the current government in Georgia. In Serbia, for example, Moscow's deteriorating standing in the Balkans means that Putin is likely to be even more intent on maintaining a Russian foothold in the region. Putin also has an incentive to stoke historical tensions between Serbia and Kosovo because doing so can stress limited NATO resources, undermine the alliance's influence in the region, and pull attention away from his war in Ukraine.[26] Belarus, too, has arguably taken on increased importance to Russia as a buffer between it and NATO, and the Kremlin will go to great lengths to ensure it maintains its influence there. Any threat of leadership change in Belarus or attempt to distance itself from Moscow could lead Russia to intervene, potentially bringing Russia ever closer to NATO's borders. And in Georgia, the Georgian Dream government has drifted closer to Moscow, while the public remains committed to deepening ties with Europe and the West. The increasing chasm between Georgians and their current government raises the risk that the two sides will clash over their visions of their country's future. Russia's invasion of Ukraine is creating ripple effects that will reverberate across Eurasia.

While the Kremlin views maintaining Russian influence in Eurasia as critical, destroying the security order in Europe is Putin's ultimate prize. Given the degradation of Russia's military in Ukraine, Putin will have to rely for now on asymmetric tactics—for example, disinformation, sabotage, cyberattacks, GPS jamming, assassinations, support for extremist parties and actors, and nuclear intimidation—to undermine NATO and its members. Putin likely sees 2024 as a pivotal year given elections in the United States and Europe, and ongoing efforts by Western governments to ramp up defense industrial production that can boost military aid for Ukraine. Putin's outlook could look quite different in 2025 if Western publics and capitals retain the political will to support Ukraine and rising defense industrial output enables greater military assistance for Kyiv. Putin therefore will seek to increase pressure not just on the front lines in Ukraine but also on Western democratic societies to secure political outcomes that would prevent this outcome from coming to fruition.

But as Russia reconstitutes its military force, a Putin that has passed his point of no return could seek to directly test NATO. There are numerous factors working to dissuade Russia from challenging NATO. However, if Putin were to come to judge that NATO—and most importantly the United States—lacks the resolve to fight, he could be tempted to attempt to undermine NATO once and for all. There are mounting reasons that could lead Putin to calculate that the United States and NATO lack the resolve to fight. Most immediate is the outcome of the United States presidential election in November. The reelection of former president Donald Trump would raise serious questions in both the Kremlin and NATO capitals about Washington's commitment to Europe, potentially leading the Kremlin to revise its calculus about the credibility of NATO's collective defense. Similarly, the growing traction of far-right parties and leaders in Europe—many of which harbor sentiments sympathetic to Moscow—could also convince the Kremlin that NATO would struggle to reach consensus on responding to Russian aggression against a NATO member on Russia's periphery.

Perhaps most concerning of all, however, would be the effect on Putin's calculus of US engagement in a major conflict with China in the Indo-Pacific. Were the US to first become involved in a major conflict with China in Asia, the military balance in Europe could look quite different in the Kremlin, and the threat of Russian opportunistic aggression against NATO would increase. In this case, the Kremlin could judge that Washington would have neither the political interest and support nor the resources to come to Europe's defense. The Kremlin could reach a similar conclusion should the US be forced to respond to multiple smaller conflicts, for example, smaller but significant conflicts in the Middle East and on the Korean Peninsula.

Further complicating the picture is the Kremlin's propensity for both risk-taking and miscalculation. Already, the Kremlin has seriously underestimated both its ability to rapidly defeat the Ukrainian military and Western resolve in response to the invasion. Political science research shows that personalist autocrats like Putin are the most inclined to make mistakes, in part because they surround themselves with yes-men and loyalists who tell the leader what they want to hear.[27] The Russian regime remains highly personalized, and if anything, rising repression in the wake of the invasion makes it even less likely that Putin receives unvarnished advice. Although Putin is unlikely to test NATO now, opportunistic aggression intended to undermine the alliance cannot be ruled out in the coming years.

Yet even if Putin never seeks to directly test NATO, his deepening partnerships with China, Iran, and North Korea portend more turbulent times. Most immediately, Russia is increasing the capabilities and brazenness of America's adversaries. The more desperate that Russia grows in its war in Ukraine, the more the Kremlin will have to give away in return for the sustained support of its partners. Already, there are suspicions that North Korea is seeking things like Russian missile technology that would improve its intercontinental ballistic missiles (ICBMs) and make them more of a nuclear threat, as well as nuclear propulsion for its submarines, in exchange for its supply of ammunition. The deepening partnership with Moscow has also made Kim Jong Un more confident and aggressive in his relations with South Korea, contributing to growing tensions in that region. And while there does not appear to be a direct connection between Russia and Hamas's attack on Israel, Russia's deepening partnership with Iran emboldened Tehran, creating a more permissive environment for Hamas to act.

In the aftermath of its invasion, Russia has become the key catalyst of a coalescing axis among Russia, China, Iran, and North Korea—one that presents an increasingly viable alternative to the West. This is transforming the international system into one now characterized by two increasingly organized and competing orders, which will have profound effects on global stability. Already, the two years since Russia's invasion of Ukraine have proven to be particularly tumultuous. Not only did Hamas's attack on Israel threaten to engulf the wider Middle East in conflict, but Azerbaijan waged an offensive against Nagorno-Karabakh, resorting to the use of force to regain full control over the region. Tensions flared in 2023 between Serbia and Kosovo, threatening to escalate into a wider conflict, and Venezuela threatened to take territory in Guyana through military force. Moreover, although the coups that have swept across Africa are internal affairs, they speak to the new international arrangement; for many years coups were on the decline, in large part because coup plotters faced costs within a cohesive liberal international order. With an emerging alternate order, that no longer appears to be the case.

There is reason to believe this uptick in conflict will be sustained. International relations research shows that, historically, periods in which there are competing orders are characterized by a higher rate of conflict initiation than periods in which there is one dominant order. That is not to say that the proximate causes of conflict change. Wars grow out of their own unique conditions—territorial disputes, intent to protect citizens or commercial interests, defending an ally, or regime survival, for instance. But the likelihood that those conditions lead to the onset of war increases during periods of dueling orders. Research on the linkage between international order and conflict suggests that the periods in which a single international order prevailed—the Concert of Europe period and the post–Cold War period—are the least conflictual, while the post–World War I period and the Cold War—when there were multiple orders present—were the most war prone.[28] Russia's efforts to fuel this emerging axis of upheaval is likely to have profound implications for the United States and its allies.

The Paradox

Paradoxically, Putin's efforts to dismantle the European and global orders run the risk of dismantling his own regime. For the last twenty-four years Putin has sought to concentrate power in his own hands. And yet, the actions he has taken since the invasion have accelerated centrifugal forces that raise the risk of a more violent and chaotic political transition in Russia. The overconcentration of power and fear within the system has slowed decision-making, leading to indecision and inaction that provides the space for small issues to spiral into larger problems for the regime. Most vividly, Putin was slow (or unwilling) to address the problems that Yevgeny Prigozhin, leader of the Wagner Group, was creating within the political system, enabling the most significant challenge the Putin regime had faced since coming to power. Similarly, in the aftermath of Hamas's attack on Israel, a wave of anti-Semitic and anti-Israeli protests swept across the North Caucasus. Local and regional authorities did little to respond, afraid to take actions in the absence of cues from the central government and/or specific directives from Moscow.[29] The events culminated in a high-profile riot at an airport in Dagestan where hundreds of people stormed the runway to protest against a flight arriving from Israel. The overconcentration of power and fear within the system that Putin has instilled raises the risk of inaction that could allow seemingly small events to develop into issues the regime cannot control.

Moreover, Putin's fear of instability has led him to loosen his monopoly over the use of force in Russia, presumably to better equip the security services to maintain control. Putin, for example, has allowed regional governors to stand up their own private military companies to deal with domestic unrest.[30] Putin's national guard—the Rosgvardia—can now access heavy arms.[31] And, as a result of the war in Ukraine, large numbers of fighters and their weapons are now returning to Russia, many of them with mental health issues or drug addictions. The increasingly rigid political system that is prone to inaction and increasing militarization of Russian society is increasing the risk of more turbulent times. Research on the way that longtime leaders like Putin exit supports this. Aside from exiting office as a result of dying of natural causes (the most common way that such longtime leaders leave office), leaders like Putin are most likely to be ousted by bottom-up forces like civil war.[32]

US policy cannot hinge on the hope that such tumult in Russia would produce a substantially weaker or less antagonistic country. But now that Putin has passed his point of no return in his confrontation with the West, Western policymakers must be prepared to face a more aggressive and tumultuous Russia—perhaps for many years to come.

NOTES

1. Joseph R. Biden, "Remarks by President Biden on the United Efforts of the Free World to Support the People of Ukraine" (speech, Warsaw, March 26, 2022), https://www.whitehouse.gov/briefing-room/speeches-remarks/2022/03/26/remarks-by-president-biden-on-the-united-efforts-of-the-free-world-to-support-the-people-of-ukraine/.

2. Antony J. Blinken, "Russia's Strategic Failure and Ukraine's Secure Future" (speech, Helsinki, June 2, 2023), https://www.state.gov/russias-strategic-failure-and-ukraines-secure-future/.

3. Jim Garamone, "Russia Suffers 'Catastrophic Strategic Disaster' in Ukraine," US Department of Defense, November 9, 2022, https://www.defense.gov/News/News-Stories/Article/Article/3214909/russia-suffers-catastrophic-strategic.

4. Alexandra Prokopenko, "Putin's Unsustainable Spending Spree," *Foreign Affairs,* January 8, 2024, https://www.foreignaffairs.com/russian-federation/putins-unsustainable-spending-spree.

5. Andrea Kendall-Taylor and Erica Frantz, "After Putin: Lessons from Autocratic Leadership Transitions," *Washington Quarterly* 45, no. 1 (April 2022): 79–96.

6. Abel Escribà-Folch, "Regression, Political Threats, and Survival under Autocracy," *International Political Science Review* 34, no. 5 (July 2013): 543–560, https://doi.org/10.1177/0192512113488259.

7. Maria Snegovaya, Michael Kimmage, and Jade McGlynn, "Putin the Ideologue," *Foreign Affairs*, November 16, 2023, https://www.foreignaffairs.com/russian-federation/putin-ideologue.

8. Andrei Kolesnikov, "Putin's War Party," *Foreign Affairs,* December 1, 2023, https://www.foreignaffairs.com/eastern-europe-and-former-soviet-union/putins-war-party.

9. Tim Lister and Katharina Krebs, "From Playgrounds to Parade Grounds: Russian Schools Are Becoming Increasingly Militarized," *CNN*, September 25, 2023, https://www.cnn.com/2023/09/24/europe/russia-schools-pro-war-parade-grounds-intl/index.html.

10. Guy Faulconbridge, "Kremlin Aide Rewrites Russian History for a Society at War," *Reuters*, August 10, 2023, https://www.reuters.com/world/europe/kremlin-aide -rewrites-russian-history-society-war-2023-08-10/.

11. Ian Garner, "Russia's Frighteningly Fascist Youth," *Foreign Policy*, May 21, 2023, https://foreignpolicy.com/2023/05/21/russia-fascist-putin-war-youth-ian-garner-book-z -generation/.

12. Patricia Cohen, "Russia's Economy Is Increasingly Structured Around Its War in Ukraine," *New York Times*, October 9, 2023, https://www.nytimes.com/2023/10/09 /business/economy/russia-economy-ukraine-war.html.

13. "Russian Defense Chief Says Military Factories Working 'Around the Clock,'" *Moscow Times*, January 2, 2023, https://www.themoscowtimes.com/2023/01/02/russian -defense-chief-says-military-factories-working-around-the-clock-a79864.

14. Julian E. Barnes, Eric Schmitt, and Thomas Gibbons-Neff, "Russia Overcomes Sanctions to Expand Missile Production, Officials Say," *New York Times*, September 13, 2023, https://www.nytimes.com/2023/09/13/us/politics/russia-sanctions-missile -production.html.

15. Eric Schmidt, "Ukraine Is Losing the Drone War," *Foreign Affairs*, January 22, 2024, https://www.foreignaffairs.com/ukraine/ukraine-losing-drone-war-eric-schmidt.

16. Nicolas Camut, "Putin Could Attack NATO in '5 to 8 years,' German Defense Minister Warns," *Politico*, January 19, 2024, https://www.politico.eu/article/vladimir -putin-russia-germany-boris-pistorius-nato/.

17. Agence France-Presse, "China, Russia Trade Soared in 2023 as Commerce with US Sank," *Voice of America*, January 12, 2024, https://www.voanews.com/a/china-russia -trade-soared-in-2023-as-commerce-with-us-sank-/7437001.html.

18. Robin Brooks (@robin_j_brooks), "China's exports to Russia of machinery and electrical equipment reached a new all-time high in December of last year. China has become—by far—the single biggest exporter to Russia," X, January 18, 2024, 4:39 a.m., https://twitter.com/RobinBrooksIIF/status/174791666.

19. Justin Porter, "Tuesday Briefing: North Korean Missiles in Ukraine," *New York Times*, January 22, 2024, https://www.nytimes.com/2024/01/22/briefing/north-korea -ukraine-india-temple-china-landslide.html.

20. Kolesnikov, "Putin's War Party."

21. Kendall-Taylor and Frantz, "After Putin."

22. Andrea Kendall-Taylor and Erica Frantz, "When Dictators Die," *Journal of Democracy* 27, no. 4 (October 2016): 159–171.

23. Sarah E. Croco, "The Decider's Dilemma: Leader Culpability, War Outcomes, and Domestic Punishment," *American Political Science Review* 105, no. 3 (August 2011): 457–477.

24. Andrea Kendall-Taylor and Erica Frantz, "The Treacherous Path to a Better Russia," *Foreign Affairs*, June 20, 2023.

25. Kimberly Marten et al., *Potential Russian Uses of Paramilitaries in Eurasia* (Washington, DC: Center for a New American Security, January 17, 2024), https:// www.cnas.org/publications/reports/potential-russian-uses-of-paramilitaries-in -eurasia.

26. David Shedd and Ivana Stradner, "Russia's Second Front in Europe," *Foreign Affairs*, November 7, 2023, https://www.foreignaffairs.com/united-states/russias-second-front-europe.

27. Erica Frantz and Natasha Ezrow, *The Politics of Dictatorship: Institutions and Outcomes in Authoritarian Regimes* (Boulder, CO: Lynne Rienner Publishers, 2011).

28. Bear F. Braumoeller, *Only the Dead: The Persistence of War in the Modern Age* (New York: Oxford University Press, 2019).

29. "R.Politik Bulletin No. 19 (127) 2023," *R.Politik*, November 13, 2023, https://rpolitik.com/the-bulletin/bulletin-no-19-127-2023/.

30. Aditya Pareek and Alex Petric, "State Duma Amendments to Laws Signal Russia Is Planning for Protracted Confrontation with the West," *Janes*, August 2, 2023, https://www.janes.com/defence-news/news-detail/state-duma-amendments-to-laws-signal-russia-is-planning-for-protracted-confrontation-with-the-west.

31. Ellie Cook, "Putin Reinforces Rosgvardia Troops with Heavy Armor after Wagner Coup," *Newsweek*, August 8, 2023, https://www.newsweek.com/russia-ukraine-rosgvardia-national-guard-vladimir-putin-wagner-group-mutiny-1818187.

32. Kendall-Taylor and Frantz, "The Treacherous Path to a Better Russia."

Chapter Fourteen

Accelerating Profound Changes Unseen in a Century

Chinese Assessments of and Responses to Russia's Invasion of Ukraine

Bonny Lin and Brian Hart

Russia's war in Ukraine marked a turning point for the People's Republic of China (PRC). The invasion occurred shortly after Chinese president Xi Jinping and Russian leader Vladimir Putin held a historic meeting in early February 2022 at which the two announced a "no limits" partnership.[1] This upgraded relationship showcased two countries increasingly aligned in assessments of external threats from the West and in shared foreign policy values, goals, and activities. It was thus not a surprise that Beijing responded to Russia's invasion of Ukraine by politically siding with Russia, blaming NATO and the United States for causing the conflict, and legitimatizing Russian security concerns. China has also strongly opposed economic sanctions against Russia, but it has been cautious about exposing itself to costs. Beijing has largely abided by the letter of sanctions and has not provided direct military support to Russia.

At the start of the war, a number of Chinese experts assessed that the war in Ukraine would be short and would only have limited international impact. They were quickly proved wrong.

Bonny Lin is director of the China Power Project and senior fellow for Asian security at the Center for Strategic and International Studies (CSIS). She also teaches at Yale University and is a member of the Council on Foreign Relations. Previously, she worked at the RAND Corporation and the Department of Defense. Brian Hart is a fellow with the China Power Project at CSIS, where he researches China's foreign policy and military, US-China relations, and Taiwan security issues. He also supports *Hidden Reach*, a CSIS special initiative tracking China's global influence through open-source data and satellite imagery.

The war's profound significance has led to extensive PRC government–directed or government-encouraged studies of its implications. This chapter analyzes the lessons China is likely drawing from the war, relying heavily on insights from leading PRC scholars and institutions that are well connected with the Chinese government. First, the chapter explores Chinese assessments of how the war has undermined the international order and increased global instability. Next, it unpacks the lessons Beijing has drawn from a US "proxy war" in Ukraine and from Russian experiences on the battlefield and examines the implications for a future war over Taiwan. Finally, it explores how China is responding to shore up its security and prepare for a potential conflict.

A Fragmented, Unstable, and Dangerous International Environment

There is now consensus among Chinese scholars that the Ukraine conflict has uprooted the global order, resulting in uncertainty and a new contest for power that is reshaping the international landscape. Some Chinese experts, such as Zhu Feng, describe Russia's invasion of Ukraine as starting a new "post-post–Cold War era."[2] Chinese officials and strategists note that the Ukraine conflict has accelerated Xi Jinping's assessment that the world is undergoing "profound changes unseen in a century (百年变局)" and that international dynamics are becoming even more complicated.[3] This creates challenges but also opportunities for Beijing to strengthen its position.

A More Divided, Fragmented World

This new post-Ukraine international landscape is still emerging, but it has several defining features. First, it is a more divided world in which Western leadership is increasingly contested. Chinese experts note that the prior balance between four major international actors—the United States, Europe, China, and Russia—no longer exists. Europe is more aligned with the United States, and both are in open confrontation against Russia. Russia has aligned itself more with China, and China has provided Russia with economic and diplomatic support. All the while, the United States continues to prioritize China as its top challenge.

This division is also economic. According to China, the Western "weaponization" of the global economy and unprecedented sanctions against Russia have fragmented global financial markets and supply chains.[4] This has been accompanied by a rise in protectionism and a retreat from globalization as countries seek to shield themselves from future economic disruptions.

Beyond the leading powers, Chinese experts see much of the Global South maintaining normal relations with Russia and refusing to take sides in the war. Beijing views developing countries as critical partners in resisting Western-led sanctions on Russia, pushing for a peaceful solution to the conflict, and sustaining existing supply chains, free trade, and economic globalization. The Global South's positioning on the Ukraine war, as well as its continued growth in relative economic power and population size, has strengthened Beijing's belief that China should work with this community to counter US hegemony and secure the critical resources needed for China's development.[5]

The war further affirms two key trends that Beijing has long believed. The first is the trend toward multipolarity. The divisions at the top and the rise of the Global South support this, though the international order is still far from a true, balanced multipolar system.

The second trend is the PRC's belief that the East is rising and the West is declining (but at present the West is still stronger). Chinese experts write that the power gap between the United States and China is shrinking, and the war has taken a significant toll on Russia and Europe. There appears to be some disagreement about whether the Ukraine conflict temporarily bolstered US leadership.[6] However, the official PRC line remains that the long-term trend is relative US decline as China grows stronger.

WEAK OR INEFFECTIVE GLOBAL INSTITUTIONS

Second, the war has sped up the sidelining of existing international institutions. Chinese experts discuss the lack of US and Western interest in reforming the United Nations to make it more effective and representative. Instead, they see the West as trying to remove Russia from the Security Council and circumventing the Security Council by leveraging the General Assembly for action related to Ukraine.[7] They also view the United States as politicizing the G20 by repeatedly pushing it to take stances on Ukraine and other issues, making it less effective in contributing to global governance.

Concurrently, leading powers are increasingly relying on smaller blocs of like-minded countries to advance their objectives. The Ukraine war has revitalized NATO and fostered closer partnerships between NATO and Indo-Pacific countries such as Japan, South Korea, Australia, and New Zealand. The United States has also "politicized" the G7 economic grouping to sanction Russia or criticize China and strengthened minilaterals such as the Quad, AUKUS, and the US-Japan-ROK trilateral.[8] In China's view, the United States is sowing division by pushing a Cold War–style narrative of democracies versus autocracies, demonizing China and Russia as the anchor of a threatening axis.

Increased Global Risk of Instability and Turmoil

Third, Chinese experts worry the Ukraine war has widespread cascading first- and second-order effects. The war derailed the global economy's recovery from COVID-19, disrupted global food supply chains, hiked energy prices, and contributed to inflation—all of which can undermine the ability of governments to rule and maintain order. This risk may be particularly acute in developing countries that face high rates of poverty and starvation.[9] Within developed countries, Chinese experts see the rise of right-wing parties, which has, in the past, led to more xenophobia and domestic violence.[10]

Chinese experts are also monitoring the sweeping impacts of the Ukraine war on Russia's confrontation with the West. China is wary that escalated global competition between the United States, Europe, and Russia could be destabilizing. This is manifested in more jockeying for influence in the Global South and Russian willingness to partner with countries that are opposed to the West in order to create problems for the United States and to support Russia's war in Ukraine.

Intensified competition risks major powers stirring up trouble and smaller actors engaging in opportunistic behavior. The risk of instability is high in Africa, where Russia is active. Chinese experts have also tracked Putin's intervention in the Israel-Hamas conflict and Hamas's release of Russians in recognition of Putin's efforts.[11] China is closely watching growing Russia-North Korea ties and has expressed reservations that Russian intentions for the Korean Peninsula differ from those of China. Moscow's preoccupation with Ukraine has also reduced Russian influence in Central Asia and South Caucasus, and actors in those regions have taken advantage of that to use violence to press for their interests.

A More Dangerous Environment for China

Fourth, the war has reinforced concerns that Beijing is facing a more dangerous external environment. China viewed NATO's military expansion and the West's quest for "absolute security" as the key reason why Moscow had no choice but to use force. Beijing believes Washington is doing the same around China and is concerned NATO could expand to the Indo-Pacific.[12] From Beijing's perspective, Western inability to sympathize with Russia demonstrates that the United States may never consider China's security concerns.

Indeed, shortly after Russia invaded Ukraine, one of the headlines that dominated US news was whether China would invade Taiwan next. Beijing views these two flashpoints as completely unrelated. The headlines thus showcased inflated US threat perceptions and Washington's fixation on China.

Overall, as Beijing looks at the international landscape, it assesses the transition to multipolarity as chaotic, dangerous, and bringing heightened risks of conflict. This post-post–Cold War order could break down even further.

China Rethinks Use of Military Force

In addition to these larger geopolitical shifts, the Ukraine conflict is offering China insights on modern warfare. On one hand, China is observing how the United States "used" Ukraine to wage a proxy war against Russia. On the other hand, China is assessing what worked and did not work in Russia's invasion of a weak neighbor.

Lessons Learned from Ukraine as a US Proxy War

China views the Ukraine conflict as a proxy war (代理人战争) between the United States and its allies on one side and Russia on the other.[13] Chinese analysts believe the war demonstrates that the United States may increasingly resort to proxy warfare as an asymmetric approach to gain advantage in major power competition.[14] They argue that direct US military confrontation against China and Russia is too dangerous and costly because of both countries' conventional and nuclear capabilities and China's economic heft. Proxy wars via third parties, however, could undermine an opponent's overall power, lock opponents in a cycle of warfare, and isolate them from the international community. US leaders are less likely to face as much domestic pushback for supporting proxy wars as they would sending US troops to intervene. The "limited" US involvement provides Washington with flexibility to escalate or deescalate.[15]

Although Chinese scholars view proxy wars as having major drawbacks, most do not believe that this dampens US willingness to use this asymmetric option. They believe that Washington has not seriously considered putting pressure on Ukraine to end the war.[16] There is particular concern that the United States could leverage pro-independence forces in Taiwan as a proxy against China to draw Beijing into a costly conflict.[17] This was voiced by the PRC government: China's August 2022 white paper on Taiwan states that "external forces are using Taiwan as a pawn to undermine China's development and progress and obstruct the rejuvenation of the Chinese nation."[18]

Revitalized US Alliances and Large US-Led Coalition

US "proxy warfare" against Russia thus offers a template for how the United States could act against China. First, Chinese experts believe that the United States not only brought together a large coalition to support Ukraine but also used and amplified the Russian threat and China-Russia axis to revitalize alliances in Europe and the Indo-Pacific. They explain that this differs from the Cold War, when proxy wars were localized and waged by proxies that were largely (if not exclusively) supported by the United States or Soviet Union. Instead, since the 2003 Iraq War, the United States has increasingly relied on coalitions because Washington recognizes that proxy wars are not always cheap or easy.

"Avatar Warfare": Unprecedented, Encompassing US and Allied Aid

Second, the United States and its allies have provided very public and unprecedented levels of support to Kyiv. This contrasts with Cold War proxy war efforts that were mainly under the radar. Chinese scholars point out that the United States trained, armed, and equipped its proxy (Ukraine) for years. They document US involvement beginning after Russia seized Crimea in 2014, which improved the ability of Ukrainian "grassroots commanders," leveled up Ukrainian special forces, and reduced corruption and mismanagement of Ukraine's military.[19]

Since Russia's 2022 invasion, support for Ukraine has included an extraordinary diversity of weapons and equipment, a fast pace of delivery of such goods, and the use of non-peacetime US authorities, such as Presidential Drawdown Authority. And US assistance has extended far beyond military support. Accurate and early public releases of intelligence helped convince allies and partners to stop fence-sitting and take steps against Russia. This put Moscow on the defensive, forcing Russia to deny and deflect from actions it had not yet taken.[20] The sharing of unclassified and open-source intelligence via US-owned social media platforms also helped expose Russian activities and spread pro-Ukrainian narratives.

According to Chinese experts, assistance to Ukraine expanded from February 2022 onwards. US intelligence allowed Ukraine to successfully defend and attack Russian military targets. This information came not only from Western governments but also from Western satellite and information technology companies. At the same time, Russia and China publicly accused the United States of direct intervention in the conflict by launching cyberattacks against Russia from Ukrainian territory.

Some Chinese strategists have coined a new term for enhanced proxy warfare, "avatar warfare" (分身战), to capture the notion that comprehensive assistance has completely remade Ukraine such that fighting Ukraine resembles directly fighting a weaker and smaller version of the United States.[21] The United States has had to provide the whole operational system to facilitate Ukraine's war, including weapons, intelligence, battlefield situational awareness, logistics support, and command and control. The rise of "avatar warfare" represents a new development in major power confrontation.[22]

Unprecedented Economic Sanctions

Chinese scholars have dissected Western sanctions on Russia, blaming the United States for using its hegemonic position within the international financial system to punish Russia. The sanctions on Russia were not just unprecedented in scope and scale; even longtime neutral European countries—Switzerland, Austria, Sweden, Finland, and Ireland—joined. Over a thousand multinational companies voluntarily left or scaled back operations in Russia, marking the first time private companies participated in sanctions at this scale.[23]

The West's ability to assemble sanctions beyond what the markets or Russia considered possible worries Beijing. On the one hand, Chinese scholars recognize that Russia is smaller and less central to the US and global economy than China and therefore easier to sanction. It would be more difficult for the United States to put together a similar sanctions package against the PRC.[24] On the other hand, if the United States could exceed expectations and sanction China, China is more vulnerable than Russia. China's larger economy and dependence on imports would make sanctions much more destructive. Russia has long suffered sanctions from the West and built up economic defenses since its 2014 seizure of Crimea. Of key concern for Beijing is the fact that there is no single country that can be an economic lifeline for China in the way that China has supported Russia. Even if official sanctions are not biting, the departure of multinational companies and investors from China would be devastating. This leaves China no choice but to prepare for the worst.

Chinese experts are also seeing some decreased international support for the war as the conflict drags on. They are closely watching the internal debates within the United States and Europe and are likely waiting to see how long the United States and Europe can sustain the fight.

Lessons Learned from Russian Military Operations in Ukraine

Chinese military strategists have pored over Russia's military campaign against Ukraine. Looking at Russian operations as a whole, there are several major PRC strategic lessons learned. First, an invasion of a weaker neighbor could become protracted, with spillover effects well beyond the territories involved. As a result, China needs to be prepared and resilient enough for a long conflict. Politically and economically, PRC scholars have studied how Russia has maintained social stability and internal resilience, how it has tried to shield its economy, and Moscow's efforts to reorient its foreign policy to support the war and its larger strategy.[25] Militarily, having sufficient precision munitions and a large war reserve is critical to shortening the fight and sustaining combat. Chinese military analysts note that Russia failed to use enough firepower in its initial operations; the number of missiles it launched daily against Ukraine in the first two months of the 2022 war was substantially lower than US use of precision-guided weapons during the Gulf War or the Iraq War.[26]

Second, Russia's military performance was not what Putin or the international community expected. Russia did not execute its military campaign according to its own doctrine, and its military was underprepared. Russia's lengthy buildup along the Ukraine border afforded the United States and its allies time to prepare and warn the international community. Once the invasion started, Russian failures were manifold. Russia's limited use of precision-guided weapons failed to dismantle Ukraine's air defenses, shore-based anti-ship missile batteries, and command, control, communications, computers, intelligence, surveillance, and reconnaissance (C4ISR) assets. Russian forces failed to use electronic warfare capabilities to decapitate Ukraine's command and control systems. These shortcomings meant Russia did not establish what People's Liberation Army (PLA) writings refer to as the "three dominances" (三权), which is superiority in the information, air, and maritime domains.[27] Russian difficulties were exacerbated by its poorly trained and equipped troops. They also were stymied by poor logistics lines and officers who lacked the ability and willingness to experiment and take initiative due to a rigid command hierarchy.

Third, the Ukraine conflict has likely reinforced Beijing's view that nuclear weapons are useful to some extent. PRC scholars believe that Russia's nuclear saber rattling worked as a strategic deterrent to keep the United States and its allies from sending troops into Ukraine.[28] At the same time, Moscow has not yet assessed that detonating a nuclear weapon would bring it more advantages than costs.

Chinese scholars also assess that the Ukraine conflict has increased the risk of nuclear proliferation. First, they see that others (such as North Korea, South Korea, and Japan) are learning from Ukraine and seeking to strengthen their nuclear capabilities or acquire nuclear weapons. Such a weakening of the "nuclear taboo" is likely to complicate China's immediate strategic environment and could facilitate further deepening of US military ties with countries around China.[29] Second, Chinese analysts have observed the threats posed to Ukrainian nuclear power plants.[30] China and other East Asian countries have many nuclear power plants. A lowering of the nuclear threshold could increase the chances that nuclear power plants are attacked during a conflict, which could afford countries without nuclear weapons a way to impose catastrophic cost on China.

These dynamics have led to debate within China on its nuclear capabilities. Some nationalist commentators such as Song Zhongping argue that China should significantly expand its nuclear capabilities and establish a more robust nuclear triad akin to US and Russian forces.[31] Others explain that some expansion is warranted, but US-China strategic stability is not (and should not be) built on the Cold War concepts of mutually assured destruction that require comparable nuclear arsenals.

How China Is Responding

Given the lessons learned from the war in Ukraine, how is Beijing responding? This section first examines initial PRC responses—which were mainly at home—and then explores changes in the PRC's external behavior.

STRENGTHENING NATIONAL SECURITY AND SANCTION-PROOFING CHINA

One of the first and immediate steps Beijing took was to strengthen national security at home. Xi Jinping's October 2022 report at the Chinese Communist Party's Twentieth National Congress warned of "external attempts to suppress and contain China" and featured an all-new section on national security that emphasized a "multidimensional" and expansive conception of national security to include issues like food, energy, and supply chain resilience.[32]

China tightened the reins soon after. In April 2023, the National People's Congress passed a revised Counter-Espionage Law, which has been accompanied by public arrests of foreign nationals accused of spying. In May, the Central National Security Commission held a meeting during which (among other things) it approved a directive on enhancing public education on national security. This is part of an overarching effort by the Chinese leadership to better prepare the Chinese public for crises and improve civilian mobilization for national defense. China's Ministry of State Security also took on a more prominent public profile, including launching a new account on the popular social media app WeChat and participating in high-profile crackdowns on foreign firms.[33]

The PRC has likewise taken measures to shore up its economic resilience. In 2023, Chinese authorities provided incentives to increase the amount of land available for crops and encouraged the adoption of new and experimental measures to boost crop yields.[34] PRC government budget for grain reserves also grew nearly 14% in 2023.[35]

Energy security has received similar attention. Shortly after the war, Chinese industry leaders and experts called for diversifying the country's energy supply, increasing its energy independence, and promoting the use of China's renminbi (RMB) for pricing and settling international energy transactions.[36] In 2023 alone, China's installed solar power capacity rose a staggering 55%, and its installed wind power capacity rose by almost 21%.[37] PRC officials also announced new efforts to expand reserves of key energy commodities.[38]

To shield against financial sanctions, China is accelerating efforts to internationalize the RMB. This includes using Belt and Road Initiative (BRI) loans to promote payment in RMB, contributing to a greater share of China's trade with Russia and some other countries now being settled in RMB. According to SWIFT, the leading organization that facilitates international payments, the RMB reached a record high share of international payments (4.6%) in November 2023.[39]

Yet prioritization of securitization has come at a cost as foreigners have become warier of investing in China. Faced with slumping economic activity in 2023, the party's flagship newspaper *People's Daily* stated in early February 2024 that "development and security should be given equal attention."[40] Beijing recognizes the contradictions and will need to balance between achieving both national objectives.

Enhancing Efforts to Deter and Prepare for Conflict with the United States and Its Allies

Linked to China's greater national security focus is enhanced PRC efforts to deter and prepare for conflict with the United States. First, Beijing likely seeks to minimize US ability to arm and equip Taiwan to be a "proxy" against China and sees parallels between US efforts to deepen ties with Taiwan and NATO's assistance to Ukraine prior to the 2022 invasion. Beijing has scaled up efforts to respond to US engagements with Taiwan. This includes two large-scale PRC exercises in August 2022 and April 2023 surrounding Taiwan to punish Taiwan for what China views as provocative US and Taiwan efforts to deepen ties. In December 2022, China also held large-scale military exercises near Taiwan in response to President Joe Biden's signing of the National Defense Authorization Act, which included programs to support Taiwan's defense.[41]

Second, China has continued to make sweeping investments to modernize the PLA. Military modernization programs long predate the Ukraine conflict, but the war has accelerated the assessment that China's global and external environment is deteriorating fast and China needs to be prepared. The US Department of Defense assesses that the PLA continued to build up its inventory of conventionally armed ballistic missiles in 2022 and warned that the PRC may be exploring the development of conventionally armed intercontinental-range missiles (which are typically only nuclear-armed). In 2022, the PLA significantly stepped up the integration of civilian assets, including roll-on/roll-off ferries, to support PLA amphibious force employment. The Pentagon also assesses that the PLA now has over five hundred nuclear warheads and will probably have over a thousand operational warheads by 2030.[42]

The PLA is making important reforms to improve personnel as well. In March 2022, the PLA put forth new regulations to increase combat effectiveness, and in August 2022, the PLA increased the age limit by which university graduates could join the military. In April 2023, China revised rules to allow the PLA to adjust conscription requirements at will after issuing a national defense mobilization order, including specifically calling up more experienced former soldiers to support active units.[43]

Third, China has purged top military officials, most notably former Minister of Defense Li Shangfu and several generals with ties to the PLA Rocket Force—likely due to corruption. Xi Jinping has made anticorruption campaigns a highly visible part of his tenure, yet this latest round of purges indicates that previous campaigns have not rooted out serious corruption within the PLA. Given the role that corruption has played in Russia's failures in Ukraine, Xi likely feels a greater sense of urgency to manage graft within his own forces.

Casting China as a Better Leader than the United States

Externally, China views the turbulence resulting from the Ukraine war as an opportunity for Beijing to step up. After initial PRC efforts to cast itself as neutral failed to prevent the United States and Europe from viewing China more negatively, China became more active in presenting an alternative leadership model.

In its September 2023 white paper titled "A Global Community of Shared Future," Beijing criticized the peace, development, security, and government "deficits" the global community faced under US and Western leadership.[44] Beijing called for a "new type" of international relations, global governance, and economic globalization that emphasizes greater openness, inclusion, equity, and cooperation. China has encouraged countries to adopt to "shared future" initiatives that involve agreeing to China's vision and participation in several key PRC foreign policy efforts.

The first is Xi's signature BRI. Over 150 countries have signed on to this decade-old initiative, the vast majority of which are developing countries. Since 2023, China has pivoted the BRI away from large-scale infrastructure megaprojects toward smaller projects with an emphasis on digital connectivity, cooperation on science and technology, and "green" development.[45] Beijing aims to make the project more palatable and sustainable so that it can continue to be a primary mechanism for building influence in the Global South.

The second is what PRC experts refer to as the three global initiatives started by Xi: the 2021 Global Development Initiative (GDI), the 2022 Global Security Initiative (GSI), and the 2023 Global Civilization Initiative (GCI). Of these, the GSI has taken on particular importance amid the Ukraine war. Rolled out two months after Russia invaded Ukraine, the GSI seeks to challenge US-dominated norms on global security issues and articulate a vision of security more friendly to Beijing's interests.[46] This includes advocating peacefully negotiated solutions to tensions (instead of what Beijing views as the United States adding fuel to the fire in Ukraine). In line with this, China released its position paper on Ukraine in February 2023 to cast itself as trying to bring the conflict to a peaceful end. Soon after, in March 2023, China brokered an agreement between Saudi Arabia and Iran to reestablish relations. Going forward, China is likely to seek similar opportunities to demonstrate its ability to bring about peace.

Similarly, China's GCI provides an alternative way to view the world as made up of diverse civilizations living in harmony instead of the democracy versus autocracy lens. It seeks to undermine the narrative that modernization is the same as "westernization."[47] The GCI's civilization umbrella has helped the Chinese Communist Party use party-to-party diplomacy to make inroads in the Middle East, Africa, and other regions.[48]

STRENGTHENING ALTERNATIVE MULTILATERAL INSTITUTIONS

In addition to the China-centered initiatives above, China has beefed up key multilateral organizations to serve as an alternative for Western-led groupings. In August 2023, China championed the expansion of the BRICS grouping by inviting six resource-rich countries to join: Argentina, Egypt, Ethiopia, Iran, Saudi Arabia, and the United Arab Emirates. Beijing aims to elevate the organization's ability to serve as a counterweight against the US-led G7 economies. Similarly, China and Russia have pushed to expand membership of the Shanghai Cooperation Organization (SCO) by bringing in Iran and Belarus, and the SCO is increasingly taking on economic dimensions as many of its members look to sidestep Western economic sanctions.

Strengthening Ties with Russia and Others

Beyond pursuing global leadership, China also recognizes that it needs to build a stronger network of friends should the United States seek to sanction or use force against China. Top among this list is Russia, a major power and neighbor that shares China's concerns about problematic US and Western behavior.

Since Russia's invasion of Ukraine, China has deepened its relationship with Russia. In 2023, two-way trade hit a historic high of $240 billion, largely as a result of China's record purchases of Russian oil.[49] Chinese companies have also sold Russia critical dual-use technologies like semiconductors.[50] Militarily, the two countries have conducted additional joint military exercises—including with third-country partners—to demonstrate opposition to US or allied activities.

China continues to double down on the relationship. Xi Jinping has met with Vladimir Putin in person three times and held multiple virtual meetings and calls since the start of the war. Most recently, in October 2023, Putin met with Xi in Beijing, where Xi called for strengthening ties further in 2024 and emphasized China's "long-term commitment" to the relationship and committed to greater cooperation on the world stage.[51]

To date there are no signs that Beijing seeks a traditional military alliance with Russia or any other country. Instead, China is strengthening relations with as many countries as possible that could support PRC interests, particularly those in the Global South that have remained neutral in the Ukraine war and autocracies that share China's concerns about the United States.

Recalibrating Relations with the United States and Europe

The final and more recent element of China's response to the Ukraine war has been its attempts to stabilize relations with the United States and Europe. Throughout much of 2022 and early 2023, China suffered from declining relations with the United States and Europe. This was due to a variety of factors including Chinese support for Russia, intensified US-China competition, as well as tensions in the Taiwan Strait, the South China Sea, and elsewhere. China's sluggish economic growth and dependence on trade have compounded pressure on Beijing to mend its relations with major economies.

Within this context, China renewed diplomatic outreach. In early 2023, China began a charm offensive toward Europe with Chinese leaders traveling to the region to praise the importance of globalization and tout China as open to European companies. In high-level meetings with European Union leaders, Xi emphasized his hope that the European Union can be "a key partner in economic and trade cooperation."[52] China is also piloting a visa-free entry program into China for seven different European countries.[53]

Similarly, the PRC has sought to reduce tensions with the United States. Throughout 2023, the two sides held several cabinet-level meetings culminating in a summit between President Xi and President Biden in San Francisco in November. While the meeting did not fundamentally reset relations, it put US-China relations on a more positive footing and reestablished critical communication channels and some cooperation.

Beijing is under no illusions that its relationships with the United States and Europe can come close to "win-win" cooperation. Instead, Beijing's goal is to reverse and slow growing anti-China sentiment in Europe and prevent US-China relations from spiraling toward confrontation. This helps Beijing better protect PRC interests within a more uncertain, unstable, and dangerous international environment.

Conclusion

Overall, Russia's war in Ukraine broke—and is now reshaping—the international order. Chinese experts view the world as increasingly divided, unstable, and dangerous. The war showcased how the United States could use proxies, expand alliances, leverage like-minded blocs, and wield unprecedented sanctions against China in the event of a future US-China conflict.

China is responding across the board. Internally, China has doubled down on national security and resilience, at some costs to economic development. China is continuing to upgrade the PLA and root out its weaknesses. Externally, China is trying to position itself as a more responsible, worthy leader compared to the United States, and it is particularly focusing on gaining influence in the Global South. China continues to strengthen ties with Russia and other strong global partners to support China against the West. Beijing is also trying to stabilize relations with the United States and Europe to provide China more space to develop and grow.

NOTES

1. Presidential Administration of Russia, "Joint Statement of the Russian Federation and the People's Republic of China on the International Relations Entering a New Era and the Global Sustainable Development," February 4, 2022, http://en.kremlin.ru /supplement/5770.

2. Zhu Feng, "Zhu Feng: The 'Post-Post–Cold War Era' Has Officially Begun! Where Do Countries around the World Go in This Period of Turbulent Change?" [朱锋: "后后冷战时代" 正式开启! 动荡变革期的世界各国何去何从?], Institute for Global Cooperation and Understanding, Peking University, September 22, 2023, https://www.igcu.pku .edu.cn/info/1026/6087.htm.

3. Wang Honggang, "Wang Honggang: 'Reviewing' the World in 2023—Crossing through the Chaotic Clouds, Gazing upon New Heights" [王鸿刚: "复盘"世界2023——乱云飞渡, 又踏层峰望眼开], *Cfisnet*, December 28, 2023, http://comment.cfisnet.com /2023/1228/1329222.html.

4. "China Institutes for Contemporary International Relations Annual Report: Global Strategy and Security Risks in 2024" [现代院年度报告: 2024年全球战略与安全风险], *Cfisnet*, January 12, 2024, http://comment.cfisnet.com/2024/0112/1329320.html.

5. Niu Haibin et al., "The Rise of the Global South and China's Role" [全球南方崛起与中国的角色], Shanghai Institutes for International Studies (November 2023): 1–8, https://www.siis.org.cn/updates/cms/cms/202312/05145516jydf.pdf.

6. Some PRC experts assess that the war has allowed Washington to demonstrate temporary leadership and that US hard power has endured while its soft power has declined. Others believe that the United States is becoming overstretched in Ukraine while also dealing with the Israel-Hamas conflict. See Zou Zhibo and Xiao He in *Annual Report on International Politics and Security (2024)* [全球政治与安全报告 (2024)] (Beijing: Social Sciences Academic Press, 2024), 2–5, https://xianxiao.ssap.com.cn /bibliography/1882873.html.

7. Ren Lin and Su Shanyue in *Annual Report on International Politics and Security (2024)* [全球政治与安全报告 (2024)] (Beijing: Social Sciences Academic Press, 2024), https://xianxiao.ssap.com.cn/reader/?resource_id=7020625&resource_type=2.

8. "The United States Manipulates the G7 to Protect Hegemony and Cause Division" [美国操纵七国集团护霸权搞分裂]," *Xinhua*, May 21, 2023, http://www.news .cn/world/2023-05/21/c_1129634846.htm.

9. Fu Xiaoqiang, "China and the World at the 'Crossroads' of History" [历史"十字路口"处的中国与世界], China Institutes of Contemporary International Relations, December 31, 2023, http://www.cicir.ac.cn/NEW/opinion.html?id=5f83a5df-2d7e-45a4 -931d-52cf7f21b923.

10. Fu Yuming and Tian Ying, "Xinhua Headlines: Europe Faces Worrying Trend as Far-Right Parties Grow," *Xinhua*, September 14, 2018, http://www.xinhuanet.com /english/2018-09/14/c_137468359.htm.

11. Ye Tianle, "Russia's Strategic Considerations in the Palestinian-Israel Conflict" [巴以冲突中的俄罗斯战略考量], China Institutes of Contemporary International Relations, December 6, 2023, http://www.cicir.ac.cn/NEW/opinion.html?id=1fdc5a64 -4ad4-44ba-800f-e229e86037d3.

12. "Russia-Ukraine Conflict Can Be Regarded as a 'Preview' of US' Possible Acts in Asia: Zheng Yongnian," *Global Times,* March 17, 2022, https://www.globaltimes.cn/page /202203/1255162.shtml.

13. Ministry of Foreign Affairs of the People's Republic of China, *US Hegemony and Its Perils,* February 20, 2023, https://www.fmprc.gov.cn/mfa_eng/wjbxw/202302 /t20230220_11027664.html.

14. Yang Guanghai, "U.S. Proxy War in Ukraine: Motivations, Actions, and Implication" [美国在乌克兰的代理人战争: 动因、举措与启示], *Journal on Peace and Development,* no. 1 (2023): 1–42, https://www.caifc.org.cn/uploadfile/2023/0309 /20230309034816415.pdf.

15. "Instigating Proxy Wars: The United States Seriously Disrupting International Order [策动代理人战争, 美国严重扰乱国际秩序]," *Xinhua,* July 11, 2022, http://www .xinhuanet.com/mil/2022-07/11/c_1211665839.htm.

16. Chen Xiang, "Russia-Ukraine Conflict and the Evolution of America's Proxy War" [俄乌冲突与美国代理人战争的走向]," *Journal of International Relations,* no. 2 (2023): 47–49, https://d.wanfangdata.com.cn/periodical/gjgxyj202302003.

17. "China Taiwan Net: U.S. Setting a 'Time Trap' for Taiwan Strait Conflict Is a Rhetoric to Contain China's Development" [中国台湾网: 美设置台海冲突'时间陷阱'是 遏制中国发展的话术], *Shanghai Observer,* March 24, 2023, https://www.jfdaily.com /staticsg/res/html/web/newsDetail.html?id=596033.

18. "Full Text: The Taiwan Question and China's Reunification in the New Era," *Xinhua,* August 10, 2022, https://english.news.cn/20220810/df9d3b8702154b34bbf1d451 b99bf64a/c.html.

19. Li Chen, "Analysis of U.S. Military Assistance to Ukraine Since the Russia-Ukraine Conflict" [俄乌冲突以来美国对乌克兰军事援助评析], Center for International Security and Strategy Tsinghua University, January 2023, https://ciss.tsinghua.edu.cn /info/zlyaq/6142.

20. Nate Beach-Westmoreland, *Sharpening the Spear: China's Information Warfare Lessons from Ukraine* (Piscataway, NJ: Institute of Electrical and Electronics Engineers, 2023): 399–415, https://ieeexplore.ieee.org/document/10181559.

21. Dong Shengli, "The Dangerous Evolution of Major Power Proxy Wars" ['分身战': 大国'代理人战'的危险演进], *China Social Sciences Net,* March 16, 2023, https://www .cssn.cn/jsx/jsx_jqlw/202303/t20230316_5608092.shtml.

22. "Outlook on Nine Global Trends for 2023" [2023年全球九大趋势展望], *China Social Sciences Net,* February 2, 2023, https://www.cssn.cn/gjgc/202302/t20230202 _5585623.shtml.

23. "Over 1,000 Companies Have Curtailed Operations in Russia—But Some Remain," Chief Executive Leadership Institute of Yale School of Management, accessed February 16, 2024, https://som.yale.edu/story/2022/over-1000-companies-have-curtailed -operations-russia-some-remain.

24. Zhang Wenzong and Wang Jingyuan, "Changes and Revelations in the U.S. 'Dual Containment' Strategy towards China and Russia" [美国对中俄实施"双遏制"战略 的变化及启示], *Journal on Peace and Development,* no. 4 (2022): 1–21, https://www.caifc .org.cn/uploadfile/2023/0214/20230214033146937.pdf.

25. Ma Qiang, "Russia's Social Resilience in the Context of Russia-Ukraine Conflict" [俄乌冲突背景下俄罗斯的社会韧性], *Russian Studies*, no. 5 (2023): 127–157, https://chn.oversea.cnki.net/kcms/detail/detail.aspx?DBCode=CJFD&DBName =CJFDLAST2023&fileName=ELSY202305005.

26. Wang Yalin et al., "Research on the Use of Precision Strike Weapons between China and Russia in the Russia-Ukraine Conflict" [俄乌冲突中俄精确打击武器运用研 究], *Tactical Missile Technology*, June 13, 2022, https://www.auvsc.com/page210?article _id=2401&pagenum=all.

27. Joel Wuthnow, "Rightsizing Chinese Military: Lessons from Ukraine," *Strategic Forum* 311 (September 1, 2022), https://ndupress.ndu.edu/Media/News/News-Article -View/Article/3146628/rightsizing-chinese-military-lessons-from-ukraine/.

28. Jin Ning and Ma Jianguang, "Strategic Deterrence and Impacts of U.S.-Russia Strategies in the Context of Great Power Competition" [大国博弈背景下的美俄战略威慑与 影响], *Russian, East European & Central Asian Studies* 12, no. 3 (2022): 42–62, http://www .oyyj-oys.org/UploadFile/Issue/201605310001/2022/6//20220601064318WU_FILE_0.pdf.

29. Chen Dongxiao, "Chen Xiaodong Wrote for *Jiefang Daily*, Speaking of Evolutions of International Security in 2023" [陈东晓在解放日报撰文, 谈2023年国际局势的演变], Shanghai Institutes for International Studies, https://www.siis.org.cn/sp/15367.jhtml.

30. Wu Chunsi, "Impact of the Russia-Ukraine Conflict on International Nuclear Arms Control and Disarmament" [俄乌冲突对国际核军控和裁军的影响], Shanghai Institutes for International Studies (2022): 36, https://www.siis.org.cn/dbfile.svl?n= /updates/cms/cms/202205/09163615vuuy.pdf.

31. Minnie Chan, "Upgrades for China's Nuclear Triad as Xi Jinping Pushes for Stronger Strategic Deterrence: Analysts," *South China Morning Post*, October 29, 2022, https://www.scmp.com/news/china/military/article/3197705/upgrades-chinas-nuclear -triad-xi-jinping-pushes-stronger-strategic-deterrence-analysts.

32. Bonny Lin et al., "China's 20th Party Congress Report: Doubling Down in the Face of External Threats," Center for Strategic and International Studies, October 19, 2022, https://www.csis.org/analysis/chinas-20th-party-congress-report-doubling-down -face-external-threats.

33. Sheena Chestnut Greitens, "National Security after China's 20th Party Con-gress: Trends in Discourse and Policy," *China Leadership Monitor*, August 29, 2023, https://www.prcleader.org/post/national-security-after-china-s-20th-party-congress -trends-in-discourse-and-policy.

34. Luna Sun, "China Vows to Boost Farm Output, Seed Research in Renewed Food Security, Tech Self-Reliance Push," *South China Morning Post*, February 4, 2024, https://www.scmp.com/economy/china-economy/article/3250889/china-vows-boost -farm-output-seed-research-renewed-food-security-tech-self-reliance-push.

35. Mandy Zuo, "China Food Security: Budget for Grain Reserves Grows by 13.6 Per Cent amid Self-Sufficiency Push," *South China Morning Post*, March 6, 2023, https:// www.scmp.com/economy/china-economy/article/3212519/china-food-security-budget -grain-reserves-grows-136-cent-amid-self-sufficiency-push.

36. Xu Jin, "Ten Revelations from the Russia-Ukraine Conflict concerning China's Energy Security" [俄乌冲突给我国能源安全的十大启示], Center for Strategic and

International Studies, *Interpret: China*, May 10, 2022, https://interpret.csis.org/translations
/ten-revelations-from-the-russia-ukraine-conflict-concerning-chinas-energy-security/.

37. "China's Installed Solar Power Capacity Rises 55.2% in 2023," *Reuters*, January 26, 2024, https://www.reuters.com/business/energy/chinas-installed-solar-power
-capacity-rises-552-2023-2024-01-26/.

38. "China Vows to Step Up Capacity of Energy Supply, Reserves," *Reuters*, October 17, 2022, https://www.reuters.com/markets/asia/china-vows-boost-domestic-energy
-supplies-step-up-risk-control-official-2022-10-17/.

39. Society for Worldwide Interbank Financial Telecommunication, *RMB Tracker*, accessed February 5, 2024, https://www.swift.com/our-solutions/compliance-and
-shared-services/business-intelligence/renminbi/rmb-tracker/rmb-tracker-document
-centre.

40. Zhong Caiwen, "We Must Adhere to High-Quality Development and High-Level Security and Benign Interaction" [必须坚持高质量发展和高水平安全良性互动], *People's Daily*, February 1, 2024, http://paper.people.com.cn/rmrb/html/2024-02/01/nw
.D110000renmrb_20240201_2-02.htm.

41. Eric Cheung, Jessie Yeung, and Emiko Jozuka, "China Carries Out Military Exercises near Taiwan and Japan, Sending 47 Aircraft across Taiwan Strait in 'Strike Drill'," *CNN*, December 26, 2022, https://www.cnn.com/2022/12/25/asia/taiwan-china
-aircraft-incursions-intl-hnk/index.html.

42. US Department of Defense, *Annual Report to Congress: Military and Security Developments Involving the People's Republic of China, 2023*, October 19, 2023, https://
media.defense.gov/2023/Oct/19/2003323409/-1/-1/1/2023-military-and-security
-developments-involving-the-peoples-republic-of-china.pdf.

43. Thomas Corbett and Peter W. Singer, "China's New Conscription Rules Reveal Concerns," *Defense One*, June 8, 2023, https://www.defenseone.com/ideas/2023/06
/chinas-new-conscription-regulations-reveal-what-worries-pla/387292/.

44. State Council Information Office of the People's Republic of China, *A Global Community of Shared Future*, September 26, 2023, http://english.scio.gov.cn/node
_9004328.html.

45. Bonny Lin et al., "Analyzing the Latest Xi-Putin Meeting and China's Belt and Road Forum," Center for Strategic and International Studies, October 23, 2023, https://www.csis.org/analysis/analyzing-latest-xi-putin-meeting-and-chinas-belt-and
-road-forum.

46. Ministry of Foreign Affairs of the People's Republic of China, *The Global Security Initiative Concept Paper*, February 21, 2023, https://www.mfa.gov.cn/eng/wjbxw
/202302/t20230221_11028348.html.

47. Li Gang, "GCI Injects New Vitality into China-Europe Exchanges," *China Focus*, October 27, 2023, http://www.cnfocus.com/gci-injects-new-vitality-into-chinaeurope
-exchanges/.

48. Dominik Mierzejewski and Przemysław Ciborek, "Gaining Influence in the United Nations and China's Global Aspirations," Casimir Pulaski Foundation, May 18, 2023, https://pulaski.pl/en/pulaski-policy-paper-gaining-influence-in-the-united-nations
-and-chinas-global-aspirations-2/.

49. "China-Russia 2023 Trade Value Hits Record High of $240 Billion—Chinese Customs," *Reuters*, January 12, 2024, https://www.reuters.com/markets/china-russia -2023-trade-value-hits-record-high-240-bln-chinese-customs-2024-01-12/.

50. Office of the Director of National Intelligence, *Support Provided by the People's Republic of China to Russia*, July 2023, https://democrats-intelligence.house.gov /uploadedfiles/odni_report_on_chinese_support_to_russia.pdf.

51. Lin et al., "Xi-Putin Meeting and China's Belt and Road Forum."

52. Ministry of Foreign Affairs of the People's Republic of China, "President Xi Jinping Meets European Council President Charles Michel and European Commission President Ursula von der Leyen," press release, December 7, 2023, https://www.fmprc .gov.cn/mfa_eng/wjdt_665385/wshd_665389/202312/t20231207_11196623.html.

53. The seven European countries are France, Germany, Italy, the Netherlands, Spain, Ireland, and Switzerland. See Angela Symons, "China Extends Visa-Free Entry to Two More European Countries in a Bid to Boost Tourism," *Euronews*, January 19, 2024, https://www.euronews.com/travel/2024/01/19/china-aims-to-boost-tourism-by -giving-visa-free-entry-to-these-five-european-countries.

Chapter Fifteen

The European Union as a War Project

Five Pathways toward a Geopolitical Europe

Mark Leonard

For the last seventy years, the driving force of European integration has been the quest for peace. But since February 24, 2022, the unification of Europe has emerged as a direct response to the return of war. The shift from the European Union (EU) as a peace project to a war project is forcing European governments to rethink some of their most important principles.

The big question for the EU from the war in Ukraine is whether we are seeing the emergence of a geopolitical Europe, one capable of defending itself against threats and able to pursue its collective interests on the world stage. Previous conflicts (some in Europe's immediate neighborhood, some farther away) have come and gone, leaving behind well-meaning initiatives in foreign policy and defense, most of which promptly withered away as Europeans returned to the familiar comfort of America's security umbrella.

If you look at the question of capabilities—which we will do below—the results are mixed. In the first phase of the war, the United States provided the bulk of equipment and was also indispensable in providing Ukraine with intelligence and helping plan operations. Even when it comes to military spending, the

Mark Leonard is a cofounder and the director of the European Council on Foreign Relations, the first pan-European think tank. He is also the current Henry A. Kissinger Chair in Foreign Policy and International Relations at the US Library of Congress, Washington, DC. His topics of focus include geopolitics and geoeconomics, China, and politics and institutions of the European Union.

European Defence Agency estimates that the EU is spending only 1.5% of its collective gross domestic product on defense, well shy of the 2% NATO target agreed to in 2014.[1]

I would argue, though, that to understand Europe's long-term trajectory, looking at capabilities and institutions is not enough. After the Balkan wars rattled Europe's post–Cold War confidence, Europeans initially focused on building up institutions and acquiring capabilities. The EU launched the European Common Security and Defence Policy and set up the European Defence Agency and the Military Staff. After Russia's invasion of Crimea in 2014, Europeans went through the same motions, vowing to do more on defense through initiatives such as Permanent Structured Cooperation or the European Commission–led European Defence Fund. But the initiatives were always underfunded and had no buy-in from member states. As a result, they were more symbolic politics than a real attempt to substantially increase European capabilities. Ultimately, these attempts to build a geopolitical Europe from above had ignored deeper and more fundamental shapers of defense: the identity and politics of the continent.

The fact that these factors did not fundamentally change is what caused Europe to continue to fail as a geopolitical actor. France may have proposed a European Intervention Initiative, but Emmanuel Macron still vetoed North Macedonia and Albania's EU accession. Germany promised to spend more on defense but allowed itself to be locked into energy dependency with Russia. Brussels had amassed global economic power, but it saw the economy as separate from politics and therefore wasn't willing to use it collectively to reinforce its foreign policy.

That short-term national interests often trumped a bigger strategy reflected the core problem: most European countries could not imagine a war breaking out between European states. Today, there is a chance that things will be different. Vladimir Putin's invasion of Ukraine in February 2022 was a challenge of entirely novel dimensions. Unlike the wars in Yugoslavia, which were seen as civil wars precipitated by the breakup of an empire, this was a war of aggression against a state whose sovereignty had been firmly established. And for the very first time, it didn't just change the policy debates in Europe. It changed the way that many of its core nations think about their identity. And through these deeper changes to the identity of key capitals, the outlines of a truly geopolitical Europe have not just become discernible but have begun taking shape. Substantial challenges remain, but internal political dynamics are combining with external necessity to fundamentally reshape the European security order and the idea of Europe along with it.

Europe's Identity Crisis

The invasion of Ukraine was never simply a security crisis. It was just as much an identity crisis, and it forced the EU to reinvent itself, to move from a peace project to a war project. In the weeks following the invasion, many of the core concepts at the heart of the EU's identity were called into question.

Before the war, Europeans had viewed their project as essentially post-national and universal. Now they were forced to confront the fact that the European project was exceptional and to define Europe's borders more clearly. After the Cold War there had been an assumption that a new European order could be built around laws and treaties, which would encompass all the great powers of Europe. But as Europeans cheered on and assisted Ukraine's heroic defense, it was impossible not to recognize that the EU rule-based model was exceptional rather than universal—and that many European countries did not accept it. From now on, Europeans needed to accept that they lived in a multipolar Europe and that different rules applied inside the EU sphere of influence and outside it. This made the question of borders existential.

Whereas Europe once felt comfortable relying mainly on its soft power (within the comfort of an American security blanket), it now had to concern itself with hard power. This was as true of arms and ammunitions as it was of other aspects of the EU system. With its multiple sanctions packages against Russia, Europe turned its economy into a weapon and developed an embryonic war economy—complete with rationing and price controls, as we saw in the winter of 2022.

Europeans also had to rethink the concept of interdependence. European integration had previously reflected the belief that economic links among countries would create a foundation for political reconciliation. This was the driving factor behind Germany's decision to continue relying on Russia for energy. But Europeans have since learned that interdependence can also enable blackmail.

Another aspect of the identity crisis had to do with whether Brussels, a seat of the EU, destroyed or enhanced national sovereignty. Many European political forces had seen Brussels as the ultimate enemy of national sovereignty. And it is certainly true that the founders of the EU had seen national sovereignty as a problem that needed to be tamed. Yet faced with an existential crisis in Ukraine, many countries realized that the only way to defend their sovereignty was by coming together. This move toward embracing European sovereignty began with a growing sense of the negative consequences of Brexit and was enhanced by the challenges of Donald J. Trump's unilateralism, the growing assertiveness of Xi

Jinping during the pandemic, and the war in Ukraine. Whereas previous geopolitical awakenings had tended to be exclusively national, these crises had created a sense in public opinion of the emergence of a "community of common European destiny." One study, conducted shortly before Russia's invasion of Ukraine, saw a majority of Europeans agreeing that Russia's approach to Ukraine represented a security threat to Europe as a whole in a variety of domains.[2]

The final aspect of the identity question was about seeing a geopolitical Europe as something that strengthened, rather than weakened, the West. Previously, Europeans had often been split between those who wanted to follow the Gaullist vision of building a geopolitical Europe as a counterpart to the United States and those whose commitment to the transatlantic alliance made them want to dilute European unity out of fear that it would push Washington out of Europe. But polling conducted by the European Council on Foreign Relations (which I direct) has demonstrated a clear shift toward a recognition that a strong West requires a strong Europe. This polling revealed that Europeans expected not just NATO, but also the EU, to step up to defend Ukraine in the event of a Russian invasion. Another study conducted a year after the invasion found that Europeans had united behind a common threat perception since the war began.[3]

The upshot of this two-year-long identity crisis is the idea of building a "geopolitical Europe" that combines the old instincts of the peace project with the imperatives of fighting a war. Fortunately, the domestic trajectories of some of the most important countries are already moving in this direction (albeit for different reasons). Each has a piece of the puzzle—together they form five different paths toward a geopolitical Europe, created out of a synthesis of EU values with contemporary realities rather than an abnegation of Europe's founding ideals.

A geopolitical Europe will combine universalism with exceptionalism. It needs, first, to have clearly defined borders that separate the postmodern world of treaty-based security from a tougher world based on deterrence and the balance of power. Second, a geopolitical Europe will mix soft and hard power. It should be able to defend itself by investing in defense, developing new technologies, and socializing risk. Third, it will integrate national sovereignty and European leadership. A Europe with legitimate political leadership will be able to make tough choices and find compromises more quickly. Fourth, a geopolitical Europe will be able to de-risk interdependence through geoeconomics. Europe must be willing to use its economic weight to pursue its foreign policy interests. Finally, Europe will achieve security only if it develops a new relationship with the United States. It cannot build its new identity if set against Washington without also splitting itself, yet it can also no longer depend on Washington to the extent that it did before. Changes in Washington and London make this new synthesis possible.

In the sections below, I outline how these five paths toward a geopolitical Europe run through Paris, Berlin, Brussels, Warsaw and Rome, and Washington and London, in turn.

Paris: Embracing "European Exceptionalism" through Enlargement

The old post–Cold War idea of security was based on the idea that peace would be secured through economic and legal interdependence and institutions. Europeans hoped to build a cooperative order around a perpetually expanding EU and NATO. Instead of creating new institutions, they sought to bind their neighbors to the old institutions (or versions of them, like the European Neighbourhood Policy, the Four Common Spaces with Russia, or the NATO-Russia Council). But this vision of a unipolar Europe was fatally damaged by the invasion of Georgia in 2008. And when accession negotiations with Turkey broke down, it was clear that there were two major European powers that didn't buy into this vision. It took a long time for Europeans to move away from this preference for a cooperative, universal, and unipolar idea of Europe back toward an idea of a multipolar Europe with different security actors and spheres of influence.

One of the biggest lessons of the war in Ukraine was the need to make a radical distinction between life inside the bloc and life outside it. Within the EU, security is guaranteed by law and economic interdependence rather than by force and by hedging. Sovereignty is enhanced by sharing and pooling it rather than protecting it. Maintaining this dichotomy between inside and outside is important since many of the things that make the EU work internally can become vulnerabilities and sources of weakness outside the bloc. In the post–Cold War years, the EU was convinced that its model would spread osmotically to the rest of the continent and beyond. But it is now clear that the distinction of who is in and who is out matters, making the question of Europe's borders an existential one.

For many years, Western leaders gave mixed messages about whether countries such as Ukraine, Georgia, and Moldova would be allowed to join the Western institutions. The ambiguity displayed at the 2008 Bucharest NATO summit when the West decided to leave Georgia and Ukraine in limbo, with a "membership perspective" for NATO, left both states with the worst of both worlds.

Russia's full-scale invasion of Ukraine changed this thinking and led European leaders to understand that the space for ambiguity had disappeared and that Ukrainians (not to mention Moldovans) passionately want to build their future on the

EU side of the border. This shift in Europe's thinking is driving the idea of a "double enlargement," which concedes that Ukraine's destiny ultimately lies within both NATO and the EU. Admitting Kyiv to both organizations in the long run is probably the best way to ensure that Ukraine won't find itself stuck in perpetual conflict with Russia or trapped in a "forever war."

Nothing is more evocative of the shift in European thinking than the Damascene conversion undergone over the first two years of the war by French president Emmanuel Macron. Prior to the war in Ukraine, Macron had made clear his skepticism on enlargement. Macron's aversion was always part of a broader historical tendency whereby France never really embraced the EU's various enlargement rounds.

Concerned that enlargement could dilute the bloc's decision-making processes and undermine its ability to act effectively on the global stage, he went so far as to veto North Macedonia and Albania's EU accession negotiations, sending shock waves through Europe's eastern neighborhood (although both countries were allowed to join NATO). This was still Macron's position when Putin invaded Ukraine on February 22, 2022. Eastern Europeans, long skeptical of the Russophile strain among France's foreign policy establishment, looked askance at Macron as he continued to talk to Putin in the early months of the war, convinced that he could somehow negotiate a ceasefire, and they criticized his statement in June that "we must not humiliate Russia."[4]

A year later, Macron was suddenly singing a completely different tune. At the GLOBSEC forum in Bratislava in 2023, he attempted to dispel Eastern European skepticism about France's reliability once and for all, telling his audience, "Some said you had missed an opportunity to shut up. I think we also lost an opportunity to listen to you. This time is over," a reference to Jacques Chirac's dismissal of Eastern European support for the United States over the war in Iraq in 2003.[5] Earlier that year, speaking to French media on the sidelines of the Munich Security Conference, he had said, "I want Russia to be defeated in Ukraine," a stunning admission given his previous comments on not humiliating Russia.[6] Moreover, at the Vilnius NATO summit in July 2023, Macron appeared more open to a NATO accession for Ukraine than the German and US leaders.[7]

This new language went hand in hand with a new French policy of embracing enlargement, starting with Ukraine's eventual accession to the bloc. It is crucial to underline what a truly fundamental change these two shifts, one on Russia, one on enlargement, imply. Whereas France had previously associated enlargement with a weaker EU, less capable of acting in its own interests, the war in Ukraine has created a new geopolitical reality whereby enlargement is the single-most-important tool Europe has to define, once and for all, the borders of Europe in relation to Russia. What Macron's conversion enabled was a re-foundation of Europe by embracing the strategic logic of enlargement for the first time.

He realized that it was precisely the ambiguity of where countries like Ukraine belonged that led to Russian aggression. Enlargement allows Europe to end this ambiguity once and for all by binding the countries in between Russia and the EU into a European security community. In this sense, the enlargement debate is about clarifying the borders of the European sphere of influence and making it clear that Ukraine and Moldova have a European future instead of being doomed to existing as buffer states.

Many challenges to enlargement remain. While France embraced a strategic approach, Germany insisted on a more plodding, legalistic one. The danger is that such an accession process could lead to negotiations disconnected from the short-term imperatives of fighting a war and kick-starting the Ukrainian economy, and from there to mutual antipathy. Internal opposition from the likes of French farmers or Polish industry could also complicate the process so that membership negotiations turn into a bridge to nowhere. But intent and political will do matter in these contests over Europe's future, and this is precisely what France's turn has given Europe.

Berlin: Seeing Hard Power as a Prerequisite for Soft Power

Since the failure of the European Defence Community in 1954, European states have done a much better job at talking about European defense integration than at implementing it. Every major crisis produced new attempts to bring about integration through new frameworks or institutions. The fact that nothing concrete materialized from these efforts was due to the fact that European countries had long been beholden to a number of unproductive instincts, foremost among them the urge to free-ride on the United States. But there have also been significant philosophical and historical barriers that prevented the sort of relationship with their armed forces that other countries around the world have, not least among them World War II's legacy.

Germany, in particular, has rejected the militarism once central to its history in favor of a gentler approach to foreign policy. In the early days of German postwar reconstruction, its foes-turned-allies deliberately sought to "keep it down [militarily]," in the words of Lord Ismay, NATO's first secretary general. West Germany from 1955 to 1989 provided the bulk of NATO land forces during the Cold War and advocated for the deployment of Euromissiles, but Germany was careful not to set itself up as an autonomous actor. After the Cold War, Germany's phobia of militarism prevented it from behaving in a manner congruent with its geopolitical status. In fact, it often played the role of a spoiler, watering down more ambitious proposals from the French under the cover of wanting an "inclusive approach."

Now the hope is that Europe is on a different path. There are three dimensions to this. For one, by training Ukrainian troops, expanding the European Peace Facility, and mobilizing funds to bolster defense industries, the European Commission stepped up and became the solution instead of wrapping the problem up in red tape, as had sometimes been the case. Some US Congress members might be surprised to learn that, by 2024, Europe had committed twice as much aid to Ukraine as had the United States, excluding the cost of welcoming five million refugees.[8]

Second is the question of the long-term transformation of European defense establishments. Twenty of the twenty-three EU members of NATO were on track to reach the 2% target by the 75th anniversary NATO summit in July 2024—and Germany was on course to meet it by the end of 2024.[9] Nonaligned countries like Sweden, Finland, Ireland, Austria, and even Switzerland have become less neutral or even joined NATO. Penny-pinchers on defense have become less miserly, and those who were spending lots of money are spending even more (like Poland, which was set to spend 4% of its GDP on defense in 2024).[10]

The third dimension is the institutional one. In the past, divisions between NATO and the EU provided excuses for inaction. Theological debates about avoiding duplication now mostly have disappeared, partly because EU members Sweden and Finland having joined the alliance meant there was less daylight between the two organizations and also because NATO sought to avoid becoming directly involved in the war in Ukraine.

What has fundamentally changed the equation, though, is that since the invasion of Ukraine, Europe's biggest economy and its biggest laggard whenever it has come to stepping up on defense has undergone a fundamental shift in its strategic objectives. This shift is of course encapsulated in one word, *Zeitenwende*, which Chancellor Olaf Scholz used in a speech to the Bundestag three days after Putin's invasion to outline a fundamentally new approach in German defense policy. An allocation of €100 million went to a special fund for the Bundeswehr, and Scholz committed Germany thenceforth to meeting NATO's 2% spending target. Since then, Germany scrapped its earlier plans to replace its aging Tornado fleet with cheaper F/A-18 aircraft, instead committing itself to buying thirty-five F-35s.[11] Berlin agreed to permanently deploy a brigade to Lithuania, the first permanent stationing of troops outside its borders since World War II (previous deployments had taken place on a rotational basis).[12] Perhaps most significantly in the context of the war in Ukraine, it abandoned its earlier policy of eschewing weapons deliveries by spearheading European efforts to arm Ukraine and turning itself into Kyiv's second-biggest supplier of military equipment, edged out only by the United States.[13]

Some grumble that Germany's current statistics on defense spending are still disappointing and that an emphasis on top-tier, so-called exquisite systems, like the F-35, has come at the expense of more prosaic articles like artillery rounds and thermal underwear. These valid criticisms shouldn't detract from the significance of Berlin's shift in so short a period. Institutional barriers to change still exist, but the discourse around defense and defense issues has changed completely and on both a party- and society-wide level. The arguments not to do certain things, which relied on a pacifistic political discourse and on the historical relationship with Russia, no longer work. Even if Berlin chooses not to move, it does not argue in principle against the idea of arming Ukraine but instead uses second-order arguments not to send certain types of equipment. Similarly, critique in the media is about whether Germany is doing its fair share and not whether there should be a *Zeitenwende* or not, marking quite a difference from earlier periods. In the realm of defense and security, Germany's basic identity has finally become that of a normal state. Like an oil tanker, it may still take some time for Germany to complete its 180-degree turn. But when it does, it will bring the resources of Europe's largest economy to the defense of the continent.

Brussels: De-risking Interdependence through Integration

The EU used to have a neo-Marxian belief in the power of interdependence. It believed that it was possible to create a common economic base by removing barriers to trade and that this economic base would form the foundation for a political superstructure, turning former enemies into friends. The war in Ukraine has meant the end of that illusion, as the EU and its member states have realized that the *nature* of interdependence matters and that it can easily be susceptible to bullying and blackmail if you let your guard down. The result of this shift has been the European Commission's effort to de-risk its most complicated relationships around the globe. On the EU level, an iron curtain long divided economic and security policy. Both were dictated by different and incompatible logics. In 2007, when the Russian government introduced sanctions against Georgian wine, I asked a senior EU trade official whether the EU might consider granting Georgian wine barrier-free access in order to stick it to the Russians and demonstrate our support for Tbilisi. He responded that it was a nice idea but that Georgia was such an insignificant market that he could never justify allocating any effort within his directorate to such an issue. The economic benefits of talking to the Chinese were simply exponentially greater.

The official's approach was indicative of what the think tank Bruegel called "Europe's fragmented power" that same year.[14] Trade, foreign policy, defense, and technology were treated as silos, and states were divided among themselves to boot. But with the coming of the war in Ukraine, the EU is undergoing a revolution from fragmented to integrated power. Under its president Ursula von der Leyen, who from the first day of her term sought to lead a "geopolitical commission," what began as a piece of political spin was turned into a reality by external events. Over the last few years, the bloc has injected foreign policy into its competition policy, export controls, and industrial policy. Through relatively small but targeted investments, it has sought to remove some of the barriers that had previously prevented common European action. The archetype of this model is the European Peace Facility, which socializes costs and allows member states to supply Ukraine and get a share of their expenses refunded from an extra-budgetary EU mechanism. This has been transformative for poorer member states like Estonia that have been able to make a major contribution. Even on big-picture issues like lessening dependence on Russian energy or financing the post-pandemic recovery, the European Commission has emerged as the key player in spreading risk and allowing member states to get rid of blockages. In other words, there is now widespread recognition that security policy today is not just about missiles, tanks, and planes. It is just as much about economic tools, technology, migration, and energy policy.

Warsaw and Rome: European Solidarity as a Force for National Sovereignty

In recent years, the EU has increasingly been split between political forces that want greater integration and those that saw Brussels as the biggest enemy of national sovereignty. But the war in Ukraine fundamentally changed the calculus in many member states—and led some of the most Eurosceptic forces to see European action as a multiplier rather than a destroyer of national sovereignty.

The driving force of integration used to be the Franco-German motor. But under Scholz and Macron, the relationship turned toxic, and the ability of the two states to move the rest of the EU also declined. Disputes over which country to buy missile defense systems from as part of Berlin's European Sky Shield Initiative were front and center in the headlines, but the two argued over practically every major issue, from the bloc's China policy and the EU's fiscal rules to which technologies should count as renewables. But even when they do agree on a pan-European issue, Paris and Berlin do not have much legitimacy in an enlarged EU—especially with respect to Russia and Ukraine. The ensuing political vacuum has been filled at least partially by President von der Leyen, who showed true leadership on COVID-19, the war in Ukraine, and China and who managed to get quite a few victories under her belt. Still, the European Commission, as a de facto unelected bureaucracy, suffers from a legitimacy deficit and cannot provide a firm foundation on which to build.

On the other hand, many of the most Eurosceptic leaders in Europe have had to reposition themselves in the wake of Brexit, COVID-19, and the war in Ukraine. Far-right leaders like Marine Le Pen have given up on their pledges to drop the euro and leave the EU—and have had to backtrack from their support of Putin. Moreover, two big political developments, in two capitals that had the biggest problems with Brussels, have made it possible to envisage a new kind of political leadership.

The return of a liberal Poland to the European stage has the potential to create a new foundation on which to build real geopolitical consensus on a truly European level. In Donald Tusk, Poland found a leader who combines deep knowledge of the EU's institutions with a strong domestic power base. Under Tusk, the EU regained domestic legitimacy and provided the continent with sorely lacking political leadership. For the first time in almost a decade, Eastern Europe's most important country, Poland, was led by a government that didn't see its country as part of Europe only when handouts were involved; rather, when its leaders said *us*, they meant Europe and not Poland.

The return of Polish liberalism is complemented by developments in Italy, where Giorgia Meloni became emblematic of the neutering of the strong pro-Russian element that once plagued the European far right and Southern Europe. Italy, specifically, was a hotbed of Russian activity and pro-Russian sentiment. As the third-largest EU country by population, it has always had the potential to be a big spoiler. When Meloni came to power in late 2022 at the head of a coalition including the Fratelli d'Italia, Lega Nord, and Forza Italia, many were worried that she would fatally undermine Europe's support for Ukraine. But on the contrary, by taking as strong a pro-Ukraine and pro-Atlanticist stance as anyone, Meloni effectively took the wind from the sails of those who sought to build up a critical mass of pro-Russian countries.

To be sure, Europe still has elements like Germany's Alternative für Deutschland party and Hungarian prime minister Viktor Orbán, which are vocal in their love for Putin. But Orbán's isolation in the European Council demonstrates that he can at most be a temporary spoiler. In fact, his decision finally to unblock €50 billion in aid for Ukraine in February 2024 was reportedly due in no small part to the personal intervention of Meloni, who coaxed Orbán over the line ahead of a summit of EU leaders.[15]

Part of her behavior can be attributed to her Atlanticism. But one of the striking things about her is that she went from a super-Eurosceptic force to one that was actively constructive on the European stage. Italian domestic politics was mostly to thank for this shift. On the one hand, Meloni de-risked her party to demonstrate that her government was capable of fiscal orthodoxy (necessary to get much-needed EU funds). On the other hand, with Berlusconi's death, a massive space opened up in the center-right of Italian (and by extension, European) politics, which Meloni believes she is well placed to fill. As a result, she made an unexpected alliance with von der Leyen on migration and sees Brussels as a defender of Italy's borders and sovereignty rather than as an enemy.

Some worry that she could change her tune on Ukraine and the EU if Trump returns to power. It is also possible that her coalition partners could pull out of the government. But for the moment, domestic political developments in Poland and Italy—two countries that traditionally served as bugbears for proponents of a stronger union—have played a major role in strengthening the EU's role as a geopolitical actor. Crucially, Meloni and Tusk have managed to unite traditionally skeptical electorates behind a vision of a geopolitical Europe (at least temporarily). And they have made it politically viable to advocate for a geopolitical Europe united at last in its threat perceptions and a shared understanding of its European identity.

London and Washington: Ending the Conflict between the West and Europe

When Donald Rumsfeld split the European continent into "new" and "old" member states, he confirmed that relations with the United States have the potential to be the most divisive issue in European foreign policy—and that Washington has often chosen to divide and rule European states. One of the reasons why Europe has struggled to develop into a geopolitical actor was its ambivalence about its links with the United States. Ever since the Suez crisis in 1956, the two most powerful European military powers—France and the United Kingdom—have adopted radically different approaches. While the United Kingdom decided to hug America tightly, France sought strategic autonomy. Washington has often used that difference to further its own leadership, sometimes even pushing for what has been called the "vassalization of Europe."

One of the best illustrations of this dynamic took place when Trump was in the White House. In an attempt to get Europeans to take responsibility for their own affairs and to complain about the lack of reliability of the US and Turkish allies in Syria, French president Macron gave an interview to the *Economist* and declared NATO "brain dead." This did not act as the rallying cry to pursue autonomy that he had hoped, however. Instead, he faced a barrage of criticism from NATO's secretary general, the German chancellor, and a slew of Central and Eastern European leaders. Instead of advancing the European debate about strategic sovereignty, he set it back.

But the war in Ukraine, coupled with changes on both sides of the Atlantic, could change this picture. For one, the United States has realized that its biggest problem is not an independent Europe but rather an overdependent Europe. This was true under Trump, who pushed Europeans to do more, but it is equally true of Joe Biden, who wants Europe to be a partner that is more capable of pulling its weight. Washington still ends up micromanaging European problems, but this is happening less and less often. This new attitude might even extend to weapons, where many American strategists would prefer that Europeans had *any* weapons rather than depending on US weapon deliveries when Washington might have other priorities.

On the other hand, the seriousness of the geopolitical challenge and the pivotal role played by the Biden administration have made it clear in Europe that it would be impossible to unite the EU against the United States. The reason why the *Zeitenwende* has been possible is because it has been framed as an Atlanticist project. And Macron (for all his Gaullist language) has been one of the European leaders who has worked most closely with Washington.

Finally, in a strange way, the war in Ukraine has also clarified the British position in a way that makes European unity more likely. Despite Brexit, the United Kingdom still views the whole of Europe as one security community. It did not want to leave that role even under Boris Johnson. The growing likelihood of political change makes a much greater alignment between London and the EU on security and defense policy probable in the medium term, with the leader of the opposition, Keir Starmer, declaring that he would like to sign a security and defense pact with Brussels. If Trump wins the 2024 presidential election, Starmer's UK would much rather band together with Europe than become the United States' 51st state. So, ironically, despite all the dangers and ominous consequences for Ukraine, Trump's return could conceivably create a framework for more European cooperation.

This is perhaps the most dramatic change: to see European unity as a force multiplier for the West rather than a barrier to Western unity. It means, possibly, that Atlanticists will increasingly need to work to build the European pillar of NATO rather than fearing that European capabilities could lead to a self-fulfilling prophecy of US disengagement.

Conclusion: Will This Time Be Different?

It is still too early to tell whether the Europe that emerges from the war in Ukraine will truly deserve to be called *geopolitical*. There have been half a dozen attempts to create such a Europe over the years, and some (such as the failed European Defense Community in the 1950s, which envisioned a level of supranational control impossible to imagine today, with a common budget, centralized military procurement, and institutions) came very close indeed. Ultimately, though, none of these attempts to move forward succeeded because the core identity of the European project was about an escape from history—and about using integration to drive geopolitical thinking out of the continent's DNA.

A betting person might expect the current drive toward a geopolitical Europe to be as chimerical as previous ones. And it is certainly true that all of the five pathways I laid out in this essay could run into roadblocks. National politics is volatile, and it is extremely hard to bring about the sort of cultural change that Europe needs to experience. There are reasons, however, to believe that this time could be different.

This is visible in some of the policies the EU has adopted—but it is even more evident in changes to the core identity of the EU's members. As the bloc embarks on a massive expansion project over the next decade, the paths toward a geopolitical Europe, which I have outlined, that run through its biggest countries have the potential to create a union that eliminates the problematic buffer zone between Europe and Russia via expansion and a sharp definition of Europe's borders, a union able to defend itself against military threats, wield its economic power more effectively, renew itself politically while maintaining its legitimacy, and emerge as an equal partner to the United States.

NOTES

1. European Defence Agency, *Defence Data, 2022: Key Findings and Analysis*, 2023, https://eda.europa.eu/docs/default-source/brochures/2022-eda_defencedata_web.pdf.

2. Ivan Krastev and Mark Leonard, *The Crisis of European Security: What Europeans Think about the War in Ukraine* (Berlin: European Council on Foreign Relations, 2022), https://ecfr.eu/publication/the-crisis-of-european-security-what-europeans-think-about-the-war-in-ukraine/.

3. Ivan Krastev and Mark Leonard, *Fragile Unity: Why Europeans Are Coming Together on Ukraine (and What Might Drive Them Apart)* (Berlin: European Council on Foreign Relations, 2022), https://ecfr.eu/publication/fragile-unity-why-europeans-are-coming-together-on-ukraine/.

4. John Irish, "Russia Must Not Be Humiliated despite Putin's 'Historic' Mistake, Macron Says," *Reuters*, June 4, 2022, https://www.reuters.com/world/europe/russia-must-not-be-humiliated-despite-putins-historic-mistake-macron-2022-06-04/.

5. Michel Rose, "Macron Tells Eastern Europe—We Should Have Listened to You over Russia," *Reuters*, May 31, 2023, https://www.reuters.com/world/europe/frances-macron-offers-mea-culpa-eastern-eu-nations-russia-2023-05-31/.

6. Phelan Chatterjee and Matt Murphy, "Ukraine War: Russia Must Be Defeated but Not Crushed, Macron Says," *BBC*, February 19, 2023, https://www.bbc.co.uk/news/uk-64693691.

7. Leila Abboud, Raphael Minder, and Henry Foy, "Emmanuel Macron Backs NATO Membership 'Path' for Ukraine," *Financial Times*, May 31, 2023, https://www.ft.com/content/2cf5609d-3a2a-4177-8c3b-2336fc61cfa4.

8. Kiel Institute for the World Economy, "Ukraine Support Tracker" [database], https://www.ifw-kiel.de/topics/war-against-ukraine/ukraine-support-tracker.

9. Boris Ruge, "Age of Confrontation: How Do NATO and the EU Cope with Crises, Conflicts, and Long-Term Competition?" (lecture, European Council on Foreign Relations, Berlin, February 1, 2024).

10. "Poland's 2024 Budget to See Big Spending on Defence, Social Benefits," *Reuters*, August 24, 2023, https://www.reuters.com/world/europe/polands-2024-budget-see-big-spending-defence-social-benefits-2023-08-24/.

11. "Germany Approves 10 Bln Euro F-35 Jet Deal with U.S.," *Reuters*, December 14, 2022, https://www.reuters.com/business/aerospace-defense/german-budget-committee-approves-f-35-fighter-jet-deal-with-us-sources-2022-12-14/.

12. "Agreement on German Brigade in Lithuania Is Historic—German Defence Minister," *Reuters*, December 18, 2023, https://www.reuters.com/world/europe/agreement-german-brigade-lithuania-is-historic-german-defence-minister-2023-12-18/.

13. Kiel Institute for the World Economy, "Ukraine Support Tracker."

14. André Sapir, *Fragmented Power: Europe and the Global Economy* (Brussels: Bruegel, 2007).

15. Barbara Moens, "How Giorgia Meloni and French Hospitality Got Orbán to OK Ukraine Aid," *Politico*, February 1, 2024, https://www.politico.eu/article/how-eu-leaders-pushed-hungary-orban-ukraine-aid-support-meloni-italy/.

Chapter Sixteen

Lose-Lose

The Economic Sanctions of the Russo-Ukrainian War

Daniel W. Drezner

T he proximate origin of the Russo-Ukrainian war dates back to an early 2010s clash of economic statecraft. Ukraine found itself being courted by two considerably larger economies. The European Union (EU) offered association agreements with a number of post-Soviet states, which would reorient their economies toward the West. Russia, in turn, conceived of the Eurasian Union as a regional counterweight to the EU, a means to ensure that its neighboring states would stay within Russia's geoeconomic orbit. In the fall of 2013, Vladimir Putin threatened Ukrainian president Viktor Yanukovych with economic sanctions and the use of force unless he rejected the EU deal in favor of joining the Eurasian Union. Eventually Yanukovych acquiesced to Putin, setting off large-scale protests in Kyiv that subsequently triggered regime change in Ukraine. In response, Putin forcibly annexed the Crimean peninsula and incited military action in the Donbas, paving the way for the war to expand eight years later.

The more intense phase of the Russo-Ukrainian war from February 2022 onward has featured a mix of new and old military tactics: 21st-century drone warfare combined with 20th-century artillery barrages. The war has also generated a

Daniel W. Drezner is a professor of international politics at the Fletcher School of Law and Diplomacy at Tufts University and a nonresident senior fellow at the Chicago Council on Global Affairs. He is the codirector of Fletcher's Russia and Eurasia program.

I am grateful to Christopher Miller for his feedback on an earlier draft and to the participants of the February 2024 America in the World conference for their thoughtful comments as well.

mix of old and new in its economic sanctions: traditional 20th-century trade embargoes combined with 21st-century attempts at weaponized interdependence.

Any *ex ante* scholarly evaluation of the ability of sanctions to affect the Russo-Ukrainian war would be pessimistic. For most of the 20th century, the economic sanctions literature was largely dismissive of them as an instrument of statecraft.[1] Using sanctions as a means of deterring or of compelling a great power to relinquish territory has produced mostly failed outcomes. Beginning with the end of the Cold War and accelerating after the September 11th terrorist attacks, however, US policymakers enthusiastically embraced economic coercion as a policy option of first resort.[2] Two years into the Russo-Ukrainian war, what have we learned about the role of economic statecraft in a 21st-century militarized dispute?

Evaluating the utility of economic statecraft during an ongoing dispute is empirically challenging. The United States is the world's most active user of economic sanctions, but its federal government has acknowledged that it does not assess the effectiveness of its coercive measures during an ongoing dispute.[3] Any assessment of the myriad uses of economic statecraft during the Russo-Ukrainian war must be acknowledged to be preliminary as of this writing.

Despite this caveat, it is difficult not to conclude that the array of economic sanctions employed by both Russia and the US-led coalition opposing Russia's invasion of Ukraine has been largely unsuccessful in achieving its goals. From the US perspective, we know that economic sanctions failed at two of three aims: deterrence and coercion. Western efforts to hinder Russia's ability to prosecute its war of aggression have been more successful, but those sanctions have not been a pivotal factor affecting the war itself. The Russian Federation's countersanctions meant to pressure Europe into remaining neutral have also not worked as intended, as European support for Ukraine has persisted. To be sure, all of these sanctions have imposed significant economic costs on their intended targets. Those economic costs, however, have not translated into political concessions. Furthermore, both sides have still engaged in significant amounts of energy trade despite the imposition of sanctions and countersanctions.

Does this assessment mean that the sanctions employed during the war have been in vain? That is a more complicated question. For the United States and its allies, sanctions are an important part of norm enforcement, and the Russo-Ukrainian war challenges one of the most important norms in international relations. The sanctions against Russia also create long-term stresses on the Russian economy, which could serve Western interests. For both the European Union and Russia, the sanctions are a tool of geoeconomics enabling a reorientation of their foreign economic policies. The war has revealed both the hard limits of economic sanctions between great powers and why they are nonetheless a persistent feature of 21st-century world politics.

Deterrence Failures in the Russo-Ukrainian War

In response to Russia's occupation and subsequent annexation of Crimea, the United States and the European Union imposed an escalating series of sanctions. At the time, officials of Barack Obama's administration designed the measures to encourage Russia to take an "off-ramp" and de-escalate the crisis following Putin's loss of influence in Kyiv. These sanctions failed—if anything, Russia escalated the conflict in the Donbas. Obama administration officials have subsequently argued that the threat of delisting Russia's entire banking sector from SWIFT (Society for Worldwide Interbank Financial Telecommunication)—thereby making cross-border financial transactions prohibitively difficult—did deter Russia from further expanding the conflict.[4] The empirical veracity of this claim is difficult to ascertain, but it is safe to say that even if it was true at the time, that deterrence was decidedly ephemeral.

One reason for this was the lack of transatlantic policy coordination in implementing sanctions. For the entirety of the post–Cold War era, there had been tensions between the European Union and the United States over sanctions against perceived adversaries. The United States generally wanted to ratchet up economic pressure; European allies, which often had larger trading relationships with targets like Iran or Russia, resisted such measures. Only after the shoot down of Malaysia Airlines flight 17 did the European Union prove more willing to sanction. At the same time, US officials had repeatedly warned European leaders that Russia's control of energy pipelines represented an implicit coercive threat, echoing Cold War transatlantic tensions. These tensions spilled over into public view frequently, undoubtedly sending a signal to Putin that multilateral cooperation on substantive economic sanctions was fragile at best. As Walter Russell Mead scornfully wrote in 2014, "The disunity and economic selfishness of the western response has made the West look ridiculous. France will deliver warships, Germany will buy gas, and Britain's banks are open for Russian business. Putin must be quaking in his boots at this awesome display of resolve."[5]

By the fall of 2021, US officials had intelligence confirming Putin's intentions to widen the war. In the months before the February 24 invasion, Western officials repeatedly and consistently threatened punishing sanctions if Russia escalated the conflict.[6] In December of that year, NATO secretary general Jens Stoltenberg warned of severe economic consequences if Russia invaded Ukraine. Secretary of State Antony Blinken said, "We've made it clear to the Kremlin that we will respond resolutely, including with a range of high impact economic measures that we have refrained from pursuing in the past."[7] President Joe Biden relayed the same message directly to Putin in a video recording later that week.[8] In January 2022, the Biden White House reiterated that threat, with Biden suggesting personal sanctions against Vladimir Putin and one senior US official warning of economic sanctions "with massive consequences" for Russia. French president Emmanuel Macron echoed Biden, asserting that "if there is aggression, there will be retaliation and the cost will be very high."[9]

Officials of the United States and the United Kingdom were explicit about threatening economic sanctions as a means to deter Russian aggression. Daleep Singh, US deputy national security advisor, explained, "The best sanctions are the ones that never have to get used, so by signaling as clearly as we could that these were going to be the most severe sanctions ever on a large economy, perhaps we can deter Putin." United Kingdom foreign minister Liz Truss concurred: "We were thinking, 'What is the maximum we can do in the time available? How can we send a very clear signal and warning that this would not be some kind of walkover, and that the West would not just accept it?'"[10] Russian technocrats briefed Putin a month before the war, warning in no uncertain terms that the costs of sanctions would be severe.[11]

Clearly, Russia's February 24 invasion demonstrates that sanctions failed as a form of deterrence. There are multiple causes for this failure. The most obvious factor has little to do with Western economic statecraft. Imperial control over Ukraine has long been the top strategic priority of Vladimir Putin.[12] Putin had demonstrated a persistent belief that Ukrainian sovereignty was a fiction and that the country was part of "Novorossiya."[13] While Russia's annexation of Crimea and occupation of the Donbas represented tactical victories, they came at the strategic cost of reorienting the rest of Ukraine toward the West. Ukraine's relatively robust democratic norms also represented a subversive challenge to Putin's more autocratic form of governance. With a waning window of opportunity to influence events in Ukraine, it is unlikely that any purely economic threat, no matter how accurately it was signaled, would have deterred Russian aggression.

In regard to the economic statecraft calculus, Putin's perception of the cost-benefit calculation likely caused him to dismiss the sanctions threat. After the

2014 round of sanctions against Russia, Putin pursued a policy explicitly designed to "sanction-proof" the economy.[14] This included accumulating currency reserves in excess of $600 billion, reducing reliance on external borrowing to finance Russian debt, diversifying away from the dollar, and reorienting trade toward China. Russian countersanctions against Europe after 2014 spurred additional import substitution in agricultural goods, reinforcing the perception of a resilient Russian economy. These efforts proved to be hollow; Russian manufacturing and finances remained dependent on access to the outside world. Nonetheless, both Putin and outside observers believed that Russian resilience efforts had been successful. By February 2022, experts had concluded that "[Russian economic officials] are pretty proud, and have good reasons to be, for the work they have done to make the Russian economy more immune to sanctions."[15] At the same time, European reliance on Russian energy likely convinced Putin that Russia possessed escalation dominance on the question of economic sanctions.[16]

Finally, the probability of strong multilateral cooperation in advance of sanctions was murky prior to the invasion. European leaders offered enough rhetorical wiggle room for Russia to downgrade the probability of collective pressure. For example, in Macron's January 2022 speech to the European Parliament, he said, "It's good for Europe and the U.S. to coordinate, but it is vital that Europe has its own dialogue with Russia." In the same speech he proposed that the EU negotiate a separate security agreement with Moscow.[17] This rhetoric, combined with his frantic shuttle diplomacy with Putin, revealed Macron's preference for an independent European approach. Similarly, German chancellor Olaf Scholz repeatedly waffled on whether Germany would respond to a Russian invasion with a suspension of the Nord Stream 2 pipeline.[18] While transatlantic policy coordination was in fact significant, it was difficult to signal that to Moscow without also signaling the tactical sanctions plan. It was understandable that Russia underestimated the potency of the economic sanctions that were actually imposed.

Compellence Failures in the Russo-Ukrainian War

After the invasion on February 24, the United States, European Union, and allied nations implemented an escalating series of economic sanctions designed to punish the Russian economy. These measures included kicking major Russian financial institutions off of SWIFT, freezing Russian assets held in sanctioning countries, and imposing an array of import and export restrictions. Russian officials publicly acknowledged that they were surprised by the scope and depth of the sanctions that were imposed after the February invasion.[19]

Two elements surprised Russian officials the most. The first was the coordinated freeze of approximately $300 billion in Russian central bank reserves held in the jurisdiction of sanctioning countries. While Russia had taken care to move assets away from the United States, officials were unprepared for European officials acting in a similar and coordinated manner. The second was the wave of Western multinational corporations announcing withdrawals or divestment from the Russian economy. These announcements generated something of a contagion effect; their number rapidly increased from 250 to 1,000 over a few months.[20]

The immediate effect of the sanctions on the Russian economy was considerable. The ruble plunged in value relative to the dollar, crashing from a prewar exchange rate of 75 rubles to the dollar to a low of 143 rubles to the dollar on March 3. Muscovites waited in long lines at ATM machines to withdraw their savings, triggering concerns about bank runs. The Central Bank of Russia had little choice but to raise its discount rate by more than a thousand basis points to over 20%.

US and allied officials began to conceive of economic coercion forcing Russia to halt its invasion. One way that imposed sanctions can succeed is if the economic pain imposed exceeds the target state's expectations.[21] Furthermore, there are additional pathways for economic sanctions to compel a shift in behavior beyond the target's rational cost-benefit analysis of its national interest. If the targeted leader fears either elite or mass unrest, for example, that leader could be compelled to acquiesce as a means of staying in power. In the first weeks of the war, the *New York Times* reported that this seemed to be the hope for both US and European officials:

> As they impose historic sanctions on Russia, the Biden administration and European governments have set new goals: devastate the Russian economy as punishment for the world to witness, and create domestic pressure on President Vladimir V. Putin to halt his war in Ukraine, current and former U.S. officials say. . . .
>
> The thinking among some U.S. and European officials is that Mr. Putin might stop the war if enough Russians protest in the streets and enough tycoons turn on him. . . .
>
> The moves have also ignited questions in Washington and in European capitals over whether cascading events in Russia could lead to "regime change," or rulership collapse.[22]

Again, however, these hopes proved to be unfounded. Less than a week later, US and European officials acknowledged that they had adjusted their expectations toward a protracted conflict.[23] Russia evinced minimal interest in ending the war. In subsequent interviews, Biden administration officials made it clear that the purpose of the ongoing sanctions regime had shifted from coercion to denial.

The reasons that economic coercion failed parallel the reasons that deterrence failed. As a general rule, compellence is always more difficult than deterrence because it is politically more costly to retreat from a policy than never to implement it in the first place. The moment Russia decided to launch its full-scale invasion, what had been a challenging situation for economic statecraft became even more difficult. This was particularly true given the stakes for Russia in its invasion of Ukraine. When faced with such demands, even the weakest and poorest target governments have the capacity to resist economic pressure. In the past half-decade US-led sanctions crippled both the Iranian and Venezuelan economies, generating considerable domestic unrest in both countries. Nonetheless, neither target regime responded with appreciable concessions.

Russia is a stronger, more powerful actor than either Iran or Venezuela. Putin's regime responded to the sanctions with a mixture of economic and repressive policies. On the economic side, the government and central bank initiated a raft of microeconomic and macroeconomic responses designed to prevent bank runs and tamp down inflationary pressures. The government banned Russians from transferring hard currency abroad, including for servicing foreign loans. Federal spending increased to counteract the drop-off in business investment and consumer spending. Politically, Putin's government launched a ferocious crackdown on domestic unrest, arresting protestors and censoring negative coverage of the conflict. As economist Sergei Guriev explained, "the central bank is backed by riot police."[24]

In retrospect, the hope for Russia to acquiesce to Western economic pressure was misplaced. However, it should be noted that Russian economic pressure on European countries also failed to yield any concessions in their support of Ukraine. At the start of the war there were deep-seated concerns that a Russian cutoff of energy exports would trigger domestic pressure in these countries to reach an accommodation with Moscow. Russia periodically suspended energy shipments to Europe in 2022, claiming technical difficulties with pipelines.[25] Despite this economic pressure, European Union assistance to Ukraine continued unimpeded. The EU's resistance to economic pressure equaled that of Russia.

Sanctions as a Tool of Denial in the Russo-Ukrainian War

By the spring of 2022 the messaging from US and European officials shifted from employing economic sanctions as a tool of coercion to employing them as a tool of denial—that is, to contain and harm the Russian state. This denial strategy had two prongs. The first was to limit Russia's ability to prosecute the war in Ukraine by impairing its ability to replace military hardware destroyed in the war. It is not a coincidence that the first sector-specific sanctions imposed after the February 24 invasion were targeted at Russia's defense industrial base. Despite rising tensions over the previous decade, Russia had become extremely dependent on imported semiconductor chips to fuel its defense sector and lacked the indigenous capacity for substitution.[26] The intent to harm Russia's military-industrial complex was made explicit in official US and EU discourse.

The second aim was to weaken the Russia economy more generally. Two months after the invasion, Secretary of Defense Lloyd Austin said, "We want to see Russia weakened to the degree that it can't do the kinds of things that it has done in invading Ukraine."[27] Russia under Putin has been keen to play the role of spoiler in world politics, attempting to influence elections in Europe and regimes across the Global South. Any policy that could weaken Russian capabilities would not just reduce the Russian military threat; it would also mitigate Russia's revisionist aims across the globe.

How well have sanctions worked as a tool of denying Russian military and power-projection capabilities? The evidence here is mixed. The greatest success seems to have been limiting Russia's ability to procure the high-tech inputs—precision machine tools and semiconductor chips—necessary for a war-fighting strategy. While Russian officials have publicly dismissed the effect of Western sanctions, multiple officials, including Putin, have acknowledged the pain caused by the sanctions on high-technology goods.[28]

This does not mean that Russia has been unable to procure high-end technological components. Multiple reports have highlighted channels through which these components are getting into Russia. These pathways include the following: a reliance on outsourced production facilities in states with weaker export controls, the importation of dual-use goods that allow the cannibalization of computer chips, the development of third-party trade routes, and a surge of imports from China.[29] Nonetheless, even these reports suggest that Russia has been unable to procure its prewar demand for imported components.[30] This appears to be the sector where denial has been the most successful.

That said, the denial strategy has hampered but not debilitated Russia's military efforts in Ukraine. In part this is because Russia has found substitutes for its own military tech via the "Coalition of the Sanctioned"—in other words, Russia has imported military hardware from other states facing heavy US sanctions. Both

Iran and North Korea have been eager to function as "black knights" by exporting significant weaponry to Russia. Iran has licensed Russia to produce an improved version of the Iranian Shahed-136 attack drone in the Alabuga special economic zone. The stated goal is to produce six thousand drones by 2025.[31] North Korea has supplied Russia with significant amounts of artillery. According to Ukrainian intelligence, the North Korean imports enabled Russia to avoid a catastrophic situation on the battlefield.[32]

The evidence is also mixed on the overall weakening of the Russian economy. Despite the March 2022 predictions that Russia's economy would shrink between 10% and 15% in the first year after sanctions were imposed, the actual number was much smaller: approximately 2%. In the second year of the war, Russia's gross domestic product was projected to grow between 2% and 3%. Increased government largesse over the past two years has severely mitigated the macroeconomic impact of the sanctions. Russia's oil exports—including to European countries—enabled the country to continue earning considerable export revenue.

It should be noted that the Russian economy faces significant problems going forward. After recovering from the initial shock of sanctions, the ruble slid in value relative to the dollar throughout most of 2023, in no small part because inflation has topped 7%. There are acute labor shortages throughout the economy. Former Russian central bank official Alexandra Prokopenko describes Putin as facing an impossible trilemma: funding the ongoing war against Ukraine, maintaining consumer living standards, and safeguarding macroeconomic stability.[33] Still, the hardships facing the Russian economy are more a product of the ongoing war in Ukraine than the effect of the sanctions. It is not hard to find media reports suggesting that sanctions alone have had minimal effects on the Russian economy.[34] Public opinion polling at the beginning of 2023 showed that a supermajority of Russians were unconcerned about the sanctions.[35]

Why have sanctions not worked better as a tool of denial? Long-standing goods embargoes create different political dynamics than do financial sanctions. The United States' government has been able to weaponize the dollar due to the dominance of US capital markets in global finance. The cooperation of other key financial hubs makes these sanctions even easier to implement. Over the past quarter-century, systemically important banks have invested considerable sums in sanctions compliance.[36] The combined effect is to ensure that most US-led financial sanctions will result in immediate and significant economic costs.

Strategic embargoes, however, have different necessary conditions to have a significant economic impact. Multilateral cooperation is much more important to ensuring that all producers of targeted goods are in compliance. This includes countries that could act as transit corridors between the sanctioning states and the target. Coordination with the private sector is also of obvious importance. Finally, if the goal is to harm the target's macroeconomy, sanctioning states have to be willing to prioritize that goal above all else. This means that sanctioning countries must be willing to incur costs that might impair their own economy's health.

In looking at the denial sanctions against Russia, almost none of these criteria are met. Beyond Iran and North Korea, key manufacturing countries like China are in less than full compliance with the sanctions. There are multiple observable transit corridors between manufacturing exporters and Russia in the South Caucasus, Central Asia, Middle East, and Far East. Private sector compliance is also not as robust as in the financial sector—not least of all because some of these firms are still moving along the learning curve on sanctions compliance and export controls. For example, in response to reports on US-produced semiconductors reaching the Russian defense sector, the Semiconductor Industry Association explained, "We have rigorous protocols to remove bad actors from our supply chains, but with one trillion chips sold globally each year, it's not as simple as flipping a switch."[37] It is possible that over time firms in non-financial sectors will adopt stronger compliance mechanisms. It is worth remembering, however, that private sector preferences in high-tech trade can clash with the preferences of sanctioning states.[38] Additionally, the penalties for violating export controls are less severe than those faced by the financial sector.

Finally, the G7 (Group of Seven) countries intentionally moved slowly to restrict energy imports from Russia and institute a price cap on that country's oil exports. While the United States did impose some immediate restrictions, they had insignificant effects on energy markets. The European Union took almost a year before banning sea-based oil imports, nearly as long as it took for the G7 to attempt a price cap on Russian oil exports. The European Union eventually imposed severe restrictions on oil, petroleum, liquefied natural gas, and coal imports from Russia—but in 2023 the EU imported record amounts of Russian liquefied natural gas.[39]

None of this is terribly surprising. There is ample evidence that even between warring states, trade can persist in sectors that do not have an immediate impact on the battlefield. Sanctioning Russian oil exports in early 2022 would have roiled global energy markets and had a catastrophic effect on European economies. The US State Department explained, "We do not have a strategic interest in reducing the global supply of energy, which would raise energy prices around the world and pad Putin's profits."[40] The G7 price cap was designed to keep Russian oil in the global market while reducing Russian profits. Russia, in turn, has used a shadow tanker fleet to evade sanctions—but it has not halted energy exports. As Mariya Grinberg notes, trade between warring states can still be a logical outcome: "states continue to trade in products that are essential to the domestic economy but that can be obtained only from the opponent, because sacrificing this trade would impair the state's long-term security."[41] Once expectations of a longer conflict set in, however, adversaries will take measures to reduce cross-border and third-party trade. By the end of 2023, the EU and member governments were pursuing a variety of different strategies to reduce Russian energy imports.[42] The EU announced its intention to wean itself from Russian energy by 2027.

As Europe has diversified its energy sources, it is worth noting that Russia's denial capabilities have, in turn, failed too. While countries like India and China are perfectly happy to buy Russian oil, they are willing to do so because they can purchase it at a steep discount due to the G7 price cap. Furthermore, European reductions of natural gas purchases will hurt Russia's economy for quite some time. Russia cannot simply redirect its natural gas to China or other buyers without building the requisite pipelines. That will take at least a decade to happen. At the end of 2022, the International Energy Agency concluded, "Russia's invasion of Ukraine is prompting a wholesale reorientation of global energy trade, leaving Russia with a much-diminished position. . . . [T]he rupture has come with a speed that few imagined possible. . . . Russia is unsuccessful in finding markets for all of the flows that previously went to Europe."[43] Russia also overestimated its ability to use countersanctions as a tool of denial.

Conclusions

There are ongoing disputes within the sanctions literature about their relative efficacy as an instrument of statecraft. There is a consensus, however, that—all else being equal—sanctioning great powers is less likely to work. Great powers are most likely to possess the strategic reserves and capacities necessary to withstand sustained economic pressure. Furthermore, almost by definition, great powers will anticipate frequent conflicts with the rivals that are sanctioning them. Expectations of future conflict reduce the probability of successful coercive bargaining even further. Finally, sanctions are particularly unlikely to cause targeted great powers to relinquish territory won through the expenditure of blood and treasure. In the history of economic statecraft, the number of instances in which a state—much less a great power—agreed to concede territory in response to economic sanctions is vanishingly small. The likelier outcome in response to maximum economic pressure is either military escalation by the target (as with Japan in 1941) or the sender (as with the United States with Iraq and the Balkans in the 1990s). It is therefore unsurprising that sanctions failed as a tool of deterrence and compellence in the Russo-Ukrainian war.

Increasingly, Western countries view sanctions as a tool of denial: that is, weakening the aggregate power of the targeted actor. The Russo-Ukrainian case highlights multiple policy challenges for using sanctions as a form of denial with a great power. Such a strategy creates dynamics different from those for sanctions employed as a tool of deterrence or compellence. For a denial strategy to work, multilateral cooperation is essential to ensure that the target cannot find alternatives for sanctioned goods. That, in turn, requires an institutional machinery to make cooperation sustainable and enforceable over the long run. The private sector needs to have the necessary compliance mechanisms to enforce the sanctions. And the sanctions have to be incentive-compatible, meaning that the senders do not incur long-term economic costs in the process of sanctioning.

Most of these conditions have not existed in the sanctions involving Russia and Ukraine. Russia has failed to meet any of these criteria in its countersanctions against the West. The United States has faced difficulties meeting these criteria. Multilateral cooperation has been robust in the West, but it has been neither global in scope nor institutionalized to any degree. The private sector has been behind the curve in implementation and enforcement. And the nature of Russian-European trade militates against total embargo.

Does this mean that sanctions have been counterproductive? Not necessarily. While sanctions may not have deterred Russia, it remains possible that they succeeded as a more general form of deterrence. If other actors contemplated similar irredentist violations of territorial sovereignty but were persuaded by the punitive nature of the Russia sanctions, that would be a significant policy accomplishment.[44] Relatedly, sanctions also serve as a means of norm enforcement. Violations of Westphalian territorial sovereignty are among the most transgressive acts in modern world politics. It makes sense that states defending those norms would need to use sanctions. Finally, the sanctions might accelerate—on both sides—a degree of necessary economic autonomy. The less dependent that Europe is on imports of Russian energy, for example, the less anxiety there is on the continent about the future.

These are all secondary arguments in favor of the sanctions imposed after Russia's invasion of Ukraine, however. Regarding the primary arguments, sanctions failed as a form of deterrence or compellence. They proved to be modestly useful as a tool of denial. Russia's use of countersanctions also failed. In retrospect, the expectation that sanctions would affect the course of the Russo-Ukrainian war proved to be unfounded.

NOTES

1. For a longer discussion of the economic sanctions literature, please see Daniel W. Drezner, "Global Economic Sanctions," *Annual Review of Political Science* 27 (forthcoming).

2. See, for example, Juan Zarate, *Treasury's War: The Unleashing of a New Era of Financial Warfare* (New York: PublicAffairs, 2013); Robert Blackwill and Jennifer Harris, *War by Other Means: Geoeconomics and Statecraft* (Cambridge, MA: Harvard University Press, 2016); Richard Nephew, *The Art of Sanctions: A View from the Field* (New York: Columbia University Press, 2017).

3. US Government Accountability Office, *Economic Sanctions*, GAO-20-145 (Washington, DC, October 2, 2019).

4. See, for example, Phil McCausland, "Russia Sanctions Are a 'Big Deal,' Experts Say. But Effects Could Take Years," *NBC News*, February 25, 2022, https://www.nbcnews.com/news/us-news/russia-sanctions-are-big-deal-experts-say-effects-take-years-rcna17380; Edward Wong and Michael Crowley, "Putin Insulated Russia's Economy. Will Biden's Sanctions Hold Him Back in Ukraine?," *New York Times*, February 22, 2022.

5. Walter Russell Mead, "Russia Blows Past Obama's 'Off Ramp,'" *American Interest*, March 6, 2014, https://www.the-american-interest.com/2014/03/06/russia-blows-past-obamas-off-ramp/.

6. For an excellent timeline of economic sanctions threatened and implemented against Russia, see Chad P. Bown, "Russia's War on Ukraine: A Sanctions Timeline," Peterson Institute for International Economics, December 31, 2023, https://www.piie.com/blogs/realtime-economics/russias-war-ukraine-sanctions-timeline.

7. Dan De Luce and Abigail Williams, "Biden Admin Threatens Harsh Sanctions against Russia If It Invades Ukraine," *NBC News*, December 1, 2021, https://www.nbcnews.com/politics/national-security/biden-admin-threatens-harsh-sanctions-russia-invades-ukraine-rcna7261.

8. Paul Sonne, Ashley Parker, and Isabelle Khurshudyan, "Biden Threatens Putin with Economic Sanctions If He Further Invades Ukraine," *Washington Post*, December 7, 2021.

9. Julian Borger, "Biden Threatens Putin with Personal Sanctions If Russia Invades Ukraine," *The Guardian*, January 26, 2022.

10. Both quotes from Erin Banco et al., "'Something Was Badly Wrong': When Washington Realized Russia Was Actually Invading Ukraine," *Politico*, February 24, 2023.

11. Max Seddon and Polina Ivanova, "How Putin's Technocrats Saved the Economy to Fight a War They Opposed," *Financial Times*, December 16, 2022.

12. See the chapter by McFaul and Person in this volume.

13. Serhii Plokhy, *The Russo-Ukrainian War: The Return of History* (New York: W. W. Norton, 2023), 120–138; see also Vladimir Putin, "On the Historical Unity of Russians and Ukrainians," Presidential Administration of Russia, July 12, 2021, http://en.kremlin .ru/events/president/news/66181.

14. Chris Miller, *Putinomics: Power and Money in Resurgent Russia* (Chapel Hill: University of North Carolina Press, 2018).

15. Alexander Gabuev, quoted in Max Fisher, "Putin, Facing Sanction Threats, Has Been Saving for This Day," *New York Times*, February 3, 2022.

16. Christina Stoelzel Chadwick and Andrew Long, "Foreign Policy Alignment and Russia's Energy Weapon," *Foreign Policy Analysis* 19, no. 2 (April 2023).

17. Jamie Dettmer, "Macron's Call for EU Talks with Kremlin Unnerves European Allies," *Voice of America*, January 20, 2022, https://www.voanews.com/a/macron-s-call -for-eu-talks-with-kremlin-unnerves-european-allies-/6405475.html.

18. Katrin Bennhold, "Where Is Germany in the Ukraine Standoff? Its Allies Wonder," *New York Times*, January 25, 2022.

19. Victor Jack, "Sergey Lavrov Admits Russia Was Surprised by Scale of Western Sanctions," *Politico Europe*, March 23, 2022, https://www.politico.eu/article/lavrov -admits-no-one-could-have-predicted-scale-of-western-sanctions/.

20. Jeffrey Sonnenfeld et al., "Business Retreats and Sanctions Are Crippling the Russian Economy" (working paper, S&P Global Market Intelligence, 2022), https://ssrn .com/abstract=4167193.

21. Jon Hovi, Robert Huseby, and Detlef F. Sprinz, "When Do (Imposed) Economic Sanctions Work?," *World Politics* 57, no. 4 (July 2005): 479–499.

22. Edward Wong and Michael Crowley, "With Sanctions, U.S. and Europe Aim to Punish Putin and Fuel Russian Unrest," *New York Times*, March 4, 2022.

23. Ashley Parker et al., "'No Off-Ramps': U.S. and European Officials Don't See a Clear Endgame in Ukraine," *Washington Post*, March 10, 2022.

24. Seddon and Ivanova, "How Putin's Technocrats Saved the Economy."

25. See, for example, Georgi Kantchev, "Russia Halts Nord Stream Gas Pipeline, Ratcheting Up Pressure on Europe," *Wall Street Journal*, August 31, 2022.

26. James Byrne et al., *Silicon Lifeline: Western Electronics at the Heart of Russia's War Machine* (London: Royal United Services Institute, August 2022); Daria Talanova, "Last Chance Saloon," *Novaya Gazeta*, September 18, 2023, https://novayagazeta.eu/articles /2023/09/18/last-chance-saloon; Alena Popova, "How to Exploit Russia's Addiction to Western Technology," *Foreign Affairs*, November 3, 2023, https://www.foreignaffairs.com /china/how-exploit-russias-addiction-western-technology.

27. Missy Ryan and Annabelle Timsit, "U.S. Wants Russian Military 'Weakened' from Ukraine Invasion, Austin Says," *Washington Post*, April 25, 2022.

28. Marcus Parekh and Berny Torre, "Putin Admits Kremlin Facing 'Colossal' High-Tech Problems due to Sanctions," *The Telegraph*, July 18, 2022.

29. Ana Swanson and Matina Stevis-Gridneff, "Russia Is Importing Western Weapons Technology, Bypassing Sanctions," *New York Times*, April 18, 2023; Chris Cook, "Moscow Imports a Third of Battlefield Tech from Western Companies," *Financial Times*, January 11, 2024; Dalton Bennett et al., "Precision Equipment for Russian Arms Makers Came from U.S.-Allied Taiwan," *Washington Post*, February 1, 2024.

30. Zoya Sheftalovich and Laurens Cerulus, "The Chips Are Down: Putin Scrambles for High-Tech Parts as His Arsenal Goes Up in Smoke," *Politico*, September 5, 2022.

31. Dalton Bennett and Mary Ilyushina, "Inside the Russian Effort to Build 6,000 Attack Drones with Iran's Help," *Washington Post*, August 17, 2023. Russia will fall short of that goal because even Iranian drones require Western-produced semiconductor chips.

32. Christopher Miller, "Kyrylo Budanov: The Ukrainian Military Spy Chief Who 'Likes the Darkness,'" *Financial Times*, January 21, 2024.

33. Alexandra Prokopenko, "Putin's Unsustainable Spending Spree," *Foreign Affairs*, January 8, 2024.

34. See, for example, "Russia's Key Economic Sectors Shrug Off Sanctions," *Bloomberg*, November 15, 2023. For an opposing perspective, see Georgi Kantchev, "Putin's Warped Wartime Economy, as Seen through a Carton of Eggs," *Wall Street Journal*, January 18, 2024.

35. Emily Sullivan, Dina Smeltz, Denis Volkov, and Stepan Goncharov, "Few Russians Are Anxious about Western Sanctions," Chicago Council on Global Affairs, January 2023.

36. Julia Morse, *The Bankers' Blacklist: Unofficial Market Enforcement and the Global Fight against Illicit Financing* (Ithaca, NY: Cornell University Press, 2022).

37. Quoted in Swanson and Stevis-Gridneff, "Russia Is Importing Western Weapons Technology."

38. Ling Chen and Miles Evers, "'Wars without Gun Smoke': Global Supply Chains, Power Transitions, and Economic Statecraft," *International Security* 48, no. 2 (Fall 2023): 164–204.

39. Alice Hancock and Shotaro Tani, "EU Imports Record Volumes of Liquefied Natural Gas from Russia," *Financial Times*, August 30, 2023.

40. Shotaro Tani, Ian Johnston, and James Politi, "US Seeks to Thwart Russia's Ambition to Become a Major LNG Exporter," *Financial Times*, November 12, 2023.

41. Mariya Grinberg, "Wartime Commercial Policy and Trade between Enemies," *International Security* 46, no. 1 (Summer 2021): 10.

42. Alice Hancock, "EU to Give Member States Power to Block Russian Gas Imports," *Financial Times*, December 8, 2023.

43. International Energy Agency, *World Energy Outlook 2022*, last modified November 24, 2022, https://www.iea.org/reports/world-energy-outlook-2022.

44. See the chapter by Lin and Hart in this volume for more on this topic.

Chapter Seventeen

America's Global Role in the Shadow of the Ukraine Conflict

Peter D. Feaver and William Inboden

The Ukraine War revived and sharpened a long-standing debate over America's role in the world. What should America's global posture be, and how—if at all—should the United States' power be employed outside American borders? Such domestic disputations have occurred in some form or another regularly since America's founding. The arguments have taken place during war and peace; cut across political party lines and also divided parties from within; occurred over issues such as trade, aid, military spending, alliances, and interventions; and appealed to both high principle and low politics.

Two years after the Ukraine War started, many of these issues surfaced in debates over American aid to Ukraine. To bring some analytical clarity, this chapter primarily addresses the question of American economic and military aid to partner forces. It focuses more on the expenditure of American treasure than American blood. Other instances of American engagement abroad, such as alliance

Peter D. Feaver is a professor of political science and public policy at Duke University, where he runs the Program in American Grand Strategy and is the co–principal investigator of the America in the World Consortium. He is the author of *Thanks for Your Service: The Causes and Consequences of Public Confidence in the US Military* (Oxford University Press, 2023). William Inboden is a professor and the director of the Alexander Hamilton Center at the University of Florida and is a Peterson Senior Fellow with the Kissinger Center for Global Affairs at the Johns Hopkins School of Advanced International Studies. His previous service includes positions at the State Department and on the staff of the National Security Council.

memberships or overt military interventions, are also considered where they help illuminate the larger questions.

American aid rather than boots on ground is a useful proxy for broader debates over isolationism versus internationalism, precisely because it is an incessant question that beset American foreign policy in every decade from the 1910s to the present. It first emerged during World War I over whether the United States should stay scrupulously neutral or aid the Allies; continued in the 1920s in numerous places including China, Latin America, and Europe; and surged in the late 1930s with the Neutrality Acts and debates over aid to the Allies against Nazi Germany.[1] And so forth into the Cold War and beyond, up to our present moment with Ukraine.

Debates around American aid are revealing precisely because they do not entail actual deployment of American forces. As damaging as the conflicts can be for the people fighting in them, they are less costly for Americans, who are asked only to contribute treasure without risking American blood. Rather, such debates are illuminating proxies for how much influence and leadership the United States seeks to exert in the world, even at comparatively low cost.

Low cost does not mean no cost, however. It is true that every dollar spent abroad could instead be spent at home (even though almost all of the Ukrainian defense aid is, in fact, spent buying weapons made in American factories by American workers). But low costs sometimes increase the prospect of higher costs. The depletion of stockpiles augurs the need for higher spending (and higher borrowing costs) in the future. And American support for one side in a conflict necessarily increases the risk of retaliation against America by the other side. Moreover, on occasion, military aid can presage significant American troop deployments such as in the case of the Vietnam War.

Still, even in the recent post–Cold War history of American interventions, the Ukraine War and the American aid program should be put in context. It did not entail a US-led bombing campaign like Bosnia or Kosovo or Libya. It was not a large-scale invasion with conventional forces like the first or second Gulf Wars. Nor was it a Special Operations–led operation with a light footprint like the campaign against ISIL (Islamic State of Iraq and the Levant) or the original phases of Operation Enduring Freedom in Afghanistan. The Ukraine debates were simply about whether the United States should provide economic and military assistance to the Ukrainian forces.

The Ukraine War

In strategic and political terms, Russia invaded Ukraine at a complicated time for the United States. The invasion was well timed to revive the Biden administration's national security reputation after a difficult first year marked by the calamitous withdrawal from Afghanistan. Ukraine initially gave President Joe Biden a galvanizing opportunity to marshal bipartisan support at home along with an unprecedented and vigorous allied response abroad. Yet it was also poorly timed because when Ukraine defied expectations in both directions—fending off Russia longer than expected in 2022 but then failing to deliver the expected knockout blow in the 2023 counteroffensive—the war dragged into a stalemate that merged with the 2024 presidential elections. As the election campaign heated up, Biden's effort to support Ukraine appeared to be one more casualty of the political polarization that had stymied American leaders in recent years.

President Biden's response to the invasion, which marked a significant kinetic escalation in the new era of great-power conflict that had been simmering for a decade, raised important questions about the domestic political foundations of US foreign policy. Its disposition will also do much to determine the trajectory of a grand strategy of defending a global order favorable to US interests.

Putin's Gamble and Initial US Response

Russia's invasion came just as President Biden's handling of national security reached its low point following the Afghanistan pullout. Biden's stubborn insistence on fulfilling President Donald J. Trump's misguided plan for Afghanistan withdrawal regardless of the costs had the predicted effect of surrendering the entire nation to the Taliban—a "strategic defeat" in the words of Biden's own chairman of the Joint Chiefs of Staff, General Mark Milley. The humiliating images, reminiscent of the last American helicopters fleeing Saigon in 1975, euthanized the "honeymoon" of favorable public approval that Biden had enjoyed since inauguration, a disapproval that persisted into 2024.

Biden initially received favorable evaluations of his handling of the Ukraine crisis from experts and in the elite media. By most accounts, Biden's early response—from the pre-invasion information campaign designed to expose Russian president Vladimir Putin's disinformation to the tougher-than-expected sanctions to even the incremental but not inconsequential military aid—showed skill and sophistication. Moreover, Biden's expressions of steadfast support and the sweeping geostrategic rationale he articulated constituted a reversal from the retrenchment logic he had used to justify the Afghanistan retreat.

Ukraine's vigorous defense of its territory quickly exposed Putin's invasion as a catastrophic blunder. Prodded by Biden, NATO responded with surprising speed and forcefulness, and within weeks the United States and its allies began providing Ukraine the financial, material, and political support that Kyiv had begged for to little avail since 2014. Led by a surprisingly resolute and inspiring Ukrainian president, Volodymyr Zelensky, Ukraine outperformed expectations throughout 2022. By a year into the war, Putin faced setbacks on all sides. The easy victory he had expected eluded him; he lost much of the territory he had gained in the initial invasion; he paid inordinate costs in further offensives; and he faced a larger and revitalized NATO alliance.

And then, 2023 proved as disappointing for Ukraine and its supporters as 2022 had been encouraging. As the war dragged on without a decisive victory in view, the weaknesses and vulnerabilities of Biden's ambivalent Ukraine policy became apparent. For starters, the gap between the ambitious military aid that Ukraine requested and the grudging military aid that Biden granted became glaringly large—perhaps large enough to metaphorically swallow up operational success in Ukraine's counteroffensive. Moreover, an unflattering pattern emerged in which Ukraine requested a specific weapon system, then Biden denied it on the grounds that it was not needed or posed too serious a risk of escalation, only to reluctantly reverse his decision and grant the same system much later. This incessant vacillation belied the Biden administration's talking points and fueled hawkish concerns that Ukraine was getting just enough help to lose slowly rather than to prevail.

Meanwhile, the domestic political foundations of Biden's Ukraine policy were exposed as brittle. Domestic opponents of American aid to Ukraine became more vocal, and the drumbeat of anti-Zelensky/pro-Putin talking points emanating from the far-right fringe of the Republican Party gradually began to have an effect on public opinion. Whereas, in March 2022, Republicans favored support for Ukraine by as much as 80%, by March 2023 Republican support had plummeted to 53%, and by December 2023 nearly half of Republican respondents were saying that the United States was providing "too much" support while only 13% were saying "too little."[2] Ukraine still enjoyed bipartisan support, especially among the Senate and some Republican House committee chairs, but the vocal Republican opponents in the House of Representatives imposed a poison pill deal that blocked further aid to Ukraine. As the 2024 campaign season came into full swing, Ukraine appeared to be a foreign policy political burden rather than a boon—the sort of issue raised more by opponents of President Biden than by his supporters.

The Long Twilight Struggle between American Isolationism and Internationalism

While the domestic debate over Ukraine had unmistakable Trumpian undertones, it channeled a much longer dialectic within American politics. These strains have their own distinct yet often overlapping lineages within both American conservatism and progressivism. Whether wittingly or not, some social media influencers and pundits, those who sought to convince the public that Putin's aggression was mostly the fault of the Ukrainians themselves or even the West as a whole, eerily echoed the arguments of the original "America Firsters," who argued in the 1930s that America had no legitimate interest in aiding the victims of Hitler's aggression—if anything, American interests aligned more closely with Berlin's and only war profiteers would argue otherwise. Thus, the notoriously inflammatory Father Charles Coughlin critiqued the status quo, claiming that American "foreign policy, devoid of all fine phrases, was one blueprinted to defend international capitalism and British imperialism, no matter what the cost might be in traditions, in dollars and in blood to the citizens of our country."[3]

Similar sentiments today are articulated by the likes of pundit Tucker Carlson, who just months before the invasion declared, "Why do I care what is going on in the conflict between Ukraine and Russia? I'm serious. Why do I care? Why shouldn't I root for Russia? Which I am." A few months after Russia invaded Ukraine, Carlson claimed that the Biden administration's support for Ukraine sprang merely from crass partisanship. "We arm Ukraine so that we can punish Russia. Why? For stealing Hillary Clinton's coronation," he averred, referring to Russian intervention to support Donald Trump in the 2016 election.[4]

The Japanese attack on Pearl Harbor awakened America's martial spirit to enter World War II. Yet in the wake of the great victories over German fascism and Japanese imperialism, the impulse to return to a more modest global role reemerged, and by late 1945 US forces were demanding to be demobilized. Despite a series of Soviet provocations, the administration of Harry S. Truman struggled at first to forge robust domestic support behind a containment strategy that required the United States to serve as a global guarantor of security, stationing troops abroad and defending sea lanes and borders thousands of miles away from the US homeland.

Again, in this immediate postwar era, some of the most foundational debates occurred not over the actual use of American force but rather over whether the United States should provide money and weapons to other partners seeking to deter or defeat aggression. These debates cut across customary partisan lines. Progressive Democrats such as Henry Wallace found common cause with right-wing Republicans such as Robert Taft in resisting the Truman Doctrine of providing aid to anticommunist forces in Greece and Turkey, the Marshall Plan, and the creation of NATO. On an issue where Republicans were more united, such as aiding the Chinese nationalists in the civil war against Mao Zedong's communists, the Democrats suffered acrimonious internal divisions.

As with the 1930s, undergirding the particulars of each of these debates over American aid to partners abroad were more fundamental divides over America's priorities and international role. Should American resources be devoted solely to needs at home or also be sent overseas to support American interests, values, and friends? Should the United States focus all its energies on domestic concerns, or should it try to exert its influence abroad to shape a new international order? And were the costs and risks of doing the latter worth the potential benefits?

North Korea's surprise invasion of South Korea in 1950 seemed initially to galvanize American internationalism behind President Truman's deployment of American troops. Yet within a year, as that war sunk into a bloody stalemate, the calls, especially within the Republican Party, for an American retreat from global commitments returned. They grew loud enough in 1952 for General Dwight D. Eisenhower to step down as NATO leader and declare himself a Republican presidential candidate so as to thwart the presidential ambitions of the neo-isolationist Taft.

America's decades-long involvement in Vietnam emerged as a costly cautionary tale. What began in the 1950s under Eisenhower as merely an economic and military aid program to South Vietnam turned in the early 1960s into the growing deployment of American ground troops. Vietnam's eventual tragedies included over fifty-eight thousand dead Americans, the humiliation of America's first lost war in history, and a rallying cry ever since for critics of American internationalism. By 1972, the war and the larger geopolitical burdens it represented were so unpopular that the Democratic nominee for president, Senator George McGovern, made "Come home, America" the central theme of his platform.

The post-Vietnam rise of the New Left in American politics in the 1970s, especially its growing influence in the Democratic Party, brought a renewed aversion to American internationalism, particularly to American support for anticommunist forces abroad. Thus in 1975 the Democratic Congress terminated all US military assistance for South Vietnam and the next year passed the Clark Amendment prohibiting any US aid to anticommunist forces in Angola. Such progressive voices also pressured the Carter administration to end its support for the anticommunist Shah of Iran and the Somoza regime in Nicaragua.

Meanwhile the Republican Party suffered its own deep rifts through the 1970s. Unlike the isolationism dividing the Democrats, the GOP debate pitted two different camps of internationalists against each other: The Nixon-Ford-Kissinger wing, which favored reduced tensions with the Soviet Union through détente while maintaining American international leadership in Asia and the Middle East, may have initially succeeded in defeating the isolationism of McGovern Democrats. But these Republicans soon found themselves squaring off against Ronald Reagan's conservative internationalist camp advocating for a more confrontational posture toward the Soviet Union and a renewed commitment to promoting liberty abroad.

Reagan's 1980 election victory showed broad support for his hawkishness toward Moscow—and also triggered a new round of domestic acrimony over American aid to anticommunist forces abroad. Quite cautious about the actual use of force, especially the deployment of American troops in combat, Reagan nonetheless determined to resist the further expansion of communism abroad. He developed what became known as the Reagan Doctrine, which involved providing American economic and military aid to anticommunist insurgents in Nicaragua, Afghanistan, Cambodia, and Angola, in addition to providing American aid to anticommunist governments such as those in El Salvador, South Korea, Philippines, and Taiwan. During the Reagan years many progressive Democrats resisted the Reagan Doctrine and tried to block American support for the government of El Salvador, and for a time they successfully banned American aid to the anticommunist Contra forces in Nicaragua. Nonetheless, America's peaceful victory in the Cold War immediately following Reagan's presidency seemed to vindicate American internationalism.[5]

Yet the end of the Cold War and the quest for a "peace dividend" revived the neo-isolationist voices that President Reagan and President George H. W. Bush had largely quelled. Despite leading the American victory in the 1991 war in the Persian Gulf, President Bush faced a surprisingly strong electoral challenge from newly remobilized right-wing critics of American internationalism, first from within the party with Pat Buchanan's primary challenge and then with Ross Perot's third-party challenge. The 1992 victor, Democrat Bill Clinton, had internationalist inclinations, and like his Republican successor, George W. Bush, Clinton saw public reluctance to bear geopolitical burdens as one of the most serious challenges his administration faced.

Public aversion to internationalism intensified in the early 2000s particularly as the costs of the prolonged wars in Iraq and Afghanistan increased. In the next three presidential elections, the electorate chose each time the finalist who called for reduced American commitments abroad. To be sure, the elections turned on domestic and other issues far removed from geopolitics. Moreover, Presidents Barack Obama and Donald Trump differed in important ways on major issues of foreign policy. But there was a common thread: the restraint-oriented foreign policy platforms of the eventual victors seemed to be a net-positive in political terms, whatever their deficiencies in policy terms. President Biden's victory in 2020, though not primarily about foreign policy, similarly was predicated on modest foreign policy goals.

Once in office, President Biden took pains to signal respect to allies and partners alike who had been bruised by rhetorical broadsides during the Trump era and to talk up democracy and human rights after Trump's repeated poor-mouthing of those traditional American values. In actual policy terms, however, the shift was far less dramatic. President Biden maintained many of Trump's signature policies at the southern border, Trump's tariff-based trade war with China, and Trump's Abraham Accords (along with the associated appeasement of Saudi Arabia's de facto leader). Aspirationally, Biden and his team sought a more dramatic reversal in certain high-profile areas, notably climate change and a revival of Obama's ill-starred Iran nuclear deal, but without much tangible success to show for it.

The continuity was most vivid in Afghanistan, where President Biden claimed, though falsely, to have an obligation to continue implementing Trump's mandated withdrawal. Biden's embrace was so dramatic that two prominent academic advocates of this restraint approach defended the Afghanistan withdrawal in a fawning review. They hoped that it may be "just the beginning," with additional retreats across a range of fronts: a dramatic restructuring of the US global military footprint, a refusal to expand NATO (where Biden had noticeably "soft-pedaled" talk of adding Ukraine), and perhaps an unwinding of US military operations against ISIL in Syria and Iraq as well as other counterterror missions in Africa and Latin America.[6]

The Ukrainian Shock and Aftershock

If President Biden was indeed flirting with such a shift, Putin put paid to it with his Ukraine aggression. The Biden administration saw the invasion coming and moved to counter it with a newfound focus and ambition. There were four lines of action, all variations on the familiar internationalist playbook conducted under the auspices of energetic American leadership—in short, the antithesis of the "restraint" reflex. First, the Biden team spoke loudly and often about the threat and about how it jeopardized vital US national interests—and shared the intelligence undergirding these assessments widely and in real time to a degree never before done by US policymakers. Second, the team built a coalition of the willing to support Ukraine and protect Eastern Europe and to warn of severe consequences for Russia if Putin persisted. Third, the team developed contingency plans for translating that rhetoric into action through defense aid to bolster Ukraine and coercive economic sanctions to punish Russia and restrict Russia's capacity to supply its war effort. Fourth, the Biden team clearly signaled its concerns about escalatory pressures and getting drawn into a kinetic conflict with Russia, and so balanced its hawkish policies with vivid redlines that spelled out what the United States would not do.

These efforts failed to deter Putin from invading, but they otherwise succeeded in galvanizing a Western response that exceeded all expectations in its breadth and depth. Under American leadership, NATO countries committed 100 billion euros in military assistance to Ukraine and adopted a multiyear program of support during the war's first two years.[7] These developments culminated in the most significant expansion of NATO in decades with the admission paths for Finland and Sweden.[8] Just as consequentially, Biden helped pull countries outside Europe into the anti-Putin coalition with significant contributions coming from Asian allies, especially South Korea and Japan. At the same time, Putin's invasion surprised in the other direction: failing catastrophically as tactical blunders compounded operational shortcomings, adding up to a massive strategic failure. Even if Russia eventually does manage to control large swaths of eastern Ukraine, it will have done so at a ghastly and disproportionate cost. Together, the assertiveness of the global coalition and the manifest strategic incompetence of Putin combined to make the first year and a half of the war something of a revival of an American-led international order.

To be sure, even during the early days there were loud domestic critics of Biden's Ukraine policy. The loudest were critics from the hawkish end of the spectrum who warned that the Biden team was too slow in sending the kinds of war-winning weapon systems that Ukraine needed to prevail. Republican Senate minority leader Mitch McConnell was quite blunt: "Our own president needs to step up his game. We're not doing nearly enough quickly enough to help the Ukrainians."[9]

There were prominent critics from the doves, conspicuously Senator Rand Paul, who proposed that Biden concede to Putin's demands that Ukraine forever be denied entrance into NATO in the hopes of buying off the invasion.[10] Paul was soon enough joined by other congressional voices, notably Senators Josh Hawley and J. D. Vance, as well as a growing right-wing cohort in the House.[11] The progressive Left echoed these critiques, with some thirty House Democrats in the Progressive Caucus sending a letter to President Biden in October 2022 urging negotiations with Russia instead of military aid to Ukraine.[12] Despite these critics, through the summer of 2023, Congress continued to approve military and economic aid to Ukraine with large bipartisan majorities.

In the fall of 2023 the fortunes of war turned, ironically not long after Putin hit his low point with the attempted coup by his mercenary leader Yevgeny Prigozhin. When Ukraine's long-touted counteroffensive fizzled, the US domestic chorus of critics grew much louder—with both the internationalists and the isolationists framing their criticisms with "I told you so." The internationalists who wanted Biden to risk Putin's escalatory wrath by arming Ukraine faster and more deeply argued that the failure of the counteroffensive could be traced back to Biden's failure to give Ukraine the help it needed. Those more wary of American involvements in conflicts overseas argued that Zelensky had tricked the West into backing a losing horse and that the sooner the United States abandoned Ukraine, the sooner the war could end. That such an end would entail at best Russia retaining all the territory it took in the 2014 and 2022 invasions—and at worst the collapse of the Ukrainian government in Kyiv, massive atrocities committed against Ukrainian civilians, and expanded Russian territorial control—was a price the isolationists did not mind paying.

The political winds in the United States shifted throughout 2023 for reasons only distantly related to Ukraine, but each new gust undercut American internationalism or bolstered the neo-isolationists. For instance, after the *Dobbs* decision ending the federal right to abortion, the Biden administration violated a half-century-long political truce against federal funding of abortion by forcing the Pentagon to pay for travel for some military women seeking abortions. Republican senator Tommy Tuberville retaliated by jettisoning the Senate norm on confirmation of flag and general officers by blocking more than five hundred nominees. The standoff continued for almost one year, with domestic political priorities preventing either side from backing down despite the severe damage incurred to American national security.

Similarly, as the House of Representatives sunk deeper into dysfunction, the beneficiaries were the factions most willing to risk extreme outcomes—a failure to pass a defense authorization bill, government shutdown, debt default—to control the legislative agenda. While these groups lacked the votes to actually pass legislation, they had enough power to block legislation, and for them, doing nothing was preferable to muddling through with yet another legislative compromise. The resulting paralysis further hindered internationalist legislative priorities.

The new anti-Ukraine version of American isolationism seemed to weave together at least four independent threads into a single confusing tapestry. These threads took age-old arguments and spun them into the neo-isolationist emperor's bespoke new clothes, which were tailored, more or less, to the present case. First was the doubt about the efficacy of US military power and the endless *reductio ad iraqum* in which every war is "another Iraq."[13] The facts that directly contradict such sloppy analogizing—Putin's blatant aggression, Ukraine's demonstrable operational capacity, and the enthusiastic support of almost all of the key NATO partners—were lost in the steady drumbeat that emphasized the failures of the American military and its partners. Whereas the call for restraint and retrenchment in the 1990s was based on claims of American strength—"we can do less because we are not facing threats abroad"—the same patent remedy was peddled as necessary because of American weakness: "we can no longer afford to police the world, not when we face so many challenges at home and abroad."

Second was the warped version of Christian nationalism that praised Putin as a hero of the faith and cursed Ukraine as apostate.[14] This form of heresy spread into many corners of otherwise orthodox theological institutions and evoked painful echoes of the corruptions of the German Catholic and Lutheran Churches in the 1930s. The evidentiary basis for this was woefully thin and, indeed, was belied by the dramatic expansion in reach and diversity of many Christian denominations in Ukraine over the past decade.[15] However, the far-fetched claims served a useful rhetorical purpose by providing a purported values-based counterargument to claims of solidarity with a Ukraine that embraced Western values and wanted to become more integrated into Europe and the liberal international order led by the United States.

Third was the firm belief that one can catalyze a virtuous circle of Europeans doing more if the United States does less, despite the evidence that it operates in exactly the opposite fashion. Biden leading by example helped push European measures and vice versa. For the neo-isolationists, however, every ally is a free-rider if it is not operating entirely on its own. Whereas "free-riding by the allies" justified leaving the allies to fend for themselves earlier in the post–Cold War era, once the allies became heavily motivated and invested in helping Ukraine, that very commitment was turned into a rationalization for letting them handle it on their own, since they care so much.

Fourth was the equally strong belief that locking in defeat and capitulation to threats in one region somehow better positioned the United States to shore up deterrence and defense in another region. Thus, one of the odder strategic arguments for abandoning Ukraine was that doing so would bolster deterrence in East Asia, as if throwing Kyiv under the bus would make Beijing think that Washington was even more resolved to defend Taipei. This argument was politically useful because it wrapped the sheep of retreat in the wolf's hide of a hawkish posture against China.[16] Of course, the argument collapsed under scrutiny, as shown by factors including Taiwan's strong appeals on behalf of Ukraine, Xi Jinping's increased threats against Taiwan amid American vacillation over Ukraine, and the erosion of deterrence and credibility that an American abandonment of Ukraine would indicate.[17]

The obvious holes in this tapestry were called out by key opinion leaders. McConnell was particularly forceful in pushing back against the neo-isolationist line.[18] President Biden was less willing to use his bully pulpit and less effective in those times when he did use it. For most of 2023, as support for Ukraine softened, the White House focused its rhetorical energies elsewhere. At best, the efforts of the pro-Ukraine caucus slowed the erosion of support—at worst they did not have much effect at all.

The relatively quick erosion of support for Ukraine is noteworthy because the neo-isolationist brief has such a weak logical foundation in general and was applied to what should be a hard case for backing its approach. If, hypothetically, US troops were dying in the unsuccessful Ukrainian counteroffensive, then the decline in support would be easily explainable: the US public is willing to tolerate the mounting human costs of war provided that the war is seen as being on a trajectory to a successful outcome.[19] Instead, it was Ukrainian blood with US (and European) treasure at risk, and President Biden was adamant in emphasizing that the United States would not commit its own troops to the conflict. Ukraine needs American weapons, not American soldiers, at least not while the fighting continues. Ironically, a ground commitment, should one ever arise, would come once peace was assured and a postwar settlement was needing stabilization—this is a reality that the neo-isolationists have not reckoned with, though one can anticipate that their answer in the moment will be to insist that the United States do the minimum or, less than that, to underwrite any post-conflict stabilization plan.

Beyond this, the Ukraine War had few of the factors that had eroded public support for the wars in Iraq and Afghanistan. Ukraine had able political and military leadership—not perfect but much better than the Iraqi and Afghan allies that US leaders had to manage. Ukrainians were willing to fight and die for their cause and proved to be capable operational and tactical innovators. Only a few elite units of the Iraqi and Afghan security forces had reached the level of proficiency that the median Ukrainian unit reached. NATO allies did not free-ride on the US military but made sizable investments of their own. That said, Ukraine did have the problem of corruption, which had proved highly corrosive to public support in Afghanistan and had a similar effect in Ukraine.

The neo-isolationist case was bolstered somewhat by an active information warfare campaign conducted by Russia and Chinese propagandists who deployed bot-farms in an effort to exploit social media algorithms and influence sectors of the Western public.[20] But while the war can be blamed on Putin and Xi, the softness of Biden's political support probably cannot be. Instead, the key factor appears to be the dysfunction in the Republican Party. Ukraine became the unlikely focal point of a genuine intramural scrum among Republicans about the future direction of the party—and thus the country.

Finally, while Ukraine exposed the GOP's painful internal fractures and uncertain commitment to internationalism, the war in Gaza exposed a similar rift within the Democratic Party. It became almost a mirror image of the Republican debate over Ukraine. After an ephemeral moment of unity and solidarity following the October 7, 2023, Hamas terrorist attacks on Israel, within weeks sizable numbers of Democrats, especially in the party's progressive base, turned vocally against US aid to Israel.[21] Once again, as with Ukraine, the question was whether the United States should provide military aid to a partner nation that was attacked by an outside force. The deployment of US troops to aid Israel was not in question. The party's grassroots and populist voices put pressure on its establishment leaders to curtail or cut off the military aid entirely. Yes, there were many ways in which the particulars of Ukraine and Israel differed, but some of the fundamental questions were the same—as were the passionate divisions they elicited within each American political party.

Whither American Internationalism

The challenge in maintaining support for Ukraine raises questions about the long-term future of American internationalism. If the United States cannot help Ukraine preserve its independence when the stakes and Russia's perfidy are this clear, and the relative costs for the United States are so low, what are the prospects that the United States could be mobilized to defend Taiwan against Chinese encroachment when actual US forces would need to deploy in the fight? More than one observer has noted that Russia's invasion of Ukraine is functioning a bit like the Spanish Civil War—a dress rehearsal to a much greater global conflagration that might yet come—and Xi Jinping is surely cheering for a rapid US retreat, which would foreshadow a much easier unraveling of the US-led international order.

The waning of the internationalist consensus is not foreordained, however. It still enjoys majority support among the public, with solid strength in both parties. The dysfunction of the razor-thin Republican majority in the House of Representatives has had the unfortunate side effect of exaggerating the political power of the neo-isolationist wing—a misperception that is belied by the considerable strength of traditional Republican hawks in the Senate.

Dramatic events can also quickly change public opinion. It was not well-crafted op-eds or speeches on the Senate floor that refuted 1930s "America First" isolationism; it was Japan's attack on Pearl Harbor. More recently, while many Republicans in 2020 voiced an eagerness to abandon Afghanistan, the calamitous withdrawal the next year, coupled with the Taliban's victory, caused many of those same Republicans suddenly to rediscover the relative merits of a stronger American posture abroad.

The emerging threat environment brings with it a sobering reality. The new coalition of tyrannies in Moscow, Tehran, Beijing, and Pyongyang spanning Eurasia pose a growing menace to the United States, our allies, and our interests. A neo-isolationist policy of retrenchment will not appease them, nor will it make the United States safer or more secure. As costly and challenging as internationalism can be, it also remains the least-bad option, grounded in the lessons of history. If the defenders of the rules-based global system prevail in Ukraine, the prospects for the American-led internationalism will improve—and that is far better for US interests and security than the alternative.

NOTES

1. Robert Kagan, *The Ghost at the Feast: America and the Collapse of World Order, 1900–1941* (New York: Knopf, 2023).

2. Scott Clement, Dan Balz, and Emily Guskin, "Most Favor Military Aid to Ukraine, but Partisan Split Grows, Poll Finds," *Washington Post*, October 4, 2023, https://www.washingtonpost.com/national-security/2023/10/04/ukraine-poll-republican-support/; Pew Research Center, "Since Russia's Invasion, Republicans Have Grown Increasingly Skeptical of U.S. Aid Level to Ukraine," December 6, 2023, https://www.pewresearch.org/short-reads/2023/12/08/about-half-of-republicans-now-say-the-us-is-providing-too-much-aid-to-ukraine/sr_23-12-07_ukraine-war_2/.

3. Father Charles Coughlin, January 5, 1942, quoted in "The Press: Crackdown on Coughlin," *Time*, April 27, 1942.

4. Chris McGreal, "Who Is Tucker Carlson Really 'Rooting for' in Ukraine?," *The Guardian*, October 2, 2022, https://www.theguardian.com/media/2022/oct/02/tucker-carlson-ukraine-vladimir-putin-propaganda.

5. William Inboden, *The Peacemaker: Ronald Reagan, the Cold War, and the World on the Brink* (New York: Dutton, 2022).

6. Joshua Shifrinson and Stephen Wertheim, "Biden the Realist: The President's Foreign Policy Is Hiding in Plain Sight," *Foreign Affairs*, September 9, 2021, https://www.foreignaffairs.com/articles/united-states/2021-09-09/biden-realist.

7. "NATO's Response to Russia's Invasion of Ukraine," North Atlantic Treaty Organization, November 6, 2023, https://www.nato.int/cps/en/natohq/topics_192648.htm.

8. Anne Kauranen and Andrew Gray, "Finland Joins NATO in Historic Shift, Russia Threatens 'Counter-measures,' " *Reuters*, April 4, 2023, https://www.reuters.com/world/europe/finland-set-join-nato-historic-shift-while-sweden-waits-2023-04-04/.

9. Burgess Everett, Olivia Beavers, and Andrew Desiderio, "Republicans Try to Out-Hawk Biden on Ukraine Aid," *Politico*, March 16, 2022, https://www.politico.com/news/2022/03/16/republicans-out-hawk-biden-ukraine-aid-00017831.

10. Andrew Desiderio, "Senate Passes Symbolic Russia Rebuke as Ukraine Threat Looms," *Politico*, February 17, 2022, https://www.politico.com/news/2022/02/17/senators-unveil-their-attempt-at-a-symbolic-reprimand-for-russia-00009692.

11. Robert Draper, "A Loud G.O.P. Minority Pledges to Make Trouble on Ukraine Military Aid," *New York Times*, May 19, 2023.

12. Alexander Ward and Matt Berg, "Progressive Caucus Retracts Ukraine Letter," *Politico*, October 25, 2022, https://www.politico.com/newsletters/national-security-daily/2022/10/25/progressive-caucus-retracts-ukraine-letter-00063310.

13. Stephen Wertheim, "The One Key Word Biden Needs to Invoke on Ukraine," *The Atlantic*, June 11, 2022.

14. Samuel Perry et al., "The Religious Right and Russia: Christian Nationalism and Americans' Views on Russia and Vladimir Putin before and after the Ukrainian Invasion," *Journal for the Scientific Study of Religion* 62, no. 2 (June 2023), 439–450.

15. Denys Brylov, Tetiana Kalenychenko, and Andrii Kryshtal, *Mapping the Religious Landscape of Ukraine* (Washington, DC: United States Institute of Peace, 2023),

https://www.usip.org/sites/default/files/2023-10/pw_193-mapping_religious_landscape
_ukraine.pdf.

16. Elbridge A. Colby and Alex Velez-Green, "Opinion: To Avert War with China, the U.S. Must Prioritize Taiwan over Ukraine," *Washington Post*, May 18, 2023.

17. Josh Rogin, "Opinion: Taiwan Is Urging the U.S. Not to Abandon Ukraine," *Washington Post*, May 10, 2023.

18. Mitch McConnell, "McConnell: Helping Defend Ukraine 'Obviously in America's Self-Interest'" (speech to Senate, Washington, DC, September 11, 2023), https://www.republicanleader.senate.gov/newsroom/remarks/mcconnell-helping-defend
-ukraine-is-obviously-in-americas-self-interest.

19. Christopher Gelpi, Peter D. Feaver, and Jason Reifler, *Paying the Human Costs of War: American Public Opinion and Casualties in Military Conflicts* (Princeton, NJ: Princeton University Press, 2009).

20. William Danvers, "Disinformation May Be One of Russia and China's Greatest Weapons," *The Hill*, April 5, 2023, https://thehill.com/opinion/national-security/3932031
-disinformation-may-be-one-of-russia-and-chinas-greatest-weapons/.

21. Russell Berman, "Why These Progressives Stopped Helping Biden," *The Atlantic*, December 6, 2023.

Index